INTERPRETING ADAM SMITH

The year 2023 marks the 300th anniversary of the birth of Adam Smith. Long known as the 'father of economics', Smith also produced many important moral and political writings, which have increasingly come to be recognised as major contributions to the Scottish, and indeed wider European, Enlightenment. In this collection of original essays, leading Smith scholars offer fresh perspectives on how to think about Smith's ideas, the nature and importance of his works, and their impact upon subsequent thinkers and ultimately the world we live in. Bringing together both leading experts and some of the most exciting new voices in the field, this collection seeks both to celebrate and to deepen our appreciation of what Adam Smith has to teach us.

PAUL SAGAR is Reader in Political Theory, Department of Political Economy, King's College London. He is the author of *The Opinion of Mankind: Sociability and the Theory of the State from Hobbes to Smith* (2018) and *Adam Smith Reconsidered: History, Liberty, and the Foundations of Modern Politics* (2022).

INTERPRETING ADAM SMITH

Critical Essays

Edited by

PAUL SAGAR

King's College London

Shaftesbury Road, Cambridge CB2 8EA, United Kingdom

One Liberty Plaza, 20th Floor, New York, NY 10006, USA

477 Williamstown Road, Port Melbourne, VIC 3207, Australia

314–321, 3rd Floor, Plot 3, Splendor Forum, Jasola District Centre, New Delhi – 110025, India

103 Penang Road, #05–06/07, Visioncrest Commercial, Singapore 238467

Cambridge University Press is part of Cambridge University Press & Assessment, a department of the University of Cambridge.

We share the University's mission to contribute to society through the pursuit of education, learning and research at the highest international levels of excellence.

www.cambridge.org
Information on this title: www.cambridge.org/9781009296304

DOI: 10.1017/9781009296335

© Paul Sagar 2023

This publication is in copyright. Subject to statutory exception and to the provisions of relevant collective licensing agreements, no reproduction of any part may take place without the written permission of Cambridge University Press & Assessment.

First published 2023
First paperback edition 2025

A catalogue record for this publication is available from the British Library

ISBN 978-1-009-29631-1 Hardback
ISBN 978-1-009-29630-4 Paperback

Cambridge University Press & Assessment has no responsibility for the persistence or accuracy of URLs for external or third-party internet websites referred to in this publication and does not guarantee that any content on such websites is, or will remain, accurate or appropriate.

CONTENTS

List of Contributors   vii
Acknowledgements   ix
Abbreviations of Works by Adam Smith   x

Introduction   1
PAUL SAGAR

1 Smith Scholarship: Past, Present, and Future   3
   GLORY M. LIU

2 The *Wealth of Nations* as a Work of Social Science   21
   CHRISTOPHER J. BERRY

3 Adam Smith's "Industrial Organization" of Religion   39
   BARRY R. WEINGAST

4 Talking to My Butcher: Self-Interest, Exchange, and Freedom in the *Wealth of Nations*   62
   SAMUEL FLEISCHACKER

5 What Did Adam Smith Mean? The Semantics of the Opening Key Principles in the *Wealth of Nations*   77
   BART J. WILSON AND GIAN MARCO FARESE

6 Adam Smith and Virtuous Business   96
   JAMES R. OTTESON

7 Adam Smith and the Morality of Political Economy: A Public Choice Reading   111
   MARIA PIA PAGANELLI

8 A Moral Philosophy for Commercial Society?   124
   ROBIN DOUGLASS

9 Adam Smith, Sufficientarian   142
   PAUL SAGAR

10	Narrowing the Scope of Resentment in Smith's *Theory of Moral Sentiments* 160	
	JOHN T. SCOTT AND MICHELLE SCHWARZE	
11	Adam Smith: Stoic *and* Epicurean 177	
	LISA HILL	
12	"Much Better Instructors": Adam Smith and the Role of Literature in Moral Education 194	
	LAUREN KOPAJTIC	
13	Sophie de Grouchy as an Activist Interpreter of Adam Smith 214	
	KATHLEEN MCCRUDDEN ILLERT	
14	Adam Smith and the Limits of Philosophy 232	
	CRAIG SMITH	

Bibliography   245
Index   269

CONTRIBUTORS

CHRISTOPHER J. BERRY is Professor (Emeritus) of Political Theory and Honorary Professorial Research Fellow at the University of Glasgow.

ROBIN DOUGLASS is Professor of Political Theory at King's College London.

GIAN MARCO FARESE is Researcher and Lecturer in English Linguistics at the University of Milan.

SAMUEL FLEISCHACKER is LAS Distinguished Professor in Philosophy at the University of Illinois, Chicago.

LISA HILL is Professor of Politics at the University of Adelaide.

LAUREN KOPAJTIC is Assistant Professor of Philosophy at Fordham University.

GLORY M. LIU is Assistant Director for the Center for Economy and Society and Assistant Research Professor at the SNF Agora Institute at Johns Hopkins University.

KATHLEEN MCCRUDDEN ILLERT is a Max Weber Fellow at the European University Institute.

JAMES R. OTTESON is John T. Ryan Jr. Professor of Business Ethics, and Rex and Alice A. Martin Faculty Director of the Notre Dame Deloitte Center for Ethical Leadership, at the University of Notre Dame.

MARIA PIA PAGANELLI is Professor of Economics at Trinity University.

PAUL SAGAR is Reader in Political Theory at King's College London.

MICHELLE SCHWARZE is Jack Miller Center Assistant Professor at the University of Wisconsin, Madison.

JOHN T. SCOTT is Distinguished Professor of Political Science at the University of California, Davis.

CRAIG SMITH is the Adam Smith Senior Lecturer in the Scottish Enlightenment at the University of Glasgow.

BARRY R. WEINGAST is Senior Fellow, Hoover Institution, and Ward C. Krebs Family Professor, Department of Political Science, Stanford University.

BART J. WILSON is the Donald P. Kennedy Endowed Chair in Economics and Law and Director of the Smith Institute for Political Economy and Philosophy at Chapman University.

ACKNOWLEDGEMENTS

I thank Robin Douglass for his support and advice in putting this collection together, and to whom I am most grateful for lending me the wisdom of his experience. Hilary Gaskin at Cambridge University Press has been a consistently helpful, encouraging, and supportive editor, and my thanks go also to Abi Sears for help in the production process. Gratitude is also due to all those who took part in the KCL workshop held in January 2022 to discuss the papers that went on to form this collection, and to the Department of Political Economy at King's College London for being such an outstanding place to read, think, and write about Adam Smith.

ABBREVIATIONS OF WORKS BY ADAM SMITH

CAS   *The Correspondence of Adam Smith*, ed. E. C. Mossner and I. S. Ross, revised ed. (Oxford: Clarendon Press, 1987), two volumes.

ED   'Early Draft' of part of the *Wealth of Nations*, in *The Glasgow Edition of the Works and Correspondence of Adam Smith: Volume V – Lectures on Jurisprudence*, ed. R. L. Meek, D. D. Raphael and P. G. Stein (Oxford: Clarendon Press, 1978).

EPS   *The Glasgow Edition of the Works and Correspondence of Adam Smith: Volume III – Essays on Philosophical Subjects*, ed. W. P. D. Wightman and J. C. Bryce (Oxford: Clarendon Press, 1980).

HA   'The History of Astronomy', in *The Glasgow Edition of the Works and Correspondence of Adam Smith: Volume III – Essays on Philosophical Subjects*, ed. W. P. D. Wightman and J. C. Bryce (Oxford: Clarendon Press, 1980).

LJ(A)   'Lectures on Jurisprudence', report of 1762–3, in *The Glasgow Edition of the Works and Correspondence of Adam Smith: Volume V – Lectures on Jurisprudence*, ed. R. L. Meek, D. D. Raphael, and P. G. Stein (Oxford: Clarendon Press, 1978).

LJ(B)   'Jurisprudence or Notes from the Lectures on Justice, Police, Revenue, and Arms Delivered in the University of Glasgow by Adam Smith, Professor of Moral Philosophy, report dated 1766', in *The Glasgow Edition of the Works and Correspondence of Adam Smith: Volume V – Lectures on Jurisprudence*, ed. R. L. Meek, D. D. Raphael, and P. G. Stein (Oxford: Clarendon Press, 1978).

LRBL   *The Glasgow Edition of the Works and Correspondence of Adam Smith: Volume IV – Lectures on Rhetoric and Belles Lettres*, ed. J. C. Bryce (Oxford: Clarendon Press, 1983).

OIA   'Of the Nature of that Imitation Which Takes Place in What Are Called the Imitative Arts', in *The Glasgow Edition of the Works and Correspondence of Adam Smith: Volume III – Essays on Philosophical Subjects*, ed. W. P. D. Wightman and J. C. Bryce (Oxford: Clarendon Press, 1980).

TMS *The Glasgow Edition of the Works and Correspondence of Adam Smith: Volume I – The Theory of Moral Sentiments*, ed. D. D. Raphael and A. L. Macfie (Oxford: Clarendon Press, 1976).

WN   *The Glasgow Edition of the Works and Correspondence of Adam Smith: Volume II – An Inquiry into the Nature and Causes of the Wealth of Nations*, ed. R. H. Campbell, A. S. Skinner, and W. B. Todd, 2 vols. (Oxford: Clarendon Press, 1975).

Introduction

PAUL SAGAR

The year 2023 marks the 300th anniversary of Adam Smith's birth. The essays collected here seek to both celebrate and reflect upon Smith's intellectual achievements at this auspicious moment.

Traditionally, an introduction to a collection of this sort might start by offering an overview of recent trends in Smith scholarship. After all, much has changed in how Smith has been received and perceived in the more than two centuries since his death. A university teacher for most of his working life, and famous during his day primarily for his contributions to moral philosophy, he was of course later canonised as the so-called 'father of economics'. Indeed, that he 'invented' a discipline called 'economics' is likely all that the lay person today knows of his legacy. Yet as Glory M. Liu shows in her opening chapter, this barely scratches the surface of how often, and in how many ways, who and what Adam Smith 'was' (and whom it has befitted to portray him as such) has changed. I thus leave the matter of Adam Smiths past to her deft treatment.

Nonetheless, it is with an eye to this long and contested history of Smith interpretation that the contributors have been assembled. I have sought to bring together both established voices within Smith scholarship – who in some cases have been shaping the field for three decades and more – as well as newer voices who are beginning to make their mark (and many who lie between those poles). Likewise, this collection attempts to reflect the broad range of ideas and (what we would now call) disciplines that Smith put his formidable mind to work on. In this regard, the results are necessarily highly incomplete: Smith simply wrote too much about too many issues, and it has not been possible to cover even close to all the topics he addressed. Nonetheless, what is lacking in breadth is hopefully compensated for by something like depth.

Thus Christopher J. Berry reflects on the *Wealth of Nations* as a work of social science (and how that relates to the question of what *science* is more fundamentally), whilst Barry R. Weingast reconstructs Adam Smith's account of first the enduring stability, and then the collapse, of equilibrated power relations between the Church, the feudal lords, and the people, in medieval Europe. Samuel Fleischacker returns to Smith's famous injunction about what we ought to expect from our butcher, and offers reasons to see what Smith is up to in a compelling new light. Bart J. Wilson and Gian Marco Farese apply the methods of Natural Semantic Metalanguage to the opening claims of *WN* to demonstrate the universality of Smith's claims, aiming to drill down to the core of what Smith meant. James R. Otteson examines the case for seeing Smith as a source of an ethics of virtuous business, whilst Maria Pia Paganelli examines the interplay between justice and incentives in *WN* from a Public Choice perspective. Robin Douglass challenges the recent consensus that *TMS* is a book about 'commercial society', and I in similar vein call into question readings of Smith as an egalitarian thinker in distributive matters, suggesting that if we are going to assimilate him to contemporary categories, then 'sufficientarian' is a more accurate label. John T. Scott and Michelle Schwarze offer a reconstruction of the logic of Smith's account of resentment, exploring its intimate but complex connections to injury and punishment in Smith's thought. Lisa Hill rejects as false the dichotomy of Smith as *either* an epicurean *or* stoic thinker, arguing that his philosophy is characterised by extensively drawing upon both traditions simultaneously. Lauren Kopajtic turns to the relatively neglected question of what Smith intended when he recommended literary authors to readers of *TMS*, and examines Smith's philosophy in the light of the early novel. Kathleen McCrudden Illert deploys new archival evidence to offer a major new interpretation of Sophie de Grouchy's 'activist translation' of Smith's *TMS*, facilitated by a redating of Grouchy's composition, and thus the correct contextual location of her intervention. Craig Smith closes proceedings by reflecting on Smith's meta-conception of philosophy itself, and thus what philosophical enquiry can (and, crucially, cannot) be finally expected to do for us, most especially when it comes to living a moral life.

1

Smith Scholarship
Past, Present, and Future

GLORY M. LIU

> There is no such thing as a new idea. It is impossible. We simply take a lot of old ideas and put them into a sort of mental kaleidoscope. We give them a turn and they make new and curious combinations. We keep on turning and making new combinations indefinitely; but they are all the same old pieces of colored glass that have been in use through all the ages.
>
> —Mark Twain

This chapter situates Smith scholarship in a long historical view. In doing so, it highlights the kaleidoscopic nature of reading and writing about Smith – that with every historical turn of our mental and moral worlds, new possibilities and new purposes emerge from the same texts and ideas that have been in use through the ages. While I do not go so far as Twain to suggest that there is no such thing as a new idea – either *from* Smith or *about* Smith – I do argue that there are few, if any, of those ideas that are fully settled or uncontested. Moreover, I suggest that the ambiguity and contestability of Smith's intentions as well as the slipperiness of the conceptual categories that he inspired have engendered shifting meanings, emergent problematics, and the enduring political relevance of his works and ideas.

To invite reflection on the past and present and perhaps even the future of Smith scholarship, I enlist Stefan Collini's "four-stages model," so to speak, of classic thinkers in order to outline and explain the trajectory of Smith's posthumous reputation. According to Collini, a thinker attains "classic" status after having passed through four major stages of reception (Collini, 1991, pp. 317–319). In the first stage, the author's works are living resources. They are immediately relevant to political debates that surround the author's life; her ideas, pronouncements, and opinions may be invoked in major discussions on substantive issues. In the second phase, discipleship is established. People begin to invoke the author's ideas and declare themselves followers, or seek to be recognized as followers, while opposition emerges in tandem. In the third stage, the intellectual authority of the author takes hold. For Collini, this is a crucial turning point; most authors, he claims, only pass through the first two stages. What distinguishes this third phase is that the symbolic value of the thinker appears to matter more than the content of her ideas; she becomes a totem, a recognizable image for followers to align themselves with or distance themselves from. Finally, the author becomes canonical. While the author and her works may have "ostensibly ... no current political resonance," they are nevertheless "recognized as having acquired some kind of classic status or to have become an object of purely scholarly inquiry" (Collini, 1991, p. 318). This model provides a rough but useful schema for understanding how and why Smith became canonized in a narrow fashion as the "father of economics." In addition, it sheds light on the central problematics that have driven and shaped writing on Smith for nearly three centuries.[1]

In that spirit, my approach here is selective rather than comprehensive. It would be both impossible and undesirable to document and summarize every trend in Smith scholarship over the last three hundred years, let alone even the last twenty or thirty. With respect to the four-stages model, my attention will be primarily devoted to the latter two stages – the invention of Smith's authority, and the tensions surrounding his status as a canonical subject and object of scholarly inquiry. For reasons of scope, economy, and expertise, my focus here is almost exclusively on anglophone scholarship on Smith.[2] Furthermore, my own disciplinary background as a political theorist and intellectual historian imposes certain biases which, though I have endeavored to shed them, will nonetheless present a narrow view of the field. This limited purview is unfortunate, but I hope that it will inspire other scholars with the right set of skills to take up a more global approach to our understanding of Smith and Smith historiography.

The idea of "Smith scholarship" as a defined and stable literature is somewhat misleading. Commentary on Smith has not always been the exclusive province of professional scholars. Politicians (most of whom were and are highly educated), popular writers, public intellectuals, and lay readers of many backgrounds have engaged with Smith's ideas and put them to different purposes. My orienting assumption is that "those who had occasion to write about Smith" are *producing knowledge about Smith*, as Keith Tribe has put it, even though what they produced might be a far cry from what we expect as scholars in the twenty-first century (Tribe, 2008, p. 515, n.5). One feature of this essay is that it suggests that Smith *scholarship* as we now know and define it is a fairly recent phenomenon, and that it is an outgrowth of a much longer intellectual tradition of thinking with, through, and against Smith's ideas. Smith's own views and views attributed *to* Smith have become so thoroughly entangled over time, and their diachronic relationship has made Smith one of

---

[1] For another adaptation and response to Collini's model of reception, see Jones, 2017.
[2] This article draws on some selective material from my lengthier treatment of Smith's reception in America in Liu, 2022. For work on Smith's reception beyond the anglophone world see Mizuta and Sugiyama, 1993; Lai, 2000.

the most challenging subjects for historical inquiry. Thus, one of my tasks here is to reflect on why that challenge has nonetheless been rewarding.

1.1 Adam Smith's Past

1.1.1 Early Engagements with Smith

During Smith's lifetime, both *The Theory of Moral Sentiments* and *The Wealth of Nations* became bestsellers (Sher, 2010). However, despite the importance that scholars and readers attribute to both works today, it is not entirely clear that either work exerted "any fundamental influence" on thinking, action, or policy at the time. Scholars have put to rest the claim that the publication of *The Wealth of Nations* had immediate causal impact on liberal trade policy, or that it was singularly responsible for Smith's fame in 1776 (Rashid, 1982; Teichgraeber, 1987). This is not to say that Smith's works were completely ignored, however. Rather, it is to suggest that the way in which both texts were important or useful during Smith's lifetime was quite different from the way in which they would eventually be read.

Initial reviews of *The Theory of Moral Sentiments* were positive but by no means extraordinary. *The Critical Review* of London applauded the "ingenuity, and (may we venture to say it) the solidity of [Smith's] reasoning" in *The Theory of Moral Sentiments*, and which the review's author believed "ought to excite the languid attention of the public, and procure him a favourable reception" when it first appeared in 1759.[3] For critics, though, the main problem with *The Theory of Moral Sentiments* seemed to be that Smith's concept of sympathy lacked a solid philosophical grounding (Klein, 2018; Liu, 2022). This apparent lack of a foundation for sympathy was the core issue and starting point for Sophie De Grouchy's *Letters on Sympathy* (1798), arguably the most extensive and famous translations and engagements with *The Theory of Moral Sentiments* in France (Scurr, 2009; Bréban and Delamotte, 2016; Schliesser and Bergé, 2019; McCrudden Illert's chapter in this volume). In America, *The Theory of Moral Sentiments* was read and considered alongside the works of other major Scottish thinkers – Francis Hutcheson's *A System of Moral Philosophy* (1755), Lord Kames' *Elements of Criticism* (1762), Thomas Reid's *An Inquiry into the Human Mind* (1764), and Dugald Stewart's *Elements of the Philosophy of the Human Mind* (1792). At least among the educated, *The Theory of Moral Sentiments* was seen as one, but certainly not the only, resource that would assist readers in "forming just notions in morality and criticism," as the physician Elihu Hubbard Smith wrote in 1792.[4]

---

[3] *The Critical Review*, vol. 7 (May 1759), p. 384.
[4] Quoted in Sher, 2010, p. 505.

Early engagements with Smith's *The Wealth of Nations* can be categorized into three major groups: (1) reviews in literary magazines such as the *Monthly Review* and *The Critical Review*, (2) written responses in both published and in private correspondence, and (3) references and applications in political debate. *The Wealth of Nations* received positive reviews, but among Smith's close readers and critics, there was no clear consensus about how popular the book would become and for what reason. Hume famously expressed his doubts about *The Wealth of Nations* becoming popular among the wider public.[5] Governor William Pownall disagreed strongly with Smith's assessment of the American colonies, and Hugh Blair, while he congratulated Smith for his "great Service to the World by overturning all that interested Sophistry of Merchants" opined that Smith's views on the colonial question tainted the work – "It is too much like a publication for the present moment" (*CAS*, p. 188). In Parliament, MPs sometimes read extracts from *The Wealth of Nations* verbatim or loosely referenced Smith's ideas when debating policies ranging from wool exportation, to commercial treaties with France, to the grazing of post office horses (Willis, 1979). In the newly founded United States, similar patterns can be observed. James Madison referred to Smith ("the friend to a very free system of commerce") in a speech in Congress on export and tonnage duties in 1789, and Madison's Smithian analysis of factions and their relation to enthusiasm can be gleaned in *Federalist 10*.[6] Jefferson referred to *The Wealth of Nations* as "the best book extant" on political economy in 1790 (Jefferson, 1961, 448–50). Most notably, Alexander Hamilton borrowed directly from Smith's analysis of banking and public credit in his "Report on Public Credit" (1790) and reproduced entire extracts on the division of labor and productivity in his "Report on Manufactures" (1791).[7] As Kirk Willis has observed, eighteenth-century politicians often treated Smith as "just another technical expert"; *The Wealth of Nations* was an important resource, but it had not yet taken on an authoritative or ideological reputation (Willis, 1979, p. 510).

Taken together, Smith's two major works, *The Theory of Moral Sentiments* (1759) and *The Wealth of Nations* (1776), were treated as major contributions to live philosophical and political debates. Perhaps what is most distinctive

---

[5] Hume wrote, "Not but that the Reading of it necessarily requires so much Attention, and the Public is disposed to give it so little, that I shall still doubt for some time of its being at first very popular" (*CAS*, p. 186).

[6] Madison, 1979, pp. 70–71. On Madison's intellectual debt to Smith, see Fleischacker, 2002, 2019b. Fleischacker's argument revisits the long-accepted argument that Madison was primarily influenced by Hume, as outlined in Adair, 1957.

[7] On Hamilton's sources, see the editors' introduction to Hamilton, 1963. Bourne (1894) helpfully compiled parallel passages between Hamilton's Reports and Smith's *The Wealth of Nations*. For further analysis of Hamilton's "Smithian" ideas, see Hacker, 1957; Somos, 2011.

about this first stage is that Smith was not yet canonized. This should come as no surprise, but it bears restating if only because so much of the subsequent work on Smith was explicitly polemical and politically charged.

The publication of Dugald Stewart's *Account of the Life and Writings of Adam Smith, LL.D.* in 1794 was the first major act of critical interpretation and reclamation of Smith's reputation and ideas. Stewart's biography (which also played the role of eulogy) worked to distance Smith from his association with radical and revolutionary ideas of political liberty in France and Great Britain (Rothschild, 1992; Buchan, 2016). Stewart neutralized the content of Smith's political economy, creating an ersatz Adam Smith whose most important opinion was that "little else is requisite to carry a state to the higher degree of opulence from the lowest barbarism, but peace, easy taxes, and a tolerable administration of justice; all the rest being brought about by the natural course of things" (*EPS*, p. 322). Thus, almost immediately after Smith's death, the biography of Smith – both the man and his ideas – began to condition the way subsequent readers and interpreters took up his ideas and constructed his legacy.

1.1.2 Discipleship

By the mid-nineteenth century, those who had the occasion to write, comment on, or engage with Smith's ideas could be sorted into categories of disciples and detractors. With the development and institutionalization of academic political economy, *The Wealth of Nations* became the agreed-upon point of departure for the discipline. New tracts, treatises, and textbooks were often compared to *The Wealth of Nations*, not only in terms of whether an author agreed with Smith's positions, but also in terms of their style, composition, and organization. Smith's reputation was sustained not "through the blindness and indifference of those who have followed him," as an anonymous writer for the *North American Review* put it, but with "the care and acumen which succeeding writers have bestowed on the *Wealth of Nations*" through their critical engagement with it (North American Review, 1823, p. 427).[8]

But discipleship and detraction were also political. In the North Atlantic, free trade and *laissez-faire* became the defining issues that separated those who saw themselves as followers of Smith and hence champions of free trade, and those who saw themselves as opponents, who declared "The system of Adam Smith and Co. to be erroneous" (List, 1827, p. 6). The German economist Friedrich List (1789–1846), for instance, outlined what he called the "American System," which rejected Smith's "cosmopolitical" political

---

[8] For helpful introductions to the origins of academic political economy in the United States, see O'Connor, 1944; Conkin, 1980; Barber, 1993.

economy and instead embraced a project of economic nationalism and protection on the basis that the management of an economy had to take into account the particular historical, cultural contingencies of a nation. List's critique of Smith was highly influential in the United States, where his ideas were adopted by major proponents of economic nationalism and protectionism such as Henry C. Carey.[9] Debates about trade policy in the United States reinforced divisions between those who saw themselves as "the disciples of the celebrated Adam Smith" and those who adhered to the "preeminence of the agricultural and exclusive system."[10] Among the heavyweights of the older German Historical School, Bruno Hildebrand (1812–1878) wrote in his *Die Nationalökonomie der Gegenwart und Zukunft* ("The National Economy of the Present and Future") of not just Smith himself, but of the "Smithsche System," the "Smithsche Lehre," the "Smithsche Doktrin," and the "Smithsche Schüler." Where the system, teachings, doctrines, and students of Smith were egoist, materialist, hyperrational, and universalizing, Hildebrand's vision of a political economy was historical, national, and ethical.[11]

To be sure, many of Smith's ideas were continually debated in earnest. In the antebellum debates in the United States, for example, congressmen expressed genuine uncertainty about the nation's economic future and were often paralyzed over the best course of action. But as time wore on and industrialization set into motion a different political machinery, commentary on Smith thinned out. People turned to Smith's works not so much because they believed in the independent intellectual merits of his works, or because they were trying to open up new intellectual terrain. Rather, Smith had become a recognizable symbol who marked the development of academic political economy and, more importantly, the politics of free trade.

1.1.3 Authority

The exact point at which Smith became an authority is difficult to pin down. However, Collini's definition helps shed some light on the conditions that demarcate discipleship from the establishment of authority. According to Collini, an author can be said to have become an authority when she becomes "a symbol or part of a tradition" in more general cultural terms; immediate

---

[9] On List's influence in North America, Britain, and Germany, see Tribe, 1995, chap. 3; Palen, 2016.

[10] *Annals of Congress*, Senate, May 4, 1820, pp. 668–669. On the significance of Smith's reputation and ideas in American trade debates, see Liu, 2018, 2022.

[11] Emma Rothschild explores the transmission of "Smithianismus" among the German Historical Thinkers in her unpublished manuscript, "Smithianismus and Enlightenment in 19th Century Europe." Centre for History and Economics, University of Cambridge.

political debates can often throw an author's authority into high relief, when her name and ideas are invoked to "align oneself with (or, conversely, distance oneself from)" (Collini, 1991, p. 318). With respect to Smith, this is evident in debates about the tariff and *laissez-faire* in the last quarter of the nineteenth century. The *Wealth of Nations* Centenary celebrations in England and in the United States in 1876 reveal the political significance of Smith amidst the free trade fervor. In New York, attendees of the Centennial gathered to celebrate the "principles of freedom taught in that immortal work" (*The Wealth of Nations*) and its argument for free trade was hailed as the "commercial gospel."[12] Crucially, however, Smith's authority was available to people on both sides of the free trade debate. One American senator declared in 1893 that "Free trade as an economic science, in the judgment of the world, is a dismal failure," and that "even the highest authority on free trade" admitted that a decrease in manufactures would diminish the size of the home market (Congressional Record, 1893, p. 203). It was less the content of Smith's arguments themselves and more the authority which Smith's name conferred that mattered. Exploiting ambiguities, inconsistencies, and even seeming contradictions in Smith's views was thus a political strategy for delegitimizing the policy of *laissez-faire*, but it nevertheless reinforced Smith's authoritative status (Palen, 2016; Liu, 2018). Such uses underscore an important point that Collini makes about the transition to this stage of being an "authority:" that at some point, "it becomes in everyone's interest, no matter what their political allegiance, to attempt to appropriate [the author], or at least to establish where they stand in relation to him" (Collini, 1991, p. 319).

Perhaps the most famous example of the uses (and, one could say, abuses) of Smith's authority are those associated with the Chicago School of economics in the late twentieth century. Decorated economists such as Milton Friedman and George Stigler frequently appealed to Smith's ideas in their academic publications as well as their popular and polemical writing. Smith, on their terms, was an intellectual forerunner of Chicago Price Theory. For Stigler, Smith's elaboration of self-interest provided a "theorem of almost unlimited power on the behavior of man" (Stigler, 1976, p. 1212). For Friedman, the invisible hand, which illustrated how the "voluntary acts of millions of individuals each pursuing his own objectives could be coordinated, without central direction, through a price mechanism," established *The Wealth of Nations* as "the beginning of scientific economics" (Friedman, 1977, p. 4). This interpretation placed Smith at the founding of a tradition

---

[12] "Free Trader's Centennial. The One Hundredth Anniversary of Adam Smith's 'Wealth of Nations': Grand Dinner at Delmonico's." *New York Herald*, December 13, 1876; "Adam Smith. Centennial Celebration of the Publication of 'The Wealth of Nations': Speeches by William Cullen Bryant, Parke Godwin, David A. Wells, Professor Sumner, Mr. Atkinson and Others." *Evening Post*, December 13, 1876.

whose direct descendants were Stigler, Friedman, and their Chicago colleagues. Reinterpreting Smith's ideas in this way not only enabled economists like Stigler and Friedman to make claims about being legitimate heirs to Smith's legacy, but it also provided the scientific rationale for Chicago's unique brand of free-market advocacy in the twentieth century (Medema, 2010; Burgin, 2012; Jones, 2014; Liu, 2020, 2022).

1.1.4 Canonization

This brings us to the last phase. At least today, scholars are all too familiar with positioning their arguments to prove that Smith was *not* a "Chicago-style economist *avant la lettre*," and that he was "not anarcho-capitalist or a promoter of no government intervention" (Hont, 2005, p. 100; Paganelli, 2020, p. 189). It is not just contestation over Smith's authority, but also a dedication to recovering Smith's ideas, intentions, and reputation from alleged "abuse" that has generated much of what we now call "Smith scholarship" today. With reference to Collini's model, this most closely resembles the fourth stage, in which the author "ostensibly has no current political resonance, but is recognized as having acquired some kind of classic status or to have become an object of purely scholarly enquiry" (Collini, 1991, p. 318). Smith, in other words, has become an analytical construct: scholars debate what properly belongs to Smith, who or what counts as "Smithian," what lines of influence and reception flow to and from Smith, and the like. There's no question that Smith, both in academic and in public discourse, has the status of a "classic" thinker; but that he is (and has been) an object of scholarly inquiry in no way precludes the political resonances or practical import of his ideas.

The first major attempts to historically situate, analyze, and interpret Smith's works began in the late nineteenth century. This first wave of scholarship was driven in large part by two major developments. One was the discovery and organization of new elements of Smith's corpus, chief among them being the discovery of the first set of student notes on Smith's Lectures on Justice, Police, and Arms in 1895 (now part of the *Lectures on Jurisprudence*). The publication of James Bonar's *Catalogue of Adam Smith's Library* was published in 1894, and John Rae's *Life of Adam Smith* (1895) – the first major biography in English since Stewart's *Account* – enabled and reflected a thirst for serious historical studies of Smith. Another development was the emergence and diffusion of new interpretive problems, most notably Das Adam Smith Problem. While earlier commentary had argued for the unity of Smith's works (such as the first two volumes of Henry Buckle's *History of Civilization in England* (1861), or Albert Delatour's *Adam Smith, Sa vie, ses travaus, ses doctrines* (1886)), what was unique about Das Adam Smith Problem was that rather than settling older debates, it introduced a new problematic for Smith's readers: were *The Theory of Moral Sentiments* and

The Wealth of Nations "two entirely independent works," or were they "a comprehensive exposition of [Smith's] moral philosophy" when read together? (Oncken, 1897, p. 444). However mistaken it might have been, Das Adam Smith Problem nevertheless stimulated debates about the consistency and coherence of Smith's works and has since become an almost permanent feature of Smith scholarship to this day (Montes, 2003; Tribe, 2008, 2021).

The second and perhaps most recognizable wave of Smith scholarship arose almost a century later. As was the case in the 1890s, this latter wave gained momentum from the discovery and collation of textual material, most importantly (again, for anglophone readers) the Glasgow Editions of the Works and Correspondence of Adam Smith, whose publication began in 1976. "The tools for a proper reading are now available," remarked the American historian Garry Wills (1978). The textual advance that the Glasgow Editions marked was unprecedented: in addition to the two new editions of *TMS* and *WN*, the publication of Smith's *Lectures on Jurisprudence* included the second set of student notes on Smith's lectures. Smith's correspondence, the few essays that Smith spared from the flames before his death (the *Essays on Philosophical Subjects*), and a volume on Smith's lectures on rhetoric were also published. However, compared to the earlier wave of scholarship in the 1880s and 1890s, the historiography beginning in the 1970s was more explicitly revisionist. One aim was to put to rest Das Adam Smith Problem, which the editors of the Glasgow Edition of *The Theory of Moral Sentiments* dismissed as a "pseudo-problem based on ignorance and misunderstanding" (*TMS*, introduction, 20). Another aim concerned something more immediate and prevalent: the assimilation of Smith to a "liberal-capitalist" tradition – of which the Chicago Smith was *a* but not *the* sole representation – that legitimized the separation of economy from politics and the hegemony of markets over the state (Winch, 1978). Influential works by Donald Winch, István Hont and Michael Ignatieff, Knud Haakonssen, J. G. A. Pocock, Duncan Forbes, and many others reveal the markedly historical key in which revisionist Smith scholarship was being written (Forbes, 1975; Winch, 1978; Haakonssen, 1981; Hont and Ignatieff, 1983a, 1983b; Pocock, 1985). These works served an important rehabilitative purpose, contending that Smith was steeped in the eighteenth-century language of republican virtue, natural jurisprudence, and of modern liberty, in ways that contemporary economistic reconstructions occluded.

Given the prominence of these contributions (and the likelihood that most readers of this volume are quite familiar with them), I will spare my readers superfluous commentary here. But two points are worth underscoring. First, the revisionist historiography that emerged in the 1970s and 1980s was not unprecedented, but its development ought to be understood as a concerted effort to correct at least two perceived problems: the lack of a complete, updated, and accessible scholarly edition of Smith's works on the one hand, and the persistence of "misreadings" stemming from Das Adam Smith

Problem or even the "Chicago Smith Problem" on the other. Second, despite major advances in the understanding of intertextual relations among *TMS*, *LJ*, and Smith's lesser-known works, scholarship around the bicentenary was still predominantly focused on *WN*.[13] The stubbornness of Smith's popular reputation as a free-market economist continues to be a target for those studying and writing on Smith today, but within the last three decades (roughly speaking), scholarship on Smith has undergone something of a renaissance.

1.2 Adam Smith's Present

There are several distinguishing features of the ongoing Smith renaissance. First, the "new Smith scholarship" has moved away from hagiography and legacy claiming; Smith scholars are now much more interested in recovery than recruitment. Of course, one can still find a healthy supply of publications that "recruit" Smith, but these tend to signal a methodological orientation of an academic discipline, rather than a political position.[14] One related consequence is that the center of gravity of Smith scholarship has slowly shifted from economics and toward the fields of political science, philosophy, and history. Additionally, scholars seem much more willing to treat Smith as an eclectic thinker who floated freely across our contemporary disciplinary boundaries, rather than providing an explicit definition of who Smith was (or was not) in terms that align with contemporary labels (e.g. "development economist," "analytic philosopher," "political scientist"). Casting Smith as an "ambitious social scientist" (as his most recent biographer, the late Nicholas Phillipson, described him) not only gives scholars greater access to the mental universe in which Smith operated, but also illuminates the distance between Smith's enlightened way of thinking and the intellectually siloed contexts in which most contemporary scholars operate.

A second feature of the new Smith scholarship has been the growing orientation toward Smith's texts as works of *philosophy*, or at least works that are philosophically interesting, and can be engaged with as such contemporaneously. This stands in contrast to much of the earliest revisionist scholarship that was largely historical. Close readings of key Smithian concepts – such as sympathy, the imagination, the impartial spectator, and conscience – have illuminated both the sentimental bases and cognitive processes involved in Smith's epistemology and account of moral approval (Griswold, 1999;

---

[13] For instance, in the *Essays on Adam Smith*, the entire second part of the volume (some sixteen essays) was almost exclusively focused on *The Wealth of Nations* or some aspect of Smith's political economy. On the impact of the bicentenary on the output of Smith scholarship, see Recktenwald, 1978; Wight, 2002.

[14] Examples of such recruitment in economics include Ashraf, Camerer and Loewenstein, 2005; Machovec, 2012; Easterly, 2021.

Fleischacker, 2004a, 2004b, 2021; Broadie, 2006; Fricke, 2013; Debes, 2016; Schliesser, 2017). At least within the discipline of philosophy, efforts to defend the empirical validity and normativity of sentimentalist approaches to ethics have encouraged scholars to revisit the place of Smith's (and Hume's) moral sentimentalism in the history of ethics more generally. Smith has thus become a prominent reference in debates surrounding the foundations of moral sentimentalism, moral psychology, and ethics of empathy (Kelly, 2013; Debes and Stueber, 2017; Fleischacker, 2019a). Additionally, careful reconstructions of Smith's philosophy of science have reframed and refined the scope and aims of Smithian philosophy and social science. For philosopher Samuel Fleischacker, Smith's "system of scientific systems" captures a realist, fallibilist view of scientific theorizing and reinforces the Smithian view that in philosophy, "the work of soothing the imagination is never done," (Fleischacker 2004b, p. 33, 2021, p. 50). For Eric Schliesser, the aim of Smithian philosophy – of "systematizing systems" – is somewhat more ambitious: to persuade the public of the right sort of systems for understanding and governing human life (Schliesser, 2017). What these rigorously philosophical approaches offer the general reader, therefore, is a way to recognize the methodological affinities across Smith's texts: Smith's alternate model of political economy in *WN* is rooted in sentimentalist moral philosophy, and his moral philosophy is an extension of a system of scientific thinking that is both philosophically satisfying and self-conscious about the limits of scientific theorizing.

A third feature is the central place of *TMS* in Smith's corpus. Though distinct from the revival of interest in Smith's philosophy and Smith *as* philosopher, recent scholarship has focused the spotlight on the unique descriptive and normative functions of Smith's first major published work. This is a significant shift from the earlier revisionist scholarship around the bicentenary of *WN*, which had thoroughly refuted Das Adam Smith Problem but did not necessarily give pride of place to Smith's earlier book on ethics. Donald Winch, for example, summarily dismissed the Problem in the opening pages of *Adam Smith's Politics*, but remarked that the relationship between *TMS* and *WN* "does not provide warrant ... for regarding the *Theory of Moral Sentiments* as a court of higher appeal on all disputed matters" (Winch, 1978, p. 10). However, a large body of scholarship has treated *TMS* as the key to unlocking the mysteries of Smith's larger project, or as an explanatory text which underwrites Smiths' views on commerce and policy. Jack Russell Weinstein's *Adam Smith's Pluralism* argues for the prioritization of *TMS* "over [Smith's] other work" and for using *TMS* as the "'legend' to Smith's systematic map" in which "universal opulence and natural liberty are themselves components of a much more elaborate moral system" (Weinstein, 2013, pp. 2–3) Jerry Evensky's *Adam Smith's Moral Philosophy* approaches Smith's works – primarily *TMS* and *WN* – as an integrated explanation of "human nature and the co-evolution of individual and society, and of human society as a multidimensional, simultaneous, evolving system." Smith's moral philosophy, Evensky argues, was constructed to resolve a Hobbesian dilemma of wanting to unleash the productive powers of individuals following their self-interest, but without "unleashing ... a war of all against all" (Evensky, 2005a, p. 29). Perhaps the most methodologically pure instance of this trend is found in Bart J. Wilson and Vernon Smith's recent volume, *Humanomics,* in which the authors draw on evidence from experimental economics to show how Smith's insights into human sentiments, affections, and other-regarding impulses are much better approximations of human behavior than utility maximization (Smith and Wilson, 2019).

One way to interpret this trend is that it functions as a constructive critique of the economistic tunnel-vision that dominated Smith interpretation for much of the nineteenth and twentieth century. For scholars such as Evensky, Wilson, Smith, and Deirdre McCloskey, Smith's "humanomics" delivers a powerful counterpunch against the Chicago paradigm and *homo economicus* of high neoclassicism (Evensky, 2005b; McCloskey, 2016). But this dramatic shift in focus towards *TMS* also evinces another feature of the new Smith scholarship, which is its function as immanent critique of contemporary politics and society.[15] This is particularly evident in a burst of scholarship written around the 2008 Financial Crisis. Influential works by political theorists Dennis Rasmussen and Ryan Hanley, for example, re-centered scholarly analysis of Smith's moral philosophy around his normative concerns about commercial modernity (Rasmussen, 2006, 2008, 2016; Hanley, 2008, 2009). Smith was "no detached student of economic and ethical phenomena," but committed to ethical and prescriptive analysis, the cultivation of virtue, and defending the prospects of commercial society on moral grounds (Hanley, 2009, p. 6).

The more important consequence of these interventions, though, has been the renewed attention to and appreciation of a wide range of politically salient topics ranging from Smith's views on poverty and inequality, to moral corruption and the normative stakes of economic growth (Herzog, 2011, 2014; Boucoyannis, 2013; Sen, 2013, 2016; Rasmussen, 2016; Hill, 2017; Schwarze and Scott, 2019). Smith scholarship in its latest form thus treats revisionism as more than a project of historical recovery, but one that has immediate practical and political import, too. These interpretive strategies have also raised questions about the limits of reading *TMS* as a *critique* of commercial society and have exposed a temptation to overinterpret the connections between *WN* and *TMS* more generally, as Robin Douglass's essay in this volume suggests.

---

[15] Keith Tribe (1999) observed a similar trend in his review of Smith literature in the 1990s.

This "rediscovery" of *The Theory of Moral Sentiments* relates to a fourth trend in the new Smith scholarship. As an extension of early revisionist historiography, new scholarship has reconfigured Smith's contribution to liberalism and its histories. As Duncan Bell has remarked, the volume of scholarship on what liberalism *is* (or *was*) has rendered it "a hyper-inflated, multi-faceted, body of thought – a deep reservoir of ideological contradictions" that is impossible to ignore, especially among political theorists and historians of political thought (Bell, 2014, p. 691). Grand historical narratives of liberalism's inherent contradictions, its lost moral commitments, its postwar ascendancy, and its preordained failures, have forced scholars to reckon with their own political, moral, and intellectual commitments.[16] As a result, Smith's position within these liberal currents has undergone constant reappraisal. In addition to disentangling Smith from *neo*liberalism (Chicago-style or otherwise) and the "liberal-capitalist" tradition that Winch identified, the new Smith scholarship has placed Smith within a variety of liberal traditions. Jennifer Pitts's *A Turn to Empire*, for instance, placed Smith at the beginning of the liberal critique of imperialism before the imperial turn from the 1830s forward, best exemplified in the thought of John Stuart Mill. Alongside Edmund Burke, Jeremy Bentham, and Benjamin Constant, Adam Smith thus represents a different strand of liberalism – one in which imperial expansionism was neither inevitable nor essential to its program (Pitts, 2006). Pitts also emphasizes an important interpretive move of the new Smith scholarship around the theme of liberalism: that is, the centrality of Smith's moral philosophy for understanding his political thought. For Pitts, Smith's liberal critique of empire is evident not only in his depictions of the violence of the East India company or his doubts about Great Britain's prospects in America. Smith's *Theory of Moral Sentiments* showed how Britons' moral imaginations were historically and culturally constrained, while Smith's stadial model of history revealed an open-mindedness toward cultural difference and contingency.

Revisiting Smith's moral philosophy of sympathy, care, and judgment from the standpoint of international thought has also placed him at the center of debates about liberal cosmopolitanism and globalization. Amartya Sen has argued that Smith's virtue ethics highlights Smith's concerns for poverty and inequality, and that Smith's impartial spectator is a mode of reasoning about social justice on a global scale (Sen, 1986, 2009, 2013, 2016). Smith is pivotal in Martha Nussbaum's recent work on the cosmopolitan tradition; by emphasizing the importance of the material conditions needed to develop human capabilities, Smith paved the way for thinking about obligations to preserve

---

[16] See, for example, Manent and Seigel, 1996; Ryan, 2012; Fawcett, 2014; Deneen, 2018; Forrester, 2019; Rosenblatt, 2019.

and promote human dignity on a transnational scale (Nussbaum, 2019). However, following Fonna Forman-Barzilai's *Adam Smith and the Circles of Sympathy*, any ethical cosmopolitanism is riddled with the problems of overcoming particularism and cultural bias which permeate Smith's moral psychology (Forman-Barzilai, 2010). Smith's (or rather, Smithian) liberalism, on these accounts, is not limited to the analysis of self-interest in markets and the sanctity of private property; a spatially expansive treatment of Smith's moral philosophy and political economy probes the ethical, geographic, and political limits of liberalism in both theory and practice.

But Smith's liberal cosmopolitanism or anti-cosmopolitanism is just one of many liberal traditions in which Smith is being reinterpreted. Readers now face a dizzying array of liberalisms that Smith can be said to have founded, participated in, or anticipated: sympathetic liberalism, liberal pluralism, reform liberalism, liberal egalitarianism, pragmatic liberalism, and so on.[17] A cynical view of this trend is that scholars are simply using Smith to redefine, articulate, and defend their own preferred version of liberalism. But a less cynical and slightly more nuanced view is that one of the primary starting points of the new Smith scholarship is a shared assumption that Smith might offer a corrective to the wide-ranging deficiencies of contemporary liberalism. Where liberal rationalism (of the epistemological sort) fails to account for other-regarding motives, Smith's liberalism injects affect, spectatorial resentment, and passions to not only explain but also rectify injustice (Schwarze, 2020). Where a different type of liberal rationalism (of the political sort) narrowly focuses on the uses of state power in relation to individual freedom, Smith's pluralism is both distrustful of state authority and espouses the positive freedoms of associational life (Levy, 2015). And where market neoliberalism maximizes efficiency in the abstract, Smith's pragmatic liberalism maximizes positive liberty, happiness, and the well-being of ordinary people (Hill, 2020). Such slippery, elusive, and at times contradictory usage of the same terms might call into question the very usefulness of reaching for Smith as a guide for the dilemmas of contemporary liberalism. Yet they also serve as an index of the way "liberal languages emerge, evolve, and come into conflict with one another" (Bell, 2014, p. 689).

---

[17] Stephen Darwall's term, "sympathetic liberalism," is the idea that Smith's theory of justice was anchored in moral sentiments – especially that of resentment – and amounted to "a system of mutual accountability in which all express a respect for others as equals" (Darwall, 1999). It should be noted that the "pluralism" of Weinstein (2013) and Levy (2015) are quite different. Weinstein is concerned mostly with Smith's *ethical* pluralism, which he claims anticipates contemporary systems of diversity. Levy, by contrast, slots Smith into a tradition of liberal pluralism *contra* liberal rationalism, with the former championing an associational vision of society and the link between rules of associations and individual liberty. For reform-minded liberalism, see Schliesser, 2017, 2022. For liberal egalitarianism, see Fleischacker, 2013, 2016.

A final feature of the new Smith scholarship is its reformulation of older problematics and categories of analysis. The category of "Smith's politics," for instance, was left open-ended in Winch's work, neither explaining Smith's political attitudes nor approximating his partisan positions, but rather clarifying the terms that comprised Smith's general orientation to the study of straightforwardly political topics. The more recent wave of Smith scholarship, however, has deepened the study of Smith's political *theory* by looking to his analysis of political leadership (Schliesser, 2021), the heuristics of political judgment (Oprea, 2022), his conception of legitimate state action (Hanley, 2014), and his theory of opinion as the basis of political authority (Sagar, 2018b).

One important category of analysis that has regained traction is that of "commercial society." Made most famous by István Hont, the usage of "commercial society" – as opposed to "capitalism" – was intended to protect the autonomy and integrity of a historical category which Smith himself had used. But the boundaries between Smith's "commercial society" and capitalism, both nascent and contemporary, have been blurred.[18] What is more, the questions asked *of* Smith's concept of commercial society have subtly shifted over time. In their landmark 1983 essay, "Needs and Justice in *The Wealth of Nations*," István Hont and Michael Ignatieff posed what they called the "paradox of commercial society:" "How was extreme inequality of distribution in modern society compatible with the satisfaction of the needs of its poorest working members?" (Hont and Ignatieff, 1983a, p. 4). A significant strand of recent revisionist scholarship approaches the familiar paradox from a different angle: how could Smith have reconciled the material benefits of commercial society with its moral costs? One consequence of this reframing has been the contraction between commercial society and "capitalism." Sometimes, this is a term of convenience: "And Smith thinks that the commercial system (what we today call 'capitalism') does that better than any other system," writes Samuel Fleischacker (Fleischacker, 2021, p. 300). At other times, commercial society prefigures capitalism, with Smith's version of the "moral economy" resulting in his measured, but nonetheless optimistic prognosis of commercial modernity (Schwarze and Scott, 2019).

Here, the ambivalence and ambiguity of Smith's normative assessment of commercial society resurfaces. New categories of "Left Smith" and "Right Smith," which have been in use among Smith scholars for at least the last decade or so, have become effective winnowing devices for Smith interpreters. "Left Smith" has come to represent a broad family of interpretations which emphasizes Smith's radical moral egalitarianism and his concern for the poor,

---

[18] Paul Cheney (2022) has recently argued that Hont's category of "commercial society" was inflected with his own presentist views of global economic orders in the twentieth century.

but also the role of the state power to limit private power and achieve the ends of distributive and social justice. "Right Smith" maps even less neatly onto conventional political positions, but rather emphasizes Smith's decentralism in both moral and political systems, his skepticism of expertise, and his faith in local knowledge.[19] The conceptual and theoretical core of these different categories stem from a protracted debate about the place of distributive justice in Smith's works. Hont and Ignatieff's "Needs and Justice" essay had introduced the question of what obligation government had to protect the rights and meet the needs of the poor. *The Wealth of Nations* was undeniably and principally concerned with a question of justice, but the answer to that question was found not in government but in market mechanism.[20] However, subsequent work by thinkers ranging from the Nobel Prize–winning economist Amartya Sen to contemporary philosophers Samuel Fleischacker and Elizabeth Anderson have substantially modernized Smith's notion of distributive and social justice. Smith's moral orientation toward the poor, his "humane vision" of commercial society and its emancipatory potential, and his willingness to allow government to have a role in promoting or enforcing the social virtues of distributive justice are all features to be categorized as "Left" or "Right."[21]

As Craig Smith has observed, what appears to be at stake in the Left/Right debates is not only the extent to which Smith can be distanced from his reputation with the "Right" and "conservative economics," but also how far he might become "associated with the contemporary left's concerns with fairness, equality, and social justice" (Smith, 2013b, p. 784). This orientation to Smith as a contemporary interlocutor on matters of distributive and social justice underscores a further point that Collini makes about this stage of canonization: we should be wary of thinking that Smith as an object of "detailed scholarly enquiry" is somehow "incompatible with an enduring political resonance" (Collini, 1991, p. 319). We might even go further and

---

[19] Of course, one must recognize the anachronistic nature of the Left/Right designation. For standard treatment of these labels as "cluster terms," see Fleischacker, 2016; Otteson, 2016; C. Smith, 2013b, 2013a.

[20] On Smith's jurisprudential distinction between distributive and commutative justice, see Winch, 1978; Haakonssen, 1981; Hont and Ignatieff, 1983a; Young and Gordon, 1996. For Smith as a modern egalitarian theorist of social justice, see Fleischacker, 2004a, 2004b, 2013, 2016. Craig Smith (2013b) provides an excellent synopsis of the distributive justice and Left/Right debate. Maria Pia Paganelli's essay in this volume offers a revised, public-choice-inspired take on *The Wealth of Nations* being centrally concerned with justice.

[21] On Smith as a theorist of global justice and poverty, see Sen, 2013, 2016. Anderson (2016, 2017) represents one of the most recent and probably most explicit arguments for markets that is nonetheless aligned with the values of the "Left," and appeals to Adam Smith in the process.

suggest that a persistent belief that Smith *must* have an enduring political resonance – or, as Jesse Norman flamboyantly put it, that Smith might offer a "new master-narrative for our times" (Norman, 2018, p. 324) – is one reason why people are so eager to marshal Smith in their political and philosophical debates.

To be sure, this is a far cry from the nineteenth-century sloganeering around free trade or the invisible-hand waving of the twentieth century. Smith scholars are not simply studding their declarations of belief with references to the timeless genius of Adam Smith. Debates over the content of Smith's politics, his moral commitments, and how his politics and moral philosophy run through his economics have had an ongoing vitality. The persistence of these debates reveals how the categories of analysis and conceptual tools for understanding Smith are slippery and fraught with ambiguity. However, these qualities are precisely what have enabled Smith to be such a useful, ubiquitous, and powerful device for expressing a wide range of hopes and fears about market society, its politics, and its morality – both in the past and present.

1.3 Conclusion: The Future of Smith Studies?

Where does Smith studies go from here? What can this longer historical view of Smith scholarship afford us moving forward?

First, the "four-stages model," which I have used here to model the trajectory of Smith scholarship, is much more than an internal dynamic; rather, it is subject to external and contingent forces. The precarious nature of political and economic independence in the American Founding Era, the national and international salience of free trade debates, and the restructuring of postwar American political economy shaped the demands that readers brought to Smith's texts over time. Second, the history of reading and writing on Smith reveals the elusiveness of a genuinely historical Smith. It is a history littered with selective, narrow, and politically fashionable readings, and it offers sobering advice: reimaginings of Smith that are too presentist, too caught up in what scholars bring to their study, often do not withstand the test of time, but rather become artifacts *of* their time. Das Adam Smith Problem and the Chicago Smith are prime examples of this.

While much contemporary revisionist scholarship has challenged and refuted these readings, it has also opened two different and sometimes competing avenues for accessing Smith. One avenue seeks to understand *Smith* better, and in doing so, hopes that contemporary concerns do not obscure our view of Smith. The other seeks to understand our world better *through* Smith, and in doing so, often deliberately and self-consciously admits a certain level of present-mindedness. Smith has become an attractive resource for our contemporary questions – whether on the content and commitments of liberalism, the ethics of empathy, or the moral bases of capitalism. However, on this latter view we should be open to the possibility of being disappointed. We may have to admit that Smith does not (or cannot) answer our questions about, say, the climate crisis and our obligations to nonhuman nature, or our ongoing global reckoning with the legacy of race-based slavery and capitalism. Or if Smith does provide guidance on such questions, he may not always say what we, in the twenty-first century, hope he might.

Finally, there is an all-too-Smithian irony worth appreciating in the evolution of Smith studies. Smith predicted the beneficial consequences of the intellectual division of labor when he wrote that "In the progress of society ... Like every other employment too, [philosophy] is subdivided into a great number of different branches, each of which affords its occupation to a particular tribe or class of philosophers ... Each individual becomes more expert in his own peculiar branch, more work is done upon the whole, and the quantity of science is considerably increased by it" (WN I.1.9). There is no question that scholars worldwide have benefitted from the quantity and expertise of Smith scholarship, itself an effect of the division of labor in the academy. Yet the more recent history of Smith scholarship seems to indicate a growing sense that our disciplinary division of labor has gone *too* far, that in spite of the truth of Smith's predictions, our attempts to grasp what Smith was really up to are profoundly limited, even benighted by our disciplinary blinders. Smith represents the lost possibilities of an anti-disciplinary intellectual discipline; we long to understand not just *what* but *how* Smith was able to craft an ambitious "science of man" that smoothly traversed the boundaries we can no longer cross so easily. Whether we will be able to successfully recover and emulate Smith's ambitious "science of man," or have to resign ourselves to being unable to do what Smith did, only the future will tell.

2

The *Wealth of Nations* as a Work of Social Science

CHRISTOPHER J. BERRY

As its title indicates the focus of this investigation is the *Inquiry into the Nature and Causes of the Wealth of Nations* [WN^1] (to give its full and significant title), though I will also refer to Smith's other writings and to those of some of his contemporaries. More precisely the focus is the text of *WN* and the ultimate objective of this investigation is to refine our understanding of the book's argumentative commitments and their assumptions – focusing on *how* Smith realizes his ends rather than *why* he has those ends or *what* he hopes to achieve (these of course are not discrete questions). As I am construing it, to answer the question 'how' is to answer the question in what sense is *WN* to be understood as a work of (modern) 'science' in general and 'social science' in particular.

2.1 Moral Science

Smith the author of *WN* is also the author of *TMS*, as his self-identification as "professor of moral philosophy" on *WN*'s title page testifies. His third book *Essays on Philosophical Subjects* (*EPS*), published posthumously by Smith's executors but authorized by him, is chiefly of note because it indicates the wide range of his interests and scholarship. The most substantial essay in *EPS* is *The Principles which lead and direct Philosophical Enquiries; Illustrated by the History of Astronomy* (*HA*). Because this contains Smith's most explicitly extensive discussion of 'science' then it would seem an obvious starting-point for this enquiry. However, notwithstanding the integral nature of Smith's work in toto, some caution is required.[2] *HA* is described by Smith himself in his correspondence as a "juvenile" work (*CAS* 137/168) and, allowing for the fact that unlike other manuscripts, he selected to have it posthumously published, its remit is specific. As *HA*'s title identifies, it is an "illustration" of "principles" not some methodological blueprint. *WN* (and *TMS* for that matter) does not set out to instantiate the account of 'science' found in *HA*. This disconnection

---

[1] All unspecified quotations are to this work.
[2] Among those who identify continuities between *HA* and *WN* see especially Thomson (1965), who is followed inter alia by Redman (1993).

is reinforced when it is recalled that Smith openly declared that *HA* is not concerned with the "absurdity or probability" of astronomical theories or whether they are consistent with "truth and reality" (*EPS* 46). Moreover, more generally, it cannot be seriously entertained that *TMS* and *WN* do not represent Smith's endeavor to account accurately for how humans make moral judgments or how public opulence is generated.[3]

Yet, these points allowed, *HA* is not unrelated to Smith's corpus and there are aspects of that essay that do resonate and to which I will advert. Indeed I open by noting one passage in *WN* that echoes the terminology Smith employed in *HA*. He states that his aim in *HA* (*EPS* 34) is to consider the "nature and causes" of the three emotions of surprise, wonder, and admiration and not only does that phrase echo the full title of *WN* but in that text itself he comments that the "revolutions of the heavenly bodies ... necessarily excite wonder so they naturally call forth the curiosity of mankind to enquire into their causes" (V.i.f.24). What is significant, and what sets the scene for my discussion, is that in the following paragraph Smith refers to the development of philosophy (science) from "maxims" that lack "very distinct and methodical order" to when "different observations are connected by a few common principles ... towards a system." And though this development was first apparent in natural philosophy, it was later applied to the "maxims of common life." Smith then, reiterating his terms, states that these maxims, too, developed to become "arranged in some methodical order, and connected together by a few common principles." He now identifies the "science which pretends to investigate and explain those connecting principles ... [as] what is properly called moral philosophy" (V.i.f.25).

From this passage it is, I infer, reasonable, and contextually appropriate, to claim that Smith would regard *WN* as a species of 'moral philosophy,' the exposition of which is nothing less than a scientific enquiry into the nature and causes of the wealth of nations. If it is thus allowed that Smith is self-knowingly a moral (social) scientist, then this raises the twin questions: what does that self-knowledge tell him makes *WN* a work of 'science'? And what are the requisite criteria to sustain that assessment?

I start by picking out three features of that cited paragraph in *WN* (V.i.f.25), namely, the references to 'system' (Section 2.2), 'principles' (Section 2.3), and 'causes' (Section 2.4). Together they characterize *WN* as a scientific 'inquiry' and Section 2.5 examines the underlying role of a 'science of human nature' and Section 2.6 outlines how a properly *social* science should proceed. In my execution of this analysis, I will note Smith's elusive, or multivocal, language, but, as I will aim to bring out in Section 2.6, this elusiveness (or at least some

---

[3] Compare Aspromourgos (2009) that *WN* is not intended as a speculative exercise to soothe the mind but "a policy science" qua a "tool of the betterment of human society." To broadly similar effect see Smith (2020).

of it) is not casual inadvertence on Smith's part but rather manifests what I shall call his argumentative style and claim that this centrally informs us about his conception of social science, about 'how' he thinks an enlightening inquiry should proceed to elicit 'nature and causes.'

2.2 System

References to 'system' are ubiquitous in the eighteenth century but not uniform. D'Alembert in his *Discours préliminaire à l'Encyclopédie* (1751) sought to clarify by distinguishing "the true systematic spirit" from "the spirit of system" (D'Alembert, 2011, p. 15).[4] Although this distinction was not absolute, it was pointed. As he says later, the latter flatters the imagination rather than instructs and for that reason it has been virtually banished from the best work (p. 60). For D'Alembert, as for the Enlightenment, the best work is what produces useful knowledge where the criterion of 'useful' is improvement of human life (p. 11). It is the hallmark of good science that it fosters improvement. It is on that basis that D'Alembert identifies Bacon as a pioneer because from profound contemporary darkness he had the vision that science should be limited to what makes life better and happier rather than to the production of sterile systems (p. 48).[5]

Smith was a keen reader (and early reviewer [cf. *EPS* 246]) of *l'Encyclopédie*.[6] He shares, as we will see, D'Alembert's Baconianism and is dismissive of "speculative systems" (v.i.f.2). For his part, one of his conspicuous usages is when, perhaps echoing his teacher Hutcheson's posthumous *A System of Moral Philosophy* (1755), he employs 'system' as a classificatory device.[7] Smith uses it in that capacity in the title of Book VII of *TMS*, "Of Systems of Moral Philosophy," where he typifies as "different classes" the three accounts of virtue that he identifies (*TMS* VII.2.intro.1). Similarly *HA* identifies a process of reducing observations "into proper classes" (*EPS* 37–38).[8]

---

[4] All translations in this chapter are my own.
[5] D'Alembert has in mind not only Aristotelians and Scholastics but also the seventeenth century system builders like Malebranche, Leibniz, and Spinoza. These three are criticized by Condillac, who is acknowledged by D'Alembert as his source; indeed he says Condillac has demolished them (D'Alembert, 2011, p. 48).
[6] He bought the first seven volumes for Glasgow University Library, where they still reside.
[7] In his opening paragraph Hutcheson refers to Natural Law as "the system or collection" of laws of nature (Hutcheson, 1755).
[8] Classification is a process of association (and here Smith closely follows Hume) that locates a common connection or theme. It is when an observation seemingly defies existing classification that it stimulates the scientific quest for a connection (cf. *EPS* 37). Smith claims this was first achieved by Pythagoras and Thales who so "methodized" their doctrines that these deserved "the name of a system" (*EPS* 52; cf. *EPS* 38).

This conception of a system as a classificatory device also features in *WN*. Indeed the most salient usage of the term 'system' in that work is again titular. Book IV's subject is identified as "Of Systems of Political Oeconomy" and therein Smith presents his examination of the mercantile and the agricultural "systems." But outside that context, the term is used liberally in both a specific sense (e.g., "repairing roads" [V.i.d.9 cf. V.ii.c.10]) and a general sense (e.g., a "feudal system" [I.xi.1 cf. IV.vii.c.43, V.ii.c.10]). However, perhaps the most significant usage of the term in *WN* is in one of his most famous references – "the obvious and simple system of natural liberty" (IV.ix.51 cf. IV.vii.c.44).

'Natural liberty' is a key motif in *WN* but in what sense, if any, does it constitute a 'system'? The answer to that question must be constructed piecemeal. The initial building-block is to consider the make-up of *WN*. The book is something of a baggy monster, and it can come over as ill-disciplined, something not missed by early critics like J.R. McCulloch or Jean-Baptiste Say (McCulloch, 1889, p. xliix; Say, 1972, p. 10). It is populated by 'digressions,' most notably, because of its length, one devoted to variations in the value of silver, and most notoriously, because of its contemporary contentiousness, one on corn.[9] Beyond these explicit excursions the text is full of historical and literary references but even to a sympathetic reader their sheer number might be judged to distract from the central argument. Yet despite calling *WN* an 'inquiry' and not a 'system,' that the book is systematic was generally acknowledged even by his contemporaries.[10] What that acknowledgment implicitly recognizes is that *WN* also embodies a non-classificatory sense of system. Whereas we can identify classified or categorized systems as *static* groupings of linked themes or data (a taxonomy), it is not difficult, and without distortion, to see *WN* as also *dynamically* systematic. The latter can be identified, albeit sweepingly, on two fronts – general and specific.

Exemplifying a general system, the book as a whole, while exhibiting both analysis and historical narrative, does coherently hang together; it engages its subject synchronically and diachronically. The book analyzes a new form of social organization – not a trading republic but a commercial society where every person lives by exchanging and is "in some measure a merchant" (I.iv.1).

---

[9] Though Smith's discussion has a British focus it is unlikely that he was unaware of the extensive French debate; he owned a copy of Morellet's refutation of Galiani, who had declared the Physiocrats' principles false but more than that had argued that before their version of an equilibrium could occur people would have died from the induced famine (Galiani, 1975b, pp. 419, 510). For debates on this question and its ramifications in recent Smithian scholarship, see Hont and Ignatieff (1983a); Rothschild (2002); Hill and Montag (2014); Wooton (2018).

[10] According to Hugh Blair in *WN* Smith's "System gradually erects itself" and according to William Robertson, Smith "has formed into a regular and consistent system one of the most intricate and important parts of political science" (*CAS* 151/188; 153/192). See Schliesser (2017) for a thematic account of Smith as a "systematic philosopher."

What makes it 'new,' and in what respects, can only be grasped by comparing it to earlier forms of organization. Analytically, Smith identifies basic principles (see later). The opening chapter identifies the productivity of labor as the source of every society's "necessaries and conveniences" of life. This productivity is caused by the division of labor, which is the consequence of the universal human propensity to "truck, barter and exchange." Those activities are constitutive of a market. As history demonstrates, it is the symbiotic relation between the extensiveness of the market and the intensification of the division of labor that determines economic growth (social progress). That growth requires some institutional structures, like those that induce stability by reliably upholding justice (rule of law), which make it worthwhile to accumulate capital stock in order to invest in the future. Those structures rely on principles of public finance that themselves reflexively rely on stabilizing institutions. This system or series of connections is complemented by historical investigations, which, inter alia, supply evidence of the relative efficacy of policies (like the measures to reduce smuggling) and identify the role of accidents (unintended consequences). This general system, suffused with D'Alembert's 'systematic spirit,' demonstrates how a commercial society distinctively enjoys "universal opulence" that, contrary to the opulence enjoyed in earlier societies, enables the material well-being of all (I.i.10). Here lies Smith's Baconianism; as Bacon himself said in his *New Organon* "the real and legitimate goal" of science is to make life better (Bacon, 1853, p. 416).

This macroeconomic system (as we can loosely call it) is excitingly broad-brush but it is fair to say that the large claims made for *WN* have rested on the more particular systems (microeconomic, as again we can nontechnically label it) that he outlines. While there is a dynamic element to the macroeconomic that is conveyed by the historical story, it is at the microeconomic level that the elements of a dynamic system are evident. Since it is no part of my aim here to outline these in any depth, I will select just one well-known example – Smith's analysis of price.

In this celebrated account, Smith twice employs the metaphor that the market price "gravitates" to the natural price (I.vii.15, 20). He has defined the "natural price" of any commodity as what is required unexceptionally to pay rent, wages and profit (I.vii.4). The market price is determined by supply and effectual demand. These two prices do not necessarily coincide. But shorn of artificial restrictions (when, that is, there is "perfect liberty" [I.viii.30]), if the demand is high and supply low then the market price will be high but that will incentivize others to enter the market for that commodity thus increasing the supply, which will meet demand and the price will fall. The converse is true when supply exceeds demand. This dynamic process is systemic. The market price "reposes" around a central (i.e., the natural) price (I.viii.15). But, unlike his later followers, Smith does not treat this (equilibrating) process as an abstraction. He is acutely aware that interested parties (corporations and the like) seek to manipulate the process and "accidental variation[s]," that by hindering effectual demand might keep the market price above the natural, are possible (cf. I.vii.15/75, I.xi.g.19). Although Smith thinks that the historical record shows that in the real world such accidents, both beneficial and baleful, do clearly happen, that recognition does not undermine the analysis that beneath the phenomenological randomness of prices (the 'higgling' of the market [I.v.4]) systemic regularities are 'at work.'

Yet despite the Newtonian image of gravitation,[11] and in contrast to Galiani for whom "the laws of commerce" are as exact as the laws of gravity (Galiani, 1975a), Smith does not presume to follow Newton by labelling these 'economic regularities' laws (*pace* Hetherington, 1983). Nonetheless, Newton is a methodological influence on Smith's aspiration to provide a scientific inquiry.

2.3 Principles

The concept of a system implies there are interconnected components and, as Smith said, in order to establish an inquiry as scientific, these components need to be connected by principles, which, moreover, play a formative or foundational role. Condillac, who as we have noted was D'Alembert's major source, opened his *Traité des Systèmes* (1749) by declaring:

> A system is nothing other than the arrangement of the different components of an art or a science in a mutually supportive order, where the last are explained by the first. Those which are explanatory are called principles; and the more perfect the system the fewer the principles: even better if they could be reduced to just one.
>
> (Condillac, 1947, I, p. 121)

Not unexpectedly the inspiration behind the identifications and definitions is Newton.[12] Although Smith's library contained a copy of Condillac's *Traité*, Newton's status is so elevated that it is not surprising that Smith's view of an explanatory system is Newtonian. In his Glasgow Rhetoric lectures he commends Newton's method over Aristotle's because "it gives us pleasure to see

---

[11] Both Wooton (2018, p. 189) and Schliesser (2017, pp. 299, 305) claim that to be accurate the imagery is rather Aristotelian but even if in stricto sensu true, it is improbable that Smith (and his readers) would regard it as anything other than an allusion to Newton. Smith is far from exceptional; see, for example, Montesquieu who likens the function of the principle of honor in a monarchy to gravitation as it operates in the system of the universe (Montesquieu, 1961, I, 29 [Bk III Chap. 7]).

[12] Condillac identifies three types of systems – those based on abstract metaphysics, on imagined suppositions (hypotheses) and on observation and experiment, which is the only one worthy of the name. He gives 'gravity' as an example of a principle in this third system (Condillac, 1947, I, 122). Newton by name is cited chiefly as an opponent of Descartes.

the phenomena ... all deduced from some principle (commonly a well-known one) and all united in one chain" (*LRBL* ii.134). This glosses Newton's own First Rule – "Nature is pleased with simplicity and affects not the pomp of superfluous causes."[13] The benchmark is parsimony, to explain a lot by a little. In addition, simplicity is aesthetically pleasing, as Smith in an earlier Rhetoric lecture observed, "the most beautiful passages are generally the most simple" (*LRBL* i.74). This observation is clearly echoed in *WN* where Smith judges that the "beauty of a systematical arrangement" consists in different observations connected by "a few common principles" (V.i.f.24).

References to 'principles' are commonplace but the obverse of this popularity is, as Bentham remarked in a footnote to his own version, that "principle" is "a term of very vague and very extensive signification" (Bentham, 1948, p. 126n) and *WN* bears that out. The book is replete with identifications of 'principles.' In a typical Smithian way these cover a number of usages. Some of them are synonyms for moral convictions (such as "charity" [I.ii.2]) or non-systemic (as of "common prudence" [II.2.36]) but others connect to the notion of a 'system.' In the classificatory sense this is explicit when in Book IV he titles the first chapter 'Of the principle of the commercial or mercantile system' (IV.1) (similarly *TMS* Book VII [*TMS* VII.i.1]) and it plays a key role in the conception of a system as dynamic, as strategically in the title of chapter 2 of Book I – "Of the Principle which gives occasion to the Division of Labor." Whether the propensity to truck is an "original principle" (or a "necessary consequence" of faculties of "reason and speech" [cf. *LJ(B)* 221]) is – as Smith himself accepts – not germane. It is clear enough that the invocation of 'principle' here identifies it as possessing an elementary explanatory function (Fiori, 2012, p. 412 et passim; Schliesser, 2017, p. 4n). There is an implicit systematic causal chain: productivity is the effect of the division of labor which is the effect of the trucking principle (cf. *LJ(A)* vi.46). I will say more about causation later but here I want to investigate how the notion of a 'principle' can begin to help answer the question in what sense 'natural liberty' is a 'system.'

The systematic nature of *WN*, in both its positive argument for the way to improve human life both materially and morally and in its critique of alternative routes, rests on the presence, in a Condillacian fashion, of mutually supportive explanatory common principles. I will identify three but, by definition, it follows that these are not discrete. One has already been touched on, namely, the principle to truck, barter, and exchange. The next section will deal with another in the form of the principle of self-interest but here I focus on the third. This is "the principle" that "every man" possesses "the uniform, constant

---

[13] In Thayer, 1953. There is a large literature on Smith's relation to Newton (see, e.g., Becker, 1961; Redman, 1993a; Montes, 2013). I discuss an aspect of this in Berry, 2018b.

and uninterrupted effort ... to better his condition." I shall label this the 'betterment principle' and in the search for the principles that must ex hypothesi inform the *system* of natural liberty it plays a key role.

It is from the expression of the betterment principle that "publick and national, as well as private opulence is originally derived" but beyond that it is "frequently powerful enough to maintain the natural progress of things toward improvement, in spite both of the extravagance of government and of the greatest errors of administration" (II.iii.31 cf. almost identically IV.v.b.43). The phrase 'in spite of' here provides a clue as to why Smith refers to 'the system' of natural liberty, which he formulates as obtaining when "every man, as long as he does not violate the laws of justice, is left perfectly free to pursue his own interest his own way" (IV.ix.51).

To label natural liberty a *'system'* is, in its textual context, to highlight polemically its distinction from especially the mercantilist but also from the Physiocratic *system*. The crux of the distinction is that the latter pair are identified with systemic illiberal, unnatural restraints. They both, the mercantilists in practice and the Physiocrats in theory, had recourse to public authorities to ensure their goals but, according to Smith, in so doing, they exhibit 'extravagant government' and 'erroneous administration' and thus inhibit that 'natural progress to improvement.'[14]

By contrast, for Smith, once those 'unnatural' restrictions are removed, the system of natural liberty "establishes itself of its own accord" (IV.xi.51). That wording gives it the appearance of the default position ('natural progress'), as befits his description of it as "the obvious and simple system." From this position it follows, for Smith, that government has no duty of superintendence over private industry but is dutifully confined to the tasks of defense, internal order, and enabling public works (though, as has been well documented, in practice Smith allows plenty of scope for government action). These duties serve (note the reference to 'laws of justice' in the definition of natural

---

[14] The mercantilist system underwrote direct legislation to prohibit imports/provide subsidies which favored corporations (most egregiously with respect to the operation of the East India Company [e.g., IV.vii.c.103]) and it was thus in the interest of producers not consumers, all at odds with "perfect liberty" (I.x.c.2). The Physiocratic system was designed to promote agriculture by "imposing restraints" on manufacture (IV.ix.49) and even though they argued that individuals should be left free to choose how to spend their funds (for which Smith commended them [IV.ix.38]) yet they saw a need for a "true" and "legitimate" or "legal despot" (as opposed to an "arbitrary despotism") to give continuous oversight, see for example Quesnay (1767a, p. 7); du Pont de Nemours (1768, p. 35n); Mercier de la Rivière (1910, pp. 143–144). See Kaplan (1976, p. 228) for the "irony" of the argument of the Physiocrats (liberals) that to realize their ends "centralization was a prerequisite."

liberty)[15] to protect the betterment principle so that it can manifest its independent autopoietic 'power' to prevent and correct the "bad effects" of the "oppressive" political economy of mercantilism as well as that propounded by Quesnay (the identified target here) (IV.ix.28 cf. II.iii.36). This is an implicit acknowledgment of its causal efficacy.

2.4 Causes

Given *WN*'s full title it would be a reasonable expectation that the identification of causes would be prominent. This expectation would be further supported by Smith's Enlightenment subscription to the Baconian goal of improvement since that requires knowledge of causes, which Bacon had declared is synonymous with power (Bacon, 1853, pp. 20, 383; Hobbes, 1991, p. 36). In addition, for 'moral philosophy' to be a science it means the Newtonian injunction to be simple and eschew superfluous causes, alongside the Condillacian emphasis on limited, linked explanatory principles, has to be emulated.

The text of *WN* is littered with explicit references to 'causes.' In addition to its presumptive presence in the potency of the betterment principle, there are a variety of synonyms in terms like 'derived from' or 'necessary consequence of' as well as his use of 'occasion,' as in the title of chapter 2 of Book I quoted earlier and its repeated use in that chapter. Yet in one (admittedly long) paragraph of that *WN* chapter (I.11.2) he also uses 'occasion' several times in the sense of a circumstantial requirement, as when he refers to "the necessaries of life he has occasion for." It is not that Smith is simply imprecise but also, as we shall see, that this (multivocal) insouciance serves positively to distinguish his mode of argumentation from another contemporaneously advocated. Nonetheless, identifying causes is important to Smith and runs throughout the microeconomic analysis, as when competition between producers/consumers is an unarticulated cause of the gravitational pull from the market to the natural price. More generally, it is clear that he confines himself

---

[15] The other clear statement is again in the context of the "regulations of the mercantile system" where Smith phrases it as "the natural system of perfect liberty and justice" (IV.vii.c.44). He uses the term 'natural liberty' without tying it explicitly to a system in various places – as in his opposition to apprenticeships (IV.ii.42) but also in its justified "violation" in the case of builders and bankers (II.ii.94). These references underline the specificity of the polemical use of 'system' in IV.xi.51 and reinforce his judgment that the mercantilist and Physiocratic systems, in contrast to the system of natural liberty, fail to achieve successfully the two objects of the political economy that he identifies in the Introduction to Book IV, namely, "to supply or enable plentiful revenue and subsistence for the people, or more properly to enable them to supply such a revenue or subsistence for themselves" and "to supply the state or commonwealth with a revenue sufficient for the publick service."

to efficient causality; as a 'modern' thinker he has no room for the remaining components (formal, material and final) of the Aristotelian quartet.

When his explicit usages are examined, they are various. Some are seemingly straightforward exemplifications of efficient causes, as when he identifies "plenty of good land" and the liberty to "manage their own affairs" as the "two great causes" of the prosperity of the American colonies (IV.vii.b.16; for other examples, see V.i.a.8; III.iv.13; I.viii.57 etc.). He employs the long-standing distinction, to which Hume had given a definitive exposition in the essay "Of National Characters," between "natural" and "moral causes," and he follows the standard line that the former operate independently of human action while the latter instantiate it (Hume, 1987, pp. 197–215). The 'accidental variations' mentioned, such as "singularity of soil and situation" (I.vii.24) or seasonal variation of corn yields (I.xi.3), are openly identified examples of "natural causes," while elsewhere he explicitly invokes "moral causes" to explain, for example, the practice of government borrowing in a commercial society and the willingness of subjects to lend to it (V.iii.5).

Notwithstanding its importance, *WN* does not contain any sustained theoretical account of the causal process but his untheorized assumptions are Humean. Smith indeed explicitly cites Hume in one of the occasions when his causal reasoning is more evidently articulated.[16] Hume had argued that it was a "fallacy" to identify the quantity of money as the "cause" of a rise in prices because it "mistakes a collateral effect for a cause" (Hume, 1987, p. 294) (and likewise for a determination of the rate of interest [Hume, 1987, p. 298]). Smith similarly calls it a "fallacy" to regard the increase in the supply of gold that followed the Spanish discoveries in the West Indies as "the real cause" of the lowering of the rate of interest.[17] For Smith the cause of that reduction is competition between the owners of capital (II.iv.8,9). Like Hume, Smith, too, puts accurate causal analysis to argumentative effect, as in his demonstration that the high value of silver is, pace the "system of political economy," not proof of a country's poverty (I.xi.n.1).

The key assumption throughout *WN* is that a convincing argument relies on the correct identification of causes; the wealth of a nation, the abundant provision of necessities and conveniences, is caused by the productive powers of labor and not by the value of silver or net exports. Indeed that identification

---

[16] See also his reference (III.iv.4) to Hume prior to his [moral causal] argument that changes in "the state of property and manners" brought about the collapse of feudalism, for which he says corroboration can be found in "remote antiquities" as well as contemporary Scotland. The explanation of that concurrence is that "such effects must always flow from such causes" – they are constantly conjoined (III.iv.8 cf. *LJ*(A) iv.157.). For Hume's account of causality in 'economics,' see especially Schabas and Wennerlind (2020, chap. 2).

[17] Paganelli (2020) emphasizes Smith's alertness to distinguishing causation and correlation.

is what marks *WN* out as properly scientific, as eliciting 'general principles' and not the stuff of superficial particularistic coffee-house conversation, as Hume dismissively characterizes shallow thinking on trade and economy (Hume, 1987; Berry, 2020b). The inquiry into the wealth of nations as a species of moral philosophy assumes, like all moral sciences, that human behavior is not random but subject to regularities and open to causal explanation. On this assumption Smith sets out, in his at-times-elliptical way, in *WN* to inquire how this applies to the operation of a commercial society; an inquiry premised on the solidity of what Hume, co-opting Malebranche, called the "science of man" (Hume, 1978, p. xv) and Smith himself called "the science of human nature" (*TMS* VII.iii.2.5).

2.5 Science of Human Nature

Smith at one point (*TMS* III.2.30) refers, without specifying them, to the "unalterable principles of human nature" (Berry, 2018a). This constancy is rooted in humans' material nature – all humans enjoy pleasure and avoid pain, they are, as such, creatures of passion and desire.[18] This signals that Smith accepts the naturalization of human nature on which, for all their differences, Descartes, Spinoza, Hobbes, Locke, and others had embarked. The consequence of this naturalization is that the way to seek the truth about human nature is, in principle, no different from the way to seek the truth about nature in general.[19] In both cases it is a search for causes. But the 'causes' in question reflect the 'modern' consensus, according to which, as we have seen, when seeking explanations attention should be paid to efficient or material causes. We explain human behavior by identifying motives, that is, literally, what causes motion in us (cf. *LRBL* ii,192). In a generic sense, desires play this motivational role.

That, as social creatures, humans are responsive to others is a lynchpin of *TMS*. Each experiences pleasure in the approval of others and pain in their disapproval because, Smith claims, humans have been endowed with an "original desire to please and an original aversion to offend" (*TMS* III.2.6). This is a dynamic process as "desires and aversions become the *causes* of new desires and new aversions, new joys and new sorrows" (*TMS* III,1.3 my emphasis). As *WN* will exploit, humans are incentivized to seek pleasure

---

[18] See the explicit statement that "pleasure and pain are the great objects of desire and aversion" and are distinguishable by "immediate sense and feeling" (not reason) (*TMS* VII.iii.2.8). See next paragraph in the text for examples of the motivating force of 'desire.' This mainstream 'modernist' view runs throughout Smith's works.

[19] This is not to say there are no practical differences, as even Hume allowed (1978, pp. xviii–xix), but I have elsewhere disputed the arguments of those who starkly separate natural and moral science in Smith (Berry, 2006; Innes, 2009).

(and avoid pain) and, consistent with that quotation from *TMS*, what gives pleasure/pain is open ended, able to embrace a wide range of motivational goals. Nowhere does Smith limit these goals to the acquisition of material goods and even when they are pursued it is often by proxy for the esteem they are thought to bring to their owner and the gratification of the natural "love of distinction" (*LJ(B)* 209/488, *TMS* IV.i.8).

The betterment principle is an example of this restless dynamism. It is a ubiquitous universal 'desire,' since it is present from the womb to the grave and "there is scarce perhaps a single instant in which any man is so perfectly and completely satisfied with his situation as to be without any wish of alteration or improvement of any kind" (II.iii.28). And, in his typically qualified way, Smith goes on to remark that in "the greater part of men," this wish manifests itself as a quest for an "augmentation of fortune" (II.iii.28 cf. *TMS* VI.i.3) or, more generally, it is this particular expression of restless desire that creates the "blessing of opulence," as he terms it in his jurisprudence lectures (*LJ(A)* iii,111). The desire for betterment is truly a causal 'principle' on Condillacian grounds; it is explanatory, its multifarious effects are widely discernible and it is an inherent property, an original characteristic of human nature.

This scientific account of human nature underwrites the often subterranean explanatory system in *WN*. Its most famous outcrop is the motivation of the butcher, the brewer and the baker who will only reliably supply us with beef, beer, and bread if we appeal to "their regard to their own interest" (I.ii.2). They can, of course, at their discretion act with "humanity" but, as a consequence, beggars cannot predictably rely upon this beneficence. By contrast, the butcher can predict that if she gives all her meat away she will not survive long as a merchant. It is her own interest qua butcher that motivates her actions and this would not call forth the censure of the impartial spectator (*TMS* II.ii.1). Self-interest with betterment and trucking is the third of the principles adumbrated in Section 2.3.[20] And since, as Smith has told us, in a commercial society every person is in some measure a merchant, it follows that what Smith had in his Glasgow jurisprudence lectures explicitly called "the general principle" of self-interest, which "regulates the action of every man" (*LJ(B)* 327/538), causally explains the system of exchange. Hence at the heart of any bargain is the understanding "give me that which I want and you shall have this you want" (II.ii.2). This self-interested "concurrence of their passions," which Smith invokes immediately before the butcher passage, is not only causally sufficient but also fulfils the Newtonian injunction to be

---

[20] The term 'self-interest' itself is employed only once in *WN* in the context of Catholic clergy, whose "industry and zeal" is motivated by the revenue they obtain from confession (V.i.g.2). Its explanatory function qua 'scientific principle' is distinct from the overtly moral language of selfishness (cf. II.iii.42 "base"; III.iv.10 "vile").

parsimonious, to dispense with superfluous factors (like say beneficence) (Berry, 2020a). Writ large, this structure of motives explains the systemic dynamics at both the macro and micro level of a 'modern economy.' The three principles of self-interest, of betterment and of exchanging function in a mutually supportive way and, in so doing, comply with the systemic causally explanatory criteria of scientific enquiry.

Of course, there is nothing novel in identifying the salience and pivotal role of self-interest.[21] On Smith's own account of it, self-interested exchange is universal: bows for venison in the first hunter-gatherer 'stage' of human social organization [I.ii.3]) had been theoretically (and normatively) treated by Aristotle and other 'classic' authors. The 'modern' world, however, brings that salience and role to the fore. It is a world of marketized relations, financial instruments, and increased and profitable long-distance trade, all of which was accompanied by increasingly sophisticated analyses of credit, interest, and the like. While initially 'unscientific,' typically comprising ad hoc and ad hominem pamphleteering, there was a general acceptance of the uniformity of human behavior and the motivational force of self-interest (Berry, 2020b).

The case of the butcher is just one instantiation of the explanatory (causal) principle of self-interest at work. If we return to the 'system of natural liberty,' its positive dimension is the freedom of "every man ... to pursue his own interest." Hence, for example and illustrating the underlying pleasure/pain dynamic, "every man's interest" prompts him to seek employment that is advantageous (and shun the disadvantageous) (I.x.1, I.vii.14) (Herzog, 2013, p. 71). From many other cases, I select two for their more general significance. It is "absurd" to imagine people will work less hard for themselves than for others (I.viii48, cf. for the same locution IV.ii.15, IV.ii.35). Similarly given "tolerable security," stockholders would "be perfectly crazy" if they didn't put their stock to use (II.i.30). Why in these cases is it absurd or crazy? The wider point of significance here is that Smith is trading on commonplace or familiar assumptions about human motivation or in later language the structure of incentives.

This brings us back to the question of 'science.' Smith's references to absurdity and craziness appeal to language that is familiar in everyday experience. This recourse to nontechnical, familiar, language has a persuasive function[22] and also, not coincidentally, throws light on the type of argumentation or method employed in WN. It is also one of the places where HA can illuminate the later work.

---

[21] There is a large literature on this aspect of Smith; see, for example, the careful accounts in Fleischacker, 2004b, chap. 5; Heath, 2013; Maurer, 2019, pp. 186–195.

[22] Endres (1991, p. 84) refers to the "familiarity criterion" and notes its link to the popularization of complex systems of thought.

HA's distinctive argument is that philosophy/science "by representing the invisible chains" that bind together seemingly "disjointed objects" allays the implicitly painful "tumult of the imagination" when confronted by this disjunction. The crucial criterion of a successful (pleasing) restoration of tranquility is when the connecting principles are familiar (*EPS* 45–46). Hence, within the remit or design of *HA*, Newton's triumph over Descartes was sealed by the fact that his use of the principle of gravity as a connecting force was "so familiar" that it "completely removed all the difficulties of the imagination" (*EPS* 98 cf. 76, 104). By extension the conduct of the butcher is so familiar that there is nothing 'wonder-full' about her self-interested transactions (Hollander, 1977). On the same lines the choice of a "trifling" enterprise like pin-making is deliberate precisely because it presents a well-known, that is, familiar case where the division of labor is "easily understood" and "obvious" and because it appeals to behavior, like the temptation to saunter, that is familiar in everyday life (I.i.2).

There is of course more to it than appealing to the familiar, just as there was with Newton, whose physics was vindicated, inter alia, by the expeditions of Maupertuis and La Condamine to measure the earth. That the butcher needs to sell her sausages if she is to stay in business is an (unsurprising) 'maxim of common life' but what determines their price is not so 'obvious' or visible, especially since familiarity is not an infallible touchstone (cf. IV.i.34). There are principles at work which, as noted above, will explain the components of price and it is these that Smith the moral scientist seeks to determine. It could be said, again echoing *HA*, that he is searching for those invisible chains that will introduce order into chaos (say price fluctuations). But even then "no system" will be persuasive if the connecting principles are "not familiar to all mankind" (*EPS* 46). Hence, while very few could understand Newton's *Principia*, Smith would consider *WN* a failure if its reach was similarly restricted. Accordingly he introduces the question of value with a simple observation. He supposes in the hunter stage that it takes twice the labor to kill a beaver than it does a deer, so it is almost intuitively obvious (it gels with human nature) that one beaver should exchange for two deer (I.vi.1). On this basis it is easy for the reader to appreciate the crucial role played by labor. Having laid this groundwork Smith is enabled "to investigate the *principles* which regulate exchangeable value" (I.iv.14, my emphasis), to explain why the market price of sausages sold by that butcher on that day need not correspond with the natural price, and so on.

2.6 The Science of Society

This discursive argumentative style is not incidental but constitutive (or at least indicative) of Smith's multivocal conception of social science. One significant manifestation of this is his coolness toward what William Petty called 'political arithmetic' (IV.v.b.30 cf. *CAS* 249/288).²³ Though the term 'political arithmetic' appears in the title of several of Petty's pamphlets, he nowhere spells out what he means. Yet the thrust of his argument is his declaration that he wanted to express his viewpoint in terms of "Number, Weight and Measure" rather than "the mutable Minds, Opinions, Appetites and Passions of particular Men" (Petty, 1899, I, p. 244).²⁴ Such an approach would be, in his estimation, the best means to advance socioeconomic improvement and political stability (Buck, 1977; Slack, 2015, p. 117ff).²⁵ Smith explicitly applies this same lack of enthusiasm to Quesnay's "arithmetical formularies" as represented by the "Oeconomical Table" (IV.ix.27).²⁶ Independently of Smith's disagreement with the Physiocrats' privileging of agriculture, he balked at their arithmetical commitment to precision in what Quesnay (1764, II, p. 284), among others, called the science of economics (Quesnay, 1764, II, p. 284).²⁷

But in this antipathy lies a wider point about Smith's view of social science. It is not that he disputes the importance of data, like that which informed the Table and the analysis of which had by mid-century in England come to be identified as exercises in political arithmetic. Indeed *WN* contains many pages where Smith himself collates information (e.g., I.xi.p.10) and his correspondence reveals the importance he attached to getting up-to-date intelligence (see, e.g., *CAS* 196/235). Nor does he resile from making inferences from the use of data (Macdonald, 2019).²⁸ The sticking-point is the abstraction that the focus on arithmetical precision implies.²⁹

The advantage of 'measure' over 'opinion' as put forward by Petty was that it is relatively unambiguous. The same end could also be achieved through linguistic clarity. A 'science' to be worthy of the name needed terminological exactitude. In the Preface to his *Commerce et le Gouvernement* (1776)

---

[23] Smith, typically, never cites Petty in *WN* but he was aware of his writings (*CAS* 30/32).
[24] A contemporary observed positively that Petty had "made it appear that Mathematical Reasoning is not only applicable to Line and Numbers but also affords the best means of Judging in all concerns of humane life" (Petty, 1899, II, p. 513n).
[25] Diderot's article 'Political Arithmetic' in the *l'Encyclopedie* cites Petty as the first to use the term and states that its aim was its usefulness (Diderot, 1751, I, p. 68).
[26] Steiner (1998, p. 19) sees a methodological parallel between the Physiocrats and Petty; see also (Perrot, 1992, p. 35).
[27] Quesnay (1767b, p. 20, 1767a, p. 214) defended what he termed "the new economic science" and reaffirmed that the language of that science is "the clearest, most precise and most philosophical" as is possible and Mirabeau stated that the Table would "prove arithmetically" the different outcomes of the distribution of produce (Mirabeau, 1759, p. 9).
[28] For example, the degree of civilization can be inferred from the relative money-price of some goods in proportion to others (I.xi.n.3).
[29] Despite Phillipson's claims about Smith having a mathematical method, influenced by Euclidean geometry, *WN* does not support that (Phillipson, 2010, p. 92; cf. 42, 101).

Condillac says the science of economics still needs its own language, which it was his aim to create (Condillac, 1947, II, p. 241). Throughout his voluminous writings, he emphasizes the merits and advantages of a "well-constructed language" (1947, II, p. 420). While, in virtue of its precision, he takes algebra as the model (e.g., 1947, II, p. 420) in that it shows how a perfect language would function,[30] he does not in *Commerce* employ arithmetic, rather he relies on terminological clarity.[31] In summarizing his argument he states that he has reduced/simplified the "naturally complicated" subject of economic science to "elementary notions" that have been determined with precision (1947, II, 366).

Condillac is likely following the influential lead both theoretical and methodological of Richard Cantillon who, in the opening sentence of his *Essai sur la Nature du Commerce en général* (1755), provides clear-cut definitions of wealth, land, and labor (Cantillon, 2001, p. 1). But Cantillon upbraided political arithmeticians, explicitly citing Petty and Davenant as his most important, if critical, predecessors, because they dealt only with effects not "causes and principles" (2001, p. 16 cf. p. 27). While, as we will note, Smith's argumentative style was different, in this regard he was of a similar opinion. In line with Beccaria's judgment that, thanks to the vicissitudes of human life, "mathematical exactitude" was inapt (Beccaria, 1965, pp. 20–21), and along with Cantillon, Turgot, and others, Smith declined to adopt what Catherine Larrère has called the "mathematization of evidence" as well as being wary of taking precision to arithmetical extremes (Larrère, 1992, p. 15ff).

It is symptomatic evidence of this wariness, of his unwillingness to privilege exactitude, that throughout *WN* most of Smith's arguments are filled with qualifications and his prose is nuanced. The infamous 'invisible hand' passage is a case in point but a more pertinent illustration is the very first sentence of chapter I of Book I, where he states that improvements in productivity, etc., "seem" to have been the effects of the division of labor. This heavily load-bearing statement for his whole argument exhibits neither Quesnay's preoccupation with exactitude and precision nor the didactic "definitionism" of Cantillon or Condillac (Klein, 1985). In their differing ways, these authors leave the 'social' out of 'social science' (so to speak) with the consequence that their accounts lose in persuasiveness what they pretend to claim in clarity. This does not mean Smith countenances ambiguity. He recognizes that it is a

---

[30] I am indebted to Pedro Pimenta for impressing this point on me.
[31] While acknowledging that it not possible to reduce all the readings of a word merely by definition (Condillac, 1947, II, p. 260), he proceeds by seeking precision through stipulated distinctions (as, for example between true and artificial needs [1947, II, p. 244]) to avoid vagueness and render the science of economics intelligible (1947, II, p. 246). This is in line with the argument in his major text *Essai sur l'origine les connoissances humains* (1746) where truth is to be found in exact or "well-determined ideas" (1947, I, pp. 104–105). Of course this broad strategy is also found in, for example, Hobbes (1991, chap. 4) and Bacon (1853, p. 210).

feature of common language (V.i.f.26) and is alert to its distortive presence in "writers upon commerce" who treat money as wealth (IV.i.34). That said, it is the case that his own language and terminology can indeed be elusive, as in the much rehearsed discussion of his conflation of labor as command and as embodied (Aspromourgos, 2009, p. 96). Nonetheless this reluctance to remove the societal experiential context is not incidental to his own conception of *WN* as a work of social science.

From his perspective, the valorization of abstract exactitude can give only a partial account of social science and is, as a consequence, distorting. Humans live in societies and to comprehend and explain their behavior cannot be accurately executed by abstracting them from that evidentially warranted situation (Berry, 1997). Smith's conviction on this score underlines why ethnographic and, especially, historical data figure so much in the text of *WN* (its apparent 'bagginess'). These data reveal that a truly informative and hence useful account of inherently complicated commercial/ economic behavior cannot be reduced to abstract calculation or, pace Condillac, to simplifying elementary notions. This further underwrites, in direct contrast to Mirabeau, why Smith does not identify his social science as "the study and demonstration of the laws of nature" (Mirabeau, 1769, p. 13). Rather there is a principled recognition on Smith's part that the recourse to concrete data is not incidental to any social science, including crucially the 'science of economics.'

This science exhibits behavioral regularities that are derived experientially from the science of human nature, together with inductive generalizations derived from an array of societal data. To look for abstract precision is chimerical (to use Hume's term). Hence history is not an expendable component of *WN* as a work of a truly social science. Not only does the historical/ empirical record defy theoretical simplicity by illustrating the complicating role of luck and accidents, it also reveals causal processes. This revelation is fully compliant with Smith's (Baconian) conception of the scientific quest.[32]

2.7 Conclusion

In the opening paragraph I announced that I was seeking to investigate in what sense is *WN* to be understood as a work of 'science' in general and 'social science' in particular. The correct identification of causes and the

---

[32] The general point is captured in one of his reported university rhetoric lectures, "historicall writing ... points out the causes by which those events [of human life] were brought about and by this means points out to us by what manner and method we may produce similar good effects or avoid similar bad ones" (*LRBL* 17/90). It is on those grounds he judges that Thucydides is "preeminent among historians" because he has "more distinctly explained the causes of events" than any other author (*LRBL* ii.25/95 cf. *LRBL* ii.49/106 and V.i.a.5).

demonstration that the interactions of commercial life instantiate a few central principles (exchange, betterment, and self-interest) that constitute a system that is grounded in the predictable constancy of human nature are, in broad terms, hallmarks of an eighteenth-century notion of 'science.' This enterprise was never conceived as end in itself, it was to be put to the service of improving human life. While *WN* shares these hallmarks, it also demonstrates that a genuinely *social* science must recognize and proceed on the basis that social life is a complex historical formation resistant to simplifying abstractions. *WN*, it can be said, is not only a product of the Enlightenment, it is also, largely by dint of that recognition, an example of the Scottish Enlightenment and constitutes its major contribution to social or moral science.

3

Adam Smith's "Industrial Organization" of Religion

BARRY R. WEINGAST

> In ... the greater part of Europe during the tenth, eleventh, twelfth, and thirteenth centuries, ... the constitution of the church of Rome may be considered as the most formidable combination that ever was formed against the authority and security of civil government, as well as against the liberty, reason, and happiness of mankind, which can flourish only where civil government is able to protect them. In that constitution the grossest delusions of superstition were supported in such a manner by the private interests of so great a number of people as put them out of all danger from any assault of human reason ... Had this constitution been attacked by no other enemies but the feeble efforts of human reason, it must have endured forever.
>
> (WN V.i.g.24)

> It may be laid down as a certain maxim, that, all other things being supposed equal, the richer the church, the poorer must necessarily be, either the sovereign on the one hand, or the people on the other; and, in all cases, the less able must the state be to defend itself.
>
> (WN V.i.g.41)

3.1 Introduction

In his discussion of institutionalized religion in *WN*, Adam Smith developed a systematic theoretical approach to understanding the incentives, institutions, violence, aspects of morality and theology, and competition surrounding religion in the Middle Ages. Curiously titling his discussion, "Of the Expence of the Institutions for the Instruction of People of All Ages" (*WN* V.i.g), Smith characterized the Roman Catholic Church as a force impeding Europe's economic and political development. An enduring institution, the

---

The author gratefully acknowledges Gary Cox, Robert Ekelund, Charles Griswold, Robert Hébert, Lisa Herzog, Glory M. Liu, Jerry Muller, Josiah Ober, Jennifer Sage, Kenneth Shepsle, and Robert Tollison for helpful comments.

Church was, in Smith's words, "the most formidable combination that ever was formed against the authority and security of civil government, as well as against the liberty, reason, and happiness of mankind" (WN V.i.g.24). In many ways, the Church's survival seems – as it probably did to Smith – "miraculous" (Minowitz, 1993, p. 176). My principal question about Smith's approach is: how did the Church maintain its wealth and power as both the monopoly provider of religious services but also as one of the principal impediments to European political and economic development? This question is especially puzzling when we consider that the secular lords had a significant comparative advantage in violence. Why didn't these lords simply take the Church's wealth and prerogatives? The analysis also provides an answer to a secondary question: why was the Church so hostile to commerce and economic growth?

Smith does not pose these questions explicitly, nonetheless his approach to institutionalized religion directly relates to his theory of European development, a topic of great conversation among Smith scholars.

To address the principal question, I appeal to the theory of the firm developed in industrial organization. The theory of the firm, sometimes called the "new economics of organization," or just the "economics of organization," sits within industrial organization, traditionally focused on questions of competition and monopoly and other aspects of the economic organization of markets. More recently, scholars in this specialty address questions, such as how does the internal structure of a firm facilitate coordination of its members to achieve a common goal, such as profit maximization or the organization's survival, given that self-interested members of the organization care more about improving their own circumstances than the nominal goals of the organization? These scholars interpret complex contracts and institutions of the firm as mitigating agency costs whereby members of the firm, including the CEO, have incentives to make decisions that deviate from those of the firm's owners, namely, profits.[1]

A robust literature exists on Smith and religion. Some scholars study Smith's analysis of the incentives of the clergy (Lindgren, 1973; Anderson, 1988; West, 1990, chap. 10; Minowitz, 1993; Griswold, 1999); others, the organization of the medieval Roman Catholic Church (Anderson, 1988; Iannaccone, 1991; Minowitz, 1993; Ekelund, Hébert and Tollison, 2006). Yet Smith scholars have under-emphasized two aspects of his views on the medieval Church: how it fits in the larger secular medieval environment, including kings and lords, and, less so, the role of religious institutions in Smith's theory

---

[1] Various scholars have explored Smith's ideas about the relationship between the Church and the masses (Minowitz, 1993, p. 169), the nature of religious services sought by the people, and, in economic terms, the demand for religious services (Anderson, 1988; Griswold, 1999, p. 281), as well the role that religion plays in morality more generally (Lindgren, 1973; Haakonssen, 1981; Anderson, 1988; Muller, 1993; Griswold, 1999).

of development (but see Anderson, 1988, p. 1074; Kennedy, 2005, p. 41).[2] These questions seem particularly pressing given Smith's preoccupation with the simultaneity of political and economic freedom necessary for economic growth, as evidenced in Book III of the *Wealth of Nations*.

This chapter demonstrates not only Smith's unique answers to these questions, but the power of his approach that has been overlooked in the general Smith scholarship. It does so by turning to what a small number of pioneering scholars have termed the "industrial organization" of the Church (Anderson, 1988; Ekelund et al., 1996; Ekelund, Hébert and Tollison, 2006). In addressing these questions, Smith explained how an implicit political accommodation emerged between the secular and ecclesiastic lords whereby each respected the other's powers within their respective domain. He shows how this accommodation hinged on a third group, the masses. The masses were a potential source of disorder, for example, by rebelling against their lords. According to Smith, the secular lords were unable to pacify the masses on their own;[3] the masses presented a powerful threat to the secular lords, especially when the Church encouraged them to confront the lords. The Church gained leverage over the masses because it subsidized them; notably, providing food in years of poor harvests while offering comfort in the face of death in this life and the promise of salvation in the next (Minowitz, 1993, p. 169ff; Griswold, 1999, pp. 284–285). The Church's credible threat to withhold these goods and services afforded it power over the masses and hence indirectly over the lords.

Generally during this period, the secular and ecclesiastic lords cooperated to exploit the masses. But if a secular lord thought to challenge the Church, the Church would encourage the masses to resist and rebel. Hence, both sets of elites had incentives to cooperate with each other to keep the masses in a state of dependence, allowing the Church and the lords to exploit them.

Drawing on ideas from the new social science of religion (Anderson, 1988; Stark and Bainbridge, 1989; Iannaccone, 1990, 1991; Ekelund et al., 1996; Barro and McCleary, 2003), I show how Smith explains the Church's dominance and the subsequent European social, political, and economic order in a coherent narrative of rational cooperation and organization in a context characterized by violence and low growth.

---

[2] While scholars in the literature on the new social science of religion provide excellent models of the Church, they have not studied the questions addressed here, notably the interaction of the secular and ecclesiastic lords (e.g., Ekelund et al., 1996). Smith's work on the medieval Church can therefore be viewed as on the frontiers of this literature.

[3] "In those great landed estates, the clergy, or their bailiffs, could easily keep the peace without the support or assistance either of the king or of any other person; and neither the king nor any other person could keep the peace there without the support and assistance of the clergy" (*WN* V.i.g.22:801).

Smith's theory of institutionalized religion forms part of his larger, tripartite project of an integrated and comprehensive approach to developing a "science of man" encompassing politics, economics, and moral development (Phillipson, 2010, pp. 2–3). Smith's theoretical approach focuses on two sets of forces that kept this low-growth arrangement in place for several centuries, the constant violence of the feudal equilibrium (discussed in *WN* Book III and in *LJ*(A) i.116–146; iv.124–141; *LJ*(B) 49–63) and the Church's monopoly position as provider of religious services (discussed in *WN* V.i.g).

The Church suppressed liberty and economic growth among the masses because, over time, growth would have afforded the people power and independence, undermining the Church's authority over them; or, in Minowitz's (1993, p. 169) terms, growth would have loosened the Church's "grip" over the masses. The weakening of the Church's authority over the people, in turn, would have weakened the Church's threat over the secular lords. The Church's long-term survival therefore required that it maintain its credible threat over the lords by suppressing growth among the masses. Acemoglu and Robinson (2006) demonstrate circumstances under which incumbents choose to solidify their hold on power at the expense of growth. Keeping the people in a state of dependence rather than of liberty, freedom, and economic growth served the private goals of the ecclesiastic lords. I also discuss Smith's views on the breakdown of the Church's grip on the masses and the rise of strong competitors in what we now call the Protestant Reformation.

This chapter proceeds as follows. Section 3.2 describes Smith's views on the industrial organization of the medieval Church and its relationship to the secular powers. Section 3.3 summarizes a game theoretic account of Smith's logic of the political accommodation between the secular lords and the Church. Section 3.4 discusses the changing industrial organization of religion; that is, how organized religion adapted to changing circumstances. Section 3.5 models the changes discussed in Section 3.4 as a comparative static result derived from the game summarized in Section 3.3. My conclusions follow.

3.2 Smith's Industrial Organization of Religion

To explain the political and economic position of the medieval Church, Smith uses logic that anticipates the modern industrial organization of religion, as Anderson demonstrated three decades ago (Anderson, 1988).[4] Drawing on this modern approach, especially the collective work of Anderson (1988); Ekelund et al. (1996); Ekelund, Hébert, and Tollison (2006) – hereinafter

---

[4] Muller's analysis reflects this assessment: "Smith's analysis of religion in the *Wealth of Nations* is one of the clearest and perhaps least expected applications of his characteristic approach to the role of institutions in channelling the passions and to the unintended consequences of social action" (Muller, 1993, p. 154).

AEHT – this section studies a range of features associated with the medieval Church[5]; namely, the structure of competition and the effects of monopolization; the implications of various religious organizations and institutions; the relationship between ecclesiastical and secular authority; and the major strategic choices made by the organization, such as the activities, services, and products it provides, and the nature of the rents that it extracts.[6]

3.2.1 Secular Lords and the Church

The secular and ecclesiastic lords constituted the lion's share of the medieval elite, especially early on before the rise of the commercial elite. The elite owned most of the land, by far the most important asset in this society. They also depended on the peasants, who were tied to the land, for production.

The two components of the medieval elite differed in important ways. Perhaps the most important difference was the structure of competition and violence. Smith addresses violence among the secular lords in Book III of the *Wealth of Nations* and in his *Lectures on Jurisprudence* where he asks: why are so few countries developed?[7] Although Smith lists two causes, he focuses almost exclusively on the second, "The causes of this may be considered under these two heads, first, natural impediments [such as geography], and secondly, the oppression of civil government" (*LJ*(B) 521). In his political-economic approach to development, Smith held that violence in the feudal era prevented development (Weingast, 2017). Smith highlights again and again the negative incentives fostered by violence and "oppression of the civil government." Kings could not keep the peace and were forced of necessity to "grant the power of jurisdiction to these lords; for as he had no standing army there could be no other way of bringing the subjects to obey rules" (*LJ*(A) iv.119).

This political accommodation of decentralized power, itself based on the reality of decentralized sources of violence, had two implications: first, no uniform law could be established and enforced in the entire kingdom; second no one had the ability to enforce political arrangements that would secure peace and cooperation among the lords. This world was violent; the lords "were always at war with each other and often with the king" (*LJ*(A) iv.6). Secular lords faced considerable violent competition, both vertical (as when a vassal challenged his lord) and horizontal (as when one baron challenged

---

[5] The larger literature on the new social science of religion is rapidly expanding. See, for example, Stark and Bainbridge (1989); Iannaccone (1990, 1997); Barro and McCleary (2003); Gorski (2003); Ekelund, Hébert and Tollison (2006).

[6] Ekelund, Hébert and Tollison (2006, p. 13) explain that Smith "took a broad, industrial organization approach to religion, in which market *structure* has an important impact on individual and collective outcomes."

[7] This paragraph draws on Weingast (2017).

another). The feudal hierarchy evolved to allow the lords the ability to defend their property and to project force against other lords; but in this setting, local lords faced great difficulties establishing long-term cooperation, and instead fought each other regularly.

Regular violence had unfortunate but predictable economic effects. "In the infancey of society, as has been often observed, government must be weak and feeble, and it is long before [sic] it's authority can protect the industry of individuals from the rapacity of their neighbours. When people find themselves every moment in danger of being robbed of all they possess, they have no motive to be industrious. There could be little accumulation of stock, because the indolent, which would be the greatest number, would live upon the industrious, and spend whatever they produced. Nothing can be more an obstacle to the progress of opulence" (*LJ*(B) 522).

Violence consumed and dissipated almost all sources of rents in the secular world, including rents realized and those foregone that could be realized in the absence of violence. As Smith argues in *WN* Book III, this violent world was poor (Skinner, 1975; Weingast, 2017). Violence and predation precluded investment and the prospect for economic growth. This environment therefore afforded few gains from specialization and exchange. The main agricultural products could not be carried far over land. Attempts to save and invest risked confiscation. "[M]en in this defenceless state naturally content themselves with their necessary subsistence; because to acquire more might only tempt the injustice of their oppressors" (*WN* III.iii.12). The relative absence of specialization and exchange – the "division of labor" in Smith's famous phrase – doomed most people to live at subsistence.

In contrast to the secular lords, the Church elite were far more cooperative (*WN* V.i.g.17; see also Anderson, 1988, p. 1080; Minowitz, 1993, p. 170). "There was always much more union among the clergy than among the lay-lords. The former were under a regular discipline and subordination to the papal authority. The latter were under no regular discipline or subordination, but almost always equally jealous of one another, and of the king" (*WN* V.i.g.22).[8] Intra-Church violence, although not absent, was far less common than violence among the secular lords.

In Smith's view, two factors help us understand the Church's behavior. First, the means by which it pursued its goals of organizational maintenance, securing sufficient power and wealth to survive in a hostile world. Second, the Church's monopoly position. With respect to the first, Smith argues that religion is only one component of motivation; whereas members of the clergy were always concerned for its own private interests (Lindgren, 1973, chap. 7;

---

[8] Ekelund *et al.* (1996) provide the best analysis of the manifold dimensions of this problem.

Haakonssen, 1981, p. 175). "The [Church's] great interest is to maintain their authority with the people; and this authority depends upon the supposed certainty and importance of the whole doctrine which they inculcate, and upon the supposed necessity of adopting every part of it with the most implicit faith, in order to avoid eternal misery" (*WN* V.i.g.17). This approach proved successful. As Minowitz observes, "Smith could hardly be more emphatic about religion's grip on the masses" (Minowitz, 1993, p. 169).

With respect to the issue of monopolization, Smith explains that the Church's position arose out of times of violent political and religious conflict. The secular parties to this conflict allied with religious organizations, and the success of one side left the favored religious organization in a sufficiently strong position as to "over-awe the chiefs and leaders of their own party" (*WN* V.i.g.7). With respect to the "civil magistrate," the first demand of the clergy:

> was generally, that he should silence and subdue all their adversaries; and their second [demand], that he should bestow an independent provision on themselves ... In making this demand therefore they consulted their own ease and comfort, without troubling themselves about the effect which it might have in future times upon the influence and authority of their order.
>
> (*WN* V.i.g.7)

The Church's monopoly in Europe fostered very different behavior than that of the secular lords. For one, its "multinational monopoly" position allowed the Church to form a hierarchy that was, in comparison with the organization of the secular lords, relatively cooperative and powerful (Anderson, 1988, p. 1080; Minowitz, 1993, p. 170). The Church coordinated the activity of a great many people who pursued common goals. The Church also commanded substantial resources in the form of tithes from parishioners; benefices, indulgences, and bequests from the wealthy; and from its vast landholdings. Although it sometimes engaged in violence with the secular lords, the Church was far less violent, and different segments of the Church much less frequently fought one another. Manifest violence in the form of combat among armies was not the principal means by which the Church defended itself from the secular lords.

The secular lords and the Church at once competed and cooperated. Although the lords held obvious military advantages over the Church, the Church possessed a very different stock of weapons with which to defend itself, including resources used to gain and maintain allies among the common people but also doctrinal weapons, allowing them to impose costs on uncooperative secular leaders. The secular lords and the Church also had mutual goals, such as maintaining order, exploiting the masses, salvation, and preserving their property, wealth, and sources of income. Over time, a stable, political accommodation evolved between the two sources of power, secular and ecclesiastic, which economists call an implicit bargain or contract (Ekelund, Hébert and Tollison, 2006, p. 15).[9]

A major implication is that, in contrast to the secular lords, the Church accumulated real rents and power. Members of the organization consumed some of these rents; but much of the rents went to the poor in the form of food. The Church systematically exploited its monopoly, being less responsive to the population than otherwise. Interpreting the passages in the head notes, Anderson opines:

> Smith was, in effect, accusing the monopoly church of reducing the quality of religion supplied to consumers, whose welfare was reduced as a result. In the same passage he clearly attributes this quality reduction to the self-interested behavior of the clergy, who extracted monopoly rent from their flock both directly and indirectly by promulgating irrational doctrines that served their own interests. The consumers of religion were badly served by the monopoly purveyor of spiritual guidance, just as in the case of monopolies in the provision of more mundane goods.
>
> (Anderson, 1988, p. 1080)

Although monopoly religious organizations, such as the medieval Roman Catholic Church, do not literally compete with other organizations, nonetheless the Church had to worry about the rise of rival organizations. To use language from modern industrial organization, their monopoly was "contestable" by potential entrants (Baumol, Panzar and Willig, 1982; West, 1990). To survive, monopolists must have the tools to prevent or eliminate such rivals. In the medieval environment, the Church activity sought to protect its position, for example, by wiping out competing sects, such as the Cathars in Italy and Southern France in the thirteenth century. "Competing entrants in the supply of religion were defined as 'heretics' and systematically persecuted" (Anderson, 1988, p. 1079).

To maintain their position, leaders of religious organizations need to tailor the various attributes of their services to their members, at least to a degree (Ekelund, Hébert and Tollison, 2006; Iannaccone and Bainbridge, 2009). Put another way, sect and religious leaders to a certain extent tailor their doctrine, morals, and theology to the needs of their members. Failing to do so means that they are less likely to attract or retain members; and hence they are more vulnerable to entry by potential competitors. Similarly, Church leaders also structured their organization and institutions in ways that suited their environment so that they could deliver their services effectively.

---

[9] Smith uses the term "tacit contract" in *LJ*; for more on this concept: see, e.g., *LJ*(A) v.118: *LJ*(A) v.128–129; and *LJ*(A) v.134.

As a final issue, Smith did not view the Church as just another feudal fiefdom, but an independent player whose interests and opportunities differed considerably from those of the king and lords in feudal Europe. Smith makes several arguments about the differences. First, as discussed earlier in this section, the secular lords were only loosely hierarchical in the sense that they challenged and fought one another all the time. This violence meant that cooperation was difficult, and no one could enforce peace across all the land. In contrast, the Church was more hierarchical, coordinating tens of thousands of Church officials. In Smith's words, "The clergy of every established church constitute a great incorporation. They can act in concert, and pursue their interest upon one plan and with one spirit, as much as if they were under the direction of one man; and they are frequently too under such direction" (WN V.i.g.17; V.i.g.22).[10] Second, the Church had influence and even command over the masses in ways that feudal lords did not. The Church sought to be a very different kind of agent than the secular hierarchy by providing religious services and salvation; and charity for the poor (Lindgren, 1973, chap. 7). Third, although Smith did not put it this way, in his scheme, the Church held the *pivotal* political position in the feudal political system, able to side either with the lords against the peasants or with the peasants against the lords. Under most circumstances, the Church preferred a coalition with the lords to exploit the peasants. If some lord sought to challenge the Church, however, the Church would react strongly by withholding essential services (such as salvation) and mobilizing the peasants against the lord.

3.2.2 *Political Exchange and Equilibrium between the Church and the Lords*

The medieval setting fostered a mutually beneficial political exchange between the Church and the lords. I call the exchange political because it involves the distribution of authority and social control between these two entities, including the means of establishing and maintaining political order.

On the demand side of the market for religious services, most people wanted comfort and salvation in times of sickness and death, charity in times of economic difficulty, a community to belong to, and a morality that supports social order (Griswold, 1999, pp. 284–285). On the supply side, consider the Church and the poor. The Church helped comfort and feed the poor. Second, the Church's revenue was typically "paid in kind, in corn, wine, cattle, poultry, &c." (WN V.i.g.22). As this amounted to far more than the clergy could

---

[10] Smith restates this point: "There was always much more union among the clergy than among the lay-lords. The former were under a regular discipline and subordination to the papal authority. The latter were under no regular discipline or subordination, but almost always equally jealous of one another, and of the king" (WN V.i.g.22).

consume themselves, the Church employed it in "extensive charity. Both the hospitality and the charity of the antient clergy, accordingly, are said to have been very great. They ... maintained almost the whole poor of every kingdom" (*WN* V.i.g.22). In return, the poor attended Church and paid the tithes. They also followed the Church's rules, including the moral rules. The moral and religious teachings emphasized acceptance of the earthly order in exchange for the rewards in the afterlife.[11] Moreover, the Church held an ultimate sanction over the poor. The Church provided eternal salvation, a value that could be withheld (Minowitz, 1993, p. 169). The exchange between the Church and masses helped pacify the poor:

> In the antient state of Europe, before the establishment of arts and manufactures, the wealth of the clergy gave them the same sort of influence over the common people, which that of the great barons gave them over their respective vassals, tenants, and retainers. In the great landed estates, which the mistaken piety both of princes and private persons had bestowed upon the church, jurisdictions were established of the same kind with those of the great barons; and for the same reason. *In those great landed estates, the clergy, or their bailiffs, could easily keep the peace without the support or assistance either of the king or of any other person.*
>
> (*WN* V.i.g.21, emphasis added)

Second, consider the exchange between the Church and the secular lords. Each generally respected the other's authority in its respective domain. The Church's efforts to pacify the population benefitted the secular lords, providing security and protecting the lords' property and wealth. The Church also provided salvation for the lords. Salvation and protection, in turn, gave the Church leverage over the lords. In the exchange for the services provided by the clergy, the secular elite respected the Church and its authority in its domain rather than using violence to undermine or remove it. Further, the lords paid tithes and various benefices, supporting the Church organization and its efforts with the poor. This financial support of the Church became a permanent obligation.

Using modern language, Smith's logic constitutes a stable pattern of interaction; that is, an equilibrium. Both parties had incentives to honor and maintain this exchange. The Church had the obvious revenue incentives to serve the lords' interests, especially in providing salvation and in aiding the secular lords through maintaining order rather serving more exclusively the poor. The lords, in turn, had incentives to participate in this exchange because it helped maintain political order, lowering the probability of an existential

---

[11] Smith says, the object of "religious instruction is not so much to render the people good citizens in this world, as to prepare them for another and a better world in a life to come" (*WN* V.i.g.1). See also Minowitz (1993, p. 169); Kennedy (2005, p. 44).

threat from violence by the poor. This political exchange thus provided salvation while protecting both the lords' and the Church's property and sources of power and wealth.

Consider the threat of violence from the poor. Violence was a constant possibility, both among the poor and between the poor and the rich. Smith explains the threat from the poor to the rich:

> Wherever there is great property, there is great inequality. For one very rich man, there must be at least five hundred poor ... The affluence of the rich excites the indignation of the poor, who are often both driven by want, and prompted by envy, to invade his possessions. It is only under the shelter of the civil magistrate that the owner of that valuable property, which is acquired by the labour of many years, or perhaps of many successive generations, can sleep a single night in security. He is at all times surrounded by unknown enemies, whom, though he never provoked, he can never appease, and from whose injustice he can be protected only by the powerful arm of the civil magistrate continually held up to chastise it. The acquisition of valuable and extensive property, therefore, necessarily requires the establishment of civil government.
>
> (WN V.i.b.2:709–710)

The logic, stated in general form, applies to the Church's efforts in pacifying the poor during the Middle Ages. The Church helped sustain this political order, again, pacifying the local population, despite so many living at bare subsistence.[12]

A final aspect of the political accommodation between secular and ecclesiastic lords is that the Church held various weapons over the secular lords that could be used were the lords to challenge the Church's authority in its domain. If the sovereign sought to challenge the Church's authority, the Church fought back, employing "all the terrors of religion to oblige the people to transfer their alliance to some more orthodox and obedient prince" (WN V.i.g.17). Princes who failed to heed this reaction fared poorly: "the convulsions which, during the course of several centuries, the turbulence of the Roman clergy was continually occasioning in every part of Europe, sufficiently demonstrate how precarious and insecure must always be the situation of the sovereign who has no proper means of influencing the clergy of the established and governing religion of his country" (WN V.i.g.17).

---

[12] Muller makes this point as follows, "For Smith, religion expressed in metaphorical terms the reality that acting justly and beneficently is the source of greatest reward and happiness while acting ignobly brings its own punishment There are several like this and if they are page ranges oughts to be en rules ... The core truth of religion is that by acting justly and beneficently we fulfill the purposes of our creation. And so, Smith concludes, 'religion [helps enforce] the natural sense of duty'" (Muller, 1993, p. 154, quoting TMS III.5.12:170).

Because the Church held both the keys to salvation and the allegiance of the people, its ability to provide the former while pacifying the latter proved a double-edged sword. When the secular lords accommodated and respected the Church's interests, pacification benefitted the lords. But the same power over the people allowed the Church to rally the people against uncooperative or threatening lords.[13]

Moreover, a serious threat from a particular lord or king might lead the Church authorities to support an alternative, "more orthodox and obedient prince." As noted earlier, secular lords who challenged the Church's authority therefore risked losing everything. Smith concluded that the clergy of an "established church" were dangerous, indeed, potentially "ruinous" for secular authorities who attempted to use violence against them. Secular lords therefore had strong incentives to work with and manage the clergy, and the "means seem to consist altogether in the preferment which he has to bestow upon them" (*WN* V.i.g.19).

3.2.3 Long-Term Economic Consequences

The coalition of secular and ecclesiastic authorities directly affected the medieval society's long-term economic growth and development. As Smith makes clear about feudalism, the violence of the secular lords prevented agrarian economic development; indeed, Smith claimed that this violence forced European political-economic development into an "unnatural and retrograde order" (*WN* III.i.9; Hont, 2005, pp. 354–388).

These arrangements combined with constant violence to suppress many economic activities that might have made many much better off and more independent. Yet these economic activities threatened the elite by fostering the growth of independent sources of authority which might displace existing elites. The secular and religious authorities therefore cooperated to suppress competing ideas, organizations, and economic activities. As Smith concludes in the first head note to this paper, the Church represented a formidable barrier to development.

Smith argued that the clergy's singular interest was "to maintain their authority with the people" (*WN* V.i.g.17). Pursuing these interests, the Church kept the masses in a position of dependency. Its principal tools, as noted, involved salvation and charity during hard times. Moreover, peasants

---

[13] For example, Smith reports that, "when Robert, the second prince of the Capetian race [in France], was most unjustly excommunicated by the court of Rome, his own servants, it is said, threw the victuals which came from his table to the dogs, and refused to taste any thing themselves which had been polluted by the contact of a person in his situation. They were taught to do so, it may very safely be presumed, by the clergy of his own dominions" (*WN* V.i.g.27).

on the Church's vast landholdings – the Church was by far the biggest landholder in Western Europe – could be thrown off their land at a moment's notice and their source of livelihood withdrawn. Because all of these means – salvation, charity, and (for peasants on the Church lands) the rights to work the land – could be withheld, the Church created a system of dependency. Dissent risked ruin.[14]

The Church thus opposed economic growth and development, even within narrow confines. In discussing Smith's view of the Church as "the most formidable combination against civil government, liberty, reason, and happiness of mankind," Anderson reports that the "Roman church impeded the development of capitalism by promoting anti-commercial attitudes and barriers to trade" (Anderson, 1988, p. 1074).

In the short-term, economic growth might produce more revenue for the Church; but in the long-term, it would foster the rise of new and powerful groups whose interests opposed and potentially threatened those of the Church. For example, had the medieval Church wanted, it could have promoted greater liberty for the people through long-term leases. (Indeed, it did just this later in the period as a means of gaining more revenue.) Leases granting peasants greater security would have provided them opportunities to improve their production and position and to accumulate wealth.

Economic development produces new interests as groups formerly without resources come to obtain them. Resources, in turn, produce power. Greater liberty for the masses would allow them independence from both the secular lords and the Church. The masses would accumulate wealth and power, thus limiting their dependence on the Church for their livelihood or for charity in bad times. Independence, in turn, would remove the ability of the Church to manipulate the peasants, ultimately threatening the existing power structure, the Church in particular. Because these interests would constitute a direct threat to the Church, it sought to prevent them from gaining power.

For these reasons, the Church suppressed liberty, the foundation of markets and wealth – or, in Smith's terms, of commerce and opulence. This environment was inhospitable to the enforcement of contracts and the development of markets. Law and justice in medieval society protected the interests of the powerful. Independent courts were unknown. As exercised by both secular and ecclesiastic lords, the provision of justice involved moral hazard: in cases involving themselves or those close to them, both sets of lords biased outcomes in their favor.

---

[14] Smith's logic fits with a range of recent arguments in the political-economics of economic growth, such as Bates (2001); Acemoglu and Robinson (2006, 2012); North, Wallis and Weingast (2009, chaps. 2–3); Besley and Persson (2011).

3.3 The Political Accommodation between the Secular and Ecclesiastic Lords

In this section, I describe Smith's account of the stability of cooperation between the secular and ecclesiastic powers during the Middle Ages. Smith provides considerable insights into the strategic interests and opportunities of the various players.

The advantages of making the game explicit are fourfold. First, it allows us to see that the behavior of the major groups in society fit together in a common, interlocking logic. The behavior of each group depends on the behavior of the others, and in a particular manner emphasized by the game. Second, the game goes well beyond a verbal analysis of incentives. Because players have mixed motives – for example, some players have incentives to defect – cooperation as an equilibrium is not assured but must be demonstrated. Third, the game highlights the incentives facing each group to play their role, contingent on the other groups playing theirs. These incentives are essential to understanding the stability and equilibrium interaction among the groups. Demonstrating the existence of an equilibrium explains why this pattern of behavior is stable. Finally, the game emphasizes the logic of how authority could be divided between the secular and ecclesiastic lords in which, on balance, the two sets of authorities accommodated one another without constant conflict.

Smith's logic reveals the incentives prompting the secular lords and the Church to cooperate in respecting each other's prerogatives within their separate domains and, jointly, exploiting the masses. The critical strategic choices are as follows. The secular lord chooses to accept the accommodation with the Church by respecting its rights and privileges, including sufficiently large subsidies. The Church cooperates with the Lord by accepting the Lord's authority in the secular realm and by providing benefits to the Lord in the form of pacifying the masses. In the face of cooperation between Lord and Church, the masses are forced to acquiesce to their poor lot in life.

Although both the Lord and the Church have opportunities to defect from cooperation, each has a means of defending itself. If a Lord defects by challenging the Church's rights and privileges, the Church and the masses will coordinate and resist the Lord's challenge. The Church also can defect; that is, to resist the Lord's authority and to coordinate with the masses against the Lord. Because the Church's rights and privileges involve subsidies from the Lord, this revenue serves as part of the incentives for the Church to accept the accommodation with the Lord rather than challenge the Lord. Therefore, both the Lord and the Church choose not to exploit the other because that leads to a costly breakdown of cooperation.

Subsidies from the Lord to the Church represent a critical feature of the game, especially with respect to the Church's decision to cooperate with the

Lord or to defect. For this to hold, the subsidies from the Lord to the Church must be sufficiently large to overcome the Church's temptation to defect, where defection means that the Church chooses to challenge the Lord's authority, withhold salvation, and encourage the masses to rebel. This formulation implies that if the subsidies are too small, the Church prefers to defect. This condition gives the Church leverage over the Lord. Because this outcome is the Lord's worst alternative, it prefers to subsidize the Church sufficiently, resulting in equilibrium. The gains from cooperation between the Church and the Lord make this outcome possible.

Finally, Smith's perspective answers the question about how the Church defends itself against the lords given their comparative advantage in violence relative to the Church, the Lord's defection outcome. As just shown, the value of cooperation between Lord and Church to the Lord prevents him from using this violence potential to attempt to force the Church to grant it some of the Church's rights and privileges. A critical reason for this cooperation involves the issues of salvation and the masses. The Lord fears losing salvation in combination with rebellion by the masses, and the Church plays an important role for the Lord by providing salvation and helping to pacify the masses. When the masses are pacified, both the secular lords and the Church can exploit the masses. But this behavior by the masses is not inevitable. If the Lord threatens the Church, the Church can, instead of providing salvation and pacifying the masses, withhold salvation while urging the masses to rebel. This choice holds high risks for the Lord. The Church thus holds important weapons with which it can defend its prerogatives and authority. The logic of the game shows that cooperation between the Lord and the Church, in which each respect each other's rights, privileges, and authority within their own domains, is a stable pattern of behavior, that is, an equilibrium.

Putting these points together, the strategic incentives induce the lords to subsidize the Church and refrain from using its comparative advantage in violence against the Church. The Church, in turn, bestows benefits to the lords by providing salvation to the lords while also pacifying the masses and protecting the lords' property and income. Both elite groups thus cooperate to exploit the masses.

3.4 The Changing Industrial Organization of Religion

With the rise of powerful, alternative religious organizations during the Reformation, the Church lost its monopoly position in Europe. The Church successfully suppressed competing religious organizations throughout the Middle Ages. Why did it fail to do so during the Reformation? Smith's approach provides an answer.

3.4.1 Changes in the Environment Erode the Church's Authority

Smith's arguments tie directly to those in Book III of the *Wealth of Nations*, which studies the stability and then fall of feudalism in response to the rise of commerce and the growth of towns. An explicit political exchange between town and king underpinned town growth: the exchange granted the towns independence and liberty; and the king, more power and authority over the lords. The rise of commerce also transformed the feudal hierarchy, at least in those areas adjacent to the towns. The towns provided local security, including disarming local lords. This environment removed the need for the secular lords to maintain a large retinue to defend themselves. The security afforded by the towns to neighboring areas also underpinned the transformation of the local peasantry from poor self-sufficient, agricultural producers living at subsistence to specialists in a market whose division of labor afforded peasants higher incomes.

As Smith emphasizes, the towns also offered new opportunities for luxury, which induced the lords to exchange their expensive retainers for consumption of "trinkets and baubles." Similarly with the Church: the clergy discovered new luxury for which they could exchange their revenues.[15] These changes diminished the power and wealth of the local lords, and with it, their contributions to the Church and, ultimately, the power of the Church. At the same time, the Church reduced its charity due to declining revenue and due to increased expenditure on luxury. Less charity reduced the dependence of the masses on the Church, as did rising incomes and independence of the peasantry within the security orbit of a nearby town.

In reaction, the Church sought additional revenue from its tenants. But, given that the Church's interests already drove it to extract the maximal monopoly revenue from the peasantry, raising rents alone would not raise more revenue. Additional revenue required that the Church alter institutions and the incentives they produce. For example, by granting greater rights and benefits to its tenants, the Church could induce tenants to pay higher rents. The principal means of doing so involved extending long-term leases to the tenants. Although providing additional revenue to the Church, these leases also restricted the Church's predatory behavior. Long-term leases reduced the

---

[15] In Smith's words, "The gradual improvements of arts, manufactures, and commerce, the same causes which destroyed the power of the great barons, destroyed in the same manner, through the greater part of Europe, the whole temporal power of the clergy. In the produce of arts, manufactures, and commerce, the clergy, like the great barons, found something for which they could exchange their rude produce, and thereby discovered the means of spending their whole revenues upon their own persons, without giving any considerable share of them to other people. Their charity became gradually less extensive, their hospitality less liberal or less profuse. Their retainers became consequently less numerous, and by degrees dwindled away altogether" (*WN* V.i.g.25).

ability of the Church qua landlord to expropriate the value of investments made by tenants (*WN* V.i.g.25).[16] Smith concludes that these changes diminished the Church's power. "The ties of interest, which bound the inferior ranks of people to the clergy, were in this manner gradually broken and dissolved" (*WN* V.i.g.25).

3.4.2 The Rise of Competition among Religions

A variety of institutional and organizational changes also occurred in this environment. Recall that the Church's monopoly was not permanent but contestable. New and powerful religious sects grew up to challenge the Church's authority in what we now call the Protestant Reformation. Moreover, in many states that maintained a Catholic monopoly, such as France, the secular authorities asserted more control over the Church within its domain; for example, control over the choice of bishops and the abbots, thereby diminishing the independence of the Church.

Combining Smith's argument about the town's escape from feudal equilibrium in *WN* Book III with his argument about the decline of the Church in *WN* Book V leads to the following predictions, although Smith does not state them. Rising incomes and security of the towns, in comparison with the more stable feudal areas of the hinterland, imply that peasants in these areas should gain independence from the Church and be the most attracted to religious sects competing with the Catholic Church, particularly the ones emphasizing austerity (implying lower rent extraction by the clergy). Similarly, the clergy in and near the towns should be the most susceptible to luxury due to its availability. Long before Max Weber opened the debate about the "Protestant Ethic and the Spirit of Capitalism," Smith developed an approach that suggest the connection. The mechanism identified by Smith holds that the Church kept the peasants poor so that the Church's charity became a tool with which the Church could manipulate peasants. Economic independence would loosen the Church's grip on the masses. And independence arose first in the areas surrounding the towns.

In the face of these changes, the people no longer "looked upon that order, as they had done before, as the comforters of their distress, and the relievers of their indigence. On the contrary, they were provoked and disgusted by the

---

[16] The editors (*WN* V.i.g.25) cite Smith's argument (*LJ* (A) iii.121), "that the clergy encouraged the relaxation of the authority of the great proprietors over their villeins as a means of reducing their power and that: 'They saw too perhaps that their lands were but very ill cultivated when under the management of these villains. They therefore thought it would be more for their own advantage to emancipate their villains and enter into an agreement with them with regard to the cultivation of their lands. In this manner slavery came to be abollished.'"

vanity, luxury, and expense of the richer clergy, who appeared to spend upon their own pleasures what had always before been regarded as the patrimony of the poor" (*WN* V.i.g.25). As I have shown, Church institutions during the Middle Ages created dependency of the masses on the Church, allowing the Church to exploit them but also to force them to support the Church against secular authorities when the latter sought to challenge the Church. The institutional changes – less charity from the Church, lower revenue to the Church from the secular lords, long-term leases granting the masses greater independence, the rise of towns – altered the masses' incentives. Less dependence on the Church diminished the poor's incentives to adhere to the Church's demands. The change in the poor's behavior, in turn, altered the relationship between the secular and ecclesiastic lords: "As the clergy had now less influence over the people, so the state had more influence over the clergy. The clergy therefore had both less power and less inclination to disturb the state" (*WN* V.i.g.26–28).

In short, a series of factors combined to weaken the Church relative to the secular lords. This provides the background to understanding the rise of competitive religious sects.

3.4.3 Implications for the Changing Industrial Organization of Religion: The Rise of Competition

Smith's argument about the rise of competition among religious organizations during the Reformation is an extension of the argument just discussed about the change in relative power between secular lords and the Church. In Smith's view, the secular lords gained power at the expense of the Church before the Reformation. Thus, in Smith's view, the rise of Protestant organizations occurred subsequently to that change (*WN* V.i.g.26–28).

Power grabs by the secular lords occurred in many areas of Western Europe. In some areas, notably France and Spain, the secular authorities bargained with the Church for greater powers and control over the Church within their domain. In these areas, the Church retained influence, but on terms much more favorable to the secular authorities (*WN* V.i.g.31).

In other areas, the secular authorities allied with the new sects, allowing these authorities together to survive. "The authority of the church of Rome was in this state of declension, when the disputes which gave birth to the reformation, began in Germany, and soon spread themselves through every part of Europe. The new doctrines were every where received with a high degree of popular favour. They were propagated with all that enthusiastic zeal which commonly animates the spirit of party, when it attacks established authority" (*WN* V.i.g.29).

Tactically, the advocates of the new doctrines had several advantages over the established Church. They were better steeped in ecclesiastical history, granting them advantages in disputes (*WN* V.i.g.29). Their austerity generated support among the people, and provided a striking contrast with that of the luxury of the Church (*WN* V.i.g.29). The Church's reduced generosity combined with the appearance of self-indulgence and lavishness to put it at a further disadvantage. Indeed, the established Church seemed ill-prepared to deal with the new competitors and their alliances with local princes.

In many areas, the new doctrines succeeded in gaining adherents, especially where the princes had been on bad terms with the Church.[17] In England, Henry VIII took advantage of the weakened Church.

> [T]hough he did not embrace himself the greater part of the doctrines of the reformation, was yet enabled, by their general prevalence, to suppress all the monasteries, and to abolish the authority of the church of Rome in his dominions. That he should go so far, though he went no further, gave some satisfaction to the patrons of the reformation, who having got possession of the government in the reign of his son and successor, completed without any difficulty the work which Henry VIII had begun.
>
> (*WN* V.i.g.31)

Smith also observed that the decentralized nature of the Reformation had important consequences for governance of the new sects, including the emergence of a degree of competition, which the Catholic Church had previously been able to stifle. When doctrinal disputes arose among the new Protestant sects, for example, the absence of a central authority made it difficult to settle them. Unlike the centralized hierarchy of the Catholic Church, the decentralized, competitive nature of the new sects meant the absence of a mechanism to adjudicate doctrinal disputes.

> When the followers of the reformation in one country, therefore, happened to differ from their brethren in another, as they had no common judge to appeal to, the dispute could never be decided; and many such disputes arose among them. Those concerning the government of the church, and the right of conferring ecclesiastical benefices, were perhaps the most interesting to the peace and welfare of civil society. They gave birth accordingly to the two principal parties or sects among the followers of the reformation, the Lutheran and Calvinistic sects, the only sects among them, of which the doctrine and discipline have ever yet been established by law in any part of Europe.
>
> (*WN* V.i.g.33)

---

[17] "The court of Rome had disobliged some of the smaller princes in the northern parts of Germany, whom it had probably considered as too insignificant to be worth the managing. They universally, therefore, established the reformation in their own dominions" (*WN* V.i.g.30).

One feature of this decentralization is that it allowed members of the same sect but in different secular realms to sustain doctrinal differences. This, in turn, allowed them to adapt their doctrine to the needs of their members in a manner not possible within the more rigid hierarchy of the monopoly medieval Church (*WN* V.i.g.34).

The alliance between the princes and the new sects led each to support the other in the face of existential threats from the Catholic Church and its secular allies. Violent disputes between secular and religious authorities would advantage their mutual enemies, giving both sets of authorities to cooperate. As Smith concludes, "This system of church government was from the beginning favourable to peace and good order, and to submission to the civil sovereign" (*WN* V.i.g.34).

3.5 The Response of the Political Accommodation to Changing Circumstances

The logic discussed in Sections 3.2 and 3.3 demonstrated the existence of a stable accommodation between church and the secular lords. This section explains how the accommodation fell apart in response to the environmental changes described in Section 3.4.

The rise of towns and their expanding security umbrella transformed the local countryside. Longer leases for the masses made them, along with other tenants, less dependent on both the secular and ecclesiastic lords. The Church's expanding desire for luxury along with their diminished charity reduced the people's dependency on the Church. These changes, therefore, diminished the ability of the Church to mobilize the peasantry against the secular lords. At the same time, the power of the Church declined relative to that of the king and the secular lords. The increase in relative power of the secular authorities forced the Church to accept a redefinition of their accommodation. In France and Spain, the Church remained but on much less favorable terms to the secular lords. The princes in Northern Germany and the King of England took more radical action, kicking out the Catholic Church and allying with new sects (in Northern Germany) or helping to forge a new one (in England).

The logic of the new equilibrium shows that as the masses became more independent of the Church, their payoffs rose and their grievances with the secular lords diminished. At some point, the masses no longer preferred to challenge the secular lords, even with the urging and cooperation of the Church. Following this change in preferences, the Church lost its ability to defend its privileges and authority against the secular lords. The lords then took advantage of the Church's diminished power, challenging and absorbing rather than respecting the Church's authority.

3.6 Conclusions

In his approach to feudalism, land rights, rights in labor (slavery), and the organization of the medieval Church – and to put it in modern terms – Smith demonstrates three major conclusions. He explains, first, how these institutions created a stable accommodation lasting for several centuries; second, why the Church opposed commerce and suppressed liberty and markets; and, third, how these institutions fell apart during the Reformation as the forces supporting the accommodation between the secular and ecclesiastical lords diminished or disappeared.[18]

Smith argued that multiple sets of interrelated medieval institutions hindered the long-term development of medieval Europe. In this role, he discussed feudalism, slavery, and the Catholic Church in detail. Smith's ideas on the first two are relatively well known, while those on the third are considerably less so. To help right this imbalance, in this chapter I developed the logic of Smith's approach to the medieval Church. Smith addresses a series of questions about the Church: how the secular and ecclesiastic authorities maintained their separate powers; why the secular authorities not only refrained from using their comparative advantage in violence to capture some or all of the Church's authority but also subsidized their ecclesiastic rivals; why the Church's interests led it to suppress liberty and economic growth; and why the Church's monopoly fell apart in the Reformation.

The Church's principal interest, as with most organizations, was to maintain itself and, in this case, its monopoly position. Smith suggests that the Church sought to maintain its authority with the people. The approach of this paper demonstrates why this authority was so central to the Church's survival.

Smith addresses the principal questions by explaining the interaction of three groups, the secular authority, as embodied in the secular lords, the ecclesiastical lords, and the people. The political exchange underlying the feudal society of the tenth to thirteenth centuries involved an accommodation between the Church and the secular lords. In simple terms, the Church helped pacify the population of poor, rural peasants, tailoring its doctrines in part to serve this purpose. The Church supported the secular authority, including helping to preserve the very unequal distribution of land and wealth. In return the secular lords helped finance the Church and respected its authority within its realm. Both sides had incentives to maintain this bargain, which allowed them to exploit the peasantry.

The Church also helped maintain the people in a position of dependence through a variety of weapons. For example, Smith argued that its charity

---

[18] In two companion papers, I develop Smith's theory of the persistence of feudalism and of slavery, despite their inefficiencies; these papers complement the approach of this paper (Weingast, 2017, 2022).

maintained most of the poor; the Church provided religious services, including salvation and comfort in times of death; and, a large portion of peasants made their livelihood by working on Church land. Although each of these elements provided valuable benefits to the peasantry, the Church could withdraw these benefits if the peasants failed to cooperate with the Church. These benefits were therefore also weapons that afforded the Church a credible threat over the people; those who failed to heed its interest risked an existential threat.

Smith's logic implies that this pattern of interaction was a stable equilibrium. Were a secular lord to attempt to challenge the Church's authority, the Church would bring all its weapons to bear in retaliation. The Church would brand the lord as heretical; it would withhold its services, such as salvation; and, instead of pacifying the people, it would rally them against the lord. In the face of these threats, most lords chose not to challenge the Church, and those that did challenge it typically backed down.

Smith's approach also affords an explanation for the rise of religious competition during the Reformation. At the same time that the Church experienced losses in revenue, new forms of luxury arose along with the rise of towns and commerce. The expanding market for luxury gave Church officials new items to purchase for themselves, especially those clergy living in or near the commercial cities and towns. Charity diminished. Finally, in search of greater revenue, the Church granted peasants long-term leases, which afforded the peasants greater independence.

In combination, these three changes weakened the Church's authority and its credible threats over the people. This diminished authority, in turn, had a major implication for the relationship of the secular and ecclesiastical lords: it removed the Church's ability to mobilize the peasants and hence its credible threat over the secular lords. The lords responded to the new environment by demanding and receiving new authority over the Church (e.g., in France and Spain) or by removing the Catholic Church altogether (England and Northern Germany). The result was the Reformation and the rise of powerful competitors to the Church.

I incorporate Smith's logic into a simple game of strategic interaction among three players: the secular authorities, Church, and the people. The advantage of the game is that it demonstrates that Smith's logic underpins a stable equilibrium. The equilibrium shows why each of the three players had incentives to play their roles in maintaining the equilibrium. Smith thought systematically about the problems of religion in moral and theological terms and also in terms of power and bargaining between the Church and the secular lords. The game also provides a comparative static result that shows how, as the Church's authority over the people diminished, their credible threat over the secular lords diminished, allowing them to successfully challenge the Church.

Finally, Smith explains that the stable equilibrium surrounding the Church in the Middle Ages had long-term economic consequences. Smith characterizes the Church as a "formidable combination" against both civil authority and the rise of liberty. The Church's authority over the people was central to its credible threat over the secular authorities, granting the Church the ability to retaliate against a king or lord who sought to challenge it. During this era, fostering greater liberty and independence among the people would have removed the Church's most important weapon in its relations with the secular authorities, much to the detriment of the Church. The Church therefore suppressed liberty, economic growth, and development.

Smith's industrial organization of religion is part of his larger project on the logic underlying the differential wealth of nations; or, in modern terms, the political economics of development. Smith's approach to economic development is well known, including the division of labor and capital accumulation (Hollander, 1973; Ekelund and Hébert, 2007). Less well known are Smith's studies of political development, often because he embeds his theoretical observations in historical narratives – that is, Smith's historical jurisprudence (Haakonssen, 1996, chap. 7).

Smith's focus on a variety of medieval institutions relies on logic that presages the modern literature demonstrating the impediments to development (Acemoglu and Robinson, 2006, 2012; North, Wallis and Weingast, 2009; Besley and Persson, 2011). Smith's approach to feudalism, the medieval Church, and to medieval slavery reveals different forms of systematic impediments to development. Common to each of these topics is the idea that political interest led groups to favor institutions by suppressing growth but which further their interests. Another important aspect of Smith's work is that he also focuses on how particular groups escaped the impediments to growth, such as the rise of towns out of the feudal equilibrium or the demise of the Catholic Church's monopoly in the Reformation.

4

Talking to My Butcher
Self-Interest, Exchange, and Freedom in the Wealth of Nations

SAMUEL FLEISCHACKER

"The *Wealth of Nations* is a stupendous palace erected upon the granite of self-interest" (Stigler, 1975, p. 237). Thus George Stigler, and thus, with minor qualifications here and there, two centuries of misinterpretation of Adam Smith, especially by economists. To attribute the belief to Smith that people should, or inevitably do, act selfishly is severely to misread his text, especially in relation to other theories of human motivation at the time. That misreading arises, especially, from a misunderstanding of the famous "butcher and baker" paragraph in Book I, chapter ii of the *Wealth of Nations* – a misunderstanding that virtually inverts the true meaning of that paragraph. I have written about this paragraph before (Fleischacker, 1999, pp. 152–156, 2004b, pp. 90–94, 2021, pp. 256–257, 296–298, 316–317), but I want here to expand on what I have said previously, commenting on sections of it line by line so as to bring out fully what I take to be its overall argument. The result points, among other things, to a deep kinship, as well as certain significant differences, between Smith and Aristotle: a nexus that could still use further exploration.

4.1 Self-Interest and Exchange

> It is not from the benevolence of the butcher, the brewer, or the baker, that we expect our dinner, but from their regard to their own interest. We address ourselves, not to their humanity but to their self-love, and never talk to them of our own necessities but of their advantages. Nobody but a beggar chuses to depend chiefly upon the benevolence of his fellow-citizens.
>
> (*WN* I.ii2)

Well, *of course* we address the butcher and the baker in terms of what they can get from us! Who would have thought otherwise? If Smith's point was that people are always motivated by self-interest he should have used a less obvious example – shown us, perhaps, like Mandeville, that charitable actions are really motivated by self-interest.[1] No self-respecting person, in ordinary

---

[1] "When a Man acts on behalf of Nephews or Neices, and says they are my Brother's Children, I do it out of Charity; he deceives you: for if he is capable, it is expected from

circumstances, would dream of going into a butcher shop and begging for a cut of sirloin. Nor does Smith deny that in extraordinary circumstances people do beg: "Nobody *but* a beggar chuses to depend chiefly upon . . . benevolence," but a beggar does so choose. Hence the passage as a whole cannot possibly make the point *that* people are motivated exclusively by self-interest. If Smith wanted to advance this Mandevillian thesis, which he is elsewhere at pains to dismiss (*TMS* VII.ii), he would not have appealed to the paradigm ways in which we already expect self-interest to work. Rather, he must be using the ordinariness, the obviousness, of the appeal to self-interest in interaction with butchers and bakers as *background*, as *evidence*, for *another* point.

What other point? I suggest: that human beings can pursue even their individual interests together; that even anonymous society, where self-interest rather than any direct emotional bond to other human beings is the normal source of motivation, need not be a hostile society; that economic exchange, even among self-interested people, is not a zero-sum game. The emphasis is on the "even" in each case. No one would be surprised that people could jointly pursue activities where the tie between them was one of instinct or affection or duty or fear. What is surprising is that a joint pursuit is possible even *without* such bonds. Many animals act jointly out of instinct or affection: "[T]o gain the favour of [the one] whose service it requires[, a] puppy fawns upon its dam," says Smith later in the paragraph we are considering. But adult animals, which normally have no instinctual bond with one another, cooperate only by accident:

> Two greyhounds, in running down the same hare, have sometimes the appearance of acting in some sort of concert. . . . This, however, is not the effect of any contract, but of the accidental concurrence of their passions in the same object at that particular time.
>
> (*WN* I.ii.2)[2]

What marks us distinctively as human is a matter of cognition, not motivation: unlike the greyhounds, we know that working together with our conspecifics can improve life for each of us rather than taking from one and giving

---

him, and he does it partly for his own Sake: If he values the Esteem of the world, and is nice as to Honour and Reputation, he is obliged to have a greater Regard to them than for Strangers . . ." (Mandeville, 1988, vol. 1, p. 253).

[2] An earlier draft adds a more striking example: "The same is seen still more strongly in the manner in which the monkeys rob an orchard at the Cape of Good Hope. – But after they have very ingeniously conveyd away the apples, as they have no contract they fight (even unto death) and leave after many dead upon the spot" (*ED* p. 352). That the point is a *cognitive* one is crystal clear here: the monkeys don't *know*, don't *realize*, that the interest of each is compatible with the interest of the others. That is what differentiates their interactions from ours (at least as long as *we* don't fight other nations for illusory economic gains!).

to the other. This reading fits with the overall polemical point of the book: that town and country, one nation and another, one industry and another are not engaged in a Hobbesian struggle over wealth. They may compete on a day-to-day level, but ultimately that competition serves to increase the wealth of everyone – can indeed be regarded as just one moment in a generally cooperative effort.[3] That is why mercantilist restrictions on trade are pointless and counterproductive.

Not only does the passage make a poor proof for the claim *that* humans are self-interested, moreover, it makes little contribution to any claim that we *ought* to be self-interested. We come away from the passage with an appealing picture of relationships that do not require benevolence, of the reliable, independent relationship most of us have with our butchers and bakers, as opposed to the cloying, humiliating, and always uncertain life of a beggar. But it is the contrast of my life as a butcher's *customer* with the life of the beggar, and not the life or self-love of the butcher himself, that stands at center-stage in this passage. The main character, the character with whom we are supposed to identify, is the one who merely *appeals* to self-love: the one who is "more likely to prevail if ...," who "offers ... a bargain," who "expect[s]" his dinner, etc. It is not at all clear that *this* character is self-interested – perhaps he is making dinner for his parents, or for a friend, or a charity – and in any case, that is not the point: the point is to bring out his *strategy*, his knowledge that the butcher is most likely to give him meat if he offers something in return. Unlike the puppy or the beggar, the butcher's customer can appeal to someone else's interests rather than bleating self-pityingly about his own. Thus the argument of the passage depends on one person's being able to perceive, and address himself to, *another* person's interests. Instead of an almost Ayn Randian exaltation of self-love, we may now see these famous lines as focusing on our capacity to be other-directed. And that this is Smith's focus – that he is interested in our capacity for being aware of other people's needs and feelings – turns out to make much more sense in terms of his overall moral concerns than any kind of endorsement of self-love.

Why? The most distinctive feature of *TMS*, Smith's other major work, is the emphasis it places on how perceiving other people's feelings, and building into ourselves their perspectives on our feelings, is essential to proper moral judgment. If Smith had lived a little later, and in Germany, he might have

---

[3] Compare Werhane: "Smith notices that economic exchange cannot operate in the 'vacuum' of self-interest but requires co-operation and co-ordination. ... [F]ree trade requires the co-operation of two parties or two countries. Tradespeople often work together, sometimes even in collusion, despite their competitive relationships. This co-operation is also seen in the relationships between townspeople and farmers, according to Smith. ... In all these cases, co-operation is both natural and required for the advantage of our self-interests" (Werhane, 1991, p. 94).

called his book the "*Critique* of Moral Sentiments," since his point is not to endorse Hume's and Hutcheson's view that virtue is based directly on a sentiment or set of sentiments but to argue that this is true only in a highly qualified way: that neither a benevolence based on an immediate feeling of compassion towards others, nor a prudence based on the feeling of self-love, nor a justice based on the desire for revenge, can count as virtue. Rather, these feelings must be refracted through the eyes of the impartial spectator, such that we feel them only to the degree, and in the circumstances, truly appropriate to each of them.

One consequence of this view is that we come to an appropriate level of both self-love and benevolence by trying to have those feelings only to a degree we can express without embarrassment in front of other people:

> The person principally concerned ... longs for that relief which nothing can afford him but the entire concord of the affections of the spectators with his own. ... But he can only hope to obtain this by lowering his passion to that pitch, in which the spectators are capable of going along with him. He must flatten ... the sharpness of its natural tone, in order to reduce it to harmony and concord with the emotions of those who are about him.
>
> (*TMS* I.i.4.7)

Initially, I respond to what actual other people let me get away with. As I get older, I build a model of the normal "impartial spectator" in my society into myself out of these actual reactions (*TMS* III, *passim*). I then moderate the expression of my emotions according to that internal standard, allowing my impulse to fit into society to guide me toward a norm for balancing among self-directed and other-directed feelings.[4] Finally, in order so much as to approximate this ideal balance, I need a certain distance from both types of feeling. Only self-command, the power to control my feelings, enables me to achieve this distance, and it is thus the pre-condition for all virtue whatever.[5]

---

[4] "[T]o feel much for others and little for ourselves, ... to restrain our selfish, and to indulge our benevolent affections, constitutes the perfection of human nature; and can alone produce among mankind that *harmony* of sentiments and passions in which consists their whole grace and propriety" (*TMS* I.i.5.5; emphasis added).

[5] Smith increasingly realized this in later editions of *TMS*. Book VI, which was added in the last edition, divides virtue into three parts – self-regarding (prudence), other-regarding (justice and benevolence), and self-command – and it is fairly clear that self-command is meant to be the psychological foundation of the other two:

> [T]he man who acts according to the rules of perfect prudence, of strict justice, and of proper benevolence, may be said to be perfectly virtuous. But the most perfect knowledge of those rules will not alone enable him to act in this manner: his own passions are very apt to mislead him; sometimes to drive him and sometimes to seduce him to violate all the rules which he

Now plug all this into the "butcher and baker" passage. I may not love my butcher and baker, I may indeed have no feelings for them at all, but to get what I want from them I must at least moderate my self-centeredness down to the point at which I can present to them a plausible understanding of *their* needs, and a willingness to help fulfill those needs. If Smith's usual way of getting at the self only through the other is at work here, it is reasonable to assume both that the butcher and baker are more likely to be open to a true understanding of my concerns if I thus moderate my self-love ("lower" my passion, "flatten its tone"), and that *I* can achieve a more appropriate, better balanced sense of my own worth and just deserts by forcing myself to lessen my demands in the presence of others. Yes, I appeal to the butcher's self-love, but paradoxically that is only more likely to *lessen* his own concern for himself and his needs, to open him more to understanding me. The market, that is, provides a condition both for true benevolence and for the development of self-command. We should not lay too much stress on the first of these achievements.[6] I do not become friends with my shopkeepers merely by having commercial relationships with them, nor does Smith think I do: "In civilized society [man] stands at all times in need of the co-operation and assistance of great multitudes, while his whole life is scarce sufficient to gain the friendship of a few persons." That the market provides training in self-command, on the other hand, is strongly implied by Smith's contrast between human beings and animals, and repeated suggestion that participation in the market grants a dignity of some kind. In *LJ* he says that "nothing gives us such noble and generous notions of probity as freedom and independency," and describes commerce as making freedom and independency widely available, even to some of the poorest of "the common people" (*LJ*(A) vi.6). In the last edition of *TMS*, he tells us that "the ordinary commerce of the world" helps us achieve propriety, and identifies "the great school of self-command" with "the bustle and business of the world." (*TMS* III.3.7 and III.3.25).[7]

>himself, in all his sober and cool hours, approves of. The most perfect knowledge, *if it is not supported by the most perfect self-command*, will not always enable him to do his duty.
>
>(*TMS* VI.ii.1; my emphasis)

I do not think this is a radical change from Smith's views in earlier editions (compare, for instance, *TMS* I.v.1 and III.5.12), merely a clearer way of presenting those views.

[6] Although Allan Silver has shown, ingeniously reading this same passage, just how Smith's "society of strangers" does provide the condition of possibility for the peculiarly intimate modern form of friendship (Silver, 1997).

[7] As Craig Smith has reminded me, Smith also says that children "enter into the great school of self-command" as soon as they leave their parents or nurses and have to get along with their "play-fellows and companions" (*TMS* III.3.22). So the market is not the sole venue for that "school." But the interactions of children with their play-fellows teach self-command precisely because they require the sorts of skills and capacities that will later

I think this remarkable suggestion is in fact correct. Especially in societies that no longer emphasize martial institutions, self-command comes about first and foremost through the workings of the market.[8] Unlike some of his more nostalgic friends, Smith knew that the world of universal participation in the military was by and large over, and looked forward to a world in which war would become a less and less important element of statecraft.[9] In such a world, the self-distancing process required to make one's way through market interactions becomes the usual way by which people learn to control their emotions

---

be needed to participate in market societies: the sorts of restraint of one's own passions, and recognition of others' needs, that enable us to get along with people who are equally independent.

[8] Nicholas Phillipson makes much of this point (Phillipson, 1983). See also Pocock (1983). What I say throughout this piece has an obvious connection with the issues both Phillipson and Pocock discuss. I am not quite sure what to say, however, about Pocock's placement of Smith in response to, and rejection of, the Harringtonian legacy. Certainly Smith does not place political participation at the center of his conception of virtue. Nor does he share the agrarian emphasis of the Harringtonians, although he nods in that direction several times. But he by no means gives up on the ideal of virtue as "independence," and he retains the vision of the independent person as "practising an austerely virtuous equality with his no less independent peers" (Pocock, 1983, p. 237). What has changed is that this independent person need no longer be first and foremost a *citizen* – moral rather than political concerns are primary, for Smith – and requires neither battle-hardiness (see next note) nor an agricultural setting to develop self-command. Both Smith's sympathy for and his criticism of Harringtonian concerns comes out most sharply as regards the latter point. Through the "higgling and bargaining" (*WN* I.v.4, p.49) of commercial exchange, even common laborers can become "alltogether free and independent" (*LJ* (A) vi.7), in Smith's sense. They may be paid by a "manufacturer," but (not knowing and not, I think, anticipating the coming of the factory system) Smith saw a free labor market as ensuring that wage labor could transcend the dependency characteristic of master–servant relations. So in the commercial era, classical virtue was something everyone could attain. Smith thus adopts the ideals of the Harringtonians while rejecting their analysis of the material conditions necessary for those ideals.

[9] Donald Winch sorts out Smith's views on 1) modern military effectiveness versus 2) the military virtues extremely well (Winch, 1978, chap. 5). I think he is wrong, however, to portray Smith as "always regard[ing] the art of war as the noblest of arts" (p. 105). The main prooftext he uses for this claim, *TMS* VI.ii, is much more equivocal than Winch claims: the military virtues come off as indeed *aesthetically* admirable, but more often than not used for vile and horrific ends. When we add to this the many disparaging remarks about soldiers in *WN* (e.g., I.x.b.29, IV.ii.42) and descriptions of war as irrational and destructive to all parties (throughout II.iii, III.iv, and IV.i, among other places), it becomes clear that Smith belongs firmly with the most pacifist of eighteenth-century writers, not with those who continued to toy with the idea that war is a glorious arena of human achievement. The point of *TMS* VI.ii comes out best in its chapter 3, I think, where Smith uses the glory traditionally attaching to military accomplishments as a metaphor, whereby we might see our entire lives as a sort of military posting to "the forlorn station of the universe" (VI.ii.4). Courage and self-mastery are indeed great virtues, for Smith, but their greatest achievement comes in a stoic acceptance of our place in the world, not on the literal battlefields where nations destroy themselves to serve the vanity of foolish rulers.

and desires.[10] This provides a powerful justification for the intrinsic value of market institutions, quite independent of their contribution to the growth and spread of wealth.

4.2 Exchange and Speech

> This division of labor ... is the necessary, though very slow and gradual consequence of a certain propensity in human nature ... : the propensity to truck, barter, and exchange one thing for another.
>
> Whether this propensity be one of those original principles in human nature, of which no further account can be given; or whether, as seems more probable, it be the necessary consequence of the faculties of reason and speech, it belongs not to our present subject to enquire.
>
> (*WN* I.ii.1–2)

Why regard the market as a form of speech? A related question might have been asked earlier: why regard the market as an essentially cooperative effort, rather than a means by which individual pursuits happen to intersect with one another? If cooperation is understood to be a duty- or friendship-based pursuit of mutual interests, then by definition nothing based on mutual appeals to self-love could possibly count as cooperation. But this is too narrow an account of cooperation. We say "they're co-operating" of two students who work on a research project together, of movie producers and their directors, workers and their managers, regardless of whether they are friends or bound by some kind of obligation, as long as they (1) share their plans and tactics with one another, (2) take care not to interfere with or unnecessarily duplicate what the other(s) is doing, and (3) in some way shape their plans so as to help each other attain their ends, even if that help is from each's perspective merely a useful by-product of their separate desires and goals. Cooperation is a working together where people talk to one another and intentionally coordinate efforts based on what they have said and heard. No intention, much less desire, to help one another is required; each can be pursuing their own self-interest, the other's interests, or any other ideal or goal. The point is not that the two have the *same* goal, immediately or ultimately, but that each knows *what* immediate goal the other is aiming for, along with how they mean to get there, and that each plans their own activities around an intention to contribute, for whatever reason and to whatever degree, to the attainment of the other's objectives. What started as two questions is therefore one: cooperation

---

[10] The market is also, of course, a *better* teacher of self-command than war. Not just because it is nonviolent, but because it is far more conducive to mutual respect among its participants. I thank Craig Smith for pointing this out.

is a coordination of pursuits based on speech, so all we need to know is whether the market somehow depends on speech.

And despite the silent, impersonal way in which it often operates, the market quite clearly does depend on speech. In the first place, as economists love to say and Smith already intimates, the market is itself a signal system, a way by which human beings can share their intentions with one another. I know that you – some average "you" with whom I may not be acquainted personally – want more corn and plan to get it because the price of corn is rising. You thereby communicate with me, albeit indirectly.

In the second place, when telling us that animals do not engage in market behavior Smith writes that no one ever saw a dog "make a *fair and deliberate exchange*" with another dog. That an exchange is "fair," we know from a little later in *WN*, depends on the objects traded having a similar exchange-value, not a similar use-value, or any other kind of absolute or intrinsic value. Smith is suspicious of notions of value as absolute or intrinsic, remarking that even labor value is commonly estimated "by the higgling and bargaining of the market, according to the sort of rough equality which, though not exact, is sufficient for carrying on the business of common life" (*WN* I.v.4; p. 49). But if what it is fair to exchange for any given object depends on what is generally being exchanged for that object elsewhere in "common life," then the notion of a fair exchange is essentially a socially mediated one. So even if two dogs happened to exchange bones, they could not look upon their exchange as "fair" unless they knew what similar bones were going for among other dogs in their neighborhood. It is hard to imagine having that kind of knowledge without being able to talk.

Finally, Smith draws a considerably less glib equation between market behavior and conversation than do modern economists. He does not say that the "propensity to truck, barter, and exchange" is *identical* with our faculties of reason and speech, but that it is a *consequence* of them. The market is not itself, more than metaphorically, a *form* of speech, but it is *based* on speech. Market interactions are virtually impossible without conversation, without the sharing of habits, tastes, and ends that conversation usually brings about, and without the independence by which individuals make contributions to a conversation. Markets may not quite *be* speech, but they depend crucially upon it.

To clarify this point, let us take an example a little removed from, and I think better than, Smith's own. Normally, when we go to the butcher we do not talk much, and certainly do not need to persuade or be persuaded that a money-for-meat exchange is in our mutual interest. Any persuasion that goes into the setting up of this interaction has been done long before, and elsewhere. "Money talks," we can safely say, sums up the level of our conversation with the butcher. But shortly before first drafting this chapter I had occasion, in a butcher shop as it happens, to overhear a conversation between a potential *supplier* and the person carving meat behind the counter. "You gotta take a look at our stuff," one of the guys from the supplier was saying. To which the reluctant buyer replied: "Well, bring in a sample." "No, no, the truck is important. It makes an impression." Again the buyer: "What have you got that I don't have?" Potential supplier: "What haven't we got? Prepared products, stuffed chickens, fresh smoked turkey – gourmet stuff, elegant." Etc. The suppliers were "real salesmen" – friendly, cajoling, bantering, slightly self-mocking in a way that made their company enjoyable, and remarkably skilled at presenting themselves as having something unique and highly desirable to offer. They acted, as only great salespeople can, as if they were very interested in the buyer and what would make the buyer's business grow. At the same time they were honestly and explicitly out for their own gain: a pretense of altruism, like a plea for altruism, would only have made the retailer suspicious – and rightly so – that there was something wrong with the goods they had to offer. If business between them and the retailer in fact resulted from this conversation, moreover, their self-interested appeal to the latter's self-interest was probably based on truth: exchange was indeed in the interests of both parties. In any case, in this example there is a direct attempt to persuade, and an express appeal to mutual self-love as a basis for that persuasion. And what makes this a particularly delightful example is that the suppliers, and the buyer, were *kosher* butchers, linked by the tight networks of friendship and obligation among America's tiny Orthodox Jewish population. On some anti-Smithian views, this would have been a perfect occasion for a plea of "Come on, help us out here – we need the business" (and that is indeed a factor in some commercial interactions among Orthodox Jews). But never the slightest hint of that did I hear. Perhaps more important than this descriptive observation is a normative one: I think, and suspect the reader thinks, that it was better so. An appeal to duty or compassion in this situation would have in fact been no less self-serving and would have left a bad taste in the mouth of both parties. The appeal to the value of their product was instead forthright, dignified, and pleasing.

My main point is a different one, however. My main point is that many, many conversations of this kind serve as the underpinning of any market economy. In addition, market participants converse with one another about where good prices or good opportunities to sell are to be found, about the quality of workers and employers and sources for various products, about favorable trends and looming dangers: all the sorts of details that are essential to making good bargains. Conversation about all of these subjects, as well as conversation aimed directly at persuading others to engage in exchange, is essential to economic activity. To view the market as a kind of machine for producing or distributing goods, or for finding price-equilibria given conditions of supply and demand, is an economist's abstraction. No shrewd investor, let alone merchant or manager, lives in isolation from society. Even in this day of computerized information, no programmer who spends 90 percent of his time alone in front of a terminal can sell a successful product. Capitalism has never been made by hermits, nor are the skills of philosophical contemplation particularly useful to it. If the corn merchant, as Smith would have it, does our conserving for us (*WN* IV.v.b.25), he must both be in touch with many farmers and be aware of the ordinary consumer's psychological proclivities. The Amsterdam merchant in the *Wealth of Nations* who wants to supervise his carrying trade (*WN* IV.ii.6) will lose out to less or more suspicious merchants if he is not finely aware of both the reliability of his workers and colleagues and the efficiency of current dock workers and customs officials. Successful investment in a capitalist economy is a matter of determining people's needs with great accuracy and specificity, and meeting them with an attention to cost that only a detailed knowledge of the available labor force can yield. The knowledge, and psychological and sociological understanding of fellow members of one's society, required for these achievements is gained from conversation, from an interest in other people and an attentive listening to what they can tell you – love is not necessary – and it is in this sense that the market depends deeply on speech and persuasion.

4.3 Speech and Freedom

> Whether [the] propensity [to truck, barter, and exchange] be one of those original principles in human nature, of which no further account can be given; or whether, as seems more probable, it be the necessary consequence of the faculties of reason and speech, it belongs not to our present subject to enquire. It is common to all men, and to be found in no other race of animals ... Nobody ever saw one animal by its gestures and natural cries signify to another, this is mine, that yours; I am willing to give this for that. When an animal wants to obtain something either of a man or of another animal, it has no other means of persuasion but to gain the favour of those whose service it requires.
>
> (*WN* I.ii.2)

"No other means of *persuasion*": the possibility that commercial exchange is rooted in speech dominates this passage. Smith mentions this possibility at the beginning of this paragraph quite tentatively, just as an alternative to the idea that our trucking propensity is an "original principle ... of which no further account can be given." But in an earlier version of the passage, Smith had declared unequivocally that commercial and linguistic exchange are bound together:

> If we should enquire into the principle in the human mind on which this disposition of trucking is founded, it is clearly the naturall inclination

every one has to persuade. The offering of a shilling, which to us appears to have so plain and simple a meaning, is in reality offering an argument to persuade one to do so and so as it is for his interest. Men always endeavour to persuade others to be of their opinion even when the matter is of no consequence to them.

(*ED* 352–353)[11]

Both here and in our passage, moreover, Smith worries the distinction between human beings and other animals at great length, making particularly heavy weather of the difference between mere "natural cries and gestures" and *saying*, "This is mine, that yours; I am willing to give this for that." Finally, just before the famous lines with which we began, Smith puts just such a speech into the mouth of the person who expects his dinner from the butcher or the baker: "Give me that which I want, and you shall have this which you want." It is by such a speech, by such persuasion, that we appeal to "their regard to their own interest."

Back now to the greyhounds. Smith's argument that they do not really exchange with one another recalls one of the oldest discussions in political theory. Man is a political animal, says Aristotle. He argues for that point as follows:

> [T]hat man is more of a political animal than bees or any other gregarious animals is evident. Nature ... makes nothing in vain, and man is the only animal whom she has endowed with the gift of speech. And whereas mere voice is but an indication of pleasure or pain, and is therefore found in other animals ..., the power of speech is intended to set forth the expedient and inexpedient, and therefore likewise the just and unjust. And it is a characteristic of man that he alone has any sense of good and

---

[11] A paragraph remarkably similar to this was also added to *TMS* for the 1790 edition: "The desire of being believed, the desire of persuading, of leading and directing other people, seems to be one of the strongest of all our natural desires. It is, perhaps, the instinct upon which is founded the faculty of speech, the characteristic faculty of human nature. No other animal possesses this faculty, and we cannot discover in any other animal any desire to lead and direct the judgment and conduct of its fellows." (VII.iv.25) For discussion, see Phillipson (1983, p. 191n52).

See also Phillipson's remarks on conversation and commerce (p. 188), and on the importance of conversational clubs to Smith's model of society (pp. 198–202). In general, I agree strongly with Phillipson's characterization of Smith's moral and political writing as "a discourse on the social and ethical significance of face-to-face relationships between independently-minded individuals" (p. 198). (Lauren Kopajtic has pointed out to me that *TMS* VII.iv.25 is immediately followed by a discussion of deception, and notes, rightly, that that suggests a dark side to speech and persuasion alongside its advantages. I agree – but great vices may lurk precisely where great virtues are to be found. That the great virtues of truth-telling and truth-seeking may also make possible the evils of dishonesty and manipulation seems very likely to me.)

evil, of just and unjust, and the like, and the association of living beings who have this sense makes a family and a state.

(Aristotle, 1984, bk. I.2 1253a7–18)

Importantly, Smith's point is that *exchange*, and not political society, is something natural, but otherwise he follows Aristotle very closely. Both writers make their case by taking an animal species one might have thought to share the human propensity for social interaction and then showing (a) that that animal interaction is a mere response to built-in impulses ("the perception of pleasure and pain," for Aristotle; "passions," for Smith) rather than something requiring communication, and (b) that what looks like speech in other animals – "mere voice" or "natural cries and gestures," respectively – is not so because it is again a mere expression of impulses, not a reason-guided process (Aristotle) or something that truly "signif[ies]" (Smith). Aristotle, tying speech to "reason" in his full sense of that word, moves immediately from here to the conclusion that not communication alone but communication *about* "good and evil, ... just and unjust" is natural to man; Smith, more moderately and I think more astutely, contents himself with a demonstration that even the most childishly self-interested of human debates is based on signification and some kind of reasoning ("This is mine, that yours; I am willing to give this for that"), and that that minimal level of intelligent communication is beyond what we can attribute to animal behavior.

Now signification is a process by which arbitrary sounds or signs (a) get associated with objects that need not be present to the speaker at the time of utterance, and (b) get strung together in ways that make sense only if they can be evaluated in terms of truth and falsehood.[12] No matter what theory of language one adopts, the ability to engage in this process requires some ability to abstract oneself from present circumstances, to separate one's utterances from sounds and gestures one has a mere immediate urge to express, and to aim to satisfy norms for meaning or truth. To have meaning – to be *signs* – marks require a standard, a norm, and not merely a cause. And to understand ourselves as *using* signs, as communicating, we must see ourselves as reasonably aiming at such standards, and succeeding or failing in our aim, rather than merely being caused to accord or not accord with them. If we must presuppose free will in order to make sense of our moral deliberations, as the Kantian tradition supposes, then we must equally presuppose free will to make sense of our ability to speak – to speak intelligibly, at least, to hold ourselves accountable to norms of communication, and be held accountable to those

---

[12] Continental philosophy of language, from Saussure on, stresses the first of these conditions; Anglo-American philosophy of language, especially as developed by Donald Davidson, emphasizes the second. Either one suffices to make the point I go on to ascribe to Smith.

norms by others. This is true, moreover, regardless of whether the speech in question concerns good and evil, justice and injustice, or merely our own and others' material advantages. Simply in speaking with people rather than trying to coerce them – at least if our speech is aimed at persuading them, not cajoling, manipulating or threatening them – we express our freedom and respect theirs.

So by tying exchange to speech, and separating speech from mere animal cries by its dependence on signification and the attempt to reason or persuade, Smith brings trade into the heart of a realm to which the possibility of human freedom is central. We should not overlook the difference between Aristotle's emphasis on expressly ethical speech – about good and evil, just and unjust – and Smith's emphasis on our capacity for any kind of speech at all. For Aristotle, what makes us human is that we strive for certain virtues, which only some of us fully achieve. For Smith, what makes us human seems to be just that we are *free*, and in that respect we are also all equal. So the difference between Aristotle and Smith over the kind of speech that defines us as human goes with a difference between Aristotle's elitism and Smith's egalitarianism.

Am I making Smith too proto-Kantian? Smith does not explicitly represent freedom as central to his ethics in the way that Kant does. And from the absence of any discussion of the matter in *TMS*, we may surmise that he had no confident views on the debate over free will and determinism.[13] But we also know that he committed himself throughout his writings to the importance of civic freedom. We should therefore not take lightly his interest in connecting exchange to persuasion. The connection suggests something politically important about the very nature of market relationships.

In accordance with this reading, the word "persuasion," on its other appearances in *WN*, carries favorable connotations and opposes unfavorably loaded synonyms for "power." For example:

> The pride of man makes him love to domineer and nothing mortifies him so much as to be obliged to condescend to *persuade* his inferiors. Wherever the law allows it, and the nature of the work can afford it, therefore, he will generally prefer the service of slaves to that of freemen.
>
> (*WN* III.ii.10, emphasis added)

> [T]hough management and *persuasion* are always the easiest and the safest instruments of government, as force and violence are the worst and the most dangerous, yet such ... is the natural insolence of man, that

---

[13] We might expect such a discussion especially in *TMS* VII.iii, where Smith considers various philosophical accounts of the source of our "principle of approbation." The very brevity of this chapter, and its opening admonition that the issue is quite irrelevant in practice (intro.3) should however warn us off from attributing to Smith any view on the metaphysics of moral action.

he almost always disdains to use the good instrument, except where he cannot or dare not use the bad one.

(*WN* V.i.g.19, emphasis added)

We disdain to persuade, yet the alternative is not only ugly but ineffective. In both cases, Smith highlights the irrationality of relying on force. He also characterizes the use of force in language evoking Christian and Stoic critiques of "pride" and "insolence." And he associates persuasion, in both cases, with the treatment of other human beings as "free" or "independent," rather than slaves. In this way, and in a more general use of commerce and conversation as metaphors for one another, Smith links the freedom manifest in speech with the freedom of the market.[14] Both conversation and commerce represent, and help to bring about, the freedom of human beings with regard to their own desires, their interpersonal relationships, and the political institutions that try to oppress them. Sir Walter Scott, who as a young man knew Smith well, places a nice summary of the point in the mouth of Frank Osbaldistone:

> It is impossible, sir, for me to have higher respect for any character than I have for the commercial, even were it not yours.... It connects nation with nation, relieves the wants, and contributes to the wealth of all; and is to the general commonwealth of the civilized world *what the daily intercourse of ordinary life is to private society.*
>
> (Scott, 1995, p. 18, emphasis added)

That commerce is a form of speech, and that it thereby represents the force most opposed to the human tendency toward oppression and violence, is, I think, a great philosophical insight. By speaking to our fellow human beings, we allow them independence from us and simultaneously express our own independence from our animal impulses; we show respect to them and to

---

[14] A broader implication follows if we couple this rooting of commerce in conversation with the very end of the chapter:

> Among men ... the most dissimilar geniuses are of use to one another; the different produces of their respective talents, by the disposition to truck, barter, and exchange, being brought, as it were, into a common stock, where every man may purchase whatever part of the produce of other men's talents he has occasion for.
>
> (*WN* I.ii.5)

Not only does this make the emphasis on co-operation absolutely clear, but it suggests that exchange can take place among "geniuses" and "talents," that there can be a stock of and marketplace in intangible human qualities – ideas, sentiments, virtues – as well as in labor, rent, and material products. A possibility opens up that Smith is looking to a commerce of virtues, as well as of goods, between town and country, and among nations.

ourselves; we overcome our own, and forestall their, impulse to domineer; and we thereby pave the way for cooperation instead of flattery, deceit, or force. Thus Smith goes one better than Montesquieu: the virtues of commerce include not just peace among nations, but the moral bases of individual freedom and self-respect as well.[15]

[15] My thanks to incisive comments by Robin Douglass, Paul Sagar, Jim Otteson, Lauren Kopajtic, Glory M. Liu, Craig Smith, Kathleen McCrudden Illert, and Barry R. Weingast, which have greatly strengthened this chapter. Remaining errors and confusion are, of course, my own.

5

What Did Adam Smith Mean? The Semantics of the Opening Key Principles in the *Wealth of Nations*

BART J. WILSON AND GIAN MARCO FARESE

5.1 Introduction

One answer to the question "What did Adam Smith mean in the *Wealth of Nations*?" might be "He meant what he wrote." Between directing his literary executors to burn his incomplete manuscripts upon his death and the thirty-one years he spent revising and expanding *The Theory of Moral Sentiments* to publish six editions of his first great book, we think we can safely say that it mattered to Smith what he put in print. Nevertheless, there is room for slippage between what Adam Smith himself knew about the nature and causes of the wealth of nations and what appears as his printed words on the subject. As precise as he may have wished himself to be, we may fail his words, or his words may fail us. There is also room for surplus, as the growing literature on Adam Smith's thought testifies. Adam Smith can mean more to us – more than he ever knew – when the *Wealth of Nations* is interpreted with historical or modern conceptual frameworks derived from inductive surveys of moral philosophy and economics.[1]

While we raise the question to explicitly inquire into Smith's authorial intention, we do not mean to suggest that there is a straightforward, definitive meaning to the *Wealth of Nations,* nor do we presume to decisively answer the question. Nonetheless, we argue that there is *a* specifiable meaning expressed in the text that can be captured in a clear and precise fashion by making a semantic and textual analysis that sticks closely and strictly to Smith's words. We aim for hermeneutical precision, not exhaustion. Our response will barely even scratch the surface by focusing exclusively on the two opening chapters of a magnum opus that founded a discipline. Our less venturesome aim is to elucidate the meanings of several key ideas early in the text, including "the necessaries and conveniences of life," "power of exchanging," and "the division of labour."

---

[1] For key ideas organizing this introduction, see and compare with Frye (1957, pp. 3–32).

One axiom of our analysis is that Adam Smith could not write down everything he knew about the wealth of nations or the *Wealth of Nations*. In deploying such an axiom for our purposes, we assume that there is a structure of concepts and ideas that exist independent of Smith and his words, and that they can be reduced to a small number of core atoms of human thought – semantic primes – which are presumed to be innate to all human languages, past and present. Such conceptual primitives make communication possible not only across languages, but also across time within a language, say between today's readers and an author born three hundred years ago.

Our naïve induction is to take the original text itself as our data set and phenomenon to be explained in terms of a conceptual framework. Using the methodology of the Natural Semantic Metalanguage, we produce simple and cross-translatable semantic explications of Adam Smith's fundamental principles of economics (Wierzbicka, 1972, 1980, 1992, 1996; Goddard and Wierzbicka, 2014; Goddard, 2018). We begin by identifying key sentences from the opening chapters of the book that contain the fundamental economic principles that underpin his entire project, and then we turn those principles inside out to explicate what they mean using semantic primes that can be translated *one-to-one* into any language. The extracts from the original text function as textual evidence and conceptual reference for the explications we present. The result is a new paraphrased text composed of a series of semantic explications that is both universally applicable for humankind and understandable by non-economists and even children of the twenty-first century. This text is intended to function as a sort of explicative guide to the original phrased in simple and cross-translatable words. It is not meant to replace the original, but to be read together with it.

One reason our analysis can only dig so deep is that our lens for identifying Smith's principles is strictly semantic and specifically economic, not political scientific nor even political economic. In a real way we do not engage with Smith's treatment of nations in the *Wealth of Nations*. We can only begin the process of presenting Smith's fundamental principles of *wealth creation* in the "Plan of the Work" and the first two chapters. Given space constraints, we also cannot even begin to explore the important key economic principles in chapters III–VII.

As with any scientific inquiry, the second postulate of our inductive leap is coherence. We assume a coherence of argument on the part of Smith; that is, we assume that the introduction and the first two chapters yield a coherent overall foundation for the economic principles that undergird his entire project. Such an assumption entails that we can build a reasonably connected set of principles from the text and that the meanings that emerge from our semantic analysis form an intelligible core for his book. We further hypothesize an order to the sentences themselves that Smith constructs and an order to the paragraphs that compose the basis of his argument in the "Plan of the

Work" and the first two chapters. In other words, by inferring that the text is intelligible, we can systematically study the order of words and ideas expressed in the *Wealth of Nations*.

5.2 Explicating Economic Principles in Universal and Cross-Translatable Words

We adopt the methodology of the Natural Semantic Metalanguage (NSM) to produce such semantic explications. Lexical semanticists use the NSM to decompose and pinpoint the meaning of words. It differs from ordinary languages in that it consists of only sixty-five semantic primes, which represent a semantic core presumably shared by all languages. The criteria for identifying primes are three: (i) a prime is an indefinable concept; that is, it is impossible to say what it means without ending up with circular definitions; (ii) a prime is a basic concept, that is, a concept which cannot be further decomposed or reduced into a simpler concept; and (iii) a prime has a lexical exponent in a natural language that is directly cross-translatable. The lexical exponents of the primes represent the mini-lexicon of the NSM, presented in its English version in Table 5.1.

In addition to semantic primes, the mini-lexicon of the NSM includes a small group of *semantic molecules* indicated with [m]. These are complex concepts that are decomposable into smaller meaningful units via the primes but used as such to explicate even more complex concepts. We will make use of one universal or near-universal molecule: *living creatures*. In addition, we will also formally explicate and use as a sort of semantic and conceptual "placeholder" *exchange*, which is a conceptual and semantic common denominator in various explications (and for the rest of the book). Our semantic analysis indicates that all kinds of economic transactions discussed by Smith are based on the idea of people exchanging things.

The NSM also has its own syntax. Both primes and molecules can be combined in canonical syntactic constructions that are available in all sampled languages, and each semantic prime has specific combinatorial possibilities. For example, the available evidence suggests that the prime DO can be used in three universally available syntactic constructions: (i) "someone does something," (ii) "someone does something good/bad to someone," and (iii) "someone does something with something/with someone else"/"people do things with other people." Syntactic constructions that are available in some languages but not in others – for example, the English idiomatic construction "to do something about something") – cannot be part of the NSM syntax because they are not directly cross-translatable. Consequently, the NSM syntax allows for a limited range of expressive possibilities: it permits the expression of negation ("I don't want this"/"I don't know (it)"), but does not permit questions ("What is this?") and the use of conjunctions ("you and I"/"one or two things of one kind").

Table 5.1 *English exponents of the NSM semantic primes*

I, YOU, SOMEONE, SOMETHING~THING, PEOPLE, BODY	substantives
KINDS, PARTS	relational substantives
THIS, THE SAME, OTHER~ELSE	determiners
ONE, TWO, SOME, ALL, MUCH~MANY, LITTLE~FEW	quantifiers
GOOD, BAD	evaluators
BIG, SMALL	descriptors
KNOW, THINK, WANT, DON'T WANT, FEEL, SEE, HEAR	mental predicates
SAY, WORDS, TRUE	speech
DO, HAPPEN, MOVE	actions, events, movement
BE (SOMEWHERE), THERE IS, BE (SOMEONE/SOMETHING)	location, existence, specification
(IS) MINE	possession
LIVE, DIE	life and death
WHEN~TIME, NOW, BEFORE, AFTER, A LONG TIME, A SHORT TIME, FOR SOME TIME, MOMENT	time
WHERE~PLACE, HERE, ABOVE, BELOW, FAR, NEAR, SIDE, INSIDE, TOUCH	place
NOT, MAYBE, CAN, BECAUSE, IF	logical concepts
VERY, MORE	augmentor, intensifier
LIKE	similarity

Source: NSM website (2017, v. 19)

The mini-language and syntax of the NSM are the only tools we use to produce the semantic explications. An explication typically consists of several lines, single lines being referred to as "semantic components," and are produced following the method of reductive paraphrase. Each explication presented in this chapter is phrased exclusively in "pure" NSM, that is, using only semantic primes and three semantic molecules. To improve the readability and the flow of the text for our target readers, we have divided the longer explications into small chunks, each one consisting of only a few lines and introduced by a specific heading summarizing the content. In addition, we make a minor concession concerning the headings of the explications that include both words for semantic primes and molecules, and some ordinary words of the English vocabulary (notably, *different, make, exchange, have*). We made this stylistic choice both for reasons of space (a heading phrased only in NSM would be terribly long) and for reasons of clarity, so that the reader can know what the content of each explication is simply by reading the heading.

5.3 An Illustration

We propose the following key economic principle based on the thrice-repeated phrase on the first page of the book, "the necessaries and conveniences of life":

> **PW.1: People want to have things of many kinds to live well and to feel good.**
> (a) it is like this:
> (b) all people want to live well, all people can feel something good if they can live well
> (c) because of this, at many times people in many places want things of two kinds to be theirs
> (d) people want things of one kind to be theirs because they can't live well if they can't do something with things of this kind as they want
> (e) at the same time, people want more
> (f) they want some things of another kind to be theirs because they want to feel something good
> (g) they can feel something good if they can say about things of this other kind: "this is mine"

The key substantives of the world, and of the study of economics, are PEOPLE, PLACES, and THINGS, and these substantives form the physical basis for what it means to LIVE as a sociable human being. At the same time these substantives form the conceptual and semantic basis of "exchange" and all kinds of money-based transactions. Individuals do not live in isolation, but with other people as a community, and they all want to have many things. It is precisely the fact that people want many things of many kinds that brings them together in a place called a "market" and makes them do things together in this place so that they can obtain what they want. Four fundamental semantic primes – LIVE, WANT, FEEL, and BE SOMEONE'S – permeate the explication and are interrelated logically through the conceptual linkers BECAUSE and IF. We evaluate how we live and feel with the concept GOOD, because both can also be BAD. The present tense and the initial component "it is like this" encapsulates the gnomic/factual nature of this postulate.

The explication is based primarily on the first two sentences of the Introduction and the "Plan of the Work":

> The annual labour of every nation is the fund which originally supplies it with all the necessaries and conveniences of life which it annually consumes, and which consist always, either in the immediate produce of that labour, or in what is purchased with that produce from other nations.
>
> According, therefore, as this produce, or what is purchased with it, bears a greater or smaller proportion to the number of those who are to consume it, the nation will be better or worse supplied with all the necessaries and conveniences for which it has occasion.

But the broader context is also important. Every paragraph in the "Plan of the Work" relies on the principle that *People want to have things of many kinds to live well and to feel good*. Concern about "the abundance or scantiness of this supply," "the causes of this improvement, in the productive powers of labour," "the general welfare of the society," and so on have the significance that they do because of this first economic principle, which we propose first precisely because it is the derivational basis, conceptually and semantically, of all other principles and, indeed, the entire book (*WN* PW.3&8, I.i.title).

5.4 Stilted and Austere but Universally Comprehensible in Meaning

Our paraphrased text is quite different in style and devoid of all the rhetorical ornaments and embellishments that Smith uses. Smith makes extensive use of repetitions to stress a particular point and convince the reader, and often used metaphors and images of people, places, and situations related to ordinary life to help his readers familiarize with the topics being discussed in the text. Any paraphrased text like the one presented in this chapter is longer than the original and is not characterized by the same degree of expressivity and stylistic elaboration. On the contrary, it is written plainly and clearly. What is lost in terms of rhetorical style is gained in terms of effectiveness of the exposition and especially cross-translatability.

It is worth specifying that the text that we have produced is not written in idiomatic English. In line with the hypothesis of linguistic relativity, we presume that most words in any language, not just Smith's eighteenth-century King's English, cannot be exactly translated into another language. Semantic primes, by contrast, can be. The lexical exponents for the primes WANT, FEEL, LIVE, GOOD, BE SOMEONE'S, and so on in other languages mean exactly the same as their English exponents. Such a modern Western European concept expressed by the Latinate word *labor* with its toil, fatigue, trouble, suffering, class connotations, and sociocultural underpinnings could not possibly translate exactly into hunter-gatherer languages like Comanche or Pitjantjatjara. But stripped to its self-explanatory core, PEOPLE DO SOMETHING FOR SOME TIME BECAUSE THEY WANT SOME THINGS TO BE THEIRS can be translated one-to-one in all human languages, and, moreover, requires no further explanation.

Our text should also not be considered as the result of a special kind of "translation" of the original into a more basic English version. A translation is not necessarily clearer and simpler than the original, whereas we tried to maximize descriptive clarity, semantic accuracy, and textual intelligibility. Furthermore, a translation typically connects two specific languages at a time and consists in producing a separate text in the target language that conforms to the linguistic and cultural context of the target readers. By contrast, the text that we have produced is immediately cross-translatable in many (if not all) languages at the same time and is also – and importantly – culturally neutral.

The NSM explications are also comparable with each other. Differences in meaning can be easily identified by looking at individual components within explications and by comparing them with those posited for other explications. The semantic concepts and ideas expressed later in the text (chapters III–VII) refer back to and are demonstrably based on the illustrations of the ideas expressed in chapters I and II, thus creating an interconnected semantic web.

Immediate cross-translatability into any language comes at the cost of sounding strange to the average reader, as the first principle above illustrates. But, in principle, it is more intelligible to more general readers. The explication surely sounds stilted, austere, and a bit belabored. But it is *comprehensible*, and in the same way that it would be comprehensible to a native speaker in the exponents of Comanche or Pitjantjatjara.

We recommend that the reader try to resist the mind's (incessant) desire for English phrasing and structure on the explications. While reading an explication, try to let the concepts flow from one to another until you absorb the primes and reach the end of the schematic structure. The larger meaning will come to you.

5.5 Introduction and Plan of the Work

Much has been made, and rightly so, of the opening line to *TMS*. It clearly situates Smith's account of human sociality and morality among prior work. The first two sentences to the Introduction and the "Plan of the Work" are no less, if not more, important for *WN*. Smith makes three main points: (i) the interaction between nations through trade, (ii) the necessaries and conveniences of life, and (iii) the produce of people's work. Conceptually, the idea that people want to have some things is at the core of all three points. People work and make things in order to obtain certain things that they want to possess. At the same time, they purchase the products of other people because they want to have those things too. It is thus necessary to explicate first the idea that people want to have some things; then it is necessary to specify what these things are; and finally, it is important to include the reason why, according to Smith, people want to have these things. We would also argue that everything that follows in *WN* is built upon these facts of the human condition.

In *PW.1*, the prime KIND captures the distinction between the "necessaries" and the "conveniences" of life. Mere "possession" is not sufficient to explicate the meaning of "necessaries." After stating that these are things that people can't not-have, it is necessary to add that these are things that people can use as they want. This is an important specification made by Goddard and Wierzbicka in their paper on the semantics of "possession" (Goddard and

Wierzbicka, 2019). The meaning of the phrase "something is someone's" (e.g., *Mary's shoes*) includes not only the idea of being able to say about this thing "this is mine," but also the idea of "being able to do something with this thing as one wants," which the authors have defined as "immediate control over use" (Goddard and Wierzbicka, 2019, p. 234). In addition, there is also the idea that "other people cannot do the same," reflecting the idea of "private property."

Conveniences are introduced by the idea that "people want more." Wanting more covers two semantic and conceptual elements: (i) the "conveniences" are not strictly necessary but are equally important for people's lives; in other words, people are not happy simply with some things, they also want more: (ii) people show a particular attitude toward the accumulation of things, that of always wanting more and more, meaning that in theory there is no limit to people's desires of possession.

Differently from necessaries, conveniences are inextricably intertwined with good feelings. Although it is true that people can feel bad if they do not possess necessaries, feelings are not as central to the semantics of necessaries as they are to the semantics of conveniences. The good feelings are inherent to the core, invariant meaning of "conveniences." They represent the main reason why "people want things of this other kind to be theirs." For Smith, both kinds of things are equally necessary for people to live well, and therefore both need to be accounted for in the explication.

Smith provides the reason why people want to have both kinds of things by appending two little yet significant words: "the necessaries and conveniences *of life*." Living well is the nuclear part of his treatise. The universal fact that people want to live well and can feel good if they can live well constitutes the conceptual basis both of the "necessaries and conveniences" and of the fact that people engage in commerce with other people. Later on, Smith insists on this idea emphasizing that all people can live well if they exchange things and their talents with other people through the division of labor. If they do this, Smith writes, all people can live well with other people (see explication I.2). This is why the component stating that "all people want to live well" comes before everything else and is presented as a fact or an axiom ("it is like this"). The explication flows nicely thanks to a series of cohesive devices phrased entirely in semantic primes ("because of this," "at the same time"). In this way, we present the logical structure (cause-consequence-reason) of Smith's arguments in a coherent, clear, and precise fashion.

People want to have things, first, because it is a matter of life and death. We universally can't live well if we can't do basic things in component (d) like eat, drink, sleep, and clothe ourselves. But, at the same time we want more (component e). People also want to have other things because of a second core mental predicament universal to all humans, which is largely foreign to modern economic analysis. We want to have a second kind of things because we want to *feel* good, and we can feel good if we can call such things "mine."

The prime MINE deserves a thorough discussion. In the NSM framework, the concept of "property" is analyzed as the sum of two key primes: BE SOMEONE'S and SAY (Goddard and Wierzbicka, 2016). The claim is that semantically "having something" is based on being able to say about something "this is mine." MINE, however, is not associated only with the prime SAY in the explications, but also with THINK and especially with WANT. It is the thought "I want this/these things to be mine" that encourages people to work and to gather at a market to exchange things with other people.

Modern economic analysis likewise begins with *PW.1* but stops short with three words: People want things, full stop. It then proceeds to make three assumptions about how people desire things. Smith, however, provides a logically prior axiom for why human beings want to have things. We all want to have things *because* we all want to live well and we can feel something good if we live well. *WN* is founded on this veritable humane premise. Imagine how such a starting point would change how the rest of the modern economics textbook and course would go if the reason for the study at the outset is that human beings universally want to live well (and in harmony with one another, since individual desires are, in principle, not in conflict with those of other people) and to feel good if we can live well. A study of economics based first-and-foremost on feeling good, as proposed by Smith, would change the way we understand the discipline and its social implications. Crucially, Smith does not talk about any self-oriented search for good feelings in relation to the accumulation of things (in NSM terms, "I want to feel good, I don't want other people to feel good like I feel"). We find no textual evidence for such an idea.

In the end, we argue, Smith's inquiry culminates in the often-overlooked proposition that by living and doing things together all individuals can do something good for one another (apart from doing something good for themselves) and can feel something good. Smith expresses and repeatedly emphasizes this idea, in some parts more explicitly and in others less explicitly. The deeper one goes through the text and the clearer it becomes that when he talks about the "mutual good offices that people stand in need of," the idea of being more or less "serviceable to one another," the "universal opulence" and the "general plenty" that diffuses itself in society, Smith actually expresses anything but a self-interested view of economics (*WN* I.ii.3, I.iv.2, I.ii.1, I.i.10).

The second foundational principle of economics captures the other main point in the "Plan of the Work":

PW.2: People do something for some time and make things.
[A] WHY PEOPLE DO SOMETHING FOR SOME TIME
    (a) at many times, people think like this about something:

        "I want to say about it: 'this is mine'
        I know that I can say this if I do something for some time"

    (b) because they think like this, they do something for some time

[B] WHAT HAPPENS WHEN PEOPLE DO SOMETHING FOR SOME TIME
  (c) when they do it, it is like this:
  (d) someone does something for some time because this someone wants something to happen
  (e) this someone knows how it can happen
  (f) after some time, it can happen as this someone wants
  (g) when it happens, it is like this:
  (h) there is a thing, as this someone wanted
  (i) this thing wasn't there before this someone did something for some time
  (j) this thing couldn't be there if this someone didn't do something for some time
  (k) it is like this at many times when people do something for some time

The first way in which people can obtain the things that they want is by working, or more primitively, doing something. The semantic prime THINK in component (a) is part of a cognitive scenario phrased in first-person perspective. Together with KNOW, THINK is at the core of people's awareness of the fact that work can lead to property. Because of the way people customarily conceptualize labor in society, people think that the possibility of saying about something "this is mine" can derive from doing something for some time.

Semantically, the "produce of labour" consists of two main ideas: (i) people do something for some time and (ii) they make things. In the explication the making process differs from "doing something for some time," which refers to people's labor. Making things consists in an act of creation of something that did not exist before. In the case of people's labor, the making process implies that something happens because someone does something, and people's activities are expressly aimed at making something happen ("people want this to happen"). The component "this someone knows how it can happen" is the reduced form of "expertise" and the "ability" of the maker. To be able to make something, individuals need to know how to do it. The phrasing "it is like this" in component (g) introduces the scenario of creation. The consequence of an act of creation in component (h) is a thing that now exists: "there is a thing". The second part of component (h), "as this someone wanted," emphasizes the idea that the existence of the new thing is the result of human intervention in the physical world. Component (i) specifies that what has been created could not have been made without human intervention.

The last component states that the creation process is repeated every time people make something. People have the ability and the potential to bring something to existence if they do something for some time. The temporal aspect of the making process is an important conceptual element. The phrasing "for some time" captures the idea that things are not made simply and immediately, but result from commitment, dedication, and effort. This idea is consistent with the fact that another meaning of the word *labor* is fatigue. Smith explicitly refers to the idea that whenever people work they feel something bad in chapter V, the "toil and trouble" of labor.

5.6 Chapter I, Of the Division of Labour

The meaning of term "division of labor" isn't self-evident to non-economists or budding undergraduate economists. The question is, what is divided and how? Smith expresses three main ideas in his discussion of the term: difference, many people, and cooperation. Explication *I.1*, divided in four smaller sections, states the idea and its consequences clearly:

> *Chapter I.1: Different people do different kinds of things. Because of this, they can do much more.*
> [A] WHEN MANY PEOPLE IN A PLACE DO SOME THINGS AT SOME TIME, THEY DON'T DO THE SAME THINGS
>   (a) when many people in a place do some things at some time it can be like this:
>   someone does something of one kind, someone else does something of another kind, some other people do things of some other kinds
>   (b) because of this, they can not-do many things of many kinds at the same time, they can all do one thing of one kind for some time
> [B] WHY IT IS GOOD FOR PEOPLE IF THEY DO SOMETHING OF ONE KIND FOR SOME TIME, NOT MANY THINGS OF MANY KINDS AT THE SAME TIME
>   (c) if all these people can do something of one kind for some time, not many things of many kinds at the same time, it can be like this:
>   (d) they can all do something of one kind for some time
>   (e) when someone does something of one kind, this someone knows how to do it well
>   (f) because of this, this someone can do much more during this time
> [C] WHEN MANY PEOPLE IN A PLACE DO THINGS OF MANY KINDS AT THE SAME TIME, THEY ALL WANT THE SAME THING TO HAPPEN
>   (g) sometimes, it is like this:
>   (h) many people in a place do things of many kinds for some time
>   someone does something of one kind, someone else does something of another kind, some other people do some things of some other kinds
>   (i) at the same time, they all want the same thing to happen
>   (j) after some time, it can happen as they all want
>   (k) because of this, it is like this:
>   there are many things there as they all wanted, these things were not there before

[D] IT IS VERY GOOD FOR ALL THESE PEOPLE IF IT IS LIKE THIS
  (l) when all people in a place do something of one kind for some time, not many things of many kinds, they can all do much more during that time
  (m) this is very good for all people in this place

Smith emphasizes the fact that producing a single item often results from the cooperation of many people performing different activities. Accordingly, the explication begins by stating that when people work, every individual does something different from what many other people do, in NSM terms "one thing of one kind, not many things of many kinds at the same time." The prime MANY in component (a) is necessary to make the distinction between the various activities clearer and more meaningful. It may well be the case that in a collaborative work some people do the same job, but it is less likely that *many* people perform the same activity.

Smith makes another important point in section [B]. The division of labor permits people to perform and specialize in a single activity, not many activities at the same time. If individuals were to do everything by themselves, they would consume a lot of time and physical and cognitive energies. In consequence of the division of labor, not only is the production process considerably accelerated and simplified, but people can also apply their talents and skills to only one activity. They can develop their skills constructively and can become better and better at that activity. By doing "one thing of one kind" only, all people can work for a short time instead of working for a long time (components c and d), they know how to do it well (component e); and crucially, they can produce much more (component f).

The possibility of producing much more is the greatest advantage and outcome of the division of labor. This applies equally to the activity of single individuals and to collaborative work. The idea of "people doing things with other people" is expressed for the first time at this point in the book. *Before everything else, it is labor that brings people together and unites them in the common goal of producing something.* Section [c] explicates that when people work together, every single individual with their activity contributes to the creation of one single item (Smith insists on the idea that people "join their different arts" and that production results from "the joint labour of a great multitude of workmen" (I.i.11)). This idea is captured in section [c] of the explication. Components (i) and (j) explicate the common intent of the workers, stating that "they all want something to happen" and that after they do something for some time (each one doing something different) "it happens as they all wanted." The prime ALL is essential to the idea of a collaborative approach to the making process derived from the division of labor.

The phrasing of the component (k) is identical to that of *PW.2* (g)–(j). A major difference lies at the very end of the explication in *I.1* (component m in section D), which is an evaluative component not specifically expressed in the text. The fact that Smith repeats several times on the various benefits made possible by the division of labor, and that he emphasizes these benefits by means of comparatives ("easier and readier methods") and intensifiers ("increases *very much* the dexterity") suggests that there is an underlying moral evaluation in his discourse (I.i.8&6). Specifically, Smith's lexical elements suggest that he means to say that the division of labor is not just "good" but "very good," and that it is very good for all the people who work in a place, because by specializing in one activity only, they contribute not only to their own improvement as individuals, but also to others. This brings us to the second key principle of chapter I:

I.2: All people can live well because different people do different kinds of things for some time.
[A] PEOPLE WANT SOME THINGS OF MANY KINDS TO BE THEIRS, NOT MANY THINGS OF ONE KIND
   (a) after someone does something of one kind for some time, not like many other people, this someone can say about many things of one kind: "this is mine"
   (b) when this someone thinks about these things of one kind, this someone thinks like this:
       "I don't want all these things to be mine, because I can live well if I can say about some of these things: 'this is mine', not many
       I want some things of another kind to be mine"
   (c) someone else can say about things of this other kind 'this is mine' because this other someone did something for some time, not like many other people
   (d) when this other someone thinks about these things of another kind, this other someone thinks like this someone thinks
[B] IT IS GOOD FOR ALL PEOPLE IF THEY CAN SAY ABOUT SOME THINGS OF MANY KINDS 'THIS IS MINE'
   (e) because they think like this, they can do something in a place of one kind
   (f) after they do it, it can be like this:
       some of this someone's things are now this other someone's things, as this other someone wanted
       at the same time, some of this other someone's things are now this someone's things, as this someone wanted
   (g) this is good for this someone, at the same time it is good for this other someone
   (h) all people can do this with other people
   (i) if they do it, they can all live well because they can all say about some things of many kinds: "this is mine"
   (j) this is very good for all people

In his discussion of the division of labor, Smith does not just mention the advantages and the benefits for people's work and production, but also the general benefits for society. Section [A] of *I.2* captures two main points made by Smith in relation to this. First, as a result of the division of labor, individuals have an abundance of things of one kind, the produce of their own labor (component a). However, people do not need all the things that they themselves produce to live well, but only some things of this kind (components b–d, a significant cross-reference to *PW.1*, confirming the fact that the idea of "living well" is Smith's axiomatic point of departure). They can exchange the surplus of their work with other people so they can obtain things of other kinds (section B). Components (e) and (f) anticipate the main topic of the next explication ("people exchange things") by emphasizing the fact that people can obtain everything they want by *doing something together in a place of one kind*. By doing this, people can obtain all the things of different kinds that they want and need, and in this way they can all live well (components h–j). Economics and sociality are the warp and woof of *WN*.

The prime ALL in this case captures the "universal opulence that extends itself to the lowest ranks of the people" and the "general plenty [that] diffuses itself through all the different ranks of the society" (I.i.10). Thus, not only did Smith make an explicit connection between the division of labor and living well, but he went as far as to claim that *all* people can benefit from the division of labor, because they can all receive something from other people's work. The mentioning of the "different ranks of the people" indicates that Smith was well conscious of social class distinctions. Nonetheless, his point is precisely that conveniences of living well can extend to everyone once everyone obtains the necessaries of life. For this reason, we do not include the idea that there are "different ranks of the people" in explication *I.2*.

In this case, too, as in explication *I.1*, the last component is again a moral evaluation ("this is very good for all people") deriving from the emphasis Smith places on the benefits of the division of labor for the entire society. He repeatedly uses the words *great, plenty,* and *abundantly*. Arguably, Smith could have expressed himself without these words without affecting the meaning of the main point he is making. The repeated use of them, however, suggests that he wants to express an evaluation in terms of "this is very good," not just "this is good."

5.7 Chapter II, Of the Principle That Gives Occasion to the Division of Labor

All people *can* live well because different people do different things, but how is it possible for the stuff that people make to reach everyone? Smith continues building his model with another key principle in the study of economics – "the certain propensity in human nature ... to truck, barter, and exchange one thing for another" (I.ii.1). The principle may sound simple the way we summarize it, but as the extensive explication indicates, exchange is far from a simple concept:

Chapter II.1: All people exchange things of different kinds with other people.
[A] WHY PEOPLE WANT TO BE WITH MANY OTHER PEOPLE IN A PLACE FOR SOME TIME
   (a) people know that it is like this:
   (b) at many times, when someone thinks like this: "I want some things of some kinds to be mine,"
   not all these things can be this someone's things because this someone does something for some time
   (c) because of this, at many times this someone can't not-be with many people in a place of one kind for some time, they all want some things of some kinds to be theirs
   (d) when this someone is with many people in this place of one kind, this someone does something with these people
   (e) people know that after they do this, they can say about many things of many kinds: "this is mine," not like before
[B] HOW PEOPLE DON'T THINK WHEN THEY ARE IN THIS PLACE WITH MANY OTHER PEOPLE
   (f) when this someone is with these people in this place, this someone doesn't think like this:
   "I want some things to be mine now, these things are someone else's things
   if this someone can feel something good towards me, maybe this someone will say to me:
   'I don't want these things to be mine anymore, I want them to be yours'
   I want this"
[C] WHEN PEOPLE ARE WITH OTHER PEOPLE IN THIS PLACE, SOMETHING LIKE THIS CAN HAPPEN
   (IT IS CALLED "EXCHANGE"):
   (g) when this someone is with these people in this place, this someone says something like this to someone else:
   (h) "something like this can happen now:
   (i) I do something good for you, at the same time you do something good for me
   (j) I can say about some things of one kind: 'this is mine'
   (k) you can't say the same about these things, you want some of these things to be yours
   (l) if I say: 'I want this,' some of these things can be yours, as you want
   (m) this will be good for you

(n) at the same time, you can say about some things of another kind: 'this is mine'
(o) I can't say the same about these things, I want some of these things to be mine
(p) if you say: 'I want this,' these things can be mine, as I want
(q) this will be good for me"
(r) after this someone says this, these two people say at the same time: 'I want this'
(s) it is good for people when something like this happens
(t) all people often do this with many other people in a place, other living creatures [m] don't do this

The explication begins with people's realization that the results of their own individual labor alone cannot give them everything that they want (component b in section A) and that therefore they must be somewhere (a market) with other people (component c) and do something together (component d) so that they can obtain many things of many kinds that they want (component e).

Section [B] captures Smith's important point in relation to the exchange of things: the things that people want cannot be obtained through a *captatio benevolentiae*. It is not by operating on other people's good feelings that individuals get the things that they want. Exchanging things is a specific interpersonal, social procedure based on a series of routinized speech acts.

Section [C] explicates the actual practice of exchanging things. The prime SAY in component (g) captures the conceptual salience of language and the primary importance of words in all transactions amongst people. It states clearly that any transaction is an "act of saying" during which all the individuals involved in the exchange commit themselves to giving another person "that which you want." If all parties can obtain what they want, *all* will be satisfied and *all* will feel good, which harkens back to living well. The other person will be convinced to exchange their things if they think "this is good for me". As Smith points out, the person who proposes the exchange "will be more likely to prevail if he can interest their self-love in his favour, and shew them that it is for their own advantage to do for him what he requires of them" (I.ii.2).

In component (m) the NSM phrasing "this will be good for you," we argue, is much more easily intelligible than complex concepts like *bargain*, *self-love*, and *advantage* used in the original text. It is also, and importantly, semantically more accurate, than implying any exclusiveness and selfishness on the part of the agents ("this will be good for me, not for anyone else"). Without such a contrastive part, the interpretation of the text changes radically. In addition, component (i) emphasizes the fact that the benefits of the exchange procedure will be mutual.

Smith specifically insists on the importance of mutual agreement. Only if both people *think* "this is good for me" will they agree to exchange things by saying at the same time "I want this" (component r). If all the people involved in the exchange do not want the same, the exchange cannot take place and none of the individuals involved will be satisfied.

Components (j–p) emphasize the role of the prime BE SOMEONE's in the idea of, loosely, the passage of property. For this to take place (the conceptual role of HAPPEN characterizing the exchange of things as a specific event is emphasized in components h and s), it is necessary that the individuals involved be in the same place at the same time and also that they all want the same. The final outcome of all this in component (s) is the claim that the social practice of exchanging things can contribute to everyone's well-being. Finally, component (t) incorporates the "certain propensity of human nature," namely, that property and the passage of property is an inherently and distinctively human phenomenon (I.ii.1). No other living creature routinely exchanges one thing for another thing (Ridley, 2010; Wilson, 2015, 2020). Most introductory studies of economics do not begin with such a human axiom. Modern economists take it for granted that people, *all* people, exchange things. But such an axiom is the linchpin for an inquiry into the causes of the wealth of nations and the basis for Smith's first major logical proposition:

II.2: People do different kinds of things because they can exchange things.
[A] BECAUSE PEOPLE KNOW THAT THEY CAN EXCHANGE THINGS, THEY DO SOMETHING OF ONE KIND FOR SOME TIME, NOT MANY THINGS OF MANY KINDS
  (a) people know that it is like this:
  (b) when someone thinks like this: "I want some things of one kind to be mine,"
   if someone else can say about things of this kind: "this is mine," this someone can exchange things of another kind with this someone
  (c) after this, this someone can say about some of these things of one kind "this is mine," as this someone wanted
  (d) because of this, this someone thinks like this:
   "I want to do something of one kind for some time, not many things of many kinds
   after I do this for some time, I can say about many things of one kind 'this is mine'
   I can exchange things of this kind with someone else
   if I do this, some things of another kind can be mine
   I want this"
[B] WHEN PEOPLE EXCHANGE THINGS, THEY CAN DO SOMETHING GOOD FOR OTHER PEOPLE
  (e) if all people think like this, it can be like this:

(f) some people do something of one kind for some time, other people do something of another kind for some time
(g) all people can do something of one kind well
(h) because of this, all people can do something good for other people

The "necessary consequence" of *II.1* is that when people want something that they cannot obtain simply from the result of their own labor (component b), they can exchange for it (component c) (I.ii.2). Having explicated the semantics of exchange in *II.1*, we embed the complex concept as a semantic placeholder in component (b). The possibility of exchanging things they have for things that other people have encourages people to specialize their production (component d). If other people do the same, each person can exchange the products of their work with other people (components e–h), and this will be mutually beneficial (component h), or, as Smith says, "the mutual good offices which we stand in need of" (I.ii.3). The explication concludes with two specific propositions. If people can specialize their productions in a specific sector, they can become better and better at it (component g, "to cultivate and bring to perfection whatever talent of genius he may possess for that particular species of business" (I.ii.3)), and (ii) by doing this, every single person helps another person live well. The underlying moral evaluation lies precisely in doing something good for other people that results from the interrelation of the division of labor and the exchange of things. At the same time, the primes DO, SOMETHING, and GOOD combine beautifully at the end as the logical and moral consequence of Smith's major point of chapter II.

Smith concludes the chapter with his famous comparison of the porter and philosopher in an explicit one-way proposition:

II.3: People are different because they do different kinds of things, not the contrary.
(a) it is like this:
(b) because people do something of one kind for some time not like many other people, there are many people of many kinds
(c) people of all kinds can do something of one kind well
(d) it is not like this:
(e) there are many people of many kinds
(f) someone of one kind is not like someone of another kind
(g) because of this, someone of one kind can do something of one kind for some time well, someone of another kind can't do it well
(h) because there are people of many kinds, people do many things of many kinds for some time not like many other people

In principle, according to Smith, it is the work that we do that makes us different, not our intrinsic differences as individuals that determine the work we can or cannot do. The primes KIND, NOT, and LIKE account for both differences in people's occupations and in personality, skills, attitudes, and social class. We decompose the variety and diversity of people acknowledged by Smith as the statement in component (b) that "there are many people of many kinds." Component (d) reflects Smith's aversion to any type of predetermined natural selection and combination, so to speak, of people and occupations.

5.8 Conclusion

Our project re-humanizes the study of economics by drilling down to the core of what Adam Smith the moral philosopher meant in his most famous book (Smith and Wilson, 2019). Where modern economics makes quantities of stuff the subject of its inquiry, Smith places human beings as the subject not just of his inquiry, but of his very sentences. The cornerstone of his analysis is that (1) people want to have things of many kinds to live well and to feel good. To satisfy their desire to live well, (2) people do something for some time and make things. When people make things, (3) they do different kinds of things. Because of this, they can do much more. Taken together, the first three principles indicate that it is possible that (4) all people can live well because different people do different things for some time. How is that possible that all people can live well because different people do different things? Smith's argument rests on the axiomatic keystone that (5) all people exchange things with other people. His first key proposition is that (6) people do different kinds of things because they can exchange things. Finally, Smith makes the egalitarian claim that (7) people differ because they do different kinds of things, not the contrary. From the beginning of his magnum opus, Smith weaves a coherent economic argument about the human condition intelligible to every human being who lives it.

6

Adam Smith and Virtuous Business

JAMES R. OTTESON

6.1 Introduction

For being the reputed "father of capitalism," Adam Smith had many criticisms of commercial society. He criticized monopolies and their ability to keep prices unnaturally high, benefiting the monopolists at the expense of the public. He worried about "masters" who "are always and every where in a sort of tacit, but constant and uniform combination, not to raise the wages of labour above their actual rate" and who coordinate their conspiracies "with the utmost silence and secrecy, till the moment of execution" (*WN* I.viii.13). He lamented that "[p]eople of the same trade seldom meet together, even for merriment and diversion, but the conversation ends in a conspiracy against the publick, or in some contrivance to raise prices" (*WN* I.x.c.27). And he cautioned that a "proposal of any new law or regulation of commerce which comes from this order [i.e., employers], ought always to be listened to with great precaution, and ought never to be adopted till after having been long and carefully examined, not only with the most scrupulous, but with the most suspicious attention" because it "comes from an order of men, whose interest is never exactly the same with that of the publick, who have generally an interest to deceive and even to oppress the publick, and who accordingly have, upon many occasions, both deceived and oppressed it" (*WN* I.xi.p.10).

Smith's concerns about commercial society and businesspeople's behavior in it were so numerous, in fact, that some commentators argue that Smith is properly considered as on the political left rather than on the political right (Fleischacker, 1999, 2016; Rothschild, 2002; but see also Otteson, 2016). Even among those who interpret him as a champion of markets, most recognize that he was no unalloyed supporter of laissez-faire (Norman, 2018).

Given the seemingly unending stories of business malfeasance and corruption, many today wonder whether there can even be such a thing as what we might call "virtuous business" (Conn, 2018; Neem, 2019). Is it possible in a

---

I thank Paul Sagar for numerous constructive comments on a previous draft of this essay. I also thank the other contributors to this volume for their helpful suggestions for improvement. Remaining errors are mine alone.

market-based commercial society to engage in business activity virtuously, or is being relatively less corrupt the best we can hope for? Is the most we can expect from our institutional structures that they channel businesspeople toward creating some benefit, however unintentional, for others as they pursue their private interests, and thus perhaps minimize the damage they do to others, to their communities, to the environment, and even to their own souls in the process (Mayer, 2018)?

Despite his concerns about business, perhaps there might nevertheless be something relevant to contemporary concerns in Adam Smith. Smith recommends political-economic institutions that can provide a framework enabling us to address what a just and humane society is, as well as the role virtuous business might play in it. In this essay, I outline how the Smithian system might plausibly provide such a framework and suggest that it can offer guidance for what we might call "virtuous business."

6.2 Adam Smith's Political Economy

Adam Smith was part of a movement that departed from the tradition of political philosophy, going back at least to Plato (1992). This earlier movement first envisioned an ideal conception of society – for Plato the *kallipolis*, or ideally good city-state – and articulating several of its key idealized elements. Second, it proceeded by finding existing system(s) wanting by comparison to the imagined ideal. Third, it concluded by advocating institutional reforms intended to more closely approximate the ideal. Smith departs from this approach and proceeds instead by asking what is practicable given the facts of the human condition. If it turned out, for example, that human beings are naturally motivated by self-interest and have only limited benevolence, then a proposed system of political economy that could succeed only if its citizens were moved by nothing but benevolence would be a nonstarter. Smith's political economy thus begins with a review of empirical observations of human nature and human psychology, as well as a review of the salient features of the human condition, and asks not what is the best that can be imagined, but instead where improvements can realistically be made.

What are the empirical realities that Smith believes he observed? Regarding human nature, Smith believes we are motivated by self-interest and limited benevolence, we have a partiality toward ourselves and those we know who matter to us, our knowledge is significantly more limited – especially regarding other people and their situations – than we typically believe, and we have value pluralism, or differing schedules and rankings of values, goals, and ends (*TMS* II.ii.2.1–4; VII.iii.1.1–4; *WN* I.ii.1–5). Regarding the human condition, Smith believes our desires outstrip our available means to achieve them – in other words, we live in a world of scarcity (*WN*, I.v.1–4). Our value pluralism entails that we have conflicting ideas about how our limited resources should be allocated, and these conflicts can sometimes become violent; and because our public social institutions are administered by "limited and imperfect" human beings (*TMS* VII.ii.3.20), the institutions themselves, and the results we should expect from them, will also be imperfect. Because Smith believes these are empirical realities, he treats them as constraints for political-economic investigation: any proposed system of political economy – as well as of any large-scale public social institutions – must be consistent with and reflect these realities.

What political-economic conclusions does Smith draw from these (alleged) empirical realities? Because we are self-interested with real but limited benevolence, and because we are partial to ourselves and our own, he recommends rules respecting private property. If I have property rights in what I have, I am motivated to steward and use it efficiently, and to get the most out of it I can without exhausting or destroying it (*WN* I.xi.c.1–7; III.ii.9–11; III.iv.17–19). If others have similar rights in what they have, I am disciplined against attempting to get what I want by stealing from or defrauding others. A system of private property also helps reduce conflict because it gives individuals an arena in which they can live and act consistently with their own schedules of value, without being beholden or vulnerable to others (*WN* I.x.a.1–3; I.x.c.12, 31–33; III.iv.11–15). Smith thus goes on to recommend reducing or eliminating trade restrictions, mandatory apprenticeships (*WN* I.x.c.11–16), and legally protected monopolies or charters (*WN* I.vii.26–37; I.x. c.1–11; IV.1.20–28), because doing so would give wider scope to individual expression of people's unique private schedules of value (*WN* I.x.a.1–3; I.x. c.12), and would act as a check on people's overestimation of their knowledge of others (*TMS* VI.ii.2.16–18; *WN* IV.ii.5–11; IV.v.b.26).

In *WN*, Smith argues that in a "well-governed society" (*WN* I.i.10), people will be incentivized to pursue their own interests in ways that simultaneously, if unintentionally, benefit others as well. For Smith, a "well-governed society" is one that primarily protects justice, which he defined in *TMS* as the protection of three things: each citizen's *person* from murder, assault, and slavery; each citizen's *property* and possessions from theft, trespass, and destruction; and each citizen's voluntary contracts or *promises* from fraud, breach, and uninvited third-party interposition (*TMS* II.ii.2.2). We can think of these three protections of justice as the "3 Ps": person, property, and promise. Smith's argument for this conception of justice is primarily empirical and historical: it turns out, he argues, that no society can exist, let alone flourish, in which there is systematic violation of these 3 Ps; and a society that does protect them can subsist, whatever else it does (*TMS* II.ii.3.3). Thus, protection of the 3 Ps is both necessary and sufficient for the existence of human society. On the other hand, what Smith calls "beneficence," or the taking of positive action to benefit others, is neither necessary nor sufficient for the existence of society. Beneficence is, he says, the "ornament which embellishes" society, making it more pleasant and "comfortable"; whereas justice is "the foundation which supports" society, without which "all the bands of it are broke asunder, and the different members of which it consisted are, as it were, dissipated and scattered abroad by the violence and opposition of their discordant affections" (*TMS* II.ii.3.3).

In such a "well-governed society," people are incentivized to seek out cooperative ways to associate, trade, exchange, and partner with others to mutual benefit. The result, Smith claims, is a "universal opulence which extends itself to the lowest ranks of the people" (*WN* I.i.10). This "universal opulence" results from the division of labor to which voluntary association and partnership lead. Division of labor leads, according to Smith, to increasing production and thus surplus; surplus, other things equal, leads to decreasing prices; and decreasing prices lead, again other things equal, to ever more people being able to afford, enjoy, use, and consume ever more goods and services – that is, to increasing standards of living.[1] Thus, the division of labor that protection of the 3 Ps enables leads Smith to conclude: "Every workman has a great quantity of his own work to dispose of beyond what he himself has occasion for; and every other workman being exactly in the same situation, he is enabled to exchange a great quantity of his own goods for a great quantity, or, what comes to the same thing, for the price of a great quantity of theirs. He supplies them abundantly with what they have occasion for, and they accommodate him as amply with what he has occasion for, and a general plenty diffuses itself through all the different ranks of society" (*WN* I.i.10).

This process results, Smith argues, in extensive networks of cooperative exchange and interdependence. If you were to contemplate how many people, from how many different societies, and with how many different skills and interests, are required to provide even a modest "woollen coat" for an eighteenth-century "day-labourer," "you will perceive that the number of people of whose industry a part, though but a small part, has been employed in procuring him this accommodation, exceeds all computation" (*WN* I.i.10). Indeed: "if we examine, I say, all these things, and consider what a variety of labour is employed about each of them, we shall be sensible that without the assistance and co-operation of many thousands, the very meanest person in a civilized country could not be provided, even according to, what we very falsely imagine, the easy and simple manner in which he is commonly accommodated" (*WN* I.1.11).

Smith proceeds to build out his political economy with three related arguments, which we might call the Economizer Argument, the Local Knowledge

---

[1] Smith's definition of wealth: "Every man is rich or poor according to the degree in which he can afford the necessaries, conveniencies, and amusements of human life" (*WN* I.v.1).

Argument, and the Invisible Hand Argument. Let us look briefly at each in turn.

6.2.1 The Economizer Argument

Smith writes: "Every individual is continually exerting himself to find out the most advantageous employment for whatever capital he can command" (*WN* IV.ii.4). This claim is connected with Smith's discussion elsewhere (and repeatedly) of the "natural effort of every individual to better his own condition" (*WN* IV.v.b.43), and his (again, repeated) claim that "[i]t is the interest of every man to live as much at his ease as he can" (*WN* V.i.f.7). The Economizer Argument holds that one will assess the limited resources available to one – including one's time, one's skills and abilities, and one's money – and one will look for ways to reach one's goals, whatever they are, in the surest, fastest, most complete ways, or with the least cost to any other goals one has. We look, as it were, for the best returns on our investment of resources; in other words, we *economize*.

6.2.2 The Local Knowledge Argument

Smith writes: "What is the species of domestick industry which his capital can employ, and of which the produce is likely to be of the greatest value, every individual, it is evident, can, in his local situation, judge much better than any statesman or lawgiver can do for him" (*WN* IV.ii.10). As Smith develops it, this argument proceeds as a three-step syllogism:

Premise 1: People's individual situations, along with their values, purposes, and opportunities, are known best by individuals themselves.
Premise 2: To be made wisely, decisions about allocating resources must exploit knowledge of situation, value, purpose, and opportunity.
Conclusion: Therefore, the person best positioned to make such decisions is the individual.

Smith's claim is not that individuals are infallible, and there might be special cases – for example, children or the infirm – where individuals are not, in fact, best positioned to make decisions in their own cases. But for the vast majority of adults, Smith's claim is that their personal knowledge of their own situations exceeds that of others. Hence, if making good decisions requires utilizing this knowledge, then in the vast majority of cases the persons who should be making decisions are those persons themselves.

Smith goes on to claim: "The statesman, who should attempt to direct private people in what manner they ought to employ their capitals, would not only load himself with a most unnecessary attention, but assume an authority which could safely be trusted, not only to no single person but to no council or senate whatever, and which would be nowhere so dangerous as in the hands of a man who had folly and presumption enough to fancy himself fit to exercise it" (WN IV.ii.10). Note especially two claims Smith makes in that passage: the statesman's attention is "unnecessary," and it would result from "folly." It is "unnecessary" because, as Smith claims in his Economizer Argument, people do it already: we are naturally inclined to seek out the best return we can on our scarce resources, so the statesman does not need to attend to it. It is, moreover, "folly" because, as Smith claims in his Local Knowledge Argument, the statesman does not possess the local knowledge of individual people's circumstances, values, goals, and resources that he would need in order to make good decisions for them. His presumption that he can "direct private people" well or effectively is, therefore, "folly."

6.2.3 The Invisible Hand Argument

Smith writes: "It is his own advantage, indeed, and not that of the society, which [each person] has in view. But the study of his own advantage naturally, or rather necessarily, leads him to prefer that employment which is most advantageous to the society" (WN IV.ii.4). Smith continues that each individual "generally, indeed, neither intends to promote the publick interest, nor knows how much he is promoting it"; "by directing that industry in such a manner as its produce may be of the greatest value, he intends only his own gain, and he is in this, as in many other cases, led by an invisible hand to promote an end which was no part of his intention" (WN IV.ii.9). The "end" the individual promotes that "was no part of his intention" is the "publick interest" (WN IV.ii.9). Thus, individuals have ends, but they tend to be personal and local. Smith's claim in this famous passage is that in seeking to accomplish their personal and local ends, they are led to discover ways to serve *others'* ends as well – whether they care about, or even know, those others. The Invisible Hand Argument hence purports to find a way to achieve the lofty goal of benefiting others from the humble motivation of self-interest.

How is this feat accomplished? Recall Smith's claim that increasing standards of living result from division of labor – but only within a "well-governed society." If your person, property, and promise are protected, I cannot enslave you, steal from you, or defraud you. The only recourse I have, then, to get whatever goods or services you might be able to provide is by making you an offer. And because your 3 Ps are protected, you enjoy what we might call an "opt-out option," or the right to say "no, thank you" to any offer I might make and walk away. This requires me to consider what I can offer you that *you* would think is valuable enough to cooperate with me. Given that each of us "stands at all times in need of the cooperation and assistance of great multitudes" (WN I.ii.2), that means that each of us must, in a well-governed society, consider the value we can provide to others – which we can discover only if we are thinking about those others and not thinking only about ourselves. In such a society, Smith says, we therefore become "mutually the servants of one another" (*WN* III.i.4). The Smithian market mechanism thus purports to coordinate the disparate individual efforts of indefinitely many persons and to derive an overall benefit for society from them.

To summarize Smith's argument: because we seek to achieve our goals in the most efficient manner possible (as the Economizer Argument holds), we are incentivized to make good decisions about how to achieve our goals using the resources available to us (as the Local Knowledge Argument holds); if we are living in a well-governed society that debars us from or punishes us for acting with injustice, we are incentivized to find ways to cooperate with others in ways that will be beneficial to them as well (as the Invisible Hand Argument holds).

As noted, however, Smith is no utopian. Accordingly, Smith's argument does not guarantee that only cooperative, mutually beneficial transactions will occur in a "well-governed society" – as his worries about businesspeople's conspiratorial motivations attest. But he does seem to believe that to whatever extent justice is protected in society, to that same extent is extraction disincentivized and cooperation incentivized. If it is sufficiently costly to benefit ourselves at others' expense, then the remaining option is to seek to benefit ourselves by benefitting others. The more people whose 3 Ps are protected will thus mean the more people entering into mutually beneficial, or positive-sum, transactions, leading to more wealth that can enable even more such transactions, and so on – creating a virtuous cycle of increasing overall prosperity, Smith's "universal opulence" and "general plenty" (*WN* I.i.10).

Even if we were to grant that the institutions Smith recommended could lead to increasing overall prosperity, however, that by itself would not give a contemporary businessperson concrete guidance about how to engage in business virtuously. And Smith's own worries about the motivations and potential corruption of businesspeople, not to mention his concerns about other potentially deleterious consequences of commercial society,[2] would suggest caution in developing a conception of virtuous business. Yet perhaps we can construct a "Smithian" conception of business ethics based on his political economy.

6.3 Virtuous Business

There is no generally accepted code of ethics for business.[3] Medicine has its Hippocratic Oath, and law has a code of professional ethics as well. Some specific areas of business, like accounting, have codes, but not business in

---

[2] Including its potentially mind-numbing effects on workers' judgment and character: *WN* VI.f.51-61.

[3] Though see Stark and Davis (2001); DeMartino (2011); McCloskey and DeMartino (2016, chap. 37).

general or overall. Perhaps one reason is that there is little consensus regarding the overall *purpose* of business. One cannot know how one should behave within an organization, or hence what constitutes acceptable or unacceptable behavior for or within the organization, without knowing what the purpose of the organization is. If we say that we engage in production, exchange, and so on because we want to improve our lives by getting more of the things we want, that might be true, but it does not get us far. Because our wants vary, because our ends and values vary, and because our preferences and experiences vary, referring to "what we want" is too large a category to give any concrete guidance – and by itself would allow too great a range of potential behavior. Unjust extraction and exploitation, after all, might enable us to get "what we want" too. This wide range of differing and sometimes conflicting goals might stymie efforts to develop a general code of business ethics.

Let us draw on Smith's political economy to narrow the discussion. By identifying the connection between the kind of society we wish to have – a just and humane society – and the kind of business behavior this entails – positive-sum exchange within the constraints of justice – perhaps we can begin to construct a code of business ethics. There are three main parts of such a code: (1) the role it plays, or should play, in the mission of a firm; (2) the role it plays, or should play, in guiding the actions of the individual businessperson; and (3) the role it plays, or should play, in informing the public institutions of the society in which it operates.

6.3.1 A Firm's Mission

Smith locates the beginning of economics in cooperative association and trade for mutual benefit, and his example of pin-making (*WN* I.i.3) indicates the gains from specialization that can happen when division of labor is deployed within even small firms. What, then, might be the purpose of a firm, on a Smithian account? Perhaps to enable more cooperation, on the argument that the more people who can cooperate with one another, the more prosperity we can generate. This is reflected in Smith's claim that the division of labor is limited by the extent of the market (*WN* I.iii.1–8): the larger the market, the more division of labor that is enabled; the more division of labor, the more prosperity. Similarly, the more people who can cooperate, the more prosperity. One of the barriers to cooperation, however, is transaction costs (North, 1992). If you and I are far away from one another, cannot communicate easily, do not know or trust one another, or do not have clear property rights, it is difficult for us to cooperate. If, on the other hand, we have clear property rights and are close to one another and can communicate easily, the costs of transacting are reduced, which means the gains from cooperating can be larger. That is what a firm can do. It brings people into close proximity with one another so that they can cooperate much more effectively. It also enables people to develop and capitalize on new ideas: we discover new ways of doing things, and even new things to do, and we can both benefit.[4] The firm, then, can act as a node of cooperation, enabling and amplifying it.[5]

Thus firms can play an important role in generating prosperity. This gives us a start in understanding the purpose of a firm, but there must be more to the story. One can, for example, imagine a firm dedicated not to cooperation but to predation and extraction. Consider a criminal enterprise – a mafia or crime syndicate. There might be cooperation among the members of the syndicate, but its larger purpose is to engage in extraction from others. Its goal is to prosper not by benefitting others but at the expense of others. This kind of activity, however, is zero-sum (or even negative-sum) and thus does not lead to net increases in prosperity. It can enrich the members of the syndicate, but that is wealth reallocation, not wealth generation.

The example of a syndicate may recall Smith's worries about "conspiracies of merchants," but Smith believes such conspiracies are far more difficult to act on in market economies. Smith believes that monopolies, for example, arise primarily from governmentally bestowed privileges, and their legal protection enables them to extract higher prices than what would be possible under "free competition" (*WN* I.vii.27; see also I.vii.27–31; IV.viii.15–17). In the absence of special legal subsidies or legal protections from competition – that is, under the "obvious and simple system of natural liberty" (*WN* IV.ix.51) – the remaining way to profit is through mutually voluntary and mutually beneficial transactions.

This conception of the origin and purpose of firms can give us guidance yet today. If their purpose is to enable cooperation with the aim of mutual betterment – "Give me that which I want, and you shall have this which you want, is the meaning of every such offer" (*WN* I.ii.2) – then every firm's mission statement, regardless of the particular goods or services it aims to provide, should include the mandate to *create value that others find worthwhile*. Implied in "give me that which you want, and you shall have this which you want" is an "opt-out option" for each party to the transaction. Respecting that option disciplines firms and their members to pay attention to those they presume to benefit. This places a burden on firms, but it should. If we wish to use our resources as wisely as possible, we must continue to search for new and better ways to use whatever resources we have, and we should remain vigilant against wasteful or inefficient use of resources. One way to encourage that is to require that firms demonstrate to the rest of us the value they can contribute

---

[4] Smith claims that most innovations are "originally the inventions of common workmen," rather than their employers or the owners of firms (*WN* I.i.8).

[5] Smith claims that a ten-person pin-making factory that divides the labor could increase its production by some 23,900 percent compared to a factory in which each person individually makes pins from start to finish (see *WN* I.1.3).

with their efforts, with the implication that if they get things right, they succeed – and if they get things wrong, they fail. And a way to do that is by making sure that everyone has the right to say "no, thank you" and go elsewhere.

6.3.2 A Code of Ethics for the Businessperson

If a firm's highest-level purpose is to create value for everyone involved – owners, investors, employees, customers, clients, partners, suppliers, etc. – then what should the code of ethics for individual businesspeople be? Building on Smith's argument, I suggest two principles forming its core:

1. You should refrain from using coercion and the threat of injury. Also, as a corollary: you should refrain from fraud, deception, and unjust exploitation.
2. You should honor the terms of your promises and contracts, including your fiduciary responsibilities.

6.3.2.1 Principle One: Refraining from Coercion, Threats, and Unjust Exploitation

According to Smith, the prosperity that can ensue from mutually voluntary and mutually beneficial transactions obtains only in a "well-governed society," which requires protection of the 3 Ps of justice. The prosperity he envisions "at least would be the case in a society where things were left to follow their natural course, where there was perfect liberty, and where every man was perfectly free both to chuse what occupation he thought proper, and to change it as often as he thought proper" (*WN* I.x.a.1).

We do not want people to coerce or threaten us. By demanding the liberty to make decisions for ourselves, we declare ourselves as full and free moral agents. Smith's first principle requires us to extend the same respect that we expect for ourselves to everyone else. We may explain our positions or preferences, and we may try to convince others we are right. We are even welcome to try to talk another into exchanging or partnering with us. But this is subject to two important qualifications. First, we may not bully or intimidate others, and we may certainly not threaten or coerce others. Doing so would compromise their moral agency and result in a zero-sum rather than a positive-sum exchange. According to the "obvious and simple system of natural liberty," Smith writes, "[e]very man, as long as he does not violate the laws of justice, is left perfectly free to pursue his own interest his own way" (*WN* IV.ix.51). Second, if we are trying to convince another to exchange or partner with us, it must be for something we believe will be *mutually* beneficial – something we believe will truly create value not only for us but for others as well. As Smith writes, it must be something "that is for their own advantage," not only ours (*WN* I.ii.2).

This first principle also addresses what we might call "opportunism" (Frank, 1988). Reneging on promises, agreements, commitments, or contracts is an obvious violation of this principle, but so is looking for ways to keep to the letter of an agreement while violating its spirit. This principle calls on us to enter into agreements in good faith, and to interpret the elements of the agreement in light of what the *other* parties to it are likely to have expected or understood it to hold. Trying to "game" an agreement or look for loopholes that enable us to benefit ourselves at the other parties' expense may not be forbidden by the letter of an insufficiently exhaustive agreement, but no agreement can address all possible interpretations and contingencies. Although we cannot take full responsibility for other parties' interests – the principle of *caveat emptor* is legitimate within reason – a problem arises when we pass from "it is your responsibility to know what your interests are and how to protect and serve them" to "you cannot reasonably be assumed to have thought of or known this." Such cases are sometimes difficult to adjudicate, even in good faith. But a heuristic for determining when this important line has been crossed is to ask oneself: *Knowing what I know, would I be willing to engage in this exchange (partnership, etc.) if I were on the other side?* If the answer is "yes," then what one is proposing is likely mutually beneficial; if the answer is "no," then what one is proposing may be beneficial only to oneself and at the other's expense.

A subtler form of opportunism is when you meet both the letter and the spirit of the agreement but nevertheless do not benefit the other party as much as you discover you might be able to (Rose, 2011). If the other party expects you to do your best, then you should do your best. But that expectation too must be subject to reasonable limits. A heuristic similar to that above would also help adjudicate cases like these: *Knowing what I know, if I were in the other party's shoes, would I be happy with my efforts?* If the answer is "yes," then you are likely doing everything one could reasonably expect of you; if the answer is "no," then perhaps you should reevaluate.

The last part of the first principle is to refrain from "unjust exploitation." The qualifier "unjust" is required because "exploitation" can sometimes be neutral or even benign (Powell and Zwolinski, 2012). We speak of "exploiting" opportunities – say, when we realize there is an unmet demand in the market and we start a business or venture to address it – but this is a benign, or at least neutral, sense of "exploitation." Morally unacceptable cases of exploitation, by contrast, are when one party knows material factors the other party does not and the former uses this asymmetry of knowledge to its own advantage at the other party's expense, or when one party has undue leverage over the other and uses it to gain a one-sided advantage.

Mere differences in knowledge – like differences in skills or abilities – are not necessarily problematic. They can, as Smith argues, enable "the most dissimilar geniuses [to be] of use to one another" (*WN* I.ii.5). But there are cases in which I know that if you knew what I know, you would not agree. If I nevertheless proceed under such circumstances, I am unjustly exploiting you. A heuristic can help here as well: *Knowing what I know, would I proceed with the agreement if I were in the other party's shoes?* There are, of course, limits to this: as Smith's Local Knowledge Argument shows, others have personal, localized knowledge about their situations that I do not have, and others might also have interests, preferences, and values that differ from mine. Hence, others might be willing to do things or accept agreements that I would not. If I think there is a good chance others would not agree with what I am proposing if they knew what I know, however, then that is a red flag that should cause me to reconsider. One effective way to know is simply to inform the other prospective party of what one knows.

Exploitation of asymmetrical leverage is minimized, if not eliminated, by the "opt-out option" each person has under Smith's principles of justice. If each of us can say "no, thank you" to any offer or proposal, then our moral agencies are more nearly leveled, reducing the ability of one party to exploit the other.

6.3.2.2 Principle Two: Promises and Responsibilities

The third "P" of justice for Smith is "promises": justice must "guard what are called his personal rights, or what is due to him from the promises of others" (*TMS* II.ii.2.2). In *LJ*, Smith elaborates that justice is violated "whenever one is deprived of what he had a right to and could justly demand from others, or rather, when we do him any injury or hurt without a cause" (*LJ*(A) i.9); one aspect of such unwarranted injury, Smith claims, is when we injure another in his "estate," including "what is due to him either by loan or by contract of whatever sort, as sales, etc." (*LJ*(A), i.16; cf. *LJ*(A) i.16–23). As Smith explains, the obligation of a promise arises from the reasonable dependence it generates in the "promittee" based on what was promised. If a promiser makes "an open and plain declaration," then the "promittee" comes to depend on that promise and alters other aspects of his or her life in light of it. "The expectation and dependance of the promittee that he shall obtain what was promised is hear altogether reasonable, and such as an impartial spectator would readily go along with" (*LJ*(A), ii.43). Smith argues that such promises generate a "reasonable expectation" on the part of the person who made the promise, "reasonable" because "an impartial spectator" would approve (*LJ*(A), ii.43–44).

In Smith's view, then, when one makes a commitment to others, they then make other decisions about their lives based on that commitment. They begin to reallocate their resources – including their time, talent, and treasure – based on the commitment. If one then reneges, one will thus have imposed a cost on them, a cost for which one is now responsible. Even if one compensates them for that cost, this will typically have resulted in a net loss of resources: one is moving resources around to bring them back to where they were before, not to improve their (or one's own) situation. If one makes a habit of breaking commitments, the losses compound.

We might regard that as an economic argument: breaking promises and failing to fulfill commitments are costly. In the best case, they constitute merely forgone prosperity; in the worst case, they lead to real loss. But breaking one's commitments is also a violation of a moral mandate to treat others with respect. They trusted you and agreed to a commitment based on their trust that you would fulfill your obligation. By failing to do so, you violated their trust. Sometimes we cannot help breaking a commitment, as when unexpected or unpredictable exigencies arise. In such cases, we should do our best to indemnify the other party and to learn from the experience to minimize the chances that it could happen again in the future. But the loss is still costly and thus regrettable.

6.3.3 The Institutions Protecting Virtuous Business

The public institutions that would protect such a purpose of business and such a conception of virtuous behavior of businesspeople would be those that would disincentivize extraction, incentivize cooperation, and would protect, as a matter of justice, the bodily persons, the property and possessions, and the voluntary contracts and promises made by the members of its society. In other words, it would be the "well-governed society" Smith describes, in which the government's main duties would be: first, to protect justice against both foreign and domestic aggression; and second, to provide those "publick works" and "publick institutions" that (a) cannot be provided by private enterprise but that (b) nevertheless benefit substantially all members of society, not merely one person or group at the expense of another (*WN* IV.ix.51; Book V *passim*). This latter duty of government – providing the public works that meet both criteria (a) and (b) – allows some indeterminacy, and might vary depending on the particular circumstances of a given society. Yet the Smithian argument would hold that they would arise only once justice has been secured, that they would nevertheless be constrained by the principles of justice, and that the burden of proof would shift to the proposer to demonstrate why a particular proposal would satisfy those criteria.

6.4 Conclusion: Adam Smith and Virtuous Business

The core of a Smithian vision of virtuous business is people enjoying the security to engage in cooperative trade, exchange, and partnership to the betterment not only of themselves but of others. It involves taking positive action to use one's scarce resources in the production of prosperity, and systematically refraining from extractively benefiting oneself at others' expense. The primary institutional structures required to encourage cooperation and discourage extraction are laws and agencies designed to protect the "3 Ps" of justice. Smith's claim was that a society whose government protected the 3 Ps but did little else would see its citizens discover novel ways to create and innovate, and to partner and transact, that would lead to mutual betterment and a growing and prospering society.

Smith's argument can give today's businesspeople two-part moral guidance. First, businesspeople should commit to engaging only in cooperative and never extractive exchange. Cooperative exchange is positive-sum and leads to increasing overall prosperity, while extractive exchange is zero-sum (or even negative-sum) and generates no new prosperity. Moreover, extractive exchange involves disregarding others' "opt-out option" and overriding their moral agency, while cooperative exchange respects others' agency and thus their human dignity.

Second, they should make personal, positive commitments to use their limited time, talent, and treasure to actively seek ways to benefit themselves by simultaneously benefiting others. The first duty might be the minimum that society may demand from all its citizens. But the second duty, to engage in positive production of prosperity, is what we may hope for and even expect from each of us – what Smith calls "the becoming use of what is our own" (TMS VII.ii.1.10). We have not only the ability to refrain from injuring others in their persons, property, and promises, but we also have the ability to proactively engage in mutually voluntary and mutually beneficial activity. If we fulfill the former but fail in the latter, society might not be justified in jailing or punishing us, but we will not have contributed all we could to the improvement of our own and others' lives. Thus, the virtuous businessperson does both.

Now, even if one has been broadly persuaded by Smith's argument, one might still ask what it can concretely tell us about the particular issues the businessperson or firm faces on a day-to-day basis. An abiding concern of business ethics literature over the last few decades has been "corporate social responsibility," which argues that business should concern itself not only with increasing returns to shareholders but with the well-being of a larger scope of stakeholders, including employees, customers, clients, the community, and even the climate.[6] More recently, business ethics literature has also explored "ESG," or environment, social, and governance issues, arguing that businesses should be scored on these criteria as well, in addition to simply returns to shareholders.[7] Although Smith discusses resources and capital, he does not discuss sustainable use of resources; hence, attempting to infer a position on climate or environmental issues from Smith would be largely speculative and

---

[6] See, e.g., Williams (2014).
[7] See, e.g., Business Roundtable (2019); Schwab (2021).

perhaps fanciful. What help can Smith's argument offer us, then, regarding such questions firms and businesspeople face today?

Perhaps we can build on a claim from section 2, that every organization must begin with a conception of its purpose and that this purpose should inform all its parts and provide proper motivation to all its members. If we want a just and humane society – a society, that is, that recognizes and protects each person's dignity and equal moral agency and in which increasing proportions of people enjoy ever more opportunity to flourish – then we should also endorse the public social institutions that are required to uphold it, including Smithian institutions that protect everyone's 3 Ps of justice. Those institutions, in turn, require people to engage in business that is cooperative and never extractive, and for individuals and firms to commit to using the resources available to them to benefit not only themselves but others as well. This conception of virtuous business entails a proper professional purpose: we should actively seek out ways to provide genuine value to others and ourselves, consistent with and constitutive of the institutions supporting the just and humane society we all want to live in.

Understanding our business activity in this way will not automatically or mechanically determine what we should do in every case or how we should decide each choice we face, but it can give us parameters within which to understand our professional purpose. And it may be sufficiently flexible to allow concerns beyond merely profit, including environmental sustainability, which would respond to people's changing values. If we, as we make our daily business decisions, regularly advert to a principle of cooperative virtuous business that seeks to create genuine value both for others and ourselves, then perhaps this can orient our activities in directions that are both economically productive and morally praiseworthy. Perhaps that can constitute an attractive Smithian vision of the moral purpose of virtuous business.

7

Adam Smith and the Morality of Political Economy
A Public Choice Reading

MARIA PIA PAGANELLI

Adam Smith's *WN* has been read as a book about many things. The reading I would like to emphasize here is one that Smith himself used to describe it:

> [the account of Hume's death gave me] ten times more abuse than *the very violent attack I had made upon the whole commercial system of Great Britain*.
>
> (*CAS*, I, 251, emphasis added)

Reading *WN* as an attack against lobbying from special interest groups and cronyism, as I interpret it here, shows that Smith links arguments about justice and efficiency. In this reading, I follow in part George Stigler's interpretation of the *WN* as a book based on the granite of self-interest (Stigler, 1975). But I develop further my (2008) argument that the account of self-interest in the *WN*, when left unbridled and able to capture state power, is more of a condemnation than an ode in its favor. I also agree with Chandra (2021) and the interpretation he offers of Allyn Young (1999) that the main concern for Smith was not laissez-faire but competition, as the way to counteract special interest groups is not necessarily laissez-faire, but government-guaranteed competition.

I would also distance my reading of Smith from Stigler's as far as he accuses Smith of not seeing Public Choice problems because he fails to think of politicians as self-interested. Politicians in Smith's time were mainly wealthy landowners with relatively safe seats, thus under less electoral pressure than their democratic counterparts. That said, for Smith, they were easily fooled and captured by lobbyists and rent seekers because they had little incentive to learn about trade, but wanted to look good in the eyes of others by pretending they knew something about it. Furthermore, I believe Smith saw and used of an analysis similar to Public Choice in his descriptions of lobbying and rent

---

With thanks to Jorge Fabrega, his students, the Universidad del Desarrollo, and Fulbright Chile. Thanks also to Maria Alejandra Carrasco, Paul Sagar, Craig Smith, the participants of the Smith workshop organized by Paul Sagar, and the participants of the University of Tokyo Executive Management Program 2022 Lecture. For research assistance, thanks to Samuel Pappas.

seeking (Farrant and Paganelli, 2016; Paganelli, 2020). In this I also differ from Paul Sagar (2021a) who also sees the *WN* as an attack against mercantilism but does not highlight the Public Choice aspects of it.

Furthermore, rather than claiming that "the high priest of self-interest, like all other high priests, had a strong demand for sinners" (Stigler, 1975, p. 277), I would suggest that Smith's "strong demand" was for justice. With Deirdre McCloskey (1998), Jerry Evensky (2005b), and Steven Medema (2010), I see that with the interpretation of Stigler and of the Chicago School, there is also a parallel "good old Chicago School" Smith or a "Kirkaldy Smith," which may present a more complex Smith than a simple "high priest of self-interest." I thus concur with Henry Bitterman (1940) and James Buchanan (1978) in reading *WN* as a prescriptive book – a book that uses descriptive analysis to make prescriptive claims.

My emphasis on the moral condemnation of rent seeking and state capture of mercantilism also does not necessarily imply that for Smith justice is distributive (cf. Fleischacker, 2004b), but, like István Hont and Michael Ignatieff (1983a), that the solutions to the injustices that poverty may cause may more likely come from economic growth.

My reading of *WN* would thus suggest that for Smith there is no trade-off between efficiency and justice. The two go hand in hand. The violence and inefficiencies of the rent-seeking mercantilist policies cause harm and are thus unjust. Just policies, policies that do not privilege some at the expense of others, happen, for Smith, to be efficient.

I thus show the clarity with which Smith identifies the problem of concentrated benefits and diffused costs in the determination of public policies, in a Public Choice fashion. But I also suggest that Smith's condemnation of mercantilist policies is based on moral grounds. Rent seeking and state capture by special interest groups is not only inefficient, but it uses the (actual) "blood and treasure" of fellow citizens to enrich a few merchants and manufacturers under the false pretense of enriching the country. In my reading, the *Wealth of Nations* is therefore a moral condemnation of mercantilist policies implying that Smith sees that "justice could also be efficient" (Buchanan, 1978, pp. 70–77).

7.1 Whose Interest?

Asserting that the *Wealth of Nations* is a moral denunciation of lobbying and cronyism requires us to understand, first, the dynamics of special interest groups in Smith's analysis, and then their moral condemnation. So, the first thing to investigate when analyzing lobbying is to look for concentrated benefits and dispersed costs – the sign of special interest groups seeking rents (Tullock, 1967; Olson, 1971; Krueger, 1974). Smith is explicit about concentrated benefits and dispersed costs when he analyzes policies that benefit few at the expense of many.

From the origins of commercial societies to the most developed ones, merchants and manufacturers are identified as rent-seeking concentrated interests: they are relatively few and they are clustered in cities. In fact, Smith tells us that "The inhabitants of a town, being collected into one place, can easily combine together" (WN I.x.c.22). This proximity allows them to form corporations (guilds), or even just voluntary associations, implicitly meant to decrease competition.

On the other hand, "The inhabitants of the country, dispersed in distant places, cannot easily combine together. They have not only never been incorporated, but the corporation spirit never has prevailed among them" (WN I.x.c.23). The inhabitants of the country, as Smith repeats later when he reiterates the point, are country gentlemen and farmers, at his time, the majority of the population (WN IV.ii.21).

That merchants and manufacturers can be easily cartelized, given their concentration, is problematic for at least three additional reasons, according to Smith. First, because their interest goes in the opposite direction than the interest of society. Second, because they are willing and able to disguise their interest for the interest of society. Third, because they are willing and able to affect legislation to benefit themselves at the expense of society.

Smith indeed claims that *"The interest of the dealers, however, in any particular branch of trade or manufacturers, is always in some respect different from, and even opposite to, that of the publick"* (WN I.xi.p.10, emphasis added). Merchants and manufacturers want to expand their markets, which is not in contradiction with the interest of society, but they want to do it while also limiting competition in them. Limiting competition implies monopoly power and thus higher profits for them at the cost of higher prices and lower quantity supplied for the consumers. This desire for higher prices is the reason why, for Smith, the interest of merchants and manufacturers is always opposite to the interest of society. And the reason why it is always covered with hypocrisy. Merchants and manufacturers themselves do their business by buying where it is cheap, independently of who produces the merchandise. But they want all other people not to be allowed to do the same. People, like merchants, also want to buy from the cheapest seller. But the merchants want them to buy from them at the highest price possible. They want monopoly pricing. This is why the spirit of monopoly is always directly opposite to the interest of the great body of the people (WN IV.iii.c.10).

If the problem was limited to the interest of a group going against the interest of society, the problem would not necessarily be as serious as Smith sees it. But for Smith the problem is in fact serious because merchants and manufacturers are able to convince most people, and the statesmen, that their interest is the same as society's, and as a consequence they are able to affect legislation in their favor. Smith indeed claims that: "The clamour and sophistry of merchants and manufacturers easily persuade them that the private interest of a part, and of a subordinate part of the society, is the general interest of the whole" (*WN* I.x.c.25).

So, for Smith, believing the false claim that merchants want protections to trade for the public good is dangerous, if not actually a folly: "I have never known much good done by those who affected to trade for the publick good. ... The stateman, who should attempt to direct private people in what manner they ought to employ their capitals, would ... assume an authority which could safely be trusted, not only to no single person, but to no council or senate whatever, and which would nowhere be so *dangerous as in the hands of a man who had folly and presumption enough to fancy himself fit to exercise it*" (*WN* IV.ii.9–10, emphasis added).

But then, how is it possible to convince the people and the statesmen that the interest of a small group is the interest of society, while in reality it is not? Smith believes that the majority of the people has an intuitive sense that trade makes a country better off, but they do not understand the actual process through which this improvement takes place. Merchants play on this ignorance. "[M]erchants [address] parliaments, and ... the councils of princes, ... nobles and country gentlemen, [as] those who were supposed to understand trade, to those who were conscious to themselves that they knew nothing about the matter. That foreign trade enriches the country, experience demonstrated to the nobles and country gentlemen, as well as to the merchants, but how, or in what manner, none of them well knew. The merchants knew perfectly in what manner it enriched themselves. It was their business to know it. But to know in what manner it enriched the country, was no part of their business" (*WN* IV.i.10). And yet, they claim they do.

So we see that the merchants know how to enrich themselves and we believe their false claim that they also know how to enrich the nation. We may trust their words even because, if we take an argument that Smith makes in *TMS* seriously, we tend to believe the rich and powerful, just because they are rich and powerful (Tegos, 2014; Sagar, 2018b, chap. 5). We look up at the wealthy, we admire them, we want to be in their presence, we suffer with them, we rejoice at their good fortune, we want them to like us, we want them to look at us, so we follow their authority (*TMS* I.iii.2).

The seriousness of the problem emerges in its full power for Smith because by conflating their interest with the interest of society, while in reality they are opposite, merchants and manufacturers "*conspire against the public*" (*WN* I.x. c.27, see also *WN* IV.iii.c.10, emphasis added) to limit competition, by asking and obtaining monopolies. And while Smith's condemnation of the statesmen who fall for the clamor of the merchants is limited to ignorance and folly, the condemnation that Smith makes of the merchants and manufacturers seeking and obtaining monopoly powers is much more severe because there is a consciousness of the damage the merchants and manufacturers may impose on society to benefit themselves. The merchants and manufacturers know what they are doing, they know their own interests, and they consciously collude to achieve it.

Another way of seeing this point is that in *TMS* Smith describes a man of system who is enamored of his system and tries to implement it, forgetting that he is dealing with real people and not with inanimate pieces on a chessboard (*TMS* IV.ii.2.17). It can therefore be dangerous if he tries to move the "pieces" against their will. Here the problem is not simply that the love of system blinds the legislators. The problem is that a group sees extremely well what its interest is and uses the power of the state to get it, at the expense of society. When a special interest is able to capture the legislature, it will hurt the interest of society, even if unintentionally, and it will consciously disregard it. Unfortunately, merchants and manufacturers know their interests well, and are willing and able to get political power to implement the policies that favor them. The damage to society is not their aim, but it is a cost they are willing to ignore to enrich themselves.

Monopolies are thus even more absurd if we think that "Consumption is the sole end and purpose of all production; and the interest of the producer ought to be attended to, only so far as it may be necessary for promoting that of the consumer [...] But in the mercantile system, the interest of the consumer is almost constantly sacrificed to that of the producer; and it seems to consider production, and not consumption, as the ultimate end and object of all industry and commerce" (*WN* IV.viii.49) while the opposite is true.

If in medieval times the monopolies of merchants and manufacturers were limited to guilds and forced apprentices, with the discovery of the new world these monopolies become the base of the construction, first, and the defense later, of the entire British Empire.

In medieval times, it was relatively easy to obtain these monopolies because the merchants and manufacturers directly controlled the government of the towns (*WN* I.x.c.18). As the economy grew, especially through colonial trade, so grew the interest groups pressuring the legislation to achieve monopoly powers. The amount of wealth up for grabs thanks to monopolies, and the size of the losses should competition be reestablished, was colossal. And so the means of persuasion also escalated. They now include also force, offenses, and intimidation:

> This monopoly [of colonial trade] has so much increased the number of some particular tribes of them, that, like an overgrown standing army, they have become formidable to the government, and upon many occasions *intimidate the legislature*. The member of parliament who supports every proposal for strengthening this monopoly, is sure to acquire not only the reputation of understanding trade, but great popularity and influence with an order of men whose numbers and wealth render them of great importance. If he opposes them, on the contrary, as still more if he has authority enough to be able to thwart them, neither the most

> acknowledged probity, not the highest rank, nor the greatest publick services can protect him from *the most infamous abuse and detraction, from personal insults, not sometimes from real danger, arising from the insolent outrage of furious and disappointed monopolists.*
>
> (WN IV.ii.43, emphasis added)

The lobbying power of merchants and manufacturers is so strong, according to Smith, that they are able to create an entire economic system to promote their own interests.

> It cannot be very difficult to determine who have been the contrivers of this whole mercantile system: not the consumers, we may believe, whose interest has been entirely neglected; but the producers whose interest has been so carefully attended to; and among this latter class *our merchants and manufacturers have been by far the principal architects.*
>
> (WN IV.viii.54, emphasis added)

And that mercantile system that merchants and manufacturers have put in place is the actual colonial Empire.

> *The maintenance of this monopoly has hitherto been the principal, or more properly perhaps the sole end and purpose of the dominion which Great Britain assumes over her colonies.*
>
> (WN IV.vii.c.64, emphasis added)

And again,

> *A great empire has been established for the sole purpose of raising up a nation of consumers* who should be obliged to buy from the shops of our different producers all the goods with which these could supply them. For the sake of that little enhancement of price which this monopoly might afford our producers, the home-consumers have been burdened with the whole expense of maintaining and defending that empire.
>
> (WN IV.viii.53, emphasis added)

For Smith, this mercantile empire is different from ancient empires. Empires in antiquities were created out of the necessities to accommodate an increasing population (WN IV.vii.1–4). The mercantile empires are created by the greed of monopolists instead. In this sense, Smith expands the "mercantilist as a rent seeking society" as later described by Baysinger, Ekelund, and Tollison (2008), to include also the age of empires. And as Baysinger, Ekelund, and Tollison suggest, also for Smith, the intellectual justification of mercantilist policies is a consequence, and not a cause, of these infamous policies (cf. Magnusson 1994; Heckscher 1994).

If we stopped here, Smith's condemnation of the mercantile system, based on the convincing lobbying powers of merchants and manufacturers, could be read as a standard efficiency argument in two ways. First, one could read Smith as claiming that despite the higher costs imposed to the consumers, the benefits of the expanded markets that the monopolists achieved are overall enough to compensate them. So that Britain experiences a high growth rate, *despite* the inefficiencies of the monopolies (*WN* IV.vii.c.50). Given the status quo ante, a cost benefit analysis would justify the cronyism that Britain exhibits. Second, one could read Smith as claiming that these monopolies are inefficient, and thus, Britain would be better off without them. So, given the current status quo, less (or no) monopolies are preferred. These are the common readings of Smith and his condemnations of mercantilism.

7.2 Unjust Interest

But Smith may have looked at the situation also from a different perspective. If we take James Buchanan's interpretation of Smith seriously, without denying Smith's concerns about efficiency, he may have seen inefficiency as a side effect of injustice. Smith's primary concern may have been justice, rather than efficiency, with efficiency as a welcomed consequence of justice, but just as a consequence.

> Smith may well have conceived his masterpiece to be an argument to the effect that the system which was acknowledged to embody justice could also be efficient.
>
> (Buchanan, 1978, pp. 70–77).

The problem with special interest groups having so much political influence, as Smith claims they do, may thus be more than an inefficiency problem, but it may also be a moral problem. The mercantilist system is a system that creates injustices. Monopolists increase their wealth through the higher prices, causing harm to others. But in *TMS* Smith tells us that we should not approve the unjust behavior of those who, rather than fairly compete, harm their adversaries. In *TMS* Smith claims that in the race for wealth, if one elbows down a competitor or violates fair play, they would lose the approval of the impartial spectators and become instead the "object of their hatred and indignation" (*TMS* II.ii.2.1). What would the reaction of impartial spectators be, if they knew that merchants and manufacturers harm others to enrich themselves even by sacrificing not just the treasure but also the blood of their fellow citizens, and the life of innocent people?

In fact, for Smith, the harm that monopolists cause is not just higher prices for consumers; they also enrich themselves at the cost of the human lives that must be foregone for obtaining these higher prices. For Smith, the crony merchants and manufacturers enrich themselves with blood money.

Smith explains that merchants are perversely and dangerously clever in fooling those who believe in them. They pervert what commerce is and ought to be, according to Smith. Commerce is and ought to be "a bond of union and friendship" among nations. The wealth of one's neighbor is beneficial in trade. A rich man is a better customer than a poor one. Open ports enrich cities and towns, and do not ruin them. Amsterdam is a very good example of this. But the "passionate confidence of interested falsehood" of merchants and manufacturers is such that they make every nation look with envy at prosperity of other countries. Their faulty rhetoric transforms the merchants and manufacturers of rich nations into dangerous rivals, even if in reality their competition is beneficial to the majority of the people. Merchants and manufacturers convince people and governments that the neighbors are necessarily enemies, so that their wealth and power would inflame violence and "discord and animosity" (*WN* IV.iii.c.9).

Thus, merchants and manufacturers capture the government in such a way to lead it straight into wars (Paganelli and Schumacher, 2019). For Smith, all the recent wars have been fought to protect these monopolies. Even the very large naval force of Britain was built to guard against smuggling (*WN* IV.vii.c.64).

> To found a great empire for the sole purpose of raising up a people of customers, may at first sight appear a project fit only for a nation of shopkeepers. It is, however, a project altogether unfit for a nation of shopkeepers; but extremely fit for a nation whose government is influenced by shopkeepers. Such statesmen, and such statesmen only, are capable of fancying that they will find some advantage in *employing the blood and treasure of their fellow citizens*, to found and to maintain such empire.
>
> (*WN* IV.vii.c63, emphasis added)

This is not an accusation accidentally made. Smith repeats it. Monopolistic privileges given to the special interest groups of merchants and manufacturers are deadly:

> But the cruellest of our revenue laws, I will venture to affirm, are mild and gentle, in comparison of some of those which the clamour of our merchants and manufacturers has extorted from the legislature, for the support of their own absurd and oppressive monopolies. Like the laws of Draco, *these laws may be said to be all written in blood.*
>
> (*WN* IV.viii.17, emphasis added)

The deaths caused by mercantilist cronyism can actually be read in two ways: a direct one and an indirect one. Mercantilist privileges are written in blood, because those privileges have to be conquered and defended with wars. And for Smith the wars to build and defend the Empire are all wars wanted by merchants and manufacturers to establish and defend their privileges.

Furthermore, mercantilist privileges may cause death by increasing poverty, or retarding growth. For Smith, the exclusive companies are dreadful to both the home country and the colonies. Not only, for example, are the production of spices in the Dutch islands and of opium in Bengal kept artificially low by burning the excess that may cause a decrease in price in Europe, by destroying the extra, they make sure it will not be smuggled to Europe. But they do the same with population. Wages are kept so low as to maintain only the number of people needed to supply their garrisons (*WN* IV.iii.c.101). In a country as fertile as Bengal, hundreds of thousands of people die each year of starvation, according to Smith. The human devastation is directly attributable, for Smith, to the presence of the monopoly of the East India Company (*WN* I.viii.26).

For Smith, the monopolies of exclusive companies, the East India Company for example, create incentives to oppress people over which they preside with force. Think of the exclusive company as a government in which the members of the administration will leave, Smith says, and will leave carrying their fortune away with them. Therefore, when they leave, they are completely indifferent to the circumstance of the country, as if the whole country would be swallowed by an earthquake (*WN* IV.vii.c.105–106).

This image of the indifference of an exclusive company in front of the devastation it causes becomes even more damaging when compared to what Smith writes about the possibility of a country being completely swallowed by an earthquake in *TMS*. There, he tells us that we care more about our little finger than about the destruction of a faraway country like China. If we know that we are going to lose our little finger tomorrow, we would not be able to sleep tonight. But if we know that the entire population of China would be swallowed by an earthquake, we would snore placidly though the night. Yet, if asked to let the whole population of China die to save our little finger, we would not do it: "Human nature startles with horror at the thought, and the world, in its greatest depravity and corruption, never produced such a villain as could be capable of entertaining it" (*TMS* III.3.4). But in *WN*, Smith tells us that there are such villains: the monopolists. They impassibly let Bengal "be swallowed by an earthquake" (*WN* IV.vii.c.106) of their rapacious policies.

And so, for Smith, we need to be very careful about laws governing trade because despite their (false) claim to benefit society, they come "from an order of men, whose interest is never exactly the same with that of the publick, and who, accordingly have, upon many occasions, both deceived and oppressed it" (*WN* I.xi.p.10).

Even the entire British Empire with its colonies "was established for the sole purpose of raising up a nation of consumers" obliged to buy from the mother country's producers. "For the sake of that little enhancement of price which this monopoly might afford our producers, the home-consumers have been burdened with the whole expence of maintaining and defending the empire" (*WN* IV.viii.53). Import restrictions benefit producers at the expense of consumers who have to pay higher prices. Subsidies on exports benefit producers and hurt consumers who not only have to pay taxes for the subsidy, but also have to pay a higher price because of the decrease in domestic supply due to the increased export. Treaties of commerce benefit producers who can sell with better terms in distant places at the expense of consumers who are forced to buy more expensive and lower quality goods from those distant places rather than cheaper and better-quality ones from closer places.

Even laws such as the Corn Laws, claimed to promote the good of Britain, are laws generated by the greed of merchants to promote their own profits. By subsidizing the export of grains in good times, they increase the scarcity and the price of corn. Nobody benefits, with the exception of exporters and importers. The merchants export more in time of plenty and will import more in time of scarcity. They are the great winners of this bad policy and the greatest opponents of its abolition. Everybody else loses out, not only because they have to face a higher price of corn and a higher tax burden needed to subsidize the exports, but also because the risk of famine increases. Since the subsidized exports of corn will reduce its quantity available at home during good and bad times, in times of scarcity there will not be enough to feed everybody (*WN* IV.v.b).

Smith is concerned about an artificially high price of corn, because everybody uses corn, and corn is the most important component in the feeding of the poor. And the problem with the poor is that they are the most vulnerable people in society, especially in poor societies. Similarly, the problem of special interest groups' government capture is that their policies hinder economic growth and prolong poverty.

Poverty is a problem, for Smith, because in poor countries people unjustly die. In rich countries, on the other hand, people have more chances to live, to live longer, and to live better. In fact,

> Some countries are so miserably poor, that, from mere want, they are frequently reduced, or, at least, think themselves reduced, to the necessity sometimes of directly destroying, and sometimes of abandoning their infants, their old people, and those afflicted with lingering diseases, to perish with hunger, or to be devoured by wild beasts.
>
> (*WN* Intro, 4)

Some countries, Smith tells us, can be so poor that people "dispose of children in the streets at night," or have them "drowned like puppies" (*WN* I.viii.24). A woman in the poor parts of the Scottish Highlands usually bears twenty children, but she is lucky if only a couple survive (*WN* I.viii.23). Poverty is the unjust cause of suffering of the weakest of society; it is the weakest of society who suffer the most, it is the weakest of society who die. Poverty kills infants, the old, the sick. On the other hand, a poor worker in a wealthy nation could live better than "an African king, the absolute master of the lives and liberties of ten thousand naked savages" (*WN* I.i.11). We should understand the nature and causes of wealth, and thus understand what deters its growth, such as monopolies, because wealth is what gives us the means to live, and to live relatively longer, better, and freer lives (Paganelli, 2021).

The combination of our natural propensity to truck, barter, and exchange; our natural desire to better our condition; the division of labor; capital accumulation, and some luck allow for "the silent and insensible operations of foreign commerce" (*WN* III.iv.10) to break the chains of poverty and dependency. In Smith's view commerce brings wealth, liberty, and justice: "[Commerce brings about] order and good government, and with them, the liberty and security of individuals" (*WN* III.iv.4).

So for Smith, trade restrictions implemented by the "mean rapacity" of merchants and manufacturers are indeed inefficient, they deter growth, but they are also profoundly unjust, as they hurt many to benefit a few.

In this sense, for Smith, the North American colonies are lucky because their land is so cheap and their labor is so expensive that they can still be better off importing manufactures rather than trying to produce them themselves. But the advisors for regulations of the colony trade are the merchants themselves. British merchants and manufacturers convinced the legislature to impose high duties to prevent refined manufactures in the colonies, putting their interest above that of the colonists and of the mother country. But for Smith, "to prohibit a great people, however, from making all that they can of every part of their own produce, or from employing their stock and industry in the way that they judge most advantageous to themselves, is a *manifest violation of the most sacred rights of mankind*" (*WN* IV.vii.b.44, emphasis added). The interest of the colonies is sacrificed to the interest of the merchants. It is unjust, and it is inefficient.

Note that the prohibitions include also the one of movement of labor. Artificers are forbidden from leaving the country for fear that they would spread their knowledge. For Smith, also this is a direct violation of their liberty. Their liberty is sacrificed to the futile interests of the merchants and manufacturers (*WN* IV.viii.44–48).

Smith's normative condemnation extends to all regulations that attempt to monopolize the labor markets:

> The property which every man has in his own labour, as it is the original foundation of all other property, so it is the most sacred and inviolable. The patrimony of a poor man lies in the strength and dexterity of his hands; and to hinder him from employing this strength and dexterity in what manner he thinks proper without injury to his neighbour, is a *plain violation of this most sacred property. It is a manifest encroachment upon the just liberty* both of the workman, and of those who might be disposed to employ him. As it hinders the one from working at what he thinks proper, so it hinders the other from employing whom they think proper. To judge whether he is fit to be employed, may surely be trusted to the discretion of the employers whose interest it so much concerns.

The affected anxiety of the law-giver lest they should employ an improper person, is evidently as impertinent as it is oppressive.

(*WN* I.x.c.12, emphasis added)

And so we can see how it is possible to read Smith's condemnation of the state capture by special interest groups as grounded in justice, since Smith tells us that "To hurt in any degree the interest of any other order of citizens, for no other purpose but to promote that of some other, is evidently contrary to justice and equality of treatment which the sovereign owes to all his subjects" (*WN* IV.viii.30).

7.3 Hopeless Future?

Adam Smith's judgment of the policies in place in Britain at his time was based not only on efficiency. Smith was quite comfortable, and quite explicit too, in expressing moral judgments. His loud condemnations of the mercantile system are based on efficiency, yes, but also, on justice.

In a sense we can think of Adam Smith asking: what would a *just* system, one which also promotes the *well-being* of humankind look like, given the imperfect and *non-perfectible nature* of humankind? How do we get there? How can we preserve it (Paganelli, 2017)?

For Smith, wealth and justice are to grow hand in hand. A nation can grow wealthy only if its growth is accompanied by justice. This is why James Buchanan claimed that the *Wealth of Nations* can be read as a book about justice, about a just system that could also be an efficient system.

But Smith is well aware that the same propensity to truck, barter, and exchange, combined with the presence of government, can also create conflicts between different interest groups, and thus enrich a few at the expense of many. Smith "violent[ly] attacks" the commercial privileges bought for a few big merchants and manufacturers with the "blood and treasure" of a country's citizens. The *Wealth of Nations* can be read therefore as a great Public Choice anti-state capture, anti-cronyism, treaty. Smith seems to justify his "violent attack against the whole commercial system of Great Britain" on a moral ground, which happens to also be an appeal to efficiency.

Smith's "violent attacks" may also be grounded on the fact that once privileges are given, eliminating them is going to be extremely difficult (Tullock, 1975). For Smith, indeed, the monopoly of colonial trade broke the natural balance between all branches of industry. Now a big single channel replaces many smaller channels. This big channel decreases security. The economy looks like "a sick body with some overgrown vital parts" (*WN* IV.vii.c.43). A small blockage in a great vein that is artificially swollen is very dangerous. If a small vein busts, not much happens. But, Smith says, if a big vein breaks, we can have "convulsions, apoplexy, and even death"

(*WN* IV.vii.c.43). So people now look at a possible break of this great vein of colonial trade with more terror than they would look at the Spanish Armada. Indeed "to expect, indeed, that the freedom of trade should ever be entirely restored in Great Britain, is as absurd as to expect that an Oceana or Utopia should ever be established in it. Not only the prejudices of the publick, but what is much more unconquerable, the private interests of many individuals, irresistibly opposed it" (*WN* IV.ii.43).

Thus Adam Smith may have seen his "violent attacks against the mercantile system" in *WN* as that rope that tied Ulysses to the mast of his ship. As a rope that enabled Ulysses to survive as he sailed through the siren-infested seas (Buchanan, 1990). Smith believes there are things that have remedies and things that do not. The universal violence and injustice of rulers has no remedy. The "mean rapacity" and the monopolizing spirit of merchants also has no remedy. But it can be and it ought to be prevented from disturbing the tranquility of society because "merchants neither are, nor ought not to be the rulers of mankind" (*WN* IV.iii.c.9).

So his warning is sound and it sounds like Public Choice warning with a moral component: "The proposal of any new law or regulation of commerce which comes from this order (people who live by profits, i.e. merchants and manufacturers), ought always to be listened to with great precaution, and ought never to be adopted till after having been long and carefully examined, not only with the most scrupulous, but with the most suspicious attention. It comes from an order of men, whose interest is never exactly the same with that of the publick, who have generally an interest to deceive and even to oppress the publick, and who accordingly have, upon many occasions, both deceived and oppressed it" (*WN* I.ix.p.10). Rent seeking causes harm, it is unjust, and it happens also to be inefficient.

8

A Moral Philosophy for Commercial Society?

ROBIN DOUGLASS

A striking feature of much recent scholarship on Adam Smith is the tendency to see him as speaking to problems that liberal-capitalist societies encounter today. The idea that we can understand much about modern capitalism by turning to Smith is nothing new, of course, but where it was once Smith the economist from whom we should learn, now it is more often Smith the moral philosopher or, better still, Smith the holistic philosopher whose political economy was deeply informed by his moral philosophy.[1] One way this view plays out is in the argument that Smith was deeply alert to, and indeed sought to address, the *moral* deficiencies of modern market societies – or simply capitalism. On this line of interpretation, Smith was in fact concerned with many of the same issues that trouble us now, including the ways in which extreme economic inequality undermines morality and happiness (Rasmussen, 2016), or "the propensity of commercial society to induce and exacerbate such psychological ills as restlessness, anxiety, inauthenticity, duplicity, mediocrity, alienation, and indifference to others" (Hanley, 2009, p. 8).

Smith never refers to capitalism – a term that rose to prominence only in the nineteenth century – but he does use the phrase "commercial society," which is often regarded as a less anachronistic way of capturing how eighteenth-century thinkers classified the modern market-based societies that

---

This chapter is greatly indebted to conversations I have had with Paul Sagar over the past few years. Not only have my views on the topics addressed here been enriched by our discussions, several of the points that I develop (I am no longer sure exactly which) were originally Paul's ideas, and this chapter could profitably be read as a companion piece to the interpretation of Smith set forth in his recent book (Sagar, 2022). For helpful comments on an earlier draft of this chapter, I also thank Sam Fleischacker, Lauren Kopajtic, Glory M. Liu, John T. Scott, and Huahui Zhu.

[1] Amartya Sen (1987, pp. 22–28), for example, famously took Smith as one of his inspirations for bringing ethical considerations back to the forefront of economics. For a recent statement of the view I have in mind, see Honneth, 2021, p. 83. For a detailed survey of the developments in Smith scholarship, see Glory M. Liu's chapter in this volume, which highlights how recent scholarship has tried to avoid pigeonholing Smith around contemporary disciplinary boundaries.

we now call capitalist (Rasmussen, 2008, pp. 2–3).² If we live in commercial societies today, and if Smith was one of the earliest and greatest theorists of commercial society, then (so the argument goes) surely there is much we could learn by attending to what he had to say about the malaises of commercial society and their potential remedies.

The term commercial society is now widespread in much of the best research on eighteenth-century and especially Scottish Enlightenment thought (see especially Berry, 2013). We need look no further than the titles of many recent studies for evidence of its prevalence in Smith scholarship (e.g. Hill and McCarthy, 1999; Hanley, 2006, 2018; Rasmussen, 2008; Herzog, 2011; Hont, 2015; Tegos, 2014; Douglass, 2017, 2018; Pignol and Walraevens, 2017; Haeffele and Storr, 2019; Halikias, 2020). In this chapter, however, I suggest that we have reached a point where the term obscures more than it enlightens about Smith's thought (see also Sagar, 2022, pp. 49–51). More precisely, I contest the view that *TMS* is a book about commercial society. Nicholas Phillipson (1983, p. 182) offered one of the most striking articulations of this view forty years ago, going so far as to claim that Smith's theory of morals "is best seen, not as a general theory of morals, but as an account of the process by which men living in a commercial society acquire moral ideas and may be taught how to improve them." Smith's theory, according to Phillipson, "is redundant outside the context of a commercial society with a complex division of labour." Without necessarily endorsing this last claim, the idea that much of *TMS* analyzes commercial society remains common in recent scholarship. We see this, for example, in Ryan Patrick Hanley's argument that Part VI of *TMS* "was intended by Smith as a remedy for the challenges that he identified with the advent and progress of commercial society" (Hanley, 2009, p. 5), or Maria Pia Paganelli's claim that "TMS, like WN, can be seen as a defense or an endorsement of commercial societies" (Paganelli, 2010, p. 427). István Hont (2015, p. 35) maintains that *TMS* "was Smith's conjectural history of the origins of commercial society," while Elizabeth Anderson relies chiefly on *TMS* to outline "Smith's diagnosis of the ills of esteem inequality in commercial societies" (2016, pp. 164–66). Even when it is not the principal focus, scholars frequently turn to *TMS* when analyzing Smith's evaluation of commercial society, rarely pausing to ask whether the ideas under discussion are, in any respect, uniquely related to commercial society.³

---

² For a more critical assessment of what is at stake in choosing to use the term "commercial society" (rather than capitalism) to discuss eighteenth-century political economy, focusing especially on István Hont's work, see Cheney (2022).

³ There are too many examples to list presently, so it is perhaps best to note that I now regard some of my earlier work as having fallen short in precisely this respect (Douglass, 2017, pp. 611–617).

In this chapter, I argue that it is a mistake to read *TMS* as some sort of commentary on the morality of commercial modernity, and in so doing I seek to unsettle a certain picture of Smith's thought that holds sway over a prominent strand of scholarship. *Contra* Phillipson, *TMS* is best read as a treatise of moral philosophy, or a general theory of morals, and we risk misunderstanding Smith's arguments whenever we assume that they apply only under distinctively modern and/or commercial conditions.[4] The chapter proceeds by, first, examining what Smith and Smith scholars mean by commercial society, and whether this concept has any place in *TMS*; second, assessing whether *TMS* should be read as a response to other (supposed) theorists of modern commercial society (Mandeville and Rousseau); and, third, analyzing whether Smith's reflections on moral corruption, inequality, and prudence in *TMS* should be associated with commercial society. I conclude with some brief speculations as to why many Smith scholars superimpose the concept of commercial society onto *TMS*.

8.1 Commercial Society and *TMS*

To evaluate whether *TMS* is a book about commercial society, we first need to know what is meant by the term. This is where the difficulties begin. Smith's idea of commercial society is frequently viewed as a distinctively Western and modern phenomenon. Dennis Rasmussen (2008, p. 98), for instance, suggests that Smith regarded only certain parts of post-feudal western Europe and North America as "fully emerged" commercial societies. Hanley (2008, 2009, pp. 123–127) sometimes uses the terms "commercial society" and "commercial modernity" interchangeably, and commentators often implicitly – and occasionally explicitly (e.g. Fleischacker, 2004b, p. 55) – treat commercial society as synonymous with capitalism, with the key point being that Smith was theorizing the type of economic system under which many of us live today. When Smith scholars refer to commercial society, then, they typically have in mind the market-based societies that developed out of the feudal systems of western Europe, and which have subsequently spread throughout much of the world.

---

[4] In this chapter, I do not address the possibility that Smith unwittingly read back behavior that he observed in the commercial societies of his day onto his more general account of the moral sentiments, without realizing that such behavior was in fact unique to the particular form of society that he inhabited. The burden of proof, however, would clearly fall on showing that (e.g.) Smith was wrong to couch his analysis in terms of general principles of human nature when it really applied only to inhabitants of commercial society. Notice also that we can accept that Smith thought his analysis would be of use to people living in commercial society (his intended audience) without endorsing the further claim that his analysis applies *only* to such people (cf. Phillipson, 1983).

The term "commercial society" appears only twice across Smith's published works (*WN* I.iv.1, V.i.f.52; see also *ED* 11, 30). Once the division of labor is "thoroughly established," he writes in the most famous passage, we provide for ourselves by exchanging the surplus part of the produce of our own labor for that of other people's labor, rather than by producing everything we need for ourselves. "Every man thus lives by exchanging, or becomes in some measure a merchant, and the society itself grows to be what is properly a commercial society" (*WN* I.iv.1). This passage is often read alongside Smith's more frequent comments from *WN* on "commercial countries" and "commercial nations," many of which discuss foreign trade, together with his remarks in *LJ* on "the age of commerce," which is characterized by exchange "not only betwixt the individualls of the same society but betwixt those of different nations" (*LJ*(A) i.31–32). As Paul Sagar (2022, pp. 43–53) has recently stressed, however, Smith uses the precise phrase "commercial society" only when discussing the internal relations of a state, and there can be extensive commercial exchange within a state without any foreign trade. In this respect, for instance, Smith could have regarded China and ancient Egypt as commercial *societies*, as they acquired great wealth through their "own interior commerce," even though they "neglected foreign commerce" and should thus not be classified as commercial *nations* (*WN* IV.iii.c.11; see also I.iii.7).[5] There is nothing uniquely modern or Western about states becoming opulent through the division of labor, the development of markets in agricultural and manufacturing goods, and extensive trade.[6] Yet it remains the case that the only places Smith explicitly designates as "commercial" are parts of western Europe and the American colonies (Rasmussen 2008 p. 98, citing *WN* I.xi.e.38, I.xi.m.4, IV.i.5–6). It is thus easy to see why the term commercial society is regularly used in relation to *modern* commercial societies alone.

The phrase commercial society does not appear in *TMS*, although in one passage, added to the sixth edition of 1790, Smith contrasts the affections that people have for their remote ancestors in "pastoral countries" and "commercial countries." Where in pastoral countries, such as the Scottish Highlands at the beginning of the eighteenth century, all members of a tribe or clan regard one another as a "cousin and relation," in commercial countries, like England at the same time, the descendants of one family have no motive for staying

---

[5] For the purposes of this chapter, I largely set aside the differences between "society" and other social units (country, nation, people, city, etc.), focusing instead on how the classification "commercial" relates to other designations, such as "civilized." For a detailed analysis of the place of society in Smith's broader taxonomy, see Schliesser (2017, pp. 151–159).

[6] Drawing on Smith's reference to "an opulent and commercial society" in his early draft of *WN* (*ED* 10–11), Berry (2013, pp. 66–67) argues that the distinguishing feature of a commercial society is that opulence is spread to the lowest ranks of society. In *WN* itself, Smith makes this claim simply in relation to "a well-governed society" (*WN* I.i.10).

together and soon disperse. This is the only point in *TMS* where Smith describes a society, country, nation, or any other social unit as "commercial," and the contrast here is solely with "pastoral" countries (*TMS* VI.ii.1.12–13).[7] Two points bear emphasizing. First, Smith does not draw on the more complex four-stage model from *LJ* here, which differentiates between the ages of hunters, shepherds, agriculture, and commerce (*LJ*(A) i.27), or "hunting, pasturage, farming, and commerce" (*LJ*(B) 149). Second, while Smith uses the Scottish Highlands and England as examples, there is nothing in his description of commercial countries that should lead us to conclude that they are a uniquely modern or Western development.

When distinguishing between different stages of socioeconomic development in *TMS*, Smith more regularly contrasts "civilized" with "barbarous" nations (*TMS* II.iii.2.4, V.2.8–10, VII.iv.36), sometimes coupling "savages and barbarians" together (*TMS* V.2.9). Even though the term "savages" maps onto hunting societies and "barbarians" to pastoral ones, the differences between the two are of little consequence in *TMS*. The distinction that really matters, in the passages in question, is between civilized and uncivilized states.[8] We might think that there is a case for treating "commercial" and "civilized" as largely synonymous terms in Smith's lexicon, in which case this distinction would be equivalent to that between commercial and noncommercial states.[9] In the passage comparing pastoral and commercial countries, for example, Smith proceeds to claim that the affection people have for their remote ancestors "becomes, in every country, less and less, according as this state of civilization has been longer and more completely established," with the key determinant of civilization being whether the authority of law is sufficiently strong to ensure security for every member of the state (*TMS* VI.ii.1.13). In *WN*, Smith likewise refers to "the commercial and civilized part of the world" (*WN* I.xi.d.3) and to "a civilized and commercial society" (*WN* V.i.f.52). All commercial states should be classified as civilized, on Smith's terminology, although whether the converse is true is less clear-cut. Where debates remain about the scope of Smith's idea of commercial society, however, there

---

[7] Compare with Hanley (2009, p. 46), who takes this passage as evidence of Smith revealing "the way in which commerce promotes ethical atomism culminating in social fragmentation."

[8] Even in LJ, where Smith does articulate a four-stages theory, in many passages the relevant contrast is simply between "civilized" and either "savage" or "barbarian" states (e.g. *LJ*(A) ii.24–27, ii.95, ii.123; *LJ*(B), 22, 29–30, 137, 183, 309–310). The same is also true of many passages in *WN* (e.g. Intro.4, I.iii.5–8, I.xi.n.3, IV.i.33, V.i.a.39–44, V.i.b.5) and Smith's other works (e.g. *HA* III.1–5; *LRBL* ii.113–115; *OIA* II.1).

[9] For helpful discussion of the relation between the terms "commercial" and "civilized" in Smith and other Scottish Enlightenment thinkers, see Berry (2013, pp. 74–77). Berry notes that none of the Scots explicitly define what counts as civilization.

is no doubt that he regarded many ancient and non-Western states as civilized.[10]

Why do these distinctions matter? One reason is that the terms "commercial" and "civilized" are sometimes used interchangeably by commentators when discussing passages in *TMS* that refer only to the latter (e.g. Rasmussen, 2008, pp. 122–123). This distorts Smith's meaning insofar as it is assumed or implied that commercial society is a distinctively Western and modern phenomenon.[11] To the degree that we now use commercial society as broadly synonymous with capitalism, or as picking out a specifically modern phenomenon, then it is unhelpful to use this term in relation to *TMS*. To be sure, elsewhere Smith was concerned with understanding the transition in Europe from feudalism to the modern commercial states that would later be classified as capitalist. Smith addresses this concern at length in *WN*, yet it is irrelevant for his goals in *TMS*. In the passages from *TMS* comparing different stages of socioeconomic development, we would do better to retain Smith's generic distinction between "civilized" and "savage" or "barbarian" – or simply between civilized and uncivilized – states.[12]

Even though Smith never uses the term commercial society in *TMS*, and even if we should be reluctant to treat it as synonymous with civilized society, are there not passages that discuss commercial society indirectly, without using the precise phrase? I shall consider some possible contenders in subsequent sections, but for now it is worth examining what could be taken as the strongest textual allusion to commercial society in *TMS*. In his analysis of beneficence and justice, Smith observes that all members of society "stand in need of each others assistance." In some cases, this assistance may be performed from the generous motives of love, gratitude, friendship, and esteem, but a society may also "subsist among different men, as among different merchants, from a sense of its utility, without any mutual love or affection" (*TMS* II.ii.3.1–2). Hont (2015, pp. 9–10) claims that these passages outline different models of society, with the utility model being a "commercial society," as we can see by comparing it to Smith's later claim that a commercial

---

[10] In *WN*, Smith suggests that the earliest civilized nations were probably the ancient Egyptians, Indians, and Chinese (*WN* I.iii.5–7; see also *HA* III.4; *LJ*(A) iv.57–58).

[11] This is the case with Rasmussen, as my earlier quotation indicates. Rasmussen (2008, p. 100) also observes that it is unclear where ancient Greece and Rome fit on the four-stages theory and whether they had "attained all the characteristics of commercial society," even though they were clearly civilized societies.

[12] One reason for avoiding these terms could be due to their association with European imperialism at the time, on which see, for example, Sebastiani (2013, pp. 73–101). Insofar as we are interested in understanding Smith, I take these considerations to count in favor of retaining his terms, so as not to elide their wider connotations. In this context, see also Ince (2021), who argues that Smith's anti-imperialist credentials are not as complete as sometimes thought.

society is characterized by everyone becoming "in some measure a merchant" (*WN* I.iv.1).

Smith's main argument in these passages is that while a society can subsist without beneficence, it cannot survive long once injustice is prevalent. Justice is thus "the main pillar that upholds the whole edifice" of society (*TMS* II.ii.3.3-4).[13] Although these passages do not compare different forms of society, Hont argues that they bear upon the comparisons that Smith draws elsewhere. We need not turn to *WN* to appreciate this, however, as toward the end of *TMS* Smith claims that "the rudeness and barbarism" of some countries prevents "the natural sentiments of justice from arriving at that accuracy and precision that, in more civilized nations, they naturally attain to." Smith clearly thought that it was only in (some) civilized states that systems of positive law come anywhere close to approximating "the rules of natural justice" (*TMS* VII.iv.36). Once again, however, the salient distinction is between civilized and uncivilized states. The adjective civilized draws our attention to the regularity of the law and civil government in the state in question, rather than to the extent of the division of labor and commercial exchange. These features are not unrelated, of course, and Smith explores the complex interplay between the progression of civil government and commercial development extensively in *LJ* and parts of *WN*, where, amongst other things, he shows that this relationship has played out very differently in different times and places. This is perhaps best illustrated by his famous conclusion that, in many respects, the "natural order of things" had been "entirely inverted" in modern European states (*WN* III.i.9). In *TMS*, however, Smith usually deploys the generic distinction between civilized and uncivilized (barbarous or savage), which strongly suggests that he was not concerned there with explaining anything distinctive about the role of commercial development in modern Europe.[14]

---

[13] Hont, in fact, claims that Smith outlines three models of society in the passages under discussion, based respectively on love, fear, and utility, with the remarks on justice referring to a society based on fear (i.e., fear of punishment). If this is the case, then Smith's comment about merchants and utility is nothing more than a passing remark – after all, the section in which these passages appear is entitled "Of Justice and Beneficence", with utility discussed in Part IV. However, it is more plausible to read Smith's point as being that, once the pillar of justice is in place, people will assist one another out of a sense of utility without necessarily being motivated by more generous or benevolent sentiments.

[14] Smith does highlight the distinctively modern character of some of the topics he discusses in *TMS*, including the arts (I.ii.2.2, II.iii.3.5, V.1.5, VI.iii.26), eloquence and manners (III.3.24, VI.iii.9, VI.iii.28), and philosophy (VII.ii.I.29, VII.ii.I.48. VII.ii.I.50, VII.ii.3.3, VII.iv.12). These sometimes focus on the differences between the moderns and the ancients – i.e., between different civilized societies, rather than between civilized and uncivilized ones – and are not principally concerned with changes based on the level of commercial development.

8.2 *TMS* as a Response to Mandeville and Rousseau

Although Smith does not refer explicitly to commercial society in *TMS*, there may be other reasons for supposing that he was occupied with its moral shortcomings when completing the book. Perhaps, for example, he should be read as responding to other thinkers who were clearly analyzing commercial society. The prime candidate here is Jean-Jacques Rousseau, who (so the argument goes) offered a scathing critique of modern commercial society in the *Discourse on the Origins of Inequality among Men* (or *Second Discourse*), which Smith then addresses in parts of *TMS* and *WN*.[15]

The strongest evidence supporting this interpretation is that Smith reviewed the *Second Discourse* for the *Edinburgh Review* in 1756. There he notes that Rousseau's work was heavily indebted to the second volume of Bernard Mandeville's *The Fable of the Bees* (hereafter *Fable II*), and, after comparing the two, Smith translates some key passages from the *Second Discourse* (*EPS* 250–254). Even though he does not mention Rousseau in either *TMS* or *WN*, Smith appears to have reworked and incorporated some of the translated passages into those books (Schliesser, 2006, pp. 343–351; Rasmussen, 2008, pp. 68–89; Paganelli, Smith and Rasmussen, 2018, pp. 4–7). We should be careful not to overstate the importance of Rousseau to the development of Smith's thought (Sagar, 2022, chap. 3), but the "Letter to the *Edinburgh Review*" provides at least some evidence that Smith was interested in certain problems that he thought the *Second Discourse* revived, following as it did in Mandeville's footsteps. The important question presently is whether those problems should be understood as constituting a critique of modern commercial society.

With the risk of unsettling too many orthodoxies at once, the first point to note is that neither *Fable II* nor the *Second Discourse* in fact analyze modern commercial society – a claim that extends beyond the (far from irrelevant) observation that the phrase does not appear in either work. While considerable parts of the first volume of the *Fable* do examine the commercial states of Mandeville's day – the "Grumbling Hive" of his notorious poem, for instance, is clearly an allusion to England (Mandeville, 1988, vol. 1, p. 6) – this is far less prominent in *Fable II*. The centerpiece of the latter work is instead an extensive conjectural history of society, which charts the main steps that would have led humans to move out of "a savage state" and eventually form "a well-civiliz'd Nation" (Mandeville, 1988, vol. 2, pp. 132–133, 318). The contrast between savage and civilized peoples runs throughout *Fable II*, and Mandeville (1988, vol. 2, p. 128) acknowledges that his account of how humans came to

---

[15] For recent studies focusing on Rousseau's and Smith's views on commercial society, see Hanley (2006, 2008, 2018); Rasmussen (2008); Hont (2015); Douglass (2017, 2018); Pignol and Walraevens (2017); Schwarze and Scott (2019).

live in civilized societies with polite manners relies on the "Use of Conjectures" far more than it does on any recorded historical evidence. As a result, very little of *Fable II* should be taken as recounting details specific to the experience of any particular time or place, such as the commercial states of modern Europe.[16] For Mandeville (1988, vol. 2, pp. 268–269), the final step toward civilized society is the invention of letters, which allows for written laws and thereby places the administration of justice on a more secure footing. Once societies reach this point, the division of labor and greater economic productivity soon follow (1988, vol. 2, p. 284), yet Mandeville's conjectural history has surprisingly little to say about economic considerations or commercial development – it is not a conjectural history of *commercial* society in any meaningful sense.

Although there is more debate around the status of the historical narrative in the *Second Discourse* (Kelly, 2006), Rousseau (1992, pp. 13, 16) likewise claims to have merely "ventured some conjectures" while offering a "hypothetical history of Governments." I have argued elsewhere that Smith's most likely reason for associating the *Second Discourse* with *Fable II* is that both texts set out conjectural histories that overlap on key points (Douglass, 2017, pp. 600–606). As Smith puts it, Mandeville and Rousseau "suppose the same slow progress and gradual development of all the talents, habits, and arts which fit men to live together in society, and they both describe this progress in pretty much the same manner" (*EPS* 250–251). Rousseau does place more emphasis than Mandeville on changes to the mode of economic subsistence, arguing that the invention of agriculture and metallurgy led to the "great revolution" that resulted in the growth of property, economic dependence, and consequently inequality (Rousseau, 1992, p. 49; some of which Smith translates at *EPS* 251–252). This gave rise to the distinction between the rich and poor, which became entrenched with the instigation of civil government (Rousseau, 1992, pp. 52–54). As with Mandeville, however, Rousseau's narrative in the second part of the *Second Discourse* presents a genealogy of civilized society in general, rather than one focused on the development of modern European states in particular.

The distinction that is central to the overarching narrative of the *Second Discourse*, as it was for Mandeville in *Fable II*, is that between savage and civilized peoples. Smith appears to have recognized this. His comparison of Mandeville and Rousseau, for example, includes their contrasting depictions of

---

[16] Mandeville sometimes makes more culturally specific points, such as when he suggests that the polite manners of modern European states are "more polish'd" than they were in ancient times. In explaining the origin of politeness, however, his narrative does not focus on European states, with politeness found also in "old *Greece*, the *Roman* Empire, [and] the great Eastern Nations, that flourish'd before them." See Mandeville 1988, vol. 2: 152 and 147, respectively.

the "life of a savage," which, Smith observes, are not as different as we might initially suspect (*EPS* 251). Similarly, the passages that Smith translates from the *Second Discourse* examine the changes occasioned by the instigation of property and the subsequent rise of inequality, which build up to Rousseau's conclusion, in Smith's translation, that man "in his savage, and man in his civilized state, differ so essentially in their passions and inclinations that what makes the supreme happiness of the one, would reduce the other to despair. ... the savage lives in himself; the man of society, always outside of himself; cannot live but in the opinion of others." In illustrating this point, Rousseau compares the life of "a *Caraib*" to that of "a European minister of state" (*EPS* 253), but his argument is a far more general one about the gulf between *all* savage and civilized peoples.[17] Insofar as the *Second Discourse* was an indictment of modern commercial society, then, it was so only indirectly and by implication, given that what Rousseau set forth was a more general critique of civilized society. The "Letter to the *Edinburgh Review*" suggests that this is precisely how Smith read it.

With this discussion of Mandeville, Rousseau, and Smith's "Letter" in hand, we can return to *TMS* and examine some of the passages that may plausibly be taken as extending themes from the "Letter." In light of the foregoing discussion, one question to ask is how Smith's analysis of the differences between savage and civilized nations compares to that we find in *Fable II* and the *Second Discourse*. Smith addresses this topic in a chapter dedicated to the influence of custom and fashion upon our moral sentiments, where he argues that the virtues founded upon humanity are more cultivated in civilized nations, and the virtues founded upon self-denial in uncivilized ones. The virtues founded upon self-denial involve controlling our emotions so that other people can more easily go along with them, rather than outwardly expressing our fears and sorrows. These virtues prevail most in times of hardship and indigence, which is why they are generally found amongst "savages and barbarians" who must toil to secure the necessities of life. "A savage ... expects no sympathy from those about him," but nor does he have much sympathy for the adversity of others. By contrast, life is much easier among "civilized nations," where greater affluence and security makes it more acceptable to display one's emotions openly. The virtues founded upon humanity therefore have more space to develop in civilized nations, since these virtues involve sympathizing with the more animated sentiments of others (*TMS* V.2.8–10).

Whether or not Smith had Mandeville and Rousseau in mind, this argument clearly distances his position from theirs (Douglass, 2017, pp. 613–614).

---

[17] Cf. Hanley's (2008, p. 139 emphasis added) claim that these passages concern "the moral consequences of *commercial society* for the individual."

For both Mandeville and Rousseau, as Smith accurately summarizes (*EPS* 251), the "amiable principle" of pity "is possessed by savages" and the vulgar to a greater degree "than by those of the most polished and cultivated manners." Not so on Smith's own account, for pity and the other virtues founded upon humanity flourish most when life is not a constant struggle for survival. What is more, as the virtues of self-denial are more common amongst uncivilized peoples, it is they who are more disposed to hiding their true sentiments away from others and acquiring "habits of falsehood and dissimulation," whereas a civilized and "polished people ... become frank, open, and sincere" (*TMS* V.2.11; cf. Rousseau's view as translated at *EPS* 252). Smith's discussion of the virtues founded upon humanity and those upon self-denial, then, indicates that he firmly rejected one of the key contrasts that both Mandeville and Rousseau had drawn between savage and civilized societies.

There are other passages in *TMS* that could be read as responding to topics raised by Mandeville or Rousseau, as highlighted in the "Letter." Mandeville and Rousseau agree that "there is in man no powerful instinct which necessarily determines him to seek society for its own sake" (*EPS* 250), and Smith's account of both sympathy and the love of praiseworthiness can plausibly be read as contesting this denial of natural sociability.[18] Insofar as Smith had Mandeville and Rousseau in his sights, however, he was challenging their ideas on human nature, sociability, and the possibility of virtue, and not their analysis of commercial or civilized society.[19]

A more promising way of connecting Smith's "Letter" to commercial society is by turning to the passages he translated from the *Second Discourse*. There are two points in Part IV of *TMS* where Smith uses phrases that closely resemble his translations. The first is Rousseau's explanation of how civilized man constantly toils and labors until death, and "makes his court to the great whom he hates, and to the rich whom he despises; he spares nothing to obtain the honour of serving them" (*EPS* 253). We find echoes of this in Smith's parable of the poor man's son, who, in pursuing wealth and greatness, "makes his court to all mankind; he serves those whom he hates, and is obsequious to those whom he despises" (*TMS* IV.1.8). The second point of resemblance appears two paragraphs later. When explaining the consequences of the revolution instigated by agriculture and metallurgy, Smith translates

---

[18] For further discussion and citations to the relevant Smith scholarship, see Douglass (2017, pp. 611–613), to which should now be added Griswold (2018, pp. 93–130); Schwarze and Scott (2019, pp. 74–78).

[19] It should go without saying that general claims about human nature, sociability, and virtue are not claims about commercial society (or any other form of society) in particular. Nonetheless, there is a tendency in much scholarship to conflate claims about the basis of human sociability with an analysis of commercial society, which is especially prominent amongst those who deploy the term "commercial sociability" when analyzing Rousseau and Smith (e.g., Hont, 2015; Stimson, 2015; cf. Douglass, 2018).

Rousseau as claiming that "equality disappeared, property was introduced, labour became necessary, and the vast forrests of nature were changed into agreeable plains" (*EPS* 252). The wording here parallels Smith's own argument that our mistaken belief that wealth and greatness will bring happiness "keeps in continual motion the industry of mankind," the consequences of which "have entirely changed the whole face of the globe, [and] have turned the rude forests of nature into agreeable and fertile plains" (*TMS* IV.1.10).

These passages can plausibly be read as responding to some of Rousseau's concerns about inequality – which, unlike commercial society, *is* the subject matter of the *Second Discourse*. The poor man's son "admires the condition of the rich" and ends up fawning himself before them in a way that resembles Rousseau's analysis of civilized man (*TMS* IV.1.8).[20] Smith agrees with Rousseau that this is not the path to happiness, and this discussion presupposes economic inequality, for otherwise there would be no distinction between the poor man's son and the rich whose condition he admires. While the poor man's son shows how the pursuit of wealth can lead to misery, Smith proceeds to argue that, on aggregate, it is beneficial that we are deceived about the pleasures of wealth and greatness. Their pursuit has led to the founding of cities and commonwealths, progress in the sciences and arts, and all improvements in agriculture and industry, resulting in the earth being able "to maintain a greater multitude of inhabitants." This may well be accompanied by considerable inequality, but when it comes to the necessities of life, the rich "consume little more than the poor" and, in "what constitutes the real happiness of human life, [the poor] are in no respect inferior to those who would seem so much above them" (*TMS* IV.1.10). Although Smith does not relate this argument explicitly to different stages of society, in *WN* he does provide a more detailed explanation of why, once the cultivation of land has been improved beyond that found in "savage and barbarous nations," the "rich man consumes no more food than his poor neighbour" (*WN* I.xi.c.6–7).

We can make perfect sense of these passages from *TMS* without recourse to the concept of commercial society, relying instead on the distinction that Smith does draw in that work (following both Mandeville and Rousseau) between savage and civilized states. Nonetheless, Smith's discussion of inequality in *TMS* IV.1.10 is at least focused on how consumption and employment in societies that have cultivated the land can secure the subsistence of all – in other words, it is the closest that Smith comes in *TMS* to analyzing the type of considerations that are relevant in determining whether a society should be designated as "commercial." Insofar as these passages

---

[20] I leave aside the question of whether the psychological explanation of *why* the poor man's son pursues wealth resembles Rousseau's analysis in the *Second Discourse*. On this question, compare Hanley (2009, pp. 104–109) and Rasmussen (2008, pp. 81–82) with Sagar (2022, pp. 133–137, 173–179 and his chapter in this volume).

constitute a response to Rousseau, however, Smith seems relatively untroubled by the "proud and unfeeling" landlords or the "natural selfishness and rapacity" of the rich, given that their pursuit of wealth and greatness leads to the necessities of life being distributed amongst greater numbers than would otherwise be the case. Can we look elsewhere in *TMS*, though, for evidence that Smith was more preoccupied with the moral shortcomings of commercial society than these passages suggest?

8.3 Moral Corruption, Inequality, and Prudence

Smith made considerable additions to the sixth edition of *TMS*, published in 1790. Two aspects of these are sometimes invoked in debates about his views on the morality of commercial society. The first is the chapter added to Part I on the corruption of our moral sentiments. This follows Smith's discussion of the origin of ambition and the distinction of ranks, in which he argues that we are naturally more disposed to sympathize with the rich and powerful than with the poor and weak. "Upon this disposition of mankind," Smith claims, "is founded the distinction of ranks, and the order of society." (*TMS* I.iii.2.3) That the consequences of this disposition are not all benign was clear in earlier editions, with Smith explaining how it leads to "all the tumult and bustle, all the rapine and injustice, which avarice and ambition have introduced into this world" (*TMS* I.iii.2.8). In case there was any doubt, however, the new chapter declares that this disposition, "though necessary both to establish and to maintain the distinction of ranks and the order of society, is, at the same time, the great and most universal cause of the corruption of our moral sentiments" (I.iii.3.1).

The reason why our disposition to admire the rich and powerful corrupts our moral sentiments is straightforward: wealth and power are not fitting objects of respect and admiration, nor, conversely, are poverty and weakness fitting objects of contempt. Morally speaking, at least, it would be better if we admired the wise and virtuous, while holding folly and vice in disdain. Wealth and power do not reliably track wisdom and virtue, and poverty and weakness do not reliably track folly and vice (*TMS* I.iii.3.1–2). The scale of this problem varies in relation to different social classes. In "the middling and inferior stations of life, the road to virtue and that to fortune ... are, happily in most cases, very nearly the same." The same cannot be said, however, of "the superior stations of life," where "flattery and falsehood too often prevail over merit and abilities" (*TMS* I.iii.3.5–6). Even though moralists are right to detect the corruption of our moral sentiments in this admiration of power and wealth, Smith later insists (in another 1790 addition) that "Nature has wisely judged that the distinction of ranks, the peace and order of society, would rest more securely upon the plain and palpable difference of birth and fortune, than upon the invisible and often uncertain difference of wisdom and virtue." (*TMS* VI.ii.1.21).

As with the parable of the poor man's son, Smith's analysis of the corruption of our moral sentiments presupposes a certain level of inequality between the rich and the poor, or between the great and the humble. Drawing on these passages, Rasmussen (2016, pp. 347–350) has argued that "Smith's principal concern regarding extreme economic inequality" is the way in which it distorts our sympathies and thereby undermines morality and happiness. The question to ask presently, however, is whether this corruption should be associated especially with modern commercial societies (as is suggested, e.g., by Anderson, 2016, p. 165). The implications of this question are far-reaching. As Hanley (2009, p. 34) puts it, "if commerce corrupts 'moral sentiments,' then the effects of corruption extend to the whole range of subjects to be treated in a theory of moral sentiments." At no point in the chapter, however, does Smith even suggest that it is *commerce* that corrupts our moral sentiments. It is not the conditions of commercial society that does the work in Smith's analysis, but the dispositions of human nature (Sagar, 2022, pp. 157–163). His claim that our tendency to admire wealth and greatness, rather than wisdom and virtue, "has been the complaint of moralists *in all ages*" counts decisively against associating this corruption exclusively with *modern* commercial societies (*TMS* I.iii.3.1, emphasis added; see also Rasmussen, 2008, pp. 78, 127–128; Sagar, 2022, pp. 128, 158–160).

Even if the corruption of our moral sentiments is not unique to commercial society, we might still expect such corruption to be exacerbated under modern commercial conditions. This is especially likely if we grant that, for Smith, "no society ... was more unequal than a fully commercial society" (Robertson, 2005, p. 394), that "Smith saw a high degree of economic inequality as an inevitable result of a flourishing commercial society" (Rasmussen, 2016, p. 342), or that he "insists that the growth of inequality in commercial society inhibits sympathy and the recognition of human dignity" (Hanley, 2009, p. 52). Although Smith thought that all civilized societies were characterized by the distinction of ranks (*WN* V.i.g.10), there is no reason to assume that he saw the downsides of this inequality as being greater in commercial or civilized societies than in noncommercial or uncivilized ones. *TMS* reveals relatively little about the extent to which Smith thought different stages of society were characterized by different levels of economic inequality, but, when discussing the distinction of ranks and our propensity to revere the powerful in Part VI, he includes examples "of the most brutal and savage barbarians, of an Attila, a Gengis, or a Tamerlane," which should at least cast doubt on the idea that the disposition to admire wealth and greatness is more prominent in civilized states than uncivilized ones (*TMS* VI.iii.30). As Smith explains in *WN*, the "authority of riches ... is perhaps greatest in the rudest age of society which admits of any considerably inequality of fortune." To be sure, this "authority of fortune" remains considerable "even in an opulent and civilized society," yet it is in the "second period of society, that of shepherds," where inequalities of wealth give the greatest authority to the rich, and thus "in which authority and subordination are more perfectly established" (*WN* V.i.b.7; see also *LJ*(A) iv.8; *LJ*(B) 20–21).

On Smith's account, inequality of wealth is more of a problem in shepherding or barbarian societies than it is in civilized or commercial ones, precisely because the authority of the rich over the poor is greater in the former case.[21] This is not to deny that Smith regarded the corruption of our moral sentiments as a problem in commercial or civilized societies, since it is a problem in all societies where any distinction of ranks or inequality of wealth can be found, including commercial ones. But there is no reason to consider it a problem either distinctive to or more pronounced within commercial societies, which is probably why Smith discusses it in a treatise of moral philosophy.

The second aspect of the 1790 edition of *TMS* that might seem to bear upon Smith's analysis of commercial society is the addition of an entirely new part on "the Character of Virtue," and especially the discussion of the virtue of prudence. According to Hanley (2009, p. 5), Part VI of *TMS* represents Smith's "considered response to the ills of commercial corruption that he himself had so powerfully articulated." Yet, as we have seen, Smith's analysis of the corruption of our moral sentiments in *TMS* should not be understood in terms of *commercial* corruption. To the extent that Part VI does represent a response to this corruption, then, we should not assume that the virtues in question are associated with commercial society.[22] Without considering all the virtues presently, it is worth attending briefly to Smith's analysis of prudence, which is sometimes taken to be a distinctively "commercial virtue" (Hanley, 2009, pp. 100–131). Indeed, prudence has long been thought to tie *TMS* to *WN*, since it is "both a moral and an economic virtue" (Griswold, 1999, p. 203), with the prudent man of *TMS* being "essentially the same person assumed to be at work in commercial society" (Winch, 1996, p. 105).

---

[21] Scholars such as Hanley and Rasmussen are well aware of these considerations, of course, and offer plenty of insightful analysis of the passages from *WN* and *LJ*. At one point, for example, Hanley (2009, p. 20) observes that "the inequality of precommercial societies such as this [feudal barbarism] is infinitely more pernicious than the inequality to be found in commercial society." See also Rasmussen (2008, pp. 96–97). Yet at other points, as the quotations indicate, they both suggest that inequality is especially troublesome in commercial societies. Cf. Boucoyannis (2013), who argues that Smith thought market-based economies should reduce inequality.

[22] See also Fleischacker (2021, p. 140), who rightly observes, in response to Hanley, that Smith does not present any of his points in Part VI "as a response to critiques of commercial society."

At no point in *TMS* does Smith claim that prudence should be associated especially with commercial or civilized society, although he does suggest that it is a virtue more often found in the middling and inferior ranks of society than amongst the upper classes (*TMS* I.iii.2.5, I.iii.3.5). When discussing the virtue in Part VI, he mostly writes of the "prudent man" in very general terms, while occasionally appealing to categories from ancient philosophy to illustrate his points. The "superior prudence" displayed by great generals, statesmen, and legislators closely approximates "the character of the Academical or Peripatetic sage," with the "inferior prudence" involved in looking after oneself coming closer to "that of the Epicurean" (*TMS* VI.i.15). Epicureanism is, after all, Smith's starting point when analyzing "systems which make virtue consist in prudence" (*TMS* VII.ii.2.1), so there is no reason to regard prudence as a characteristically modern virtue in any respect.

The strongest evidence linking prudence to commercial society is found elsewhere. In *LJ*, Smith argues that where probity and punctuality are almost unknown in "a rude and barbarous country," they are "the principal virtues of a commercial nation." These virtues are associated with the "prudent dealer, who is sensible of his real interest," and when "the greater part of people are merchants they always bring probity and punctuality into fashion" (*LJ*(B) 326–328). Yet there is more to prudence than probity and punctuality. The virtue of prudence consists in the union of foresight (or "superior reason and understanding") and self-command (*TMS* IV.2.6), and Smith's discussion of the virtue in Part VI of *TMS* focuses on the qualities required to secure the health, fortune, rank, and reputation of an individual in general (*TMS* VI.i.5), without mentioning either probity or punctuality explicitly. Even if commercial development does breed prudence, Smith's discussion of the virtue in *TMS* is not concerned with understanding the dynamics of commercial society.[23] Much as Smith analyzes the relationship between probity, punctuality, and commerce more in other works, so too it is in those works – and not in *TMS* – that he addresses the "inconveniences ... arising from a commercial spirit" (*LJ*(B) 328–333), and the measures that the government should take "to prevent the almost entire corruption and degeneracy of the great body of the people ... in a civilized and commercial society" (*WN* V.i.f.49–52). The strongest evidence that Smith was concerned with weighing up the moral costs and benefits associated with the development of commerce and the division of labor, then, is nearly all found in *LJ* and *WN*, which should come

---

[23] Conversely, the virtue of prudence is not analyzed in any detail in either *LJ* or *WN*. Smith does mention prudence soon after his first reference to commercial society in *WN*, but there he writes of "every prudent man *in every period of society, after the first establishment of the division of labour*," which is presumably long before the division of labor is "*thoroughly established* ... and the society itself grows to be what is properly a commercial society" (*WN* I.iv.1–2, emphasis added).

as little surprise once we recognize that *TMS* is not, in any meaningful sense, a book about commercial society.

8.4 Conclusion

It is tempting to read our own concerns back onto past thinkers, especially those we admire. Claims that something is a distinctive feature of modernity or capitalism are commonplace, and the concept of commercial society might seem to offer a bridge from Smith's world to our own. If we read *TMS* as a book about modern commercial society, then we are liable to assume that key aspects of Smith's analysis are related to distinctively *modern* and/or distinctively *commercial* considerations. My goal in this chapter has been to show that this assumption will usually lead us astray. Smith is not concerned with diagnosing and remedying certain problems associated with commercial modernity (or capitalism) in *TMS* for the very simple reason that his overarching aim is to analyze our moral sentiments at a far more foundational level. To the extent that *TMS* still speaks to us today, it is down to the many insights Smith draws about human nature and our moral sentiments in general, which, if anything, should lead us to question whether the problems that *we* regard as distinctively modern or commercial are really such. As we have seen, for example, Smith is more plausibly read as *challenging* rather than *supporting* the notion that the corruption of our moral sentiments is exacerbated by modern commercial conditions, precisely because he does not explain this corruption by appealing to causes unique to, or more prominent within, commercial modernity.

There is something ironic about the tendency to read *TMS* as a book about commercial society. In other works, Smith maintains that many aspects of our lives are affected by the different social and economic conditions under which we live, but this is not a central theme of *TMS* and in the places where it does come into view, such as Part V, the key distinction is between "civilized" and "savage" or "barbarous" nations. The fact that *LJ* and *WN* do have a lot more to say about commercial societies or nations is one of the things that sets those texts apart from *TMS*. In much scholarship, however, the distance between these works is elided in ways that distort our understanding of Smith's thought. To end on a speculative note, I suspect that this is because a great deal of Smith scholarship still unwittingly operates under the shadow of "Das Adam Smith Problem" – not by reading *TMS* and *WN* as inconsistent works, but, instead, by pushing back too strongly in the other direction and arguing that they together "form a coherent whole" (Griswold, 1999, pp. 29–30; Fleischacker, 2021, p. 319). As Axel Honneth (2021, p. 69) has recently observed, today "hardly any leading interpreter doubts the continuity in Smith's work." Insofar as this is true, however, it should be more of a cause for concern than celebration. As I hope to have shown, projecting questions and concepts from *WN* back onto *TMS* is one path to misreading Smith's moral philosophy. If we really want to free ourselves from the shackles of "Das Adam Smith Problem," then we must avoid assuming that *TMS* and *WN* should be read as *either* contradictory *or* complementary works. This is not to deny that Smith's two great works can sometimes be profitably read alongside one another, but one danger of doing so is that we lose sight of the extent to which they address *independent* questions. And if we start by asking the wrong questions then we cannot hope to get Smith right.

9

Adam Smith, Sufficientarian

PAUL SAGAR

In normative political theory, Jeremy Waldron has encouraged us to note the distinction "between (a) a discussion of equality as an economic or social aim, and (b) a discussion of the basic equality of all humans as a premise or assumption of moral and political thought" (Waldron, 2008, p. 1). Adam Smith's work bears upon both issues.

On the more fundamental question, Waldron's (b), there is compelling evidence that Smith is a basic egalitarian. Although Smith nowhere explicitly states a commitment to universal human moral equality, the evidence is nonetheless strong that he subscribed to such a view (Griswold, 1999, pp. 12, 199–200; Darwall, 2004, p. 132; Peart and Levy, 2005; McLean, 2006; Hanley, 2009, pp. 205–206; Fleischacker, 2013; Anderson, 2016). There is his condemnation of all forms of slavery, and his contempt for any notion of the legitimacy of subordinating some humans to the institutionalised domination of others; his emphasis on adopting an impartial point of view when forming correct moral judgments that treats all human beings as moral agents and hence as presumptive equals; the absence (remarkable by eighteenth-century standards) of racist thinking in his works; and his insistence that the observable differences of rank and quality in society are less a function of inherent worth or ability than the division of labour: that the vanity of the philosopher notwithstanding, the differences between him and a street porter arise "not so much from nature, as from habit, custom, and education" (*WN* I.ii.4).

Regarding Waldron's (a), however, matters are less clear. In part this is simply because, as stated, (a) encompasses an awful lot. At the very least, it involves questions of distribution of *material resources*, but also the *relationships* that individuals stand in relation to one another (matters of respect, status, hierarchy, authority, etc.). And, as Smith recognised, these things interact in complex ways, not least because both are conditioned by, but also in turn condition, the psychological states of relevant agents. What Smith thought about egalitarianism in terms of *distributions* (not just of material goods, but of status and respect) is complex and multifaceted, and cannot straightforwardly be read off his underlying commitment to basic equality.

Regarding distributions of material holdings, Smith is evidently not any kind of strict egalitarian. He famously condones the inequality that arises from widespread market exchanges insofar as the poor in advanced market conditions are vastly better off than they would be in a situation of greater equality, but more extensive frugality: "the accommodation of an European prince does not always so much exceed that of an industrious and frugal peasant, as the accommodation of the latter exceeds that of many an African king" (WN I.i.24). Nonetheless, the fact that Smith felt the need to *offer* a justification, and one specifically in terms of the benefits accruing to the relative losers in material distributions, is significant. As Samuel Fleischacker has shown, Smith cared deeply about the plight of the poor, and was motivated to change both policy and attitudes in ways that would benefit them (Fleischacker, 2004a, pp. 62–67, 2004b, pp. 203–227). Similarly, several recent commentators have suggested that the impetus for a kind of egalitarianism can in fact be found in Smith. That even if he was not an egalitarian in matters of what we would now call distributive justice, we can nonetheless recover in his work important insights that egalitarians today might profitably work with (Pack, 1991, pp. 1, 4, 66; Kennedy, 2008, pp. 256–261; Rasmussen, 2008, pp. 101–108, 2016; Hanley, 2009, pp. 45, 199–200; Anderson, 2016). In turn, whilst Smith is a defender of societies that license significant material inequality because of their reliance on market arrangements, insofar as he cares about the losers from those arrangements and wants to improve their condition, so there is a case for a 'left' Smith against the more popularly conceived-of 'right' Smith associated with *laissez-faire*: an intellectual resource for modern defenders of (broadly speaking) social democratic welfare states, who take themselves to be various species of egalitarian in Waldron's sense (a) (e.g. Fleischacker, 2016).[1]

I am sceptical about this way of assembling the pieces. For as I read him, Smith's account is more complex than (I want to claim) has hitherto been realised, and appreciating that complexity prohibits us from telling a straightforwardly supportive story about Smith and egalitarianism. In particular, reading Smith calls into question whether an *individual* ethic regarding the holding of material wealth will be isomorphic with our *political* commitments. And insofar as these are incongruent, there seems an important gap between what Smith says about the normative implications of material distributions for individuals, and what to say in turn about the political aspects of inequality vis-à-vis society – a gap that Smith's ethical reflections alone do not help us bridge.

The reading defended in this chapter is that at the level of individual ethics Smith encourages us to be *sufficientarians*: that what matters in distributive questions is not that all approach equality on some relevant metric(s), but that one as an individual has *enough*, and that above a relevant threshold material

---

[1] For scepticism about Smith being appropriately claimed for either left *or* right, see Smith (2013b).

inequality ought not to be of pressing normative concern to the individual considered *qua* individual. In this regard Smith's position anticipates the basic argument for sufficientarianism found in Harry Frankfurt's seminal paper 'Equality as a Moral Ideal' (1987). However, Smith (to my mind) offers a *better* version of the argument, by grounding it in an astute grasp of ordinary human psychology, and indeed a willingness to give psychology a central explanatory role in what is at stake. This may seem a backhanded compliment, however, insofar as sufficientarianism is now widely viewed as theoretically inferior to various species of egalitarianism (Casal, 2007; Shields, 2020; Lippert-Rasmussen, 2021; Phillips, 2021, pp. 75–85). But again, I am not so sure. For if Smith's psychological account is correct – and my sense is that it might well be – then the sufficientarianism that he espouses may turn out to be one that we still have good reason to endorse today, *at least as an individual ethic*. Nonetheless – and the distinction here is important – there may remain good reasons to think that egalitarianism still has a claim on us as a *political* value, and regarding which Smith's considerations are ultimately indeterminate. As a result, it is not at all clear that Smith offers support for contemporary egalitarianism in the ways that recent commentators have hoped, precisely because we cannot read off of Smith's individual-level ethical analysis straightforward political implications.

The case for reading Smith as a sufficientarian in matters of individual ethical outlook centres on Part IV, chapter 1, of *TMS*, which contains Smith's account of what drives the economic consumption that gives rise to both prosperity and inequality, as well as his normative appraisal of the results. Yet it is crucial to interpret IV.1 correctly – something that, in my view, has largely not been done. This is because most readers take Smith to be arguing that consumption is driven by *vanity*, that is, a desire to attain status, in competition with others, as signalled through possession of material assets (Griswold, 1999, pp. 217–227, 292–301; Fleischacker, 2004b, chap. 6; Rasmussen, 2008, chap. 3; Hanley, 2009, pp. 18, 36–38, 52, 101–103; Luban, 2012, p. 284; Hont, 2015, pp. 91–102; Hill, 2017, p. 11). By contrast, I read Smith as arguing that what drives most consumption is what I term a 'quirk of rationality' whereby we tend to become more preoccupied with the means of utility than any actually derived utility itself. This is important, because taking a position on the underlying psychological drive to consumption, and hence the effects of that consumption on our psychology, is crucial for forming a normative assessment of the material inequality that arises from it. Whereas most readers take Smith to defer to Rousseau's view that what drives consumption is competitive *amour propre*, and thus that inequality is normatively problematic insofar as it rests upon, and in turn aggravates, domineering status differentials, my reading is that this is not what Smith is arguing. Instead I read him as *rejecting* this kind of Rousseauvian concern as being largely ill-founded, and hence beside the point, when it comes to questions of material distribution, at least regarding how to live one's individual life, and when aspiring for a state of psychological balance (i.e. happiness, on Smith's view). The implications of this bring us finally to the question of Smith's thought and its relation to egalitarianism as a political ideal.

9.1 The Motor of Consumption and the Poor Son's Perils

Part IV opens with Smith correcting Hume's view that the utility of objects pleases by bringing to mind the satisfaction that such objects will deliver, either to us personally, or to others (in which case they please via sympathy). Against Hume, Smith notes that there are many instances in which we are more concerned with acquiring the means of utility than with the actual utility delivered. As examples he gives the man who spends more effort neatly arranging the chairs in a room than could be derived from the satisfaction of the floor being clear; the lover of trinkets who lugs about many devices with more effort than those devices could possibly save him; the person who has a watch that loses two minutes in a day and is obsessed with purchasing a more expensive one which loses only a minute in a fortnight, despite both being evidently good enough for the function of telling the time. In all cases "What pleases these lovers of toys is not so much the utility, as the aptness of the machines which are fitted to promote it" (*TMS* IV.1.6).

These may seem trivial examples, but Smith insists that "Nor is it only with regard to such frivolous objects that our conduct is influenced by this principle; it is often the secret motive of the most serious and important pursuits of both private and public life" (*TMS* IV.1.7). He draws out the far-reaching consequences of this quirk of rationality – of being more preoccupied with the means of utility than with utility itself – through his famous parable of the "poor man's son, whom heaven in its anger has visited with ambition" (*TMS* IV.1.8). The problem that besets the poor man's son is that he looks at the means of utility possessed by the rich and powerful, and wishes the same for himself. Whereas he must walk, they ride in carriages; whereas he labours for himself, they have a retinue of servants; whereas he sleeps in a cottage, they slumber in a palace. If only he could have these things, he tells himself, he would be content. Accordingly, he engages in a life of toil to acquire those means of utility, but in the process expands far more effort than could ever be compensated for by their possession. This is all undertaken in the mistaken belief that "if he had attained all these, he would sit still contentedly, and be quiet, enjoying himself in the thought of the happiness and tranquillity of his situation" (*TMS* IV.1.8). But the poor man's son is caught in a trap. For once he acquires the means he discovers that they do not make him happy after all. He is fixated on a "distant idea of felicity", which he mistakenly believes will be arrived at if only he can acquire *yet more* means of utility. Rather than realising that he is on a hiding to nothing, he continues to toil away, seeking yet further means of utility. Only at the very end of his life is the poor man's son apt to realise, too late, the error of his ways: that he has wasted his life grasping for the horizon, precisely because "wealth and greatness are mere trinkets of frivolous utility, no more adapted for procuring ease of body or tranquillity of mind than the tweezer-cases of the lover of toys; and like them too, more troublesome to the person who carries them about with him than all the advantages they can afford him are commodious" (*TMS* IV.1.8).

Smith holds wealth and greatness to ultimately be mere means to utility, and hence of no greater inherent worth than a box of trinkets or a tidy room. However, we are apt to *think* that they are worth more because the conveniences of wealth and greatness are more obvious to disinterested observers. Insofar as grand estates, carriages, retinues, etc. are easily recognisable as things that promote utility, and insofar as we can all easily enter by sympathy into the imagined pleasures of the rich who possess such things, we imagine that if *we* possessed these means to utility, then *we* would be happier than we currently are. By contrast, "the curiosity of a tooth-pick, or an ear-picker, of a machine for cutting the nails, or of any other trinket of the same kind, is not so obvious". In turn, wealth and greatness are more "reasonable" subjects of "vanity than the magnificence of wealth and greatness", because everybody can see the mechanism by which wealth and greatness promote utility, so it makes sense to be prouder of these things than (say) a watch, which is interesting only to the fellow aficionado of watches. As Smith concludes, this is why wealth and greatness are in part valued *beyond* merely the utility that they are a means for promoting directly: they "more effectually gratify that love of distinction so natural to man", in a way that trinket boxes and accurate watches do not, and hence issue in a sort of psychological double-hit: once, from the utility they promote directly, and then again, from the thought of being admired for possessing such excellent means to utility by sympathetic observers (*TMS* IV.1.8).

Yet it is nonetheless at root the quirk of rationality, not the love of vanity, doing the heavy lifting in Smith's account of why we admire and pursue richness and greatness, and thus motivating the majority of individual economic consumption. He explains the point as follows. First, if we observe whether the rich and great are *actually* happier due to their wealth and greatness – their possession of multiple means of utility – we find that they are not. Revealingly, the spectator typically "does not even imagine that they [the rich and great] are really happier than other people: but he imagines that they possess more means of happiness". And from this preoccupation with the means of utility, not the actual utility experienced by the rich and great, comes the main admiration for riches and greatness. Combined with the fact that we all take pleasure, via sympathy, in being looked at approvingly by others (and hence we imagine that if *we* had wealth and greatness, then *we* would be looked at approvingly by others too, and would take pleasure from the situation accordingly), this tricks us into thinking – like the poor man's son – that if we had more riches and greatness, then we would be happier. Remarkably, Smith notes, this belief persists in spite of abundant evidence that wealth and greatness *do not* make their possessors more contented, on average, than others. In any case, although vanity *reinforces* preoccupation with the means of utility, it is, Smith insists, the quirk of rationality that is doing the major work in the psychology of economic consumption. Vanity is a secondary, and derivative, motive, one that supervenes upon the false belief that if we had more means of utility, then we would finally be content. (We will return to this point later.)

Smith is adamant that pursuing wealth and greatness is folly if one thinks such things will generate contentment. By contrast, when adopting what he calls a "splenetic philosophy" (*TMS* IV.1.9), he believes it evident that "the pleasures of the vain and empty distinctions of greatness disappear" (*TMS* IV.1.8):

> in the languor of disease and the weariness of old age, the pleasures of the vain and empty distinctions of greatness disappear ... Power and riches appear then to be, what they are, enormous and operose machines contrived to produce a few trifling conveniencies to the body, consisting of springs the most nice and delicate, which must be kept in order with the most anxious attention, and which in spite of all our care are ready every moment to burst into pieces, and to crush in their ruins their unfortunate possessor.
>
> (*TMS* IV.1.8)

The poor man's son is the most extreme example of wasting one's life in the pursuit of chimerical ends, caused by valuing the means of utility more than utility itself. But we are all prone to engaging in this kind of behaviour, Smith thinks, for it is only when caught up in moments of "splenetic" philosophy that we recognise the futility of pursuing yet more means of utility. In less melancholy moods, we happily go along with endlessly pursuing yet more means of utility in our own lives, without being troubled by the fact that sober philosophical reflection reveals that this is to grasp after the horizon. Whereas "If we consider the real satisfaction which all these things are capable of affording, by itself and separated from the beauty of that arrangement which is fitted to promote it, it will always appear in the highest degree contemptible and trifling", nonetheless in daily practice "we rarely view it in this abstract and philosophical light". Instead, "the pleasures of wealth and greatness, when considered in this complex view, strike the imagination as something grand and beautiful and noble, of which the attainment is well worth all the toil and anxiety which we are so apt to bestow upon it" (*TMS* IV.1.9). Most of the time, in other words, we are all a bit like the poor man's son. But that need not be an especially bad thing, Smith suggests, so long as we avoid the extremities that the poor man's son falls into, instead engaging in our pursuit of the means of utility in moderation, in ways that do not excessively sacrifice real contentment for the "distant idea of felicity".

Smith famously describes this psychology of endless consumption – of being more preoccupied with the means of utility than with utility itself, and thus never being satiated – as a deception. And this deception, he claims, *is a good thing*, at least at a societal level. (At the individual level, it depends: witness the poor man's son.) This is because the deception is the main motor of consumption that drives overall economic prosperity. In perpetually pursuing the means of utility, rather than just utility itself (regarding which we could long ago have been content, with far less), humanity "entirely changed the whole face of the globe" and "turned the rude forests of nature into agreeable and fertile plains, and made the trackless and barren ocean a new fund of subsistence, and the great high road of communication to the different nations of the earth. The earth by these labours of mankind has been obliged to redouble her natural fertility, and to maintain a greater multitude of inhabitants". Whilst the "proud and unfeeling" landlords who early-on gained possession of the great shares of property cared not at all about the poor, nonetheless in pursuing their own selfish gratification – the desire for ever more means of utility – they inadvertently promoted the good of all. This was because their eyes were bigger than their bellies, and whilst they imagined consuming the "whole harvest" themselves, in reality they were forced to share with others – not out of kindness or generosity, but again out of selfishness. Having too much to consume alone, they traded their surpluses. In turn, through an ironic and unintended process, the selfishness of the rich and their ceaseless pursuit of more means of utility led to increased economic activity, thus greater prosperity, and the rising tide lifted all boats. The rich "are led by an invisible hand to make nearly the same distribution of the necessaries of life, which would have been made, had the earth been divided into equal portions among all its inhabitants, and thus without intending it, without knowing it, advance the interest of the society, and afford means to the multiplication of the species". As a result, "When Providence divided the earth among a few lordly masters, it neither forgot nor abandoned those who seemed to have been left out in the partition. These last too enjoy their share of all that it produces" (*TMS* IV.1.10).

Yet Smith's final normative assessment of this state of affairs is two-pronged. The first prong is well known, and has already been noted: that insofar as the poor are made better off than they otherwise would be, the mere fact that they have less is not necessarily objectionable. But Smith concludes his discussion by offering a second consideration, referring back to what he earlier claimed regarding the disjuncture between wealth and greatness and genuine happiness:

> In what constitutes the real happiness of human life, they [the poor] are in no respect inferior to those who would seem so much above them. In ease of body and peace of mind, all the different ranks of life are nearly upon a level, and the beggar, who suns himself by the side of the highway, possesses that security which kings are fighting for (*TMS* IV.1.10).

This final remark, however, is crucial for teasing out the implications of Smith's position.

9.2 Smith's Sufficientarianism

Smith's account of the workings of the great deception is standardly read as an 'on-balance' defence of material inequality. That is: material inequality is normatively acceptable *on balance*, because although objectionable, this is outweighed by the good of making the poor vastly better off than they would be in conditions of more extensive equality, but greater overall frugality (e.g. Rasmussen, 2008, p. 171). Yet this is *not* Smith's position.

Instead of being an *on balance* matter, Smith is claiming that *not only* are the poor made vastly better off in conditions of inequality-with-prosperity than they would be under equality-with-frugality, but that they aren't anyway significantly worse off than the rich *when it comes to what really matters*. This is because what really matters on Smith's view is living a life of contentment: of achieving happiness. Why are the less well-off in advanced conditions of economic opulence not necessarily significantly worse-off than the great and wealthy? Precisely because wealth and greatness are mere "enormous and operose machines" that do not render anyone significantly happier, whereas when it comes to "ease of body and peace of mind, all the different ranks of life are nearly upon a level". Hence why, in Smith's example, the beggar sunning himself on the highway is (at least in that precise moment) better off than the king fighting for the very peace and security that the beggar (at least in that precise moment) possesses.

Smith's position is that once we realise that more wealth and more greatness do not reliably lead to more happiness, so we can also realise that as long as one has enough to secure "ease of body and peace of mind", then attaining further wealth and greatness ought to lose their appeal. Having more means of utility will not by itself make one more contented, so it is better to try and achieve contentedness with what one has. But if that is the case, then it *doesn't matter* if some have vastly more material holdings, so long as one has enough to attain "ease of body and peace of mind".

This is the basic case for reading Smith as, in modern parlance, a sufficientarian. What really matters, Smith thinks, is the achieving of contentedness, something which he sees as a question of personal psychological calibration rather than either total or relative material holdings. Certainly, a threshold of material and social goods will be required for anyone to be able to possess "ease of body and peace of mind". This is presumably a major reason why, as Fleischacker has shown, Smith cares deeply about ensuring that the poor are, indeed, able to attain enough. Having said that, Smith seems to think that the threshold for "ease of body and peace of mind" isn't especially high. We might well disagree with him about that: my observation of beggars is that their lives are, generally speaking, miserable, and Smith's use of that example is a rare occasion where his rhetoric hinders rather than helps his argument. But the important conceptual point is that wherever the threshold is finally taken to be, assuming that it has indeed been achieved, Smith's position yields the following question: how could it be normatively concerning as a matter of individual ethical living if above the threshold some have more than you do, when having more does not make a difference to happiness?

Smith's position is thus not egalitarian, but sufficientarian. Indeed, it anticipates Harry Frankfurt's argument that "With respect to the distribution of economic assets, what is important from the point of view of morality is not that everyone should have the same but that each should have enough. If everyone had enough, it would be of no moral consequence whether some had more than others" (Frankfurt, 1987, p. 21). Like Frankfurt, Smith is sensitive to the fact that it is a "false assumption that someone who is economically worse off has more important unsatisfied needs than someone who is better off" (1987, p. 34). At the end of his life of toil, the poor man's son may have grown rich, and yet be miserable and unfulfilled. By contrast the less ambitious street porter – enjoying ease of body and tranquillity of mind in his comparatively lowly station – may be far more contented, and thus ultimately better off when it comes to what matters.

Yet Smith's thought also contains the resources for a more plausible account than Frankfurt's. This is because Smith's sufficientarianism is grounded in a wider psychological matrix, one which enables him to address what are frequently taken as compelling reasons for favouring some form of egalitarianism over sufficientarianism, and that Frankfurt's account is insufficiently sensitive to: the link between material inequality and the *relational standing* of agents with different holdings in society (Lippert-Rasmussen, 2021).

The basic charge here is that material sufficiency cannot be enough, even for the individual qua individual, because whenever there is material inequality, there will necessarily be inequality in the relations that individuals stand in towards each other – and such inequality is not likely to be benign, but oppressively domineering, and of significant disadvantage to those subjected to it. In other words: if there is inequality then there is likely to be domination, and insofar as there is domination, individuals are unlikely to be able to achieve the happiness that Smith envisages for them as enabled by meeting some sufficient threshold of material holdings. Accordingly (the charge goes) sufficiency above a threshold of material assets *cannot* be enough, because above that threshold inequalities *do* still matter.

Indeed, it may be objected on these very grounds that my reading of Smith as sufficientarian cannot in fact be *Smith's* position, precisely because he registered this very form of relational egalitarian concern, and responded to it in egalitarian terms, via his engagement with Rousseau (Hanley, 2008; Rasmussen, 2008). Anderson, for example, has argued that "Smith accepts central elements of Rousseau's analysis. He agrees that vanity – the desire for the unmerited esteem of others – is the basic motive for seeking luxury ... This is one of the driving forces behind commercial society, generating both great wealth and great inequality" (Anderson, 2016, p. 164). In turn, she presents Smith as offering "moderate egalitarian remedies" to Rousseau's radical egalitarian critique (2016, p. 166). Yet my view is that this is not correct. That not only does Smith *not* agree with Rousseau's diagnosis, but that his position in *TMS* when it comes to the normative assessment of material distributions is not best characterised as egalitarian (however moderate), but sufficientarian.

9.3 Rousseau's Challenge

In the *Second Discourse* Rousseau depicts human psychology as deeply corrupted by the advent of widespread economic consumption. In the state of nature, human beings were still possessed of the natural principle of pity, and were able to engage in mutually gratifying social practices (communal dancing, dressing up in feathers and shells, etc.) designed to satiate the *amour propre* of all individuals in a positive-sum manner. But with the advent of economic exchange this happy state of affairs ended. Once humans realised that they could use material goods to signal status, their capacity for natural pity was suppressed, with *amour propre* becoming pathologically enflamed into "a black inclination to harm one another ... and always the hidden desire to profit at another's expense" (Rousseau, 1997, p. 171). Status-seeking became zero-sum, individuals hankering after ever more material goods in an endless cycle of social one-upmanship. Imbalances in economic production and consumption quickly gave rise to inequality, and thus class relations. In order to avoid nascent revolution at the hands of the now also pathologically *amour propre*-driven poor, the rich hit upon the idea of property rights as enforced by a central agency (i.e. the state). Although this was a terrible deal for the poor, they bought into the arrangement because their enflamed *amour propre* was more preoccupied with securing their meagre holdings from the perceived threat of their immediate (also poor) neighbours, rather than with recognising the systemic nature of the problem. "All ran toward their chains in the belief that they were securing their freedom; for while they had enough reason to sense the advantages of a political establishment, they had not enough experience to foresee its dangers" (Rousseau, 1997, p. 173). Under conditions of state-enforced private property and widespread material inequality, human beings were condemned to having their *amour propre* remain permanently enflamed, and thus forever a source of psychological pain due to the remorseless nature of social status competition, now coupled with a system of centralised political domination designed to keep the entire state of affairs in place. On Rousseau's account, therefore, not only is economic consumption driven primarily by status competition (enflamed *amour propre* with natural pity suppressed), but this consumption is in turn a source of social domination and individual misery – which further enflames *amour propre*, propagating a vicious cycle.

Does Smith, as many commentators maintain, fundamentally agree with Rousseau's diagnosis of what drives economic consumption, even if he disagrees with Rousseau's assessment of the downstream political outcome? As the above should already have begun to make clear, the answer is no.

In the first place, in *TMS* Part IV Smith is clear that it is *not* vanity, or status competition, that drives most economic consumption, but the quirk of rationality. Vanity is a *secondary* motive to most consumption, one which at most supervenes on the more fundamental preoccupation of acquiring ever more means of utility. Smith rejects Rousseau's account of what motivates the bulk of economic consumption.

Second, it is vital to recognise that Smith's example of the 'poor man's son' is an *extreme* case. Whereas Rousseau posits that pretty much everyone behaves like the poor man's son all of the time, Smith believes such a figure is the exception not the rule. The poor man's son is worth drawing attention to because he sharply illustrates the phenomenon under discussion, and because we are all prone to behaving like him *some* of the time. But he is not the archetype of normal behaviour. Furthermore, whilst the poor man's son is a pathological extreme we ought to be cautious not to emulate, Smith thinks it evidently *is* possible not to emulate him. Whereas Rousseau in the *Discourse* supposes that in advanced market relations characterised by extensive material inequality we cannot help but be driven by status and vanity concerns to endlessly pursue consumer goods in a never-ending cycle of competitive psychological self-harm, Smith disagrees. The entire thrust of *TMS* IV.1 is to encourage us *not* to be like the poor man's son, indicating that Smith thinks we are capable of resisting the siren song of endless consumption, at least to some adequate degree.

Third, Smith denies Rousseau's claim that because natural pity is suppressed in conditions of enflamed *amour propre* due to rampant consumption, so our vanity necessarily issues in zero-sum status competition. On the contrary, Smith makes it central to his moral psychology that our capacity for sympathy enables us to take *pleasure* in the pleasures of others – including their social status – and hence our social interactions are not necessarily zero-sum. Smith, following Hume, is clear that human beings tend to love and esteem the wealthy and powerful, rather than being competitively provoked, or psychologically harmed, by their superior standing, and that we willingly in turn defer to superiors on the basis of opinion-based natural authority (*TMS* I.iii.2.1; *WN* V.i.b.11; Sagar, 2018b, chaps. 3 and 5). Indeed, one of the reasons we are vain about our material possessions is precisely because other people take pleasure in looking at those possessions and imagining the utility they are a means to, and we in turn take pleasure from knowing that they are taking pleasure in looking at us and our material assets. The psychology of vanity as filtered through consumption is not only, for Smith, primarily predicated on the quirk of rationality (not status competition), but insofar as vanity enters the picture it is often a mutually complementary process whereby we elevate each other rather than, as Rousseau supposes, constantly doing each other down.

Rather than taking over Rousseau's concerns and recycling them in his own name, but sheepishly apologising for the evils of inequality because on balance the poor are made better off than they otherwise would be, Smith is saying something else. He is saying that Rousseau's concerns are *ill-founded*. Not only is Rousseau wrong about what motivates most economic consumption, he is also wrong about the effects of this consumption on the psychologies of ordinary people. Smith is *denying* that material inequalities necessarily lead to relational inequalities in the way that Rousseau claims. Precisely because most consumption is motivated by the quirk of rationality, not vanity, and because we take pleasure via sympathy in the riches of others and admire them for it (as they do towards us), there is no necessary link between inequality of material holdings and inequality of relations. Smith denies that we are living in the unhappy situation dramatically depicted in the *Second Discourse*. Our condition is altogether more benign, even if, from a detached philosophical perspective, it is still peculiar because founded upon the operations of a more-or-less ubiquitous deception.

This is not to say that Smith thinks relational inequality therefore does not matter, or is a non-problem. Far from it. An abiding feature of his thought is his condemnation of domination, and his advocating for political arrangements which protect the weak from the depredations of the powerful, which in practice typically *does* mean securing the poor from the ravages of the rich, who typically use their material advantages to exploit and dominate the poor (Luban, 2012; Sagar, 2021b, 2022, chaps. 2 and 5). Yet Smith thinks that the best way to achieve *that* is to establish the meaningful rule of law as a safeguard for all against domination, rather than to try and reduce material inequality. So long as the rule of law protects individuals from domination, the mere fact that some have greater material holdings than others does not automatically, on Smith's picture, generate troublesome relational inequality. This is because the functioning of sympathy entails the positive-, not zero-, sum nature of consumption in a well-ordered polity, which is anyway mostly motivated not by a desire for status, but by our preoccupation with acquiring the means of utility. Consumption again emerges as much more benign in its relational effects than Rousseau supposes. Of course, one may not be persuaded by this, but it is Smith's position.

The contrast with Rousseau thus reinforces, rather than undermines, the conclusion that Smith in *TMS* is best characterised as sufficientarian, not egalitarian. So long as one has sufficient material holdings to secure ease of body and peace of mind, and is fortunate enough to reside in a political locale where the rule of law and the regular administration of justice secure one from domination by the more powerful, Smith offers no reason to think that concomitant material inequality *ipso facto* generates relational inequality. From his perspective, there is no (relational) egalitarian case for greater material equality to answer. To be sure, from the perspective of the contemporary liberal-egalitarian left Smith's picture is liable to look woefully incomplete, given what we now know about how the formal rule of law tends *not* to be sufficient, by itself, to secure the weak and poor from domination, absent further meaningful social measures (e.g. Shklar, 1990; Waldron, 1993). But that is a distinct matter, and it ought hardly to be a surprise that a thinker of the eighteenth century failed to anticipate the concerns of post-war liberal-egalitarians.

On Smith's view, dealing with relational inequality emerges as a problem *not* directly caused by inequalities of material holdings themselves, and in turn not appropriately targeted by any form of egalitarian solution with respect to material distributions. At the societal level, Smith thinks that the problem of relational inequality is ultimately caused by the *libido dominandi*, the urge of humans to try and dominate others (Luban, 2012), and not the mere presence of material inequality. Of course, those who seek to dominate others will likely seek to employ differentials of material holdings as a *means* to enact their domination. In which case, material inequality would certainly be of concern to Smith (as it evidently is, throughout *LJ* and the historical sections of *WN*). But the problem in such cases isn't material inequality *per se*, nor its direct effects on the moral sentiments of relevant agents, but the use such inequality is being put to in a particular context, namely the domination of the weak by the strong. The relation between material inequality and domination is for Smith contingent upon wider social circumstance, which he seems to think can be effectively mitigated in conditions of modernity in a way Rousseau expressly denies. If domination is sufficiently controlled via the rule of law in a well-ordered political structure, Smith indicates that material inequality might safely proceed without deleterious effects in terms of relational inequality necessarily following, so long as those with less have enough to secure their material and social standing.

Smith's position suggests that if one is suffering psychologically under conditions of material inequality, the solution lies not in targeting the material inequality itself, but in one's psychological response to it. *TMS* is in part a guide for how best to achieve psychological balance in the extremely taxing context of having to live permanently in the gaze of others (be they richer than us or otherwise). This culminates in Smith's injunction that the goal of a healthy ethical life (which, for him, is *pari passu* a healthy psychological life) is to seek to be praiseworthy, rather than merely praised (*TMS* III.2.1–35). Praiseworthiness is, however, not a function of material holdings, but of one's psychological calibration and public comportment. Again the result is sufficientarian in implication: so long as one has enough to secure ease of body and peace of mind – which in practice means learning as far as possible to live for praiseworthiness rather than praise – so one must also avoid the trap of the poor man's son, and not become besotted with the means of utility, nor be preoccupied with the standing of the great and wealthy, but instead focus on one's personal psychological calibration. The correct solution to personal distress under conditions of material inequality no more lies in advocating for greater material equality (however moderate), than in trying to become rich. Despite attacking the problem from opposite directions, so to speak, both these responses are, from Smith's perspective, founded upon the same confusion: of thinking that the means of utility can make us contented. And again, note the sufficientarian implication: so long as you have enough, *it doesn't matter* if others have more when it comes to material distributions (provided they aren't using that inequality as a means for enacting domination), because it isn't making them any happier, let alone more praiseworthy.[2]

9.4 The Personal versus the Political

Smith in *TMS* offers a sufficientarian, rather than egalitarian, perspective. He urges us to accept that happiness is a function of personal psychological calibration, not total or relative material holdings (at least above some sufficient threshold), and what matters is not having the same as everyone else, nor having more than them, but having enough to achieve contentedness *regardless* of what others have. In this regard, the tendency (and I take it, the intended function) of *TMS* is therapeutic: Smith's message is one about how to live better in a world of material inequality, where the great deception that created that inequality (the effects of the quirk of rationality) also threatens to trick us into adopting the folly of the poor man's son.

---

[2] It may be objected that I focus here unduly on *TMS* Part IV at the expense of Part I, where Smith may appear to take an entirely more Rousseau-like position. For reasons of space I cannot address this matter here, but for relevant considerations as to why Smith is not agreeing with Rousseau in Part I any more than in Part IV, see Sagar (2022, chaps. 3 and 4).

Yet *TMS* has effectively nothing to say on the wider *political* implications of inequality, especially in terms of what governments might do (or not do) about it when it arises as a social phenomenon. And this ought not to be especially surprising. As Robin Douglass argues in this volume, despite recent commentary tending to read *TMS* as a primarily political intervention, one centrally preoccupied with defending something called 'commercial society', this is a serious distortion. *TMS* is overwhelmingly and primarily a work of ethics, focused on both explaining the form and content of moral life, and also offering suggestions for how to live well: ultimately, to seek praiseworthiness and not mere praise, and where those categories are understood as constructed out of the purely naturalistic functioning of our shared sentiments. Smith, to be sure, offers penetrating reflections on political matters at certain key points (e.g. *TMS* VI.ii.I). But his aim in *TMS* is not to guide social policy, nor to indicate how legislators might tackle any particular question. This is significant, insofar as it is not obvious, and certainly not necessarily the case, that individual-level responses to distributive questions are isomorphic with social-level ones. Whilst it may be that *as an individual* one agrees with Smith in *TMS* that what matters is sufficiency, not equality, it is an open question whether *as a social policy* one thinks some kind of egalitarianism might still be preferable to some comparative non-egalitarian arrangement.

For example, Martin O'Neill has argued that the most plausible forms of egalitarian theory are *non-intrinsic*: that what renders them persuasive (or not) is their connection to substantive normative goods, and not just the brute fact of equality in-and-of-itself (O'Neill, 2008; cf. Brooke, 2020, pp. 1407–1408). Specifically, that egalitarian theories are most plausible when seen as a way of delivering improved well-being (however conceived) to relevant individuals, which they would lack under conditions of comparable inequality.[3] By contrast, if egalitarianism is conceived of as *merely arithmetic* – as detached from the social and political situations in which (in)equality matters in substantive ways to people's lives – then it is at the very least implausible, and perhaps even unintelligible, as a normative ideal. Yet as O'Neill makes clear, what motivates leading non-intrinsic egalitarian theories, such as those of John Rawls and Thomas Scanlon, is precisely what motivated Rousseau: a concern with the allegedly deleterious effects of material inequality in terms of status competition as refracted through competitive *amour propre*, and the resulting instantiation of social domination and illegitimate hierarchy that are thought to result. O'Neill distils the point down very precisely when he suggests that

---

[3] Importantly, certain forms of equality may *themselves* be a factor in what counts as improved well-being, in which case a non-intrinsic egalitarian theory is not merely *instrumental*, not just a means to something else. It must, however, ultimately make reference to something else, besides mere equality in-and-of-itself, in order for the value of equality to make sense as a value.

non-intrinsic egalitarianism makes central what he calls "an egalitarian conception of *amour propre*", one which holds that "self-respect is inconsistent with living under conditions of domination, or of being under the arbitrary power of others", hence why he identifies non-intrinsic egalitarianism as "itself a Rousseauvian position" (O'Neill, 2008, pp. 128, 129n28). Crucially, O'Neill contends that it is a "deep social fact" that greater material equality is usually both necessary and sufficient to avoid "domination and stigmatizing differences in status" which are "offensive to the dignity and standing of human agents" (O'Neill, 2008, p. 30; Jubb, 2015, p. 681). It follows that non-intrinsic egalitarians have reason to advocate for greater equality of material conditions.

What bearing does *TMS* have on these matters? On the one hand, Smith calls into question the urgency of the call for non-intrinsic egalitarianism that O'Neill puts forward. In particular, by rejecting Rousseau's account of what motivates economic consumption, of its effects on our psychological calibration, and by positing the possibility of legitimate hierarchy amidst inequality as a function of natural authority (Sagar, 2018b, chap. 5). Smith suggests that O'Neill's "deep social fact" may not be as deep, or as worrisome, as the latter supposes. Inequality may not always be as bad, for non-intrinsic reasons, as Rousseauvian theorists are apt to presume.

On the other hand, it does not follow that Smith's sufficientarian considerations *rule out* the kinds of concerns that O'Neill highlights as central to non-intrinsic egalitarianism. One way of seeing this is to consider the different responses it is appropriate to offer an individual *qua* individual from, for example, the position of friendship, versus individual *qua* member of a political group in conditions of social contestation. Suppose a friend bemoans the fact that they make less money than others in their social circle, and that this is a source of personal unhappiness. It might be quite appropriate to give them a copy of *TMS*, urge them to take on board the lessons of Part IV, and avoid falling into the pitfalls of the poor man's son: 'Money won't make you happy!' is sometimes good advice, provided that the other person does in fact have enough at present, and assuming that you stand in the right kind of relationship to them when saying such things. By contrast, if somebody is worried that their child does not have access to a good school because their family is unable to afford to buy a house in an area which has good schools – or indeed buy a house at all, say because inequities in the property market accruing over several decades have effectively excluded lower-income households from being able to purchase houses, leaving them in precarious rental accommodation – then offering them a copy of *TMS* with the words 'Money won't make you (or your child) happy!' is not just inappropriate, but potentially insulting. It might be true that material assets alone won't make one happy, and that in our personal lives we generally do best to reconcile ourselves to what we currently have. Yet nothing necessarily follows from that about how to evaluate the social implications of inequalities, nor how we ought properly to register and respond to the concerns voiced by those negatively affected by them. Smith may be right that everyone would be better off if they adopted the outlook he urges in *TMS* Part IV. But that doesn't change the fact (as Smith himself points out in *TMS* I.iii.3) that most people *won't* adopt this perspective, and hence when it comes to politics we have to work with that fact rather than just imagining it away, or dismissing it via high-handed reflection on what we deem the correct form of the good life to be. Furthermore, what *governments* should do about such inequalities – and the political pressures that arise from them – is a further, obviously political, and enormously complex, question, and one that *TMS* simply does not offer us help in answering.

A related concern is that over time inequality is likely to interfere with sufficiency, insofar as those with more tend to concentrate that advantage and exclude those with less, precisely by using their material advantage to politically rig the system in their own favour, compounding inequality over time (Phillips, 2021, pp. 78–85). One potential – and experience indicates, likely – consequence of this is that it becomes harder for those at the bottom of the social pile to secure enough for happiness, because they find themselves living in a system increasingly structured against them. But as a result, one might turn out to have individual-level sufficientarian motivations for adopting societal-level egalitarian political measures, if the latter turns out to be required for realising the former. This is to a significant degree an empirical question, but then the point is that such matters cannot be settled via ethical reflection regarding the psychology of individuals alone.

Smith's position in *TMS* is thus *indeterminate* on questions of how we ought to view social policy. One may follow Smith in being a sufficientarian in one's private life, whilst adopting non-intrinsic egalitarianism in one's politics, or indeed some other distributive outlook entirely. Again, this ought not to be especially surprising. *TMS* is a work of ethics, not of government or social policy, and furthermore one written in the eighteenth century, that is before modern questions of distributive justice really got going following the rise of mass industrial capitalism, the enormous increase in the capacity of the modern state and its ability to provide welfare, the emergence of social phenomena like trade unions movements, and new collectivist ideological outlooks that arose partly in response to dramatic social change, but also in contestation with the increasingly dominant ideology of liberalism (Heath, 2020, pp. 116–148). Yet when we turn to that portion of Smith's corpus that *was* concerned with questions of government and social policy, what we find in *WN* is that Smith is primarily concerned with relieving the suffering of the poor in absolute terms, not their standing relative to other more advantaged social groups. This again points in the direction of Smith being better categorised as a sufficientarian, rather than an egalitarian, in distributive matters, although there is no space to make the case here (nonetheless, see *WN* V.i.f.).

Although Smith can certainly help us to sharpen our thoughts on some of the matters involved, recent efforts to claim him as a resource for the modern egalitarian left are insufficiently sensitive to the considerable difficulties involved in doing so. Those difficulties are inherent not just to the complexity of Smith's thought, as well as the historical distance that separates his context from ours, but to what is at stake when we are thinking about the demands of equality, and the truth – which it seems to me to be – that we should not expect private morality to neatly correlate with, nor straightforwardly translate into, politics.

10

Narrowing the Scope of Resentment in Smith's *Theory of Moral Sentiments*

JOHN T. SCOTT AND MICHELLE SCHWARZE

For Adam Smith, resentment is the essential feeling that motivates our concern for justice, which is in turn "the main pillar that upholds the whole edifice" of society (*TMS* II.ii.3.4).[1] But resentment is also a problematic passion in several ways. In this chapter we examine Smith's account in *TMS* of resentment in relation to justice, specifically analyzing how Smith attempts to restrict the proper expression of resentment to a similarly restricted conception of justice and injustice. Smith follows the school of modern natural jurisprudence stemming from Grotius in narrowing the scope of justice properly speaking to injuries to persons, property, and reputation. Smith's main innovation with regard to his treatment of justice is the way in which he situates our reactions to injustice understood as injury within his theory of moral spectatorship. Resentment is the natural passion we feel at experiencing or witnessing injustice and thus the basis for our natural sense of justice, according to Smith, but it is also an unruly passion that needs to be "humbled" to be considered proper by any impartial observer. Unfortunately, as Smith recognizes, we often seem to become resentful about things other than injustice, such as ingratitude, developing an excessive and improper resentment on Smith's terms. What is his argument for restricting justifiable resentment given his seeming admission that we do naturally feel resentment beyond the case of injury? To what extent is Smith successful in providing a rationale for restricting resentment within his theory of moral spectatorship?

We begin with a brief review of Smith's conceptions of justice and injustice, focusing on how he narrows the scope of justice to cases of injury and how he develops categories established in the natural law tradition. Then we turn to Smith's description of the role of resentment as the natural passion that motivates us to act in response to injuries we experience or witness, as well as how he incorporates resentment into his theory of moral spectatorship. While scholars have noted how the impartial spectator leads us to "humble" excessive indignation (Darwall, 1999, 2004; Griswold, 1999; Schwarze and Scott, 2015; Schwarze, 2020), we are more concerned here with the

---

[1] All references are to *TMS* unless otherwise specified.

phenomenon of improper resentment, which is not limited to injustice and therefore which should not be considered resentment on Smith's account. Yet Smith acknowledges that we might nevertheless feel "resentment" in various situations in which there is no injury, and not only as a descriptive matter but also in a seemingly normatively appropriate manner.

Since Smith himself never directly addresses why such resentments are inappropriate according to his own account of propriety (especially if we can imagine an impartial spectator might reasonably be expected to sympathize with them), we reconstruct a response drawn from his moral psychology and social theory. First, we explain the origins of Smith's narrow view of justice, which is drawn from the modern jurisprudential tradition. We then turn to Smith's account of resentment, explaining its purpose as the natural motive for narrow justice, but also questioning the split between Smith's descriptive and normative accounts of resentment. We ultimately argue that resentment's logical tie to punishment for Smith is a necessary but not sufficient one, and that injury and resentment are separate conditions required to justify punishment. Finally, we reconstruct Smith's normative justifications for severing the tie between improper resentments and punishment and limiting the propriety of resentment, arguing that Smith's reasons for doing so are driven by his claims about our equal status and about sociability.

10.1 Narrowing Justice: Smith and the School of Natural Jurisprudence

Smith's discussion of justice in *TMS* has produced some bewilderment because of the narrow scope he gives to the virtue despite its role as "the main pillar that upholds the whole edifice" of society (II.ii.3.4). He explains:

> Mere justice is, upon most occasions, but a negative virtue, and only hinders us from hurting our neighbour. The man who barely abstains from violating either the person, or the estate, or the reputation of his neighbours, has surely very little positive merit. He fulfills, however, all the rules of what is peculiarly called justice, and does every thing which his equals can with propriety force him to do,of which they can punish him for not doing. We may often fulfill all the rules of justice by sitting still and doing nothing.
>
> (II.ii.1.10)

In writing here of what is "peculiarly called justice," Smith signals that he is intentionally narrowing the definition and scope of justice from its possible broader meanings and applications, especially as compared to the classical tradition that emphasizes distributive justice. Many interpreters take Smith's discussion of mere justice to be the final word on the matter: justice is strictly negative (e.g., Winch, 1992, pp. 109–112; Smith, 2013b; Smith and Wilson, 2019, pp. 13–14).

Smith reveals his intentional narrowing of justice later in *TMS* when he discusses Plato's theory of moral virtue, which he attributes to Aristotle and the Scholastics as well (see VII.ii.1.4; VII.ii.1.12–14). He explains that while he has so far only discussed justice understood as the abstention from "any positive harm" of another's person, estate, or reputation, there is "another sense" of justice that positively demands that "we conceived for [our neighbor] all that love, respect, and esteem, which his character, his situation, and his connection with ourselves, render suitable and proper for us to feel, and unless we act accordingly." The first sense is what is called "commutative justice" by Aristotle and the Scholastics, and *justitia expletrix* by Grotius, whereas the second is what Grotius referred to as *justitia attributrix* "which consists in proper beneficence" and which "comprehends all the social virtues" (VII. ii.1.11). In other words, Smith's division of the virtues into justice and beneficence (II.ii.1) apportions justice as understood by the tradition of moral and political philosophy into two categories, one of which is "peculiarly called justice" and the other of which consists of beneficence.

A brief glance at the background of Smith's narrowing of justice to what is "peculiarly called justice" in the modern natural law tradition will help illuminate his reasons for adopting this narrow sense. Smith employs Grotius's distinctions when he splits the classical conception of justice into justice and beneficence, since Smith develops his teaching concerning jurisprudence by borrowing categories and terminology from the modern natural law tradition, even if he is not strictly a natural law thinker himself (Haakonssen, 1996). At the very end of *TMS*, when announcing his promised but never delivered treatise on jurisprudence, Smith states that Grotius seems to have been the first to attempt to outline a systematic theory of natural jurisprudence (VII.iv.37). Despite the "imperfections" in his theory, Smith signals his future discourse would follow in Grotius's footsteps, a suggestion made explicit in the surviving student lecture notes of *LJ*. Indeed, the second set of collected lecture notes open with an immediate reference to Grotius, in which Smith reiterates his claim about Grotius's innovations (and his imperfections) before explaining that injury is central to his "compleat system of jurisprudence," as seeking redress for injury was the cause of just war (*LJ*(B) 1–2).

Most importantly for our purposes, Grotius first articulates the narrow understanding of justice that Smith later adopts, as he establishes the perfect-imperfect rights distinction foundational for natural law theory at least through Kant. Grotius's distinction comes as part of an engagement with Aristotle in which he effectively puts old wine into new bottles, although not without the exercise of some force and not without spillage. "'Tis expletive Justice, Justice properly and strictly taken, which respects the Faculty, or perfect Right," he explains, narrowing justice to its proper and strict sense. He goes on to align this sense of justice somewhat uneasily with Aristotle's "corrective justice" and its "commutative" nature. Most importantly, the violation of perfect rights or non-fulfillment of perfect duties are enforceable by law. On the other hand, "imperfect" rights and duties comprehend virtues that are "beneficial" to others, such as liberality, mercy, and prudence. Grotius suggests imperfect rights and duties align with Aristotle's "distributive" justice, and are geometric or proportional, but whose observance is strictly voluntary (Grotius, 2005, pp. 143–145 [*De juri belli ac pacis*, I.i.8–9]). Motivating Grotius's distinction between perfect and imperfect rights is their enforceability and a consideration of the public good. Grotius, along with Pufendorf and other modern natural law theorists, sees violations of perfect rights as enforceable by law: one primary purpose of law, much like war, is to remedy those injuries done that hurt the public good in some way (2005, p. 972 [*De juri belli ac pacis*, II.xx.7–9]). As Smith characterizes this tradition in LJ, "so far, say they, as publick utility requires, so far we consent to the punishment of the criminall, and that this is the naturall intention of all punishments" (LJ(A) ii.91). Put differently, it is useful to society to punish violations of perfect rights like justice, whereas it is not useful or harmful to society to punish imperfect rights violations. We will return to this point below, as it will help illuminate some of the "imperfections" Smith saw in Grotius's theory.

Smith refers to another theorist in the modern natural law tradition, Lord Kames, and he does so precisely when he adopts and explains his definition of justice narrowly defined. Smith appeals to Kames after claiming that the "proper object of resentment" is "injury," noting that Kames (evidently the target, though Smith does not name him) insisted in this "remarkable distinction between justice and all the other social virtues" (II.ii.1.5). In his discussion of duty and obligation in the *Essays on the Principles of Morality and Natural Religion*, Kames argues that justice should be distinguished from other virtues because it alone is socially integral and thus enforceable: "benevolence and generosity are more beautiful, and more attractive of love and esteem, than justice. Yet, not being necessary to the support of society, they are left upon the general footing of approbatory pleasure; while justice, faith, trust, without which society cannot subsist, are objects of the foregoing peculiar sense, to take away all shadow of liberty, and to put us under a necessity of performance" (Kames, 2005, p. 33). Like Smith after him, then, Kames refers to justice in the "peculiar" sense. Eschewing the language of perfect and imperfect rights and duties found in Grotius and others, Kames instead terms justice a "primary" duty and benevolence and such other virtues "secondary" duties. Like Grotius, Kames insists that law and punishment is restricted to issues of justice and cannot be extended to benevolence and other similar virtues. He writes: "justice is enforced by natural sanctions of the most effectual kind, by which it becomes law in the strictest sense, a law that never can be transgressed with impunity. To extend this law to generosity and the other secondary virtues, and to make these our duty, would produce an inconsistency in human nature. It would make universal benevolence a strict duty, to which the limited capacity and more limited abilities of man, bear no proportion. Generosity, therefore, heroism, and all the extraordinary exertions of virtue, must be left to our own choice, without annexing any punishment to the forebearance" (Kames, 2005, pp. 38–39). When he references Kames, Smith paraphrases this very passage and insists that we must "carefully distinguish what is only blamable, or the proper object of disapprobation, from what force may be employed either to punish or to prevent," with lack of proper beneficence, for example, being blameworthy but not punishable (II.ii.1.6). To this degree, then, Smith follows Kames (and Grotius). Nonetheless, he does not adopt Kames' appeal to an innate moral sense motivating our concern with justice. Instead, he innovates by basing this prohibition on his account of the natural sentiment that drives us to punish injustice – resentment – and on an understanding of human beings as juridically equal.

In sum, then, in treating justice in its narrow or "peculiar" sense, Smith expressly follows the modern natural law school beginning with Grotius and comprising other thinkers, such as Pufendorf, whom he discusses in his treatments of jurisprudence, and also including Kames. Since we do not possess his planned treatise on the subject, we do not know how he might have transformed this tradition in whole or part. What matters for our present purposes is the fact that in *TMS* he adopts the narrow sense of justice developed in this tradition, and that he does so without comment much less defense. In analyzing how he brings a narrow meaning of justice together with a narrow conception of proper resentment, then, we have to take the "peculiar" sense of justice he embraces as given.

10.2 Bringing in Resentment

In Smith's theory, resentment is the passion that undergirds our concern with injustice, both with regard to the anger experienced by the victim of injustice and with regard to the indignation raised in a spectator. His originality in this respect is to marry a narrow sense of justice adopted from the modern natural law tradition with an account of resentment as a passion that motivates us to be concerned with justice. As we shall see, the marriage is not always an easy one.

10.2.1 Resentment and Moral Spectatorship

The importance of resentment in Smith's theory of moral sentiments is evident from the prominent position it plays in his presentation of the theory. Two textual features indicate this importance. The first is when Smith first defines "sympathy" near the outset of *TMS*, expanding its scope to account for our reactions to and judgments of the disagreeable passions, resentment chief among them. "Pity and compassion are words appropriated to signify our fellow-feeling with the sorrow of others. Sympathy, though its means was, perhaps, originally the same, may now, however, without much impropriety, be made use of to denote our fellow-feeling with any passion whatever" (I.i.1.5). These passions include our fellow-feeling with "disagreeable" passions, including anger and resentment (I.i.1.7; I.i.2.3). The second indication of resentment's importance in his account is the fact that the first use of the term "the impartial spectator" occurs when discussing the "most detestable" expression of unchecked anger as opposed to our entering into sympathy with properly expressed resentment: "But we admire that noble and generous resentment which governs its pursuit of the greatest injuries, not by the rage which they are apt to excite in the breast of the sufferer, but by the indignation which they naturally call forth in that of the impartial spectator . . ." (I.i.5.4). Resentment will nonetheless prove to be a difficult passion for Smith to work with in his theory of moral spectatorship.

Two difficulties regarding resentment are already hinted at in the passage quoted earlier where Smith first uses the term "the impartial spectator." First, there is the disagreeable character of resentment, especially in its immoderate expression, and thus the need to temper the passion for a spectator or the impartial spectator to enter into sympathy with it. Second, there is Smith's assertion of the strict connection between resentment and injury or injustice, leading to the challenge of limiting the unruly passion to the case of injustice. Since both difficulties are also present in Smith's main source for emphasizing resentment as the motivational spur for our concern with injustice, Joseph Butler, a brief look at his predecessor's treatment of resentment will help us identify what is unique about Smith's incorporation of resentment within his theory of moral spectatorship.

Butler's *Fifteen Sermons Preached at the Rolls Chapel*, and some other writings, offered a method of inquiring into morals that focused on human nature "from a matter of fact, namely, what the particular nature of man is, its several parts, their economy or constitution" (Butler, 2017, p. 5). Hume terms this the "experimental" approach to morals, citing Butler as an exemplar. As for Smith, he indicates Butler's influence both in his general approach and in his treatment of resentment when he states, speaking of resentment, that "the present inquiry is not concerning a matter of right, if I may say so, but concerning a matter of fact" (II.i.4.6 n.). Butler takes up resentment in the eighth and ninth sermons, beginning with a warning that he takes resentment to be a natural passion, a fact of nature, and suggests that it must have been implanted in mankind by the deity for a purpose, as a defense against injustice in this imperfect world. Recognizing the potentially unruly character of the passion, Butler distinguishes between two sorts of resentment: "hasty and sudden" and "settled and deliberate." The hasty sort is unmitigated anger, which seems to be instinctual, and while it may serve a purpose of defense against harm, it must be tempered. As for "deliberate anger or resentment," it is a moderated form of indignation directed against injury or injustice, and not mere harm, and "raises indignation, somewhat of a desire that it should be punished." He explains: "The indignation raised by cruelty and injustice, and the desire of having it punished, which persons unconcerned would feel, is by no means malice. No; it is resentment against vice and wickedness; it is one of the common bonds, by which society is held together." Butler acknowledges that such indignation sometimes "rises too high, and is beyond proportion to the particular ill actions it is exercised upon," largely due to how our partiality for ourselves tends to magnify the injury. His counsel for tempering resentment seems to be one of humility. As for the scope of proper resentment, while he does generally speak of resentment in relation to injustice, Butler sometimes seems to apply it to immoral actions more generally. For example, in the passage quoted earlier, he describes it as "resentment against vice and wickedness," and somewhat later he writes: "indignation against vice and wickedness is, and may be allowed to be, a balance to that weakness of pity, and also to anything else which would prevent the necessary methods of severity" (Butler, 2017, pp. 69–73). For Butler it seems that proper resentment, both in terms of its expression and object, requires a balance between a potential weakness in our nature seen in misapplied pity for our fellows, on the one hand, and the opposite weakness of our propensity to too much self-regard or pride, on the other. Smith will agree with Butler that resentment needs to be humbled, but he also emphatically confines proper resentment to matters of injustice understood as injury alone.

Smith takes up resentment thematically within the section of *TMS* in which he discusses our judgments of merit and demerit, and hence reward and punishment. Our reaction to merit is gratitude, which prompts us to reward, and our reaction to demerit is resentment, which "directly prompts us to punish." The difficulties in this process are suggested by the title of the second chapter in the section: "Of the *proper* objects of gratitude and resentment" (II.i.2, emphasis supplied). Restricting ourselves to resentment, the ways in which the passion can surpass its "proper" bounds are expressed most fully by Smith in a note he adds to the very end of the section. Concluding the main text by describing the "sympathetic indignation which naturally boils up in the breast of the spectator, whenever he thoroughly brings home to himself the case of the sufferer" (II.i.5.6), Smith adds a lengthy note in which he defends his embrace of resentment and in which he also reveals his debt to Butler. "To ascribe in this manner our natural sense of the ill desert of human actions to a sympathy with the resentment of the sufferer, may seem, to the greater part of people, to be a degradation of that sentiment," he begins: "Resentment is commonly regarded as so odious a passion, that they will be apt to think it impossible that so laudable a principle, as the sense of the ill desert of vice, should in any respect be founded upon it." In response, and following Butler, Smith asks the reader to distinguish between proper and excessive resentment:

resentment when it is "properly humbled and entirely brought down to the sympathetic indignation of the spectator" and the "rude and undisciplined impulse of resentment" that is not moderated and provokes the "excess" of revenge. Likewise following Butler, Smith explains that the present inquiry "is not concerning a matter of right, if I may say so, but a matter of fact" (II.i.5.6.n.). To what degree he further follows Butler by explaining resentment as being a necessary part of the plan of Nature or the Author of Nature is beyond the scope of the present inquiry (but see Schwarze and Scott, 2015). Resentment for Smith is a fact of our nature, and the challenge for him is how we can temper the unruly passion using the resources of our better nature.

Central to Smith's solution to tempering the expression of resentment is the impartial spectator. Returning to the chapter in which he first addresses the "proper" objects of gratitude and resentment, he writes: "But these, as well as all the other passions of human nature, seem proper and are approved of, when the heart of every impartial spectator entirely sympathizes with them" (II.ii.1.1–2). The distance between our initial fury at witnessing injustice and especially in experiencing it ourselves and the moderated expression of the passion that enables others to sympathize with our passion is bridged by the process of spectatorship. Discussing the "unsocial passions" of hatred and anger, Smith explains that resentment must be "humbled" for someone to be able to sympathize with it due to the distance between the fury of the original passion felt by the injured party and the necessarily lesser degree of resentment capable of being experienced by a spectator. "Before resentment, therefore, can become graceful and agreeable, it must be more humbled and brought down below that pitch to which it would naturally rise, than almost any other passion" (I.ii.3.1). The language of "humbling" used by Smith suggests that the process of lowering the pitch of our expression of resentment means moving from our initial self-concern with the injury, which is liable to be partial and exaggerated, to seeing our injury through the eyes of others, including ultimately the impartial spectator, and moderating our expression accordingly. If we succeed in this process, we bring about a proportionate accord between the extent of injury we have experienced, our expression of our resentment toward it, and the sympathetic resentment we elicit in another. "As the greater and more irreparable the evil that is done, the resentment of the sufferer runs naturally higher; so does likewise the sympathetic indignation of the spectator" (II.ii.2.3). This proportionality between injury and resentment will provide the sympathetic foundation on which Smith will build his treatment of justice.

10.2.2 Resentment and Justice

Smith first establishes the connection between resentment and justice in his introductory discussion in Part 2 of *TMS*, "Of Merit and Demerit," highlighting resentment's intimate connection with punishment: "The sentiment which most immediately and directly prompts us to reward, is gratitude; that which most immediately and directly prompts us to punish, is resentment ... To reward, is to recompense, to remunerate, to return good for good received. To punish, too, is to recompense, to remunerate, though in a different manner; it is to return evil for evil that is done" (II.i.1.2, 4). To anticipate, we see Smith following Grotius in this initial passage by separating the ancient understanding of justice into two distinct sets of virtue, and in the process excising ingratitude at beneficence from the proper scope of resentment and justice.

However uncomfortable we might be with the tie between resentment and justice, Smith insists that the link is useful because resentment prompts punishment. He claims in no uncertain terms that "the very existence of society requires that unmerited and unprovoked malice should be restrained by proper punishments; and consequently, that to inflict those punishments should be regarded as a proper and laudable action" (II.i.5.6 n.). Although Smith categorizes resentment as an "unsocial passion," in part because it is "disagreeable" for individuals to experience, he calls resentment and indignation the "guardians of justice" and useful because they make injury costly and therefore deter it (I.ii.3–4). In other words, an "unsocial passion" is paradoxically the cement of the pillar upholding society. Resentment thereby fulfils "the favourite ends of nature" of self-preservation and propagation of the species (II.i.5.6 n.). Nevertheless, as we explore more in the next section, Smith seems wary enough of resentment such that he insists it "seems to have been given to us by nature for defence, and for defence only," signaling his interest in restricting the proper scope of resentment (II.ii.1.4).

After fully articulating his controversial claim that resentment is good because it makes injury – and thus injustice (II.ii.1.9; *LJ*(A) i.1–4) – less likely, Smith finally begins to explain his narrowing of the scope of justice in section 2 of Part II of *TMS*, a section devoted to its uniqueness as a virtue. He makes this logic clear by contrasting justice and beneficence, both of which were traditionally subsumed in the broader ancient conception of justice:

> There is, however, another virtue, of which the observance is not left to the freedom of our own wills, which may be extorted by force, and of which the violation exposes to resentment, and consequently to punishment. This virtue is justice: the violation of justice is injury: it does real and positive hurt to some particular persons, from motives which are naturally disapproved of. It is, therefore, the proper object of resentment, and of punishment, which is the natural consequence of resentment. As mankind go along with, and approve of the violence employed to avenge the hurt which is done by injustice ...
>
> (II.ii.1.5)

Key to Smith's argument are three things. First, what he identifies as the *proper object* of resentment is "injury," namely, something that does "real and positive hurt to some particular persons" (or their property or reputation) and something that is done "from motives which are naturally disapproved of." As Smith later states, "upon *this* is founded that remarkable distinction between justice and all the other social virtues," noting that the origin of the limit of proper objects of justice is what "mankind" can approve of or, elsewhere, of what the "impartial spectator" can go along with (see II.ii.2.2; emphasis supplied). Second, resentment is the appropriate reaction to either suffering or witnessing such an injury. Third, punishment is the "natural consequence" of resentment. The apparently necessary connection between resentment and punishment is asserted at the beginning of the passage, when Smith states that the violation of justice "exposes to resentment, and *consequently* to punishment," and at the end of the passage, where he writes that injury is "the proper object of punishment, which is the natural *consequence* of resentment." In other words, resentment is appropriate because, antecedently, there has been "real and positive hurt" or "injury" and because, consequently, "mankind" or the impartial spectator approves of the punishment or vengeance for the injury.

Unfortunately, Smith leaves the first and last steps of his argument relatively undefended. He never explains why resentment couldn't be the proper reaction to something that is not injurious to someone but nonetheless still hurtful, especially if an impartial spectator is wont to sympathize with such resentment. Likewise, he does not clarify why resentment necessarily leads to punishment. In the passage quoted above, the apparent logic is: (1) an injury has occurred; (2) we react to the injury with resentment; (3) such resentment "consequently" leads to punishment. If we do experience resentment in cases not involving injury, and especially if doing so is justified, then it does not seem to follow that such resentment necessarily entails punishment. We take up the question of the scope of proper resentment in the next section. For now, we propose that a slight reconstruction of his argument concerning the relationship among injury, resentment, and punishment makes better sense of his logic. Namely, if we think of resentment as a necessary but not sufficient condition for punishment, and instead consider resentment as justifying punishment *if and only* a positive injury has occurred, then injury and resentment together are jointly sufficient for punishment. We turn now to his arguments for restricting the scope of resentment.

10.3 Narrowing the Scope of Resentment

Smith's attempt to limit the scope of resentment parallels his narrowing the scope of justice, as he similarly jettisons broader concerns with distributive injustice and other cases not involving injury from its circle of propriety. In his thematic discussion of beneficence and justice, Smith begins by comparing the two virtues. He initially presents the two virtues by using a parallel construction. On the one side, he states that actions of beneficence done from proper motives "seem alone to require reward; because such alone are the approved objects of gratitude, or excite the sympathetic gratitude of the spectator." On the other side, actions of "a hurtful tendency" done from improper motives "seem alone to deserve punishment," once again "because such alone are the approved objects of resentment, or excite the sympathetic resentment of the spectator" (II.ii.1.1–2). Or, as he summarizes later, "proper resentment for injustice attempted, or actually committed, is the only motive which, in the eyes of the impartial spectator, can justify our hurting or disturbing in any respect the happiness of our neighbour" (VI.2.intro.2). Thus, beneficence "requires" reward while injury "deserves" punishment. The causal link indicated by "because" is that they alone are the "approved objects" of the passion "or" they excite the sympathy of the impartial spectator, with the "or" here presumably inclusive in meaning, with the sympathy of the impartial spectator being the source of approval.

If justice is enforceable and injury deserves punishment, then Smith by contrast argues that beneficence is unenforceable. According to Smith, "beneficence is always free, it cannot be extorted by force, the mere want of it exposes to no punishment; because the mere want of beneficence tends to do no real positive evil." What about the other side of the coin: ingratitude on the part of someone who receives beneficence? Smith argues that such ingratitude may "justly" excite dislike and disapprobation, but "it cannot, however, provoke any resentment which mankind will go along with." Ingratitude may provoke "hatred," but not "resentment, a passion which is never properly called forth but by actions which tend to do real and positive hurt to some particular persons. His want of gratitude, therefore, cannot be punished" (II.ii.1.3; see also Raphael, 1973, p. 94). We see here the same logic as in the passage analyzed above concerning the causal links between injury defined as "real and positive hurt," resentment, and punishment. Since the want of beneficence does no "real positive evil" (i.e., injury), it cannot properly provoke the resentment, and therefore cannot be punished. The key premise is precisely the narrowed scope of justice Smith asserts: injustice is limited to real injury to persons, property, and reputation, and only such injury can properly elicit resentment, which, in turn, can only justify punishment. Nevertheless, we might wonder why Smith thinks resentment at ingratitude and other violations of beneficence that do not constitute real injury should still be considered improper.

Smith states that ingratitude cannot "provoke any resentment which mankind will go along with," but he never claims that ingratitude or similar cases does not provoke resentment as matter of fact, as a descriptive matter.

Indeed, he acknowledges the reality of such improper resentment in several instances in *TMS*. The question is whether such resentment, properly "humbled," is normatively appropriate as a "proper" instance of resentment properly understood.

Oftentimes when considering instances of anger evoked in cases where no positive injury has occurred through improper motives, Smith eschews the specific language of resentment, for example, stating that we are "shocked beyond all measure" at actions of ingratitude we read in histories (II.i.5.3) or that we find such actions "odious" (III.5.1). Sometimes, however, he uses the language of "indignation" when considering such cases. For example, he speaks of our "indignation" at the ingratitude of friends, suggesting that such indignation might be appropriate given its place in a section on the "sympathetic gratitude of the impartial spectator" (VI.ii.1.19). He admits that a "well-disposed mind," presumably one that has internalized the impartial spectator, will feel "the highest indignation" against those who blame an overly tender-hearted person who indulges his beneficence upon unworthy persons or objects (VI.iii.15). Finally, and going beyond the case of ingratitude, he writes of the "indignation" we experience when we witness the all-too-common disproportion between merit and reward, with virtue unrecognized or vice unpunished, but argues that it is not for human beings to rectify such injustices (III.v.9–10). A potential crux in interpreting these passages is determining whether Smith uses "resentment" and "indignation" interchangeably, including with regard to their proper expression, or whether he distinguishes them, restricting "resentment" as (normatively) applying only to cases of injury or injustice. A crucial passage we already quoted suggests that he at least sometimes uses them as synonyms: "But we admire that noble and generous *resentment* which governs its pursuit of the greatest injuries, not by the rage which they are apt to excite in the breast of the sufferer, but by the *indignation* which they naturally call forth in that of the impartial spectator ..." (I.i.5.4, emphasis supplied). We therefore occasionally see him speak of resentment even where there is no injury, for example, when he writes that when we "prefer ourselves so shamefully and so blindly to others, we become the proper objects of resentment," and moreover does so while arguing that the "eye of this impartial spectator" should correct our distorted vision of ourselves (III.3.4). (We will have more to say later about the presumption that comes from our distorted vision of ourselves in reconstructing Smith's argument.) Presumably, none of these cases of indignation are inspired by any real positive injury nor do they merit punishment. In these cases, then, we seem to have a break in the logical linkage Smith would establish between injury as real positive harm, resentment, and punishment.

In short, then, as a descriptive matter, people may feel resentment, indignation, or similarly irascible reactions at a whole host of perceived wrongs aside from real injury. Nevertheless, Smith wants to suggest that they *ought not*. One reason we have given in reconstructing Smith's argument is that punishment follows from resentment as a natural consequence *if and only if* there has been some positive injury committed from improper motives. In the case of unrequited gratitude or other cases, while Smith admits that we experience resentment, not only as a matter of fact but potentially appropriately so, then punishment or coercion is inappropriate because no injury has been committed. Nonetheless, the ground for this narrowing the prescriptive account of resentment is still not entirely clear. Why exclude indignation at ingratitude and violations of beneficence from its scope? To answer this question, we have to move beyond Smith's appeals to the impartial spectator and clarify the relationship between resentment, punishment, and justice.

10.4 Justice, Punishment, and the Problem of Improper Resentment

Smith's core concerns with rectifying injustice and humbling pride lead him to embrace a narrower conception of justice and to narrow the scope of propriety for resentment. For Smith, it is fundamentally presumptuous to attempt to rectify anything other than injustice via punishment, and rectification is the only ground for deeming any form of resentment proper. Why? First, Smith maintains that individuals have equal standing or pre-political status, and rectification of an injury to person, property, or reputation would be the only ground for violating this equality of persons. Second, Smith does consider social utility as a factor in establishing the propriety of resentment, though only in rare exceptions and while always maintaining the close tie between injury and justice. The judgment of actual and the impartial spectators still largely determines the propriety of resentments and punishments.

Smith's strongest normative argument in favor of narrowing the scope of proper resentment, as we reconstruct it, rests on his understanding of the equal status of individuals as moral agents, an equality we are wont to ignore in our selfishness and presumptuousness. Smith claims a kind of equality of pre-political rights for all persons, which shapes their juridical status later: "Among equals each individual is naturally, and antecedent to the institution of civil government, regarded as having a right both to defend himself from injuries, and to exact a certain degree of punishment for those which have been done to him" (II.ii.1.6; II.ii.1.9). In other words, individuals with equal standing have no natural or perfect right to anything other than restitution for injury from any other individual in their society. They have no natural or perfect right to demand gratitude for benefits conferred and no natural or perfect right to punish those who fail to be grateful. As Smith puts it, "even the most ordinary degree of kindness or beneficence, however, cannot, *among equals* be extorted by force" (II.ii.1.6, emphasis supplied). We might feel or think we feel resentment at being denied gratitude, but to expect gratitude from others – and to punish its omission – is to deny their fundamental equality with us in moral matters. When we do feel such resentment, we seem to consider ourselves more deserving of respect or praise than others – that is, we exhibit an excessive and pernicious pride. For this reason, Smith characterizes it as the "highest degree of insolence and presumption" to punish a lack of kindness, or ingratitude (II.ii.1.7).

Yet, much as he is aware of the reality of improper resentments, Smith understands that human beings are more likely to be presumptuous than they are to be willing to recognize their fundamental equality. Indeed, the poetic phrase Smith uses to describe human equality throughout *TMS* is his most repeated in the text: that we are "but one of the multitude, in no respect better than any other in it" (II.ii.2.1; III.3.4; VI.ii.2.2[2]). It is almost as if he is trying to remind his reader of an uncomfortable truth. Given his admissions elsewhere about "the nature of ambition" (I.iii.2) and the "love to domineer" (*WN*, III.ii.10), we can see why he might think such reminders are necessary. Smith brings up the latter in his discussion of the abhorrent and inefficient practice of slavery in the *Wealth of Nations*, where he directly attributes it to the "pride of man" (ibid.). In the LJ, Smith refers to the same phenomenon as the "love of domination and authority over others, which I am afraid is naturall to mankind, a certain desire of having others below one, and the pleasure it gives one to have some persons whom he can order to do his work rather than to be obliged to persuade others to bargain with him" (*LJ*(A) iii.130). Yet Smith is clear that this natural, excessive pride is something to be curbed rather than left alone. Just as Smith advocates for an economic system of exchange reliant on persuasion and not slave labor, it is paramount to social stability as well as justice that we respect the equal standing of others and call for neither their forced gratitude nor their punishment in its absence.

Aside from rights considerations, Smith makes clear that considerations of social utility at least influence the propriety of resentment in certain cases, even though utility itself does not motivate the punishment of injustice. He argues throughout his works that the utility of the resentment of injustice is evident. Recall that when he first introduces resentment as one of the principal "unsocial" passions, he speaks of its utility to the individual through deterrence and to society as "the guardians of justice, and of the equality of its administration" (I.ii.3.4). He elsewhere describes the "consciousness of ill-desert, those terrors of merited punishment which attend upon [justice's] violation", as the great safe-guards of the association of mankind, to protect the weak, to curb the violent, and to chastise the guilty (II.ii.3.3). In the concluding chapter of the section comparing beneficence and justice, titled "Of the utility of this constitution of nature" (II.iii.title), Smith explains that

---

[2] In Part 6, Smith changes his phrasing of the passage slightly: "but one of the multitude, in the eye of that equitable judge, of no more consequence than any other in it."

even among a proverbial society of thieves such resentment would be paramount, because "society ... cannot subsist among those who are at all times ready to hurt and injure one another" (II.iii.3). In other words, resentment of injustice, and the fear of punishment it inspires, counterintuitively makes society possible, according to Smith.

In stark contrast, Smith describes the social and individual detriment that would follow from encouraging the resentment of ingratitude or other violations of beneficence. As he explains:

> Though Nature, therefore, exhorts mankind to acts of beneficence, by the pleasing consciousness of deserved reward, she has not thought it necessary to guard and enforce the practice of it by the terrors of merited punishment in case it should be neglected. It is the ornament which embellishes, not the foundation which supports the building, and which it was, therefore, sufficient to recommend, but by no means necessary to impose.
>
> (II.ii.3.3)

Beneficence does not require "terrors of merited punishment" to incentivize it whereas justice does. And gratitude brought about by coercion would neither encourage future beneficence or appropriate expressions of gratitude nor would we be able to consider such expressions gratitude anyway (Berns, 1994, p. 84). Smith, similar to Seneca's approach in *On Benefits*, believes that ingratitude for benefits received is something nature (or Nature) will sufficiently punish instead, via the hatred or contempt of others (II.ii.1.3; see also Elster (2004, p. 154). If anything, Smith suggests that the ingratitude of recipients might lead to even more reward, in the form of additional praise and respect. According to him, "no benevolent man ever lost altogether the fruits of his benevolence," because the ingratitude of those he helps only leads other spectators to heap additional honors on him for his admirable charity *despite* such ingratitude (VI.ii.19). Permitting the resentment of violations of beneficence would, if anything, be harmful and make us less sociable.

Of course, for resentment of injustice to have its socializing effects, even the punishment it leads to has to be strictly limited. Speaking of the general rules by which most individuals regulate their conduct, Smith cautions: "There is, however, one virtue of which the general rules determine with the greatest exactness every external action which it requires. This virtue is justice. The rules of justice are accurate in the highest degree, and admit of no exceptions or modifications, but such as may be ascertained as accurately as the rules themselves ..." (III.6.10). In political societies, these exact rules are laws, which ensure proportionality in punishment when resentment is felt *and* an injury has been committed. Smith is careful to insist that injury can only consist in "every external action" attempted or committed, because there would be no way to establish proportionality – nor to tame resentment – if punishment of evil intentions were allowed. Rather, "sentiments, thoughts, intentions, would become the objects of punishment," indignation would run rampant, and "every court of judicature would become a real inquisition." He explains: "Actions, therefore, which either produce actual evil, or attempt to produce it, and thereby put us in the immediate fear of it, are by the Author of nature rendered the only proper and approved objects of human punishment and resentment" (II.iii.3.2). Here we see again the close connection between resentment and punishment with regard to the "only proper and approved objects" of resentment and punishment. In short, Smith's argument seems to depend on how the threat or execution of punishments for injuries done renders human beings sociable, while any extension of punishment beyond injuries simply increases injury, even if we may experience resentment at vicious or blameworthy intentions or harms other than proper injuries.

Because Smith uses sociability, along with the judgment of the impartial spectator, as the standard to determine propriety in the realm of resentment, we might worry that considerations of utility would inevitably trump the spectator's judgments in determining appropriate punishments. Raphael even suggests that Smith conceded "perhaps too much" to his good friend Hume, who famously claimed the considerations of social utility both motivated and made legitimate the laws of justice, allowing utility to determine the approval of punishment (Raphael, 1973, p. 94). For example, in a famous passage, Smith argues that punishment may be extended beyond the borders of injustice defined as injury by a civil magistrate "entrusted with the power not only of preserving the public peace by restraining injustice, but of promoting the prosperity of the commonwealth, by establishing good discipline, and by discouraging every sort of vice and impropriety." Such a magistrate might, though only with "the greatest delicacy and reserve," enact and enforce laws that go beyond commutative justice in service of this prosperity (II.ii.1.8). In an extreme example, Smith suggests that "when the sovereign commands what is merely indifferent, and what, antecedent to his orders, might have been omitted without any blame, it becomes not only blameable but punishable to disobey him" (II.ii.18). Isn't this simply Smith admitting that considerations of utility – or of whatever the sovereign determines the "prosperity of the commonwealth" to be – will ultimately determine proper and improper resentments and, in turn, proper and improper punishments? How does the judgment of the impartial spectator fit in here?

To put it simply, utility is not only in the eyes of the sovereign. As Smith clarifies in the same passage, and as Haakonssen (1981) perhaps most comprehensively argued, the task of a legislator is a difficult one: though they should not only be interested in preserving their commonwealth's peace but also in promoting its prosperity, they must do so within the natural limits of justice and morality. As Smith puts it, "to neglect it [prosperity] altogether exposes the commonwealth to many gross disorders and shocking enormities, and to push it too far is destructive of liberty, security, and justice" (II.ii.1.8). Smith also disagrees with both Grotius and Hume about the closeness of the connection between considerations of utility and justice. In the LJ, Smith explicitly differentiates his account of merited punishment and its origins from Grotius's on the grounds that "that which Grotius and other writers commonly allege as the orignall measure of punishments, viz the consideration of the publick good, will not *sufficiently* account for the constitution of punishments" (*LJ*(A) ii.90, emphasis supplied). And, in *TMS*, Smith disagrees with an unnamed Hume about considerations of utility alone being sufficient to support our concern with justice (II.ii.3.6), an important disagreement given that he follows his friend on the topic of justice's utility for society. As Smith clarifies in an example of a sentinel who must be put to death for falling asleep at his post, public utility clearly shapes the propriety of punishment, but it alone is not usually sufficient to deem an act "unjust." In other words, here we have a case where it is appropriate to punish even though there is apparently no resentment felt. Rather, some sort of injury has to be established for injustice to occur, and what is considered an injury is still subject to the judgments of the actual and, ultimately, the impartial spectator.

11

Adam Smith
Stoic and Epicurean

LISA HILL

During the period of Western Philosophy that was developed in Hellenistic civilisation following Aristotle (384 BC–322 BCE) and ending with Neoplatonism (205–325 AD), Epicureanism and Stoicism emerged as the two dominant schools. Long considered rivals, in Smith's hands they are reconciled in unexpected ways.

Smith was well acquainted with both Epicurean and Stoic thought. His private library contained all the major Stoic works, including the complete works of Cicero, Seneca and Epictetus, several editions of the *Meditations* of Marcus Aurelius and two different editions of Diogenes Laertius' *Lives of Eminent Philosophers* (Mizuta, 2000) which contains a detailed account of Stoic teachings. Smith cited Stoic doctrine freely and there are myriad allusions to Stoicism and Stoic thinkers throughout his corpus. Smith scholars have repeatedly adverted to Smith's debt to Stoic thought (Waszek, 1984; Clarke, 2000; Brown, 2016; Maurer, 2016) and it has even been suggested that "Stoic philosophy is the primary influence on Smith's ethical thought" (Raphael and Macfie, 1976, p. 5).

Yet, Smith was also influenced by Epicureanism (e.g. Force, 2003). Although there are fewer references to Epicureanism in Smith, this may be related to the fact that Epicureanism was regarded with far more suspicion than was Stoicism in Smith's time. Or it could simply be because no complete works by Epicurus survive and so there was less to reference.

The key ancient text for understanding ancient Epicureanism is the extended entry in Diogenes Laertius' *Lives and Opinions of Eminent Philosophers*, in which are preserved not only a compilation of quotations known as Epicurus' "Principal Doctrines" but also three complete letters composed by Epicurus as well as his last Will and Testament. The other ancient text of significance is Lucretius' *De Rerum Natura*, a philosophical poem that provides the most complete account of the Epicurean system to survive antiquity. Other reliable sources of Epicureanism available to eighteenth-century readers include Cicero's *De Finibus*, Pierre Gassendi's complete works and Thomas Stanley's translations of Epicurean thought contained in his *History of Philosophy*. All are found in Smith's personal library (see Mizuta, 2000).

177

Arguably the two most important of all the Hellenistic schools, the Stoics and Epicureans were contemporaries and obdurate rivals. The Stoics disliked the individualism and hedonism of the Epicureans and were contemptuous of their view that the only rationale for refraining from crime was to prevent anxiety about detection. The Stoics also disapproved of the Epicureans' refusal to take responsibility for the welfare of others as exemplified in their avoidance of politics on the grounds that it interfered with pleasure and *ataraxia* (tranquillity of the soul and mind). By contrast, the Stoics stressed the importance of duty and service to others and embraced public life (Diogenes Laertius, 1925, VII. 21; Cicero, 1961, III.65-68: pp. 285-289).

Well aware of their differences, nevertheless Smith did not regard Epicureanism and Stoicism as necessarily incompatible, drawing attention to the fact that Epicurean teachings were often put to good use by their supposed adversaries. It is from Epicurus, says Smith, that Cicero, "the great enemy of the Epicurean system borrows his most agreeable proofs that virtue alone is sufficient to secure happiness". Similarly, despite the fact that Seneca is a member of "the sect most opposite to that of Epicurus", he "yet quotes [Epicurus] more frequently than any other" (*TMS* VII.5). While Smith concedes that Epicureanism seems to "strip" the "amiable" virtues "of all their beauty" and the respectable "of all their grandeur", nevertheless it is equally capable with Stoicism of encouraging "the best and most laudable habits of the human mind" (*TMS* VII.iv.2-35).

Smith fuses Stoic theological sensibilities with a more modern, humanistic approach through his belief that God's will is expressed in the workings of efficient or secondary causes rather than through direct divine intervention. These secondary causes are found in the pragmatic, realist, instrumental and worldly urges endorsed by Epicureanism which Smith imports into an optimistic Deistic Stoic framework to build his own social science (Hill, 2001).

Convinced that society was "a system" benignly created and governed by social laws that invariably tended towards a positive equilibrium (Stoicism), Smith wanted to show that our inherent tendencies, even the seemingly vicious ones (Epicureanism), embody positive latent functions that keep in motion, not only the market, but the whole system of spontaneous order that regulates and equilibrates the human universe. What makes the human world tick is not universal benevolence, as per both the Stoic and Christian traditions, but Epicurean prudence and regard to our own private interest. How, then, did Smith rehabilitate Epicurean drives and make them conceptually congruent with the Stoic framework? The answer is found in Stoic theology (and theodicy) and, in particular, its response to the age-old question: "if God is good, why evil?"

Smith's political economy and his social science in general is an attempt to take conventional virtues and moralising out of the social science narrative and replace them with a focus on the real motors of human systems: our seemingly base dispositions and drives. He enlists Stoic theodicy to reconcile Epicureanism with Stoicism and to put apparently selfish drives to socially productive uses. In the process, he produces something original; a moral and political economy resistant to public opprobrium in which self-regarding human beings are still worthy, and therefore worthy of objective "scientific" study, because this is just as "the Creator" made them and for the best purposes.

11.1 Stoic Theodicy, Epicurean Desires and Smithian Theodicy

What, then, is theodicy? Any religion that insists on the omnipotence and omniscience of a benign deity must reconcile those qualities with the apparent evils of life. In other words, a theodicy is any attempt to explain the puzzle: "if God is good, why is there evil?" In order to avoid heresy, no answer should compromise the Creator's perfection or "diminish" any of "His" divine attributes (Waterman, 2002, p. 916). In other words, the prevalence of evil cannot be God's fault. The standard Christian answer to this conundrum comes down to the exercise of free will. But the Stoics before them had a far more elegant solution: to deny the existence of evil altogether. After all, "what motive" could the gods have "for impelling [us] to do evil"? asks Marcus rhetorically (Marcus Aurelius, 1987, VI.44, p. 155). Smith agrees.

Like many of his contemporaries, Smith accepted the world as a product of design, perceiving the order and regularity of human affairs as a direct result of this design and benign purpose in nature (Hill, 2001). Even apparent vice and evil are a misunderstood aspect of the divine masterplan. The Stoics taught that, since "the world was governed by the all-ruling providence of a wise, powerful and good God", we should regard "every single event ... as making a necessary part of the plan of the universe". On the Stoic account adopted and adapted by Smith "the vices and follies of mankind" make "as necessary a part of this plan as their wisdom or their virtue" and "tend equally to the prosperity and perfection of the great system of nature" (*TMS* I.ii.3.4; II.3.3). Marcus Aurelius, an early promulgator of theodicy, and with whose thought Smith was very familiar, allowed for a universe simultaneously perfect yet sometimes "distasteful" and full of "bitter pills" (Marcus Aurelius, 1987, V.8, p. 107). The "boor", the "rogue, the deceiver" and every other kind of "shameless" "wrongdoer" are as necessary "in the world" as "the rose in spring and the fruit in summer" (IX.42, p. 257). Even "disease and death and treachery", and all the other things that "gladde[n]" or "sadde[n]" the "foolish" are normal and "usual" (4.44, p. 91). Knaves and the ignorant provide valuable opportunities to exercise tolerance and to "teach and enlighten" without resentment (VI.27, p. 145) while the offensive and loathsome help us learn how to correct without impatience or "anger" (VI.29, p. 123). Everything has an adaptive function.

Extending this idea to modern commercialising societies, Smith sees our apparently vicious tendencies, "errors and evils" as fully *intended* by a benevolent Creator who implants them to perform positive latent functions at the social-systems level. The imperfections of the created universe, even its seemingly destructive and uncomfortable aspects, are accommodated within such a framework. As with Stoicism, everything exists for a benign purpose.

Although Smith insists with the Stoics (and against the Epicureans) on a benevolent and moral deity, he is aware that Stoic virtues cannot really account for the social and economic physics that need explaining. It is all very well to say that God has given us fools and "boors" to stimulate our moral education, but by what means has the Stoic Creator provided for our worldly welfare beyond the urge to mutual benevolence?

11.2 Impartial Benevolence

For the Stoics, the highest virtue is benevolence; indeed the whole point of the Stoic life is to do as much good as we can to our fellow human beings. The virtuous agent must refrain from harming others since it is impious and the universal law forbids it (Marcus Aurelius, 1987, IX.1, p. 231). It is natural for human beings to aid others (Cicero, 1961, III.63, p. 285) and it is "Nature's will that we enter into a general interchange of acts of kindness, by giving and receiving" (Cicero, 1990, I.vii.22, pp. 23–24). As Cicero remarks in *De Officiis*: "[men] are born for the sake of men, that they may be able to mutually help one another" (I.22, p. 23).

Although the Stoics agree with the Epicureans that it is natural to shrink from pain (Seneca, 1917, CXX117, pp. 405–407), and tolerated the self-regarding drives up to a point, they did not regard them as particularly important to the real business of life which is conforming with sociable Nature. Further, anyone who allowed them to dominate their actions was morally immature. The most important and "excellent thing" is "that which is akin to the other", namely "community" (Marcus Aurelius, 1987, V.21–22, p. 119). Although every human naturally starts out as a self-regarder, over time they learn to take delight in going from one "social act" to another (VI.7, p. 133). This relates to the Stoic theory of *oikeiosis* (usually translated as a sense of either affinity, familiarisation or appropriation) which maps out the natural history of the moral maturation process. In the early stages of our individual development we experience *oikeiosis* as self-awareness and self-preservation: "immediately upon birth ... a living creature feels an attachment for itself, and an impulse to preserve itself and to feel affection for its own constitution" (Cicero, 1961, III.16, pp. 233–235). But as we morally mature, this sense of affinity or of being "akin to" ourselves extends to a moral concern for our family, our community, nation, strangers and eventually all of humanity (III.62, pp. 281–283). Because our end is to live "in agreement with nature" (Diogenes Laertius, 1925, VII.87, p. 195) and because "the intelligence of the Universe is social" (Marcus Aurelius, 1987, V.30, p. 123) we can best serve our own interests by embracing this sociable nature and exercising *sympathia* (our affinity or organic relationship to one another) and *philanthropia* (benevolence).

To be self-regarding and partial towards intimates is not only contrary to natural law, it is a sign of moral underdevelopment. The true world "citizen" treats "nothing as a matter of private profit" and "exercises choice or desire" only "by reference to the whole" (Epictetus, 1989, vol. 1, II.x.1–2, p. 275). The Stoics live for others and happiness is synonymous, not with pleasure, but with wisdom and virtue (Diogenes Laertius, 1925, VI..89, p. 197).

These are high sentiments, thinks Smith, but in any properly functioning society, especially the mass, commercial societies that interested him, benevolence will not take us very far. As he put it: "nobody but a beggar chuses to depend chiefly upon the benevolence of his fellow citizens" (*TMS* I.ii.3). So Smith turns to Epicureanism for the psychogenic motors of his social system, locating God's benign intentions and action in the banal, bodily and self-regarding business of daily life; in physical and social survival, the perpetuation of the species, in the pursuit of pleasure and the avoidance of pain, and the pursuit of the "natural joy of prosperity" (*TMS* III.3.9). The Epicureans saw the self-regarding and instrumental urges as perfectly natural and they encouraged people to exercise them freely but within the bounds of prudence. Even when we seem to be choosing the virtues it is only "on account of pleasure and not for their own sake" (Diogenes Laertius, 1925, X.138, p. 663).

Although Smith agrees with the Stoics that the universe has been designed perfectly by an utterly benevolent "divine intelligence whose wisdom [governs the world] for the safety and preservation of all" (Cicero, 1967, II.132, p. 251), he does not believe that we can secure our "safety and preservation" through the exercise of perpetual, general benevolence towards others; quite the opposite.

The virtuous life is certainly commendable but it is really "self-preservation, and the propagation of the species" that "are the great ends which Nature seems to have proposed in the formation of all animals" (*TMS* II.i.5.10) and virtue has no substantive part to play here. Indeed, the benevolent affections do a very poor job of getting our needs met (*WN* I.ii.2). Self-interest yoked with prudence is what really makes the world go round. This is highly reminiscent of Epicureanism.

11.3 Prudence, Pleasure, and Self-Regard

11.3.1 *Pleasure*

The Epicureans were rationalistic utility-maximisers and individualistic self-regarders. Unlike the Stoics, they did not consider virtue to be the *summum bonum*, the "highest good"; instead, they subordinated virtue to pleasure. "Pleasure" says Epicurus, "is our first and kindred good". It is "the alpha and omega of a pleasant life" (Diogenes Laertius, 1925, X.128–129, pp. 654–655).

The greatest good is to seek pleasure in order to attain a state of tranquillity and freedom from fear (*ataraxia*) as well as absence of pain (*aponia*). As Epicurus says "the end of all our actions is to be free from pain and fear, and, when once we have attained all this, the tempest of the soul is laid" (Diogenes Laertius, 1925, X. 128–9, pp. 654–655). This is directly opposed to the Stoic view. Although they too sought *ataraxia*, individual pleasure is of no consequence, says Marcus: we were not "made ... for pleasure" but "to do what Nature bids" us and to make our part like a worker bee in "building up ... an orderly Universe" (Marcus Aurelius, 1987, V.1, p. 99). Those who pursue only "what is in their eyes congenial and advantageous ... *are mistaken*" (VI.24, p. 145). *Ataraxia* is not an end in itself, as per the Epicureans, only a by-product of virtue.

Prudence. The Epicurean system of ethics is based on the four cardinal virtues of wisdom, justice, honesty and pleasure constrained and regulated by pain. Although they sound lofty, together they merely equate to prudence. Prudence or practical wisdom (*phronesis*) is the chief of the Epicurean virtues; indeed, it "is a more precious thing even than philosophy; from it springs all other virtues, for it teaches that we cannot lead a life of pleasure which is not also a life of prudence, honour and justice; nor lead a life of prudence, honour and justice, which is not also a life of pleasure" (Diogenes Laertius, 1925, X.132, p. 657). In other words, virtue is merely a matter of instrumental prudence.

Smith dismisses Stoic beneficence (that "feeble spark") and displaces it with Epicurean "prudence", or "care for our own happiness" (*TMS* VI. 1), which he defines awkwardly as a "selfish" "virtue" (*TMS* VI.iv. 1). Although he makes prudence do much of the moral legwork in his system, Smith does admit that it is rather an inferior virtue since it is "directed merely to the health ... fortune ... rank and reputation of the individual". Accordingly "imprudence" is nothing more than "the mere want of the capacity to take care of one's-self". Prudence is "respectable" but it only commands "a certain cold esteem" (*TMS* VI.i.14).

11.3.2 Self-Regard

I have already noted that the naturalness of self-preservation is a Stoic principle as well as an Epicurean one. The difference, however, is that care of the self is a low priority for the Stoics. But for the Epicureans, as for Smith, self-care ranks very highly. Smith says that "[e]very man is ... principally recommended to his own care; and as he is fitter to take care of himself than of any other person, it is fit and right that it should be so" (*TMS* II.ii.1).

Self-preservation is the first task given to us by nature (*TMS* VII.ii.1.15), reflecting God's concern for us and "His" desire for our physical safety, security, prosperity and perpetuation. This vital set of tasks must be delegated to our completely reliable "original and immediate instincts" (*WN* I.I.i; *LJ*(B),

300–301) rather than to any altruistic imperative. In fact, self-regarding acts are far more socially useful than other-regarding acts: "By pursuing his own interest [the economic actor] frequently promotes that of the society more effectually than when he really intends to promote it" (*WN* IV.ii.9). Here Smith alludes to a central element of his theodicy: Nature's law of unintended consequences. On the one hand, there are our basic hedonic urges and, on the other, their tendency to produce "beneficent ends which the great Director of nature intended to produce by them". The Author of Nature has "endowed mankind with an appetite for the end which she proposes but likewise with an appetite for the means by which alone this end can be brought about, *for their own sakes and independent of their tendency to produce it*" (*TMS* II.i.5.10, emphasis added). By this reasoning, Smith renders the Epicurean imperative to pursue pleasure and avoid pain naturally and divinely ordained.

God's benevolent ambitions are manifested in the worldly and self-interested aspects of human life; for example, the rather prosaic "principle in the mind" that prompts us "to truck, barter and exchange ... is not marked with anything amiable" and yet it is this principle that is, in reality, the "great foundation of arts, commerce, and the division of labour" (*LJ*(B), 301–302). Similarly, the urgent sex instinct has been benignly endowed to ensure that the species perpetuates itself (*TMS* III.3.13; see also VI.ii.1.1). Our egotistical craving for social recognition and "to be observed, to be attended to, to be taken notice of" is a powerful motor of productivity, innovation and prosperity (*TMS* I.iii.2.2; IV.i.10).

Humans often evince motives and dispositions that appear vicious – or at least not particularly virtuous – but this misses the point that comprehending the dynamics of the human universe in an authentically social-scientific way is not a "matter of right" but rather of "fact" (*TMS* II.i.5.10; *LJ*(B), 300). Those "whining and melancholy moralists ... who regard as impious the natural joy of prosperity" (*TMS* III.3.9) mistake utterly God's purposes when they condemn our worldly, self-regarding and hedonistic ambitions. Ironically, those "principles of the human mind which are most beneficial to society are by no means marked by nature as the most honourable". It is unfortunate, Smith says in theodocean tones, that "[h]unger, thirst and the passion for sex" wrongly "excite[s] contempt" in moralists, when, in reality, these are the very drives that "are the great supports of the human species" (*LJ*(B), 300). More than that, they are purposive and designed, signs of God's benevolence. Indeed, those who denounce our self-regarding drives are heretics, "the enemies of God" who seem to want to "obstruct ... the scheme which the Author of nature has established for the happiness and perfection of the world" (*TMS* III.5.7).

Although Smith sees value in beneficence, this is largely because it has demonstrable utility. A populace animated by "humanity and benevolence" is more orderly because more respectful of "established powers and privileges" and "the great orders and societies, into which the state is divided" (*TMS* VI. ii.2.16). In addition, benevolence contributes to human happiness (*TMS* II.iii.1). But the truth is that our own interests always come first: "[b]efore we can feel much for others, we must in some measure be at ease ourselves" (*TMS* V. 2.9). Further, life will still roll along with or without the other-regarding virtues: "a society may subsist from a sense of its utility, without any mutual love or affection" or relations of "obligation" or "gratitude" to others because it can "still be upheld by a mercenary exchange of good offices according to an agreed valuation" (*TMS* II.3.2). Benevolence may be the "sole principle of action" in a perfect "Deity" who has no material needs but it could never be depended upon to secure the welfare of beings so imperfect and completely dependent on external goods as are humans (*WN* VII.ii.3.18). We congregate for instrumental reasons and obtain the favour of others, not through eliciting their compassion but by appealing to their own "self-love". "Give me that which I want, and you shall have this which you want" is how "we obtain from one another the far greater part of those good offices which we stand in need of" (*WN* I.ii).

On what is, in reality, a very partial reading of Stoic teachings at this point (and of which he would have been well-aware), Smith tells us that we should all imitate the "perfect confidence" in God of the Stoics and concern themselves only with the "propriety" of our own self-regarding "endeavours" while trusting in the Creator's "superior power" to "[turn] it to that great end, which he himself was most desirous of promoting" (*TMS* VII.ii.1.21; see also III.5.6–7; VI.ii.3.4). The motivations of individual agents may seem morally suspect at times yet, overall, the *system* of nature is self-evidently benign. In creating us, God's "original purpose" was not to make us good but to preserve us, "to promote happiness, and to guard against misery" (*TMS* III.5.7). It is not virtue but "opulence and freedom" that are "the two greatest blessings men can possess" (*LJ*(A) iii.111).

The self-equilibrating order and benevolence of the universe, a Stoic idea, is effected by Epicurean urges in the here and now. Like the practical Epicureans, Smith wants to understand and explain humans as they truly are, not as moralists might wish them to be. Through his theodicean social science (albeit adapted in a manner that was never intended by the Stoics) we are led to a proper understanding of what humans are really supposed to be doing and what adaptive social-systems effects they can achieve by their naturally self-regarding behaviours.

How does Epicurean justice fit with Smith's thinking here? And does Smith have any functional use for Stoic justice?

11.4 Justice and the Law

The Stoic conception of justice is closely related to our other-regarding duties. Cicero says that "the mere fact" of our "common humanity" not only inclines us but *"requires"* us to feel "akin" to one another (Cicero, 1961, III.63, p. 283 emphasis added). It is impious to harm another and the universal law forbids it (Marcus Aurelius, 1987, IX.1, p. 231). Indeed, "according to [Nature's] ruling, it is more wretched to commit than to suffer injury" (Seneca, 1917, 95.52–53, p. 91). But the negative virtue of refraining from harm is not enough: virtue must also be positive. We are duty-bound to meet the needs of our divine siblings and the morally mature person understands that she must "live for [her] neighbour" as she lives for herself (Seneca, 1917, 48.3, p. 315). Further, "[p]ains must ... be taken *to benefit as many as possible* with such kindnesses" (Cicero, 1990, II.63, p. 235 emphasis added). Consistency and impartiality require us to love each other as Zeus loves us. As Cicero reflects: "how inconsistent it would be for us to expect the immortal gods to love and cherish us, when we ourselves despise and neglect one another" (Cicero, 1961, III.xx.66, p. 287).

The Epicureans have a much thinner conception of justice; it merely consists in refraining from harming the interests of others. Further, the main reason we desist from crime is not because it is the right thing to do, but because it is prudent in order to avoid anxiety about being caught for wrongdoing. "Injustice is not in itself an evil, but only in its consequence, viz the terror which is excited by comprehension that those appointed to punish such offences will discover the injustice" (Diogenes Laertius, 1925, X.151.33, p. 675). Our motive is pleasure and the avoidance of pain, not a desire to be virtuous, or because it is God's will and an "unquestionably good" and natural thing to do (Marcus Aurelius, 1987, V.12, p. 113), as per the Stoics.

We also obey the law for another instrumental reason: self-protection. The law is simply a covenant or contract we make to avoid harm: "Natural justice is a symbol or expression of expediency, to prevent one man from harming or being harmed by another" (Diogenes Laertius, 1925, X.31, pp. 674–675). Justice is purely conventional and the contract can be suspended if it no longer serves its purpose: "There never was an absolute justice, but only an agreement made in reciprocal intercourse in whatever localities now and again from time to time, providing against the infliction or suffering of harm" (X.33, p. 675).

Smith rejects the Stoic view and gravitates towards the Epicurean account of instrumental, negative justice. A society left to regulate itself by the moral sentiments alone is untenable, for it would be riven with conflict and mutual injury (*TMS* II.ii.3.1–3). It is only a formal, commutative system of justice that makes existence between self-interested competitors possible (*TMS* III.6.9–10). As Smith decreed, "upon the impartial administration of justice depends the liberty of every individual, the sense which he has of his own security" (*WN* Vi.1.ii). The law enables us to live free and free from harm and we obey the law to gain those benefits. Smith concedes that justice is morally inferior to "beneficence" because it is merely a "negative virtue" that "only hinders us from hurting our neighbour". Indeed, it is possible to "fulfil all the rules of justice by sitting still and doing nothing" (*TMS* II.ii.1.9).

Smith's conception of justice is strictly commutative (not distributive, as per the Stoics) because it precludes any imperfect obligation of benevolence. The state may justifiably use force to prevent the injury of one person by another, but it is on shaky ground if it seeks to enforce the exercise of the benevolent virtues. By contrast, commutative justice is precise, its rules highly impersonal, impartial, predictable and "accurate in the highest degree, and admit of no exceptions or modifications ... If I owe a man ten pounds, justice requires that I should precisely pay him ten pounds" (*TMS* III.6.9–10). It therefore makes instrumental sense for us to obey the law.

But Smith adds a twist to the story, rebuking his Epicurean antecedents for missing another and more important psychological motivation. We also obey the law to avoid reputational harm (*TMS* II.ii.2.1). Smith finds it "extraordinary" that Epicurus failed to appreciate that the strongest instrumental motivation for being just relates to a "much more passionate desire or aversion" than fear of the legal "consequence", namely, to obtain and keep the good opinion of others: "[T]o be odious, to be contemptible, to be the proper object of indignation, is more dreadful than all that we can suffer in our body from hatred, contempt, or indignation" (*TMS* VII.ii.2.12). What we really dread is not to be unvirtuous but to be *seen* as unvirtuous.

By contrast, the Stoics disdained instrumental motives and had far less respect for positive, conventional laws. The moral agent will always put the laws of Zeus before those of "men" whenever a conflict between them arises, even when this imperils the well-being of the agent concerned as it frequently did in the case of Stoic disciples (Hill and Blazejak, 2021). In fact, an act is only disobedient when we refuse to carry out "right, honourable and beneficial orders" (Musonius Rufus C., 2011, 16.10). But in both the Epicurean and Smithian systems of thought, the positive laws of Caesar must always be respected because it is prudent to do so.

11.5 What Are Our Duties to Others Then?

Like the Epicureans, Smith has a very thin conception of what we might owe others. In contrast to Stoicism, as hinted at already, Smith says that we only enjoy "perfect rights" which he limits to the rights to "person", "reputation" and "estate" (*LJ*(A), i.12). But "what they call imperfect rights are those which correspond to those duties which ought to be performed to us by others but which we have not title to compel them to perform" and it is "intirely in their power to perform them or not" (*LJ*(A), i.15). He gives as his example the "beggar" who is "an object of our charity and may be said to have a right to demand it", however, "when we use the word right in this way it is not on a proper but metaphorical sense". By this Smith means it is not a right in the sense of constituting an imperfect right which denotes a right to "distributive justice". We only owe others "commutative justice" (*LJ*(A), i.15).

The imperfect rights to benevolence, altruism, hospitality and charity asserted by the Stoics are purely supererogatory for Smith; more importantly, from a social science perspective, they are superfluous and usually counterproductive because of the "universal benevolence" that inheres in the "Divine Masterplan". Smith admits that what he is saying may "shock all [our] natural sentiments" but he wants to reassure his reader that it was "established for the wisest and best purposes" (*TMS* III.5.10).

Smith's incorporation of Epicurean tendencies within an optimistic Stoic framework is replicated in his discussion of our proper relations with other nations. The same motives that ensure domestic flourishing and harmony can also be applied to our dealings with the world at large.

11.6   Cosmopolitanism

To what extent did Stoic cosmopolitanism impact Smith's outlook? Smith was certainly a cosmopolitan thinker insofar as he shared with the Stoics the long-term goal of a world society of pacific and amiably disposed states. He vastly preferred peace to war and agreed that we should exercise courtesy and forbearance towards strangers and foreigners. However he regarded Stoic moral psychology as hopelessly utopian and diverged on how and why the cosmopolis was to be achieved and sustained. Whereas, for the Stoics, world society would be a function of universal benevolence and our divine sibling-hood with the entirety of humanity, Smith had a more instrumental and prosaic method for achieving it: self-interest, prudence and the division of labour. Again, he finds inspiration in Epicurean pragmatism in order to fill out and realise the broader Stoic framework.

11.6.1   Stoic Cosmopolitanism

The Stoics are by far the most important figures in the development of cosmopolitan thought and the idea of universal, world citizenship. They argued that because reason is universal all of humanity shares in a common soul; we are all "kinsmen", the "offspring of Zeus" (Epictetus, 1989, I.13, 1-5, p. 99). Our natural kinship both with God and each other renders the "whole universe" "one Commonwealth of which both gods and men are members" (Cicero, 1988, I. vii.23, p. 323). The "wise man" knows that "every place is his country" (Seneca, 2003, vol 2, IX.7, p. 447), and we are governed by common, universal laws (Marcus Aurelius, 1987, IV.4, p. 73). Zeno argued in his *Republic*:

> All the inhabitants of this world of ours should not live differentiated by their respective rules of justice into separate cities and communities, but should consider all men to be of one community and one polity and that we should have a common life and an order common to us.
>
> (Cited in Frecer, 2015, p. 4)

Although the cosmopolis is natural, at the same time its moral obligations of impartial concern for others are extremely demanding and have to be cultivated assiduously (Hill and Blazejak, 2021). It is our duty, Cicero tells us, "to respect, defend, and maintain the common bonds of union and fellowship subsisting between all members of the human race" (Cicero, 1990, I.xlii.150, p. 153). Impartiality was the Stoic ideal and moral failure consists in an "incapacity to extend help", even to strangers (Epictetus, 1989, vols. II, Fragment 7, 4, p. 447). This is where the demandingness of Stoicism escalates. Musonius says that the "person who wrongs strangers wrongs Zeus" who is their "guardian" (Musonius Rufus C., 2011, 15.2, p. 62). It is not only neutral strangers but also those we perceive as our enemies who are entitled to our assistance. Although it is said that "the despicable man is recognized by his inability to harm his enemies ... actually he is much more easily recognized by his *inability* to help them", says Musonius (Musonius, 2011, Saying 41:88, emphasis added). Cicero decrees that we must not "listen to those who think that one should indulge in violent anger against one's political enemies and imagine that such is the attitude of a great-spirited, brave man": indeed "nothing is more commendable than courtesy and forbearance". To enter the cosmopolis "we must school ourselves to affability" and "mental poise" (Cicero, 1990, I.xxv.88, pp. 89–91). The virtues of the Stoic cosmopolite are cultivated through a disciplined refusal to give way to emotional antipathies and attachments and to anti-social passions like resentment and anger, no matter how seemingly justified.

11.6.2 Smith's Response: Epicurean Cosmopolitanism?

Although Smith was inspired by the Stoic image of a globalised, egalitarian and interdependent world of friends, he was not a thoroughgoing *moral* cosmopolitan. He agreed with the Stoics that interstate conflict, aggressive military imperialism and war were all bad (Hill, 2020), but he disagreed on what would or could replace them. He also valorised Stoic *desiderata* like tolerance, mutual-enablement, global interdependence, pacifism, non-interference and mutual forbearance and thought they were practically achievable; but only via his own, more instrumental, Epicureanised version of cosmopolitanism.

For Smith, the Stoic ideal of a cosmopolis based on universal, impartial benevolence is impossible; indeed Smith rejected the very idea that humans are capable of such a sentiment (*TMS* III.4–9). Our keener interest in ourselves first, our intimates afterwards and strangers very little at all is both reasonable and natural. Although common decency requires that strangers are "entitled to our good wishes", they have no further moral claims on us (*TMS* III. iii.9–10). We may all feel a vague sense of "good-will" towards the world in general but in reality our "effectual good offices can very seldom be extended to any wider society than that of our own country" (*TMS* VI.Ii.3.1). To feel responsible for those we are unable to effectively aid is pointless and an unnecessary emotional burden (*TMS* VI.ii.3.5; II.iii.3.3; III.4).

For most people (including the Epicureans, who were content to live under the protection of their local states (Long, 2008, p. 58)) the sovereign state is "*the greatest society* upon whose happiness or misery, our good or bad conduct can have much influence". This is because "all the objects of our kindest affections, our children, our parents, our relations, our friends, our benefactors ... are commonly comprehended within it; and their prosperity and safety depend in some measure upon its prosperity and safety" (*TMS* VI.ii.2.2). We have no obligations to strangers and especially distant strangers except to be courteous, trade with them on fair terms, offer a thin kind of commercial hospitality and otherwise leave them in peace. It turns out that the "plan" laid out for humankind by "Nature" is "altogether different" from that of the Stoics (*TMS* VII.ii.1.47).

Humans are constitutionally incapable of cultivating the kind of disciplined impartiality required by Stoicism to break down our intimate, local and national loyalties, therefore Smith substitutes moral cosmopolitanism for his own variant: commercial or economic cosmopolitanism. To Smith's mind, this was a far more achievable form of global society because it does not rely on the cultivation of dispositions that are so morally demanding as to be almost impossible. By contrast, self-interest and the equally natural cognate urges to specialise and "truck, barter and exchange" need no encouragement whatsoever; further they are already busily at work in the human universe, breaking down parochial sensibilities and encouraging us to mingle, indirectly, with strangers beyond our borders.

It is by self-interested economic means, says Smith, that the *cosmopolis* will be brought into existence. This was a form of cosmopolitanism that would not only bring immense economic benefit but even many of the political and moral outcomes desired by the idealistic Stoics. Global, pacific society could become a reality due to the natural expansion of markets. If allowed (i.e. absent mercantilism and its maladaptive, even malicious obstructions to free trade) our natural and irresistible drives – self-interest and the "trucking instinct which originally gives occasion to the division of labour" (*WN* I.ii.3) – will generate ever-increasing surpluses of exchangeable goods; as a result, markets will naturally expand outwards until "the society itself grows to be what is properly called a commercial society" (*WN* IV.1).

The term "commercial" had a particularly broad meaning in the eighteenth century, denoting not only "the market-oriented manufacture and trade of goods", but also "interaction, exchange, and communication more generally"; the "frequent crossing of borders" and the development of "navigational and communications technologies" that drew "the world closer together" and hastened "trade, capital flows and the development of transnational ... networks" (Muthu, 2008). Global trade increasingly brought unprecedented "divisions of labour and improvements of arts" enhancing the "productive powers of labour" and "with it the real revenue and wealth of the inhabitants" (*WN* IV.i.32).

That humans were self-interested was beyond doubt; that the division of labour, if allowed, would exponentially expand markets out into the known world and beyond also seemed to be beyond doubt. All governments had to do was to remove any impediments to the global market, exchange war and mercantilist imperialism for peace and trade and dismiss the idea that trade was a zero-sum game. The great conceptual error of mercantilism was its perception of international trade as a situation whereby one nation's gain is another's loss (Minowitz, 1993, p. 104). As Smith wrote: "Nothing . . . can be more absurd than this whole doctrine of the balance of trade" upon which almost all "regulations of commerce are founded". It is a most misguided notion that a nation's interest consists "in beggaring all their neighbours" (*WN* IV.iii.c.9; IV.viii.48). In fact, it is a policy that never fails to backfire (*WN* IV.iii.c.2). We should trade freely, not because we love humankind in general, but because it is against our interests not to do so. What goes around comes around, thinks Smith. The same logic applied to aggressive imperialistic expansion, mercantilism's evil twin.

Just like Zeno and the early Stoics (Erskine, 1990, p. 181), Smith abhorred empire for the injustice, exploitation and "dreadful misfortune" it necessitated (*WN* IV.vii.c.80). But he also condemned empire for practical and instrumental reasons. There was a right way and a wrong way to manage our relations with other nations and, for Smith, the British imperial project was not only economically disastrous but unjust and even unnatural. Commerce should naturally be a source of "friendship" between nations, but under the antagonising influence of mercantilism it "has become the most fertile source of discord and animosity" (*WN* iii.c.9; IV.ii.38; V.ii.g.2). European imperialism brought nothing but "savage injustice" to many "unfortunate countries" (*WN* IV.vii.a.16) and far from enriching "the mother country" it had only served to impede and even "crush" its own industry and prosperity (*WN* vii.c.81–83; IV.vii.c.65). British imperialism was a bad deal all round because the colonies yielded few benefits at vast cost to everyone (*WN* IV.vii.c.65). In order to guarantee enduring global friendship and plenty for all, there should be no limitations on the nature and extent of the market because this limits the natural growth of the division of labour.

If the system of "natural liberty" (the free market) is allowed to bring the commercial cosmopolis into existence, relationships between distant strangers will be vastly improved; they will no longer regard each other as either outsiders, potential enemies, aggressors or subjects to be conquered, but will meet one another on a more equal and respectful footing as commercial friends, potential traders and mutual needs-providers. Of course, commercial friendship is only an instrumental, ersatz type of friendship devoid of passion and warmth. It is animated by what Smith calls "necessitudo" meaning "that it was imposed by the necessity of the situation". "Colleagues in office, partners in trade" find that "[t]heir good agreement is an advantage to all; and, if they are tolerably reasonable people, they are naturally disposed to agree" (*TMS* VI. ii.1.15–16). The commercial cosmopolis is a form of amicable strangership; our fellow cosmopolites are neither friends "from whom we can expect any special favour and sympathy" nor enemies "from whom we cannot expect any sympathy at all" (Mizuta, 1976, p. 122; see also Hill, 2011). But "so what?" thinks Smith, because impersonal, instrumental friendship is infinitely preferable to the malevolent mercantilist alternative.

Therefore, although Smith disagreed with the Stoics about how much we owe to the rest of the world, he shared their desire for a world society based on amicable and respectful relations with everyone, everywhere. This would add immeasurably to happiness and prosperity but also to liberty and mobility, two conditions he held dear. Economic cosmopolites, Smith observed presciently, were the future: "He" who possesses capital "is properly a citizen of the world ... not necessarily attached to any particular country" and able to "move himself and his stock freely from place to place" (*WN* V.ii.f.6). Whereas the Stoics also valued freedom of global movement and insisted on the universal duty to offer asylum, aid and hospitality to everyone who asked for it, be they foreigner, stranger or even enemy (Cicero, 1990, I.51, pp. 55; 3.27, 295), Smith asks only that we permit the free global movement of capital, commodities and the economic cosmopolites who produced and owned them. Everyone is entitled to the "*liberi commercii*" – the "right of trafficking with those who are willing to deal with him" (*LJ*(A), i.12–13), regardless of whether they are compatriots or distant strangers. Through an international division of labour whereby nations prudently export surpluses and import shortages, productivity, prosperity and levels of material comfort will be exponentially enhanced. Best of all, famine will become a distant memory. Trade will unite "the most distant parts of the world" and enable separate nations to "relieve one another's wants", "increase one another's enjoyments" and encourage "one another's industry" (*WN* IV.vii.c.80). Accordingly, all protectionist policies and trade barriers should be revoked "and liberty of exchange ... allowed with *all nations and for all things*" (*LJ*(B), 269, emphasis added). As this happens, economic cosmopolites will suspend those irrational "national jealousies" that cause potential trading partners "to spite and ill-will each other", and irrationally "refuse to be supplied by them in any convenience of life" (*LJ*(A), vi.164–65). They will also cease to regard the prosperity of their neighbours with "malignant jealousy and envy" but will cheerfully celebrate "the internal happiness and prosperity of the other, the cultivation of its lands, the advancement of its manufactures, the increase of its commerce, the security and number of its ports and harbours" and "its proficiency in all the liberal arts and sciences" because, in the long run, the benefit of one is the benefit of all. After all, these "are all real improvements of the world we live in" and therefore, in one way or another, available to everyone everywhere (*TMS* VI.ii.2.3).

There will still be sovereign states in Smith's "liberal system" but they will operate as a single community of amicable but separate "provinces of a great empire" (*WN* IV.v.b.39). Due to the tendency of free trade to enrich all nations, members will eventually become unwilling and unable to "over-awe" other nations or violate their "rights" (*WN* IV.vii.c.80–1). Commerce, not impartial benevolence, will become the universal substitute for war and a siblinghood of amiably disposed but distant exchangers will gradually displace a universe fraught with suspicion, xenophobia and hostility. As Smith sees it, the "state of peace" is synonymous with the state of "commerce" (*WN* IV.iii.c.11).

It is important to remember, however, that despite Smith's apparent optimism here, he was still an Epicurean realist where the potential for inter-state aggression was concerned. Until economic cosmopolitanism had become fully entrenched, the natural passions of acquisitiveness and invidious comparison, coupled with the economic success of commercial societies, exposed the latter to the perpetual threat of "violence and injustice" from "other independent societies" (*WN* V.i.a.39; *WN* i.a.40). He therefore argued for a permanent system of defence as a necessary evil, the only means to guarantee that commercial states could live in peace and prosperity (*WN* V.i.a.15; IV.v.b.43). But, in the long term, he hoped that a mutual desire to trade would deter interstate conflict.

Neither did the Epicureans see much prospect for world peace or the withering away of sovereign states (Long, 2008, p. 58). But they did value the pacific life and regarded friendship as the most important good: "Of all the means that are procured ... to ensure happiness" opines Epicurus, "by far the most important is the acquisition of friends" (Diogenes Laertius, 1925, X.27, p. 673). Friends add to our pleasure but also, notably, to our safety: "Nothing enhances our security so much as friendship" (X.28, p. 673). Like Smith long after him, Epicurus was alert to the interested ambitions of foreign neighbours and taught that friendship is necessitous because the world outside the Epicurean garden is full of threat. Friendship, and the mutual forbearance that goes with it, is desirable for instrumental reasons.

> He who best knew how to meet fear of external foes made into one family all the creatures he could; and those he could not, he ... did not treat as aliens; and when he found even this impossible, he avoided all intercourse, and, so far as was expedient, kept them at a distance.
>
> (Diogenes Laertius, 1925, X.39–40, p. 677)

So, although Smith thinks the Stoics were mistaken in their expectation that the world-state or *cosmopolis* would be held together by such lofty moral and affective bonds as Stoic *philanthropia* and *sympatheia*, by importing a realist

Epicurean moral psychology into an optimistic Stoic framework, an equally desirable version could be imagined and achieved.

11.7 Conclusion

Despite his attraction to their pragmatism, Smith was a more ambitious and idealistic thinker than the Epicureans. They lacked what Stoicism was able to provide: a Deistic framework that conceived the universe as a benign, self-equilibrating system. Stoic theodicy also enabled Smith to reconcile the Epicurean strains of this thought with his own sincere belief in a designed universe. But Stoicism lacked what Epicureanism was able to provide: a convincing account of human drives and moral psychology. Smith reconfigures this unlikely combination into a plausible social scientific explanation of how individual societies and their relations with other nations should and could be managed. Benevolent impartiality towards strangers and the world at large might be impossible but happiness and prosperity was still achievable, provided it was recognised that the divine architect moves in mysterious, often counter-intuitive ways.

12

"Much Better Instructors"
Adam Smith and the Role of Literature in Moral Education

LAUREN KOPAJTIC

It is now often observed that Adam Smith had a keen interest in literature, and that his works reveal that interest and even have formal affinities with various literary forms, including theatrical drama and fictional narrative. Charles Griswold (1991, 1999) has written extensively about Smith's interest in literature as part of his pedagogical rhetoric, attending to Smith's roots as a public lecturer, and then as a professor. Griswold (2010, 2018) has also analyzed the theatrical and narrative elements of Smith's works, focusing on Smith's moral psychology as presented in *TMS*. Colin Heydt (2012) has similarly focused on the pedagogical aspects of *TMS*, showing how Smith balances concrete and abstract elements in his character descriptions in order to engage the reader in the activities of moral discernment and judgment. Several scholars, including Nancy Armstrong (2005), Stephanie Degooyer (2018), Ian Duncan (1998), Samuel Fleischacker (2019a), Rae Greiner (2010, 2012), John Mullan (1988, 1996a, 1996b), and Karen Valihora (2016) explore connections between Smith's moral philosophy and the novel, which emerged as a literary form during Smith's lifetime. These scholars are interested in how the novel, with its highly particularized characters, engaging narrative, and absorbing effects on readers, produces the processes of sympathy and spectatorship described by Smith. Finally, Deirdre Dawson (1991) and Neven Leddy (2009) have explored the lines of influence between Smith and the French novelists he names in his works.

This chapter contributes to this growing scholarship by bringing Smith's views on rhetoric and education together with his account of sympathy and spectatorship, and placing both views in the context of his recommendation of specific literary authors. In the sixth edition of *TMS*, Smith made extensive revisions to Part III, including a striking addition:

> The poets and romance writers, who best paint the refinements and delicacies of love and friendship, and of all other private and domestic affections, Racine and Voltaire; Richardson, Maurivaux [sic], and Ricciboni; are, in such cases, much better instructors than Zeno, Chrysippus, or Epictetus.
>
> (*TMS* III.3.14)

While often-cited, Smith's recommendation of these particular authors rarely receives detailed consideration. Furthermore, to my knowledge, no one has yet attended to the immediate context for this recommendation, which is an examination, heavily revised for the sixth edition, of how we learn the "hardest of all the lessons of morality," the lesson of how to "correct" the balance between our oft-excessive concern for our own affairs and our often "improper indifference" to those of others (*TMS* III.3.7–8). Smith argues that "two sets of philosophers" have tried to teach us this lesson: "The first would have us feel for others as we naturally feel for ourselves. The second would have us feel for ourselves as we naturally feel for others" (*TMS* III.3.8). The first set, dismissively called the "whining and melancholy moralists," are criticized for seeking to increase our commiseration with the distresses of others, absurdly "render[ing] a certain melancholy dejection habitual to all men" (*TMS* III.3.9). The second set, identified with the ancient Stoics, is also criticized for a kind of absurdity, in this case working against the natural and proper preferences we have for our own loved ones. As Smith writes, just prior to recommending literary authors, "the stoical apathy is, in such cases, never agreeable, and all the metaphysical sophisms by which it is supported can seldom serve any other purpose than to blow up the hard insensibility of a coxcomb to ten times its native impertinence" (*TMS* III.3.14).[1] For Smith, both systems are flawed, in part because neither makes distinctions within the class of private feelings. Smith's view, which stands opposed to the two he criticizes, is that private feelings that are responses to those we love, like "parental tenderness," "filial piety," and other "domestic affections," are often salutary and should be cultivated in high degrees (*TMS* III.3.13). And his claim in our focal passage is that some modern literary authors instructively illustrate the affections that we should cultivate in ourselves and sympathize with in others, providing a valuable aid to the sentimentalist moral philosopher who is trying to teach us this "hardest of all the lessons of morality."

Smith enlists the help of literature in his project of moral education, but he does not explain *why* or *how* literature can be so instructive. This chapter fills in this account, elucidating the instructive potential of the early novel, and showing how well suited the techniques of that form are to the goals and challenges of Smith's sentimentalist moral philosophy. Focusing primarily on Samuel Richardson's *Clarissa* (1747–1748), Pierre Marivaux's *La Vie du Marianne* (1727/1743), and Marie Jeanne Riccoboni's *Lettres de Milady*

---

[1] I do not have the space to discuss Smith's criticisms of Stoicism, but see Kopajtic (2020) for an overview of the literature on this topic, along with an argument for why Smith is not best read as holding Stoic conceptions in his sentimentalist moral philosophy. Smith is likely using the Stoics in this passage because they provide the strongest contrast with the authors he recommends.

Juliette Catesby (1759/1760),[2] I show how themes and formal features shared by these three novels can contribute to Smithian moral education.[3] Thematically, as many have shown, the prose fiction of mid-eighteenth-century France and Britain is overwhelmingly concerned with personal relationships of family, friendship, and romantic love. Given Smith's view on the biases and limitations of sympathy and spectatorship, these novels provide valuable access to perspectives, sentiments, and relationships that would otherwise be inaccessible to the spectator. Formally, I will focus on several well-documented features of the epistolary form of the novels of these three authors, showing how a reader's engagement with these features works to activate and train their spectatorial capacities.

This chapter proceeds as follows. In Section 12.1, I establish that Smith, like many of his contemporaries, held that literature played an important role in moral education because it provided entertaining and persuasive "paintings" of sentiments and character. In Section 12.2, I show *why* literature is valuable in a Smithian moral education, turning to the need for access to aspects of psychology, sentiment, and relationship that are normally blocked to spectators. Finally, in Section 12.3 I turn to the question of *how* literature performs the functions assigned to it, focusing on formal features shared by three novels,

---

[2] My choices of specific novels and editions are based on popularity during Smith's time, quality across the oeuvre, and accessibility to the present-day student of Smith. Smith had no works by any of these three authors in his library, and no specific works by any of the authors are mentioned anywhere in his corpus, including his correspondence. See Mizuta (2000) and Klein and Humphries (2019) for the catalog of Smith's library. *Clarissa* is considered to be Richardson's best novel and was an avowed favorite of several of Smith's contemporaries (including Samuel Johnson, Diderot, and Rousseau). Marivaux's *Marianne*, began in 1727 but left unfinished, was also popular in France and England. There were several attempts to continue or finish the novel, and many English translations. I rely on the most popular translation and completion of this novel during Smith's lifetime, Mary Mitchell Collyer's 1743 edition. Riccoboni's *Juliette Catesby* was published in 1759, and translated into English soon after by Frances Brooke (1760). This novel was a bestseller in France, and Brooke's translation went through several popular editions as well. In the cases of Marivaux and Riccoboni, I rely on a contemporaneous English translation for convenience, not because Smith would not have or could not have read these novels in French.

[3] My narrow focus on these three authors and on their prose writings is motivated by concerns of space, but also guided by the structure of Smith's reference. Smith's reference to the five writers includes two categories ("poets and romance writers") and then two groups of authors, separated by a semi-colon. Racine and Voltaire, I take it, are representatives of "poets", or verse writers, where Richardson, Marivaux, and Riccoboni are representatives of "romance writers," or writers of prose fiction (the terms "romance" and "novel" were used interchangeably at this time). Of the five named authors, Voltaire, Marivaux, and Riccoboni produced significant work in both categories, but Racine produced no prose, and Richardson produced virtually no verse. Further research is needed on what educational role the verse dramas of Racine and Voltaire might play in Smith's view.

and showing how the reader engages in spectatorial training in the controlled setting provided by the novel.

12.1 Painting Sentiments

In our focal passage, Smith describes the work of Richardson, Marivaux, and Riccoboni, saying that they "*paint* the refinements and delicacies of love and friendship, and of all other private and domestic affections" (*TMS* III.3.14, emphasis added). Smith's description recalls David Hume's distinction between two species of moral philosophy: that which anatomizes virtue and that which paints it. Moral painters, according to Hume,

> [P]aint [virtue] in the most amiable colours; borrowing all helps from poetry and eloquence, and treating their subject in an easy and obvious manner, and such as is best fitted to please the imagination, and engage the affections. They select the most striking observations and instances from common life; ... They make us *feel* the difference between vice and virtue; they excite and regulate our sentiments ...
>
> (Hume, 2001, 1.1)

Smith and Hume each indicate the powerful effects of rhetorical literature, literature that borrows "all helps from poetry and eloquence." By illustratively representing, or "painting" sentiments, characters, and virtues, literature can contribute to moral education.[4]

This understanding of the rhetorical power of literature was common in Smith's moment. In Smith's *LRBL*, for example, he describes good writing as "the art of painting or imitation" and claims that a good writer must "paint" their subject "in the most proper and expressive manner" (*LRBL* i.105). In their 1763 speeches on the question "Ought the Reading and Writing of Romances to be encouraged?" the student-organized Edinburgh Belles Lettres Society associates painting with the romance, arguing that "The writer of Romance has in his Power to Paint every Scene which can delight the Mind. He may mingle with his Narration the most beautiful Descriptions, and all the Charms of native Eloquence" (Bator, 1996, p. 296). Hugh Blair, in his own *Lectures on Rhetoric and Belles Lettres* (2005), describes the novel, or the "fictitious history", as providing "one of the best channels for conveying instruction, for painting human life and manners, for showing the errors into which we are betrayed by our passions, for rendering virtue amiable and vice odious" (Blair, 2005, p. 421). According to Blair, "well contrived stories" are more "useful" "vehicles of knowledge" than "simple and naked instruction"

---

[4] See Craig Smith's chapter in this volume for a related discussion of Smith's understanding of moral education.

(2005, p. 421). Literature, and especially the novel, is understood as employing vivid representative forms in order to entertain, persuade, and instruct.

Literature was thought to be a powerful vehicle for education, especially the moral education of young people. In his report to Dugald Stewart, James Millar remembered the role of literature in Smith's pedagogy,

> The best method of explaining and illustrating the various powers of the human mind ... arises from an examination of the several ways of communicating our thoughts by speech, and from an attention to the principles of those literary compositions which contribute to persuasion or entertainment. By these arts, every thing that we perceive or feel, every operation of our minds, is expressed and delineated in such a manner, that it may be clearly distinguished and remembered. There is, at the same time, no branch of literature more suited to youth at their first entrance upon philosophy than this, which lays hold of their taste and their feelings.
>
> (EPS 274)

Millar attests that Smith saw the pedagogical value of the study of rhetoric and literature, emphasizing the study of "those literary compositions which contribute to persuasion or entertainment," as well as their powers of expression, delineation, and description. Indeed, Smith's comments on the ancient moralists in *TMS* affirm that he saw that "agreeable and lively pictures" can "inflame our natural love of virtue, and increase our abhorrence of vice," thus producing "the noblest and most lasting impressions" on young and flexible minds (*TMS* VII.iv.6).

Millar and Smith do not refer specifically to novels in these passages, and indeed, acknowledgment of the rhetorical power of literature often surfaces as anxiety over the corrupting influence of novels, especially on young people.[5] James Fordyce, for example, in his *Sermons to Young Women* (1766), condemns the "vulgar story-telling tribe" who produce novels with a "pestiferous" tendency, and contain "rank treason against the royalty of Virtue" (Fordyce, 1766, pp. 145, 148). Nevertheless, many were still willing to grant the instructive potential of high-quality novels. Samuel Johnson warns, in a 1750 essay in *The Rambler*, that since novels are "written chiefly to the young, the ignorant, and the idle, to whom they serve as lectures of conduct, and introductions into life," precautions must be taken (Johnson, 2000, p. 176). The novelist should seek to secure their audience from "unjust prejudices, perverse opinions, and incongruous combinations of images," and should therefore avoid representing vicious or mixed characters and improbable events (Johnson, 2000, p. 176). But he also lauds the novelist for representing, with veracity and clarity, pictures of "life in its true state", gleaned from "accurate observation of

---

[5] For further discussion, see, inter alia, Mullan (1988, pp. 93–109).

the living world" (Johnson, 2000, p. 175). Novelists like Richardson (2011, pp. 3–4) and Henry Mackenzie (1987, pp. 99–103) also warned against inferior productions while lauding the powerfully instructive capacities of the best novels. During Smith's lifetime, novels were held to have special powers above and beyond other literary forms, and to be especially appealing to young, impressionable minds. While there were certainly concerns that these powers could be used for ill, it was widely accepted that when directed by propriety, sincerity, and delicacy, the novelist's skills could greatly influence the moral development of the novel-reader.

Statements about the instructive (or corrupting) powers of the novel are commonplace in the eighteenth century. But how exactly is this instruction understood? What is the literary "painter" doing, and how does their work contribute to the moral education of the reader? Answering these questions will be the work of the next two sections of this chapter, but for now I want to note two things. First, while the metaphor of moral painting is pervasive and evocative, it is also misleading. Reading a novel that narrates the lives of several characters, including their thoughts, feelings, relationships, and actions, is not like viewing a static painted scene. To bring the comparison closer together, reading Smith's vivid and dynamic description of the man stung by guilty conscience (TMS III.2.9) is not like viewing a painting of David Garrick in the role of guilty Macbeth, it is not even like being in the audience as Garrick delivers Macbeth's dagger soliloquy on stage. Reading a novel takes time – more time than viewing a painting or even, in most cases, than watching a play at the theater – and it is something most people do silently and privately, even in Smith's own moment.[6] In the next parts, we will examine some distinctive themes and forms of the early novel, seeking to deepen and specify these commonplace claims about the instructive potential of literary "painting."

Second, while I have canvassed the remarks of several prominent mid-eighteenth-century writers in order to show some of the common assumptions and claims, the goal of this chapter is to understand what *Smith* means when he says that novelists are "much better instructors". To that end, it is important to ask our questions about the instructive potential of the early novel from within Smith's moral framework. Smith conceives of moral education from within a naturalist, sentimentalist, virtue theoretical framework. As such, moral education will not involve indoctrination, strictly intellectual development, or the internalization of universal moral laws. Instead, it will involve: (1) the development of psychological capacities, like imagination, sympathy, and the ability to suppose and occupy other perspectives; (2) an understanding of

---

[6] For further discussion of reading practices in the eighteenth century, see Lynch (1998); Mullan (1996a).

the different affective states, the situations that give rise to them, and the levels of propriety for each; and (3) the cultivation of virtuous character traits. Smithian moral education will thus involve training over time and in a range of different venues. My argument here is thus connected to the general question of the moral importance of literature, but I am not offering a general claim about how reading novels will make you a better person. My claim is that, in the context of Smith's moral philosophy, reading certain kinds of literature contributes to the training of skilled Smithian spectators.

As I will show later, this view of moral education as involving training and cultivating various psychological capacities in a variety of venues helps to explain how novels function as vehicles of instruction. But before turning to the question of *how* novels do this work, we should ask *why* – why rely on novels for moral instruction when other forms and venues might also suffice?[7] What can a novel do that a sermon, or an encounter in the marketplace, or a course of lectures cannot do? What are the distinctive contributions of the novel as it was understood in Smith's lifetime, as a fictitious, narrative, prose form of writing focused on the lives of ordinary people?[8]

12.2 Momus's Glass

For Smith, becoming a mature moral spectator is the work of a lifetime. On Smith's account, we all develop an "idea of exact propriety and perfection," "gradually formed" from our "observations upon the character and conduct" of ourselves and others. This "slow, gradual, and progressive work" involves the development and refinement of the capacities of imagination, sympathy, and judgment in a range of settings and situations. Importantly, this work is always in progress, and the accuracy, design, and aptness of the idea we are forming is dependent upon the "delicacy and acuteness of that sensibility, with which those observations were made, and according to the care and attention employed in making them" (*TMS* VI.iii.25). But there are important situations

---

[7] Smith cites two authors of verse drama in our focal passage, so he clearly thinks they can be sources of moral instruction as well, but the question of whether the novel provides a *distinctive* form of moral education from that provided by a drama would need to examine the similarities and differences between these forms, which I do not have space to do here. See Marshall (1986) and Griswold (1999) for further discussion of drama in a Smithian setting; see Degooyer (2018) for an argument that the dyadic audience–spectator interaction enacted by drama does not best fit the "triangular" spectatorial framework in Smith, whereas, Degooyer argues, the sentimental novel does. I make a similar point later about the triadic structure of Smithian spectatorship, but I connect this with the epistolary novel.
[8] The novel was also distinguished from other forms by appearing primarily as a printed book in volumes, which could be purchased from a bookseller or borrowed from a circulating library. For further discussion of the material history of the novel, see Lynch (1998) and Stein (2020).

that will be less accessible to developing spectators.[9] Private and domestic affections, the very feelings to which Smith refers when he lauds the powers of fictional narrative and drama, will be hidden from view, at least outside of our own homes and private spaces. Furthermore, affections like parental love, sibling animosity, or romantic passion will be hard to sympathize with because of the peculiarity of the attachment, which Smith claims presents a significant obstacle to the spectator. But these private and domestic affections are ubiquitous and enormously important in our lives. So, how can a Smithian spectator "make observations" on and refine and develop their sense of these feelings?

The observations of the developing spectator are constrained by several obstructive psychological, social, and material conditions. General psychological opacity is one such obstacle. In *Tristram Shandy* (1767), Laurence Sterne has his eponymous narrator reflect on the problems of trying to understand other people. Tristram references the legend of the Greek god Momus and his complaint that humans had been foolishly fashioned out of clay, without a window to look in:

> [H]ad the said glass been there set up, nothing more would have been wanting, in order to have taken a man's character, but to have taken a chair and gone softly, as you would to a dioptrical beehive, and look'd in,- view'd the soul stark naked ... then taken your pen and ink and set down nothing but what you had seen, and could have sworn to:—But this is an advantage not to be had by the biographer in this planet ... our minds shine not through the body, but are wrapt up here in a dark covering of uncrystalized flesh and blood; so that, if we would come to the specifick characters of them, we must go some other way to work.
>
> (Sterne, 2009, pp. 59–60)

Similarly, Smith begins *TMS* with a description of our sympathetic interest in the affairs of others, immediately following this with a claim about our general opacity. Our senses, claims Smith, "never did, and never can, carry us beyond our own person." He adds that "it is by the imagination only that we can form any conception of what are his sensations" (*TMS* I.i.1.2). There may be no wishfully convenient window into the soul, but the imagination provides a way into the minds and hearts of others.

For Smith, the imagination is an associative and creative faculty which depends entirely on the input of one's own experiences and sensations (*TMS* I.i.1.2). The primary function of the imagination, as detailed in *TMS*, is to enable the work of sympathy, or "fellow-feeling with any passion whatever" (*TMS* I.i.1.5). Sympathy requires the capacity to imaginatively represent the situation of another person, and to place oneself in that situation, sometimes described by Smith as a change of place. Our interest in other people provides

---

[9] See Kopajtic (2022) for discussion of a related problem.

a continual background motivation to engage in this work, as does our desire for mutual sympathy – to feel concord and approval with whatever the other person is feeling, especially in moral matters, and to receive the same ourselves. But these efforts are made laborious by the general opacity of other people. Furthermore, they are constrained by other material and social limitations, including geographical and language barriers, and the barriers dividing people along class, gender, and racial lines. In order to gather the experiential input sufficient to allow the spectator to imagine the situations of others and subsequently to sympathize with them, we need to find ways of overcoming these obstacles, and aids for that work.

In other words, for Smith, sympathizing with another person requires an observational tool enabling one to peer through the opacity of others, and an access point. Imagination is the observational tool, but what are the access points? In the case of prudence or ambition, the access points are likely to be public and familiar – go to the market, an office, or a club – whereas the access points for loyalty or gratitude may be more private. Furthermore, depending on who one is and what areas of society one occupies, there will be instances of prudence or ambition, loyalty or gratitude that will be less visible because the individuals feeling those feelings are not within one's sympathetic orbit. These obstacles are not insurmountable, and, conveniently, the novel provides the access points and aids required. By thematizing private spaces, feelings, and relationships, the novel enables the development of the Smithian spectator.

In order to better see this, let's look at one of Smith's more infamous claims about an obstacle to sympathy – the difficulties of sympathizing with "peculiar" feelings and the relationships founded on them. Smith claims that the passions "which take their origin from a peculiar turn or habit [the imagination] has acquired, though they may be acknowledged to be perfectly natural, are, however, but little sympathized with." With these passions, "the imaginations of mankind, not having acquired that particular turn, cannot enter into them; and such passions, though they may be allowed to be almost unavoidable in some part of life, are always, in some measure, ridiculous." Romantic love is his primary example in this discussion, and Smith goes so far as to say that "all serious and strong expressions of it appear ridiculous to a third person" (*TMS* I.ii.2.1). This surprising statement is often dismissed as an oddity, perhaps tied to Smith's lifelong bachelor status, but engaging with this discussion of romantic love will help show why the novel form is a particularly valuable vehicle for moral education.

Smithian spectators are not ideal observers – they have limitations, finding it difficult, for example, to sympathize with passions that are based in the body, like hunger and thirst (*TMS* I.ii.1.1–3); and they have preferences, including a tendency to admire the rich and the powerful (*TMS* I.iii.3.1). Smith's account of moral spectatorship and judgment are built out of an empiricist moral psychology, and so, some nonideal features of human psychology come along. One of those features, according to Smith, is the fact that it is difficult, near impossible, for me to sympathize with your love for your specific beloved. This is because of the *peculiarity* of the attachment – you love a particular person, with a particular set of traits, interests, and so on. Furthermore, you have a unique history with that particular person, and much of that history takes place in private and intimate moments, moments you would not, or perhaps could not communicate to me. If I am lucky enough to love someone myself, I may have a general sense of what it is like to love, but that general sense cannot provide my imagination with the detail sufficient for me to imaginatively recreate your peculiar romantic love – my imagination does not have enough input to do the necessary work. Since Smithian sympathy depends on the imaginative construction of the situation of the other, when that imaginative construction fails, so too does the sympathy.

Crucially, while Smith holds that we cannot sympathize with a specific lover's love for their specific beloved, he holds that we *can* sympathize with their general situation: "it interests us not as a passion, but as a situation that gives occasion to other passions which interest us; to hope, to fear, and to distress of every kind" (*TMS* I.ii.2.2). Moreover, when romantic love is placed in a situation that provokes several of these passions, it can render that love "wonderfully interesting" (*TMS* I.ii.2.3). Smith claims that this is precisely the effect of "some modern romances and tragedies" – by placing the lovers in a situation that gives rise to hope and fear, we are able to sympathize more successfully with their entire situation (*TMS* I.ii.2.3). Referring to Racine's *Phèdre*, Smith writes,

> We are charmed with the love of Phaedra ... notwithstanding all the extravagance and guilt which attend it. That very extravagance and guilt may be said, in some measure, to recommend it to us. Her fear, her shame, her remorse, her horror, her despair, become thereby more natural and interesting. All the secondary passions, if I may be allowed to call them so, become more furious and violent; and it is with these secondary passions only that we can be properly said to sympathize.
>
> (*TMS* I.ii.2.4)[10]

The narrative and dramatic frame provides the details of Phaedra's situation, which importantly includes these "secondary passions" with which we can sympathize.

Thus, while we do not sympathize with the passion of romantic love, we do sympathize with the situation of romantic love. Furthermore, sympathy with

---

[10] Smith's use of examples from the plays of Voltaire and Racine suggest that he saw drama, or "poets" as also providing important access points for spectatorial training and observation. But see note 7 for further discussion of the connections between novels and drama.

the situation of romantic love is enabled by the vivid presentation of the secondary passions of love as well as the details of the situation that give rise to those secondary passions. Finally, Smith explicitly refers to literary representations of the situation of romantic love as those capable of rendering this passion accessible to spectators. Taking all of this together, we can see how the novel would be especially well-suited to providing a much-needed access point for romantic love. The novel form allows for a highly vivid and detailed presentation of the situation of romantic love, including a lengthy unfolding of the characters of the lovers, and the contrivance of the situations of distress that are necessary both for plot and pacing, as well as to make the romantic love "wonderfully interesting." It is hardly surprising, then, that the three novelists named by Smith all wrote fictional histories wherein romantic relationships are central.

Smith does not hold that other private affections, like sibling or parental love, are subject to the same limitations as romantic love, and, indeed, he argues that high degrees of such feelings often earn the sympathetic approval of the spectator (*TMS* III.3.13). Nevertheless, such affections, because of their private and domestic nature, will be less on display in the public arenas of life, and so less accessible to the spectator. The novel provides access to these other private affections by delineating, in Ian Watt's words, "the domestic life and the private experience of the characters who belong to it: the two go together – we get inside their minds as well as inside their houses" (Watt, 1957, p. 175). Readers of Richardson's *Clarissa*, for example, are let into the private spaces of Harlowe Place and the subsequent cells in which Clarissa is confined. They can cringe while Clarissa reports an especially nasty interaction with her sister Arabella, and they can feel the despair Clarissa feels when her beloved mother refuses, yet again, to see or speak with her. These domestic interactions and private moments are made accessible through the novel.

The novel, then, is a valuable vehicle for moral instruction within Smith's framework because it provides the access points and informational input needed to fully imagine the private and domestic situations that give rise to "private and domestic affections." More specifically, the novel offers access to situations like that of romantic love, which one otherwise would not be able to sympathize with; to instances of peculiar passions like parental tenderness, which one would otherwise have access to only in one's own or limited cases; and to a wider range and more instances of many passions and situations, as felt by people one does not already know. Of course, this is not to say that the novel must do such work, nor that all novels do such work. But our focus is on why Smith enlisted "poets and romance writers" for moral instruction, and one answer is that the writers of novels open windows onto familiar but new worlds. But the novel does not just open a window, it shapes how one looks through that window and what one sees. So, *how* do novels do this work?

12.3 Spectatorial Training in the Epistolary Novel

There is a quick and ready answer to the question of how novels contribute to the work of moral education in a Smithian framework – they draw the reader into created perspectives and situations, thereby producing the workings of sympathy and spectatorship.[11] I want to focus closely on both parts of this claim about the function of the novel: how exactly it *draws the reader in*, and how exactly it *produces the workings of sympathy and spectatorship*. I will structure this discussion as I set out above, looking closely at the formal features shared by three novels, each written by one of the three novelists Smith names.

Richardson, Marivaux, and Riccoboni all wrote epistolary novels, or novels composed primarily or exclusively of letters between particular correspondents. Marivaux's *Marianne*, the earliest of the three (1727/1743), is a memoir in letters, with the various entries presented as lengthy letters written by Marianne to a silent correspondent, referred to only as "Madam." The histories of other people are related by Marianne within her own history, and she frequently reports, with improbably good recall, lengthy conversations involving a wide cast of characters. Richardson's *Clarissa*, next in publication (1747–1748), is the most multi-vocal of the three novels, with two correspondences in the spotlight, the letters between Clarissa Harlowe and her close friend Anna Howe, and those between Robert Lovelace and his friend Jack Belford. Letters to and from a number of other people also pass through the hands of our main correspondents, and other letters and documents are enclosed and described. Riccoboni's *Juliette Catesby* (1759/1760) begins mono-vocally, with only Juliette's letters to her friend Henrietta, but as the correspondence continues, letters from other authors are enclosed and commented on, including two lengthy histories of events. All three novels are narrated first-personally, and primarily by the protagonists, who relate and reflect on their own experiences.

There are three features of the epistolary form that are important in a Smithian context. First, the epistolary form largely employs present-tense narration, with the correspondent relating their thoughts and feelings as closely to their occurrence as possible. While this aspect of the form has been the site for much criticism, it is also an important part of how the reader is drawn into the narrative frame. Second, the familiar letter was widely recognized in Smith's moment as a document that attested to the intimate and sincere sentiments of the writer. Reading the correspondence of another person was held to be an especially valuable way to gain insight into their

---

[11] Several scholars have made a version of this claim (Griswold, 1991, 1999; Duncan, 1998; Greiner, 2012; Valihora, 2016; Chamberlain, 2017; Degooyer, 2018; Fleischacker, 2019a).

sentiments and character. Finally, the letter explicitly provides a vehicle for narrating the "situation" of the "person principally concerned," to use Smith's terms. Marianne, Clarissa, and Juliette all respond straightforwardly and at great length to the prompting question of Smithian sympathy with distress: "What has befallen you?" (*TMS* I.i.1.9). Positioned in the place of the recipient of those letters, the reader of the novel becomes the spectator of the protagonist, listening to her detailed narrative of her situation. These three aspects of the epistolary form help to explain how readers are: (1) drawn into the novel, (2) informed and persuaded through the evidence of a supposed documentary history, and (3) thus placed in the position of the well-informed and sympathetic spectator ready to imaginatively enter into the situation of another. To see this, let us take up each aspect in turn.

While Marivaux's *Marianne* is a memoir, relying more on the intrinsic interest of the story – a beautiful young orphan who has suffered much and is now telling the full tale of her life from a position implying that things will work out – Richardson's *Clarissa* and Riccoboni's *Juliette Catesby* rely on other narrative techniques to draw the reader into the narration. *Juliette Catesby* begins *in medias res* and unfolds the history of the events preceding the first letter, using letters written in the heat of the moment, occasionally bearing the marks of an interruption and resumption of the correspondence. But Richardson is the avowed inventor of a highly effective technique for drawing readers in. In his Preface to *Clarissa*, he writes: "the letters on both sides are written while the hearts of the writers must be supposed to be wholly engaged in their subjects ... they abound not only with critical situations, but with what may be called *instantaneous descriptions and reflections*, which may be brought home to the breast of the youthful reader" (Richardson, 1985, p. 35 emphasis added). Clarissa and Lovelace are both constantly writing – "never was there such a pair of scribbling lovers as we," as Lovelace says – trying to keep up with the live reporting of their experiences and interactions (Richardson, 1985, p. 416).

While this pretense of instantaneous recording strains probability, nevertheless, the advantage of present-tense, first-personal narration is that it can involve the reader deeply in the fictional world of the novel.[12] In an 1804 piece for *The Edinburgh Review*, Francis Jeffrey describes the effect of Richardson's techniques: "with Richardson, we slip, invisible, into the domestic privacy of his characters, and hear and see every thing that is said and done among them, whether it be interesting or otherwise, and whether it gratify our curiosity or disappoint it. ... We feel for [them], as for our private friends and acquaintance, with whose whole situation we are familiar" (Jeffrey, 1844, vol. 1,

---

[12] From the publication of *Pamela*, this pretense has been much criticized; see, *inter alia* Bray (2003), Spacks (2006) and Watt (1957).

pp. 321–322). According to Jeffrey, this "slip" into the domestic privacy of Richardson's characters is accomplished through the present-tense narration as well as the "unparalleled copiousness and minuteness of his descriptions, and in the pains he takes to make us thoroughly and intimately acquainted with every particular in the character and situations of the personages with whom we are occupied" (Jeffrey, 1844, vol. 1, p. 321). Richardson's narration is immersive, detailed, and interesting, capturing the imagination of the reader and bringing them into the situations of the letter-writers.

It is also significant that the narration is accomplished entirely through personal letters. In Smith's moment, as Patricia Spacks writes, "personal letters, assumed to be intimate communication, could plausibly express their writers' hidden thoughts and deep feelings" (2006, p. 92). Blair also expresses this promise of insight into and acquaintance with another mind through their letters, but with an important note of caution:

> It is childish indeed to expect, that in Letters we are to find the whole heart of the Author unveiled. Concealment and disguise take place, more or less, in all human intercourse. But still, as Letters from one friend to another make the nearest approach to conversation, we may expect to see more of a character displayed in these than in other productions, which are studied for public view. We please ourselves with beholding the Writer in a situation which allows him to be at his ease, and to give vent occasionally to the overflowings of his heart.
>
> (Blair, 2005, p. 418)

A person's letters, while not capable of providing the magical window wished for by Momus, nevertheless carry the familiarity of a conversation between friends, allowing the reader of those letters to slip easily into that conversation, learning about the people involved.

The intimacy and sincerity of personal letters is amplified by a further common pretense of the early novel, its status as a found object, edited and published by a third party, not fabricated by an author. In his preface to *Clarissa*, Richardson styles himself the "editor" of this massive collection of letters (1985, p. 35). In Marivaux's original advertisement in *Marianne*, he claims that he received the manuscript from a friend and has only made small corrections to the original text, and in Collyer's translation, she removes this advertisement, replacing it with a "Preface" that repeatedly classifies the text as a "history" (1965, pp. 527, n3). Well into the narrative, Marianne responds to an unseen response from her correspondent, complaining about Marianne's treatment by her "perfidious" lover, Valville, writing, "Could anything be more diverting? . . . I fancy that, instead of the life of your friend, you have insensibly brought yourself to believe you were reading a romance" (1965, p. 279). Riccoboni eschews all prefatory material entirely, and there is no indication of an author or editor beyond the letter-writer, "Milady Juliette Catesby," and the recipient, "Milady Henriette Campley," on the original title page. Scholars have suggested that this authenticating pretense had the effect of encouraging and heightening immersion into the novel, or at least of "overcoming prejudice against romantic invention" (McBurney and Shugrue, 1965, p. xxii). As Lynn Hunt writes, this "created a vivid sense of reality precisely because their authorship was obscured within the letters' exchange. This made possible a heightened sense of identification, as if the character were real, not fictional" (2007, p. 42). A novel like *Clarissa*, then, with its pretense of being an authentic "History of a Young Lady" encourages the reader to take the substance of the letters seriously, reflecting on them as the documentary evidence of real (or at least plausibly realistic) people truthfully reporting on their lives, relationships, and sentiments.

The actual fictional status of the characters and their letters, however, would seem to be a mark against their instructive capacity for Smith. In *LRBL*, Smith separates the "Romance" from the "History," claiming that with the first form the aim is only to entertain, and so "it is of no consequence whether the incidents narrated be true or false." But in a history, the goal is "the instruction of | the reader. It sets before us the more interesting and important events of human life, points out the causes by which these events were brought about and by this means points out to us by what manner and method we may produce similar good effects or avoid Similar bad ones." Smith continues, even more strongly, "the facts must be real, otherwise they will not assist us in our future conduct, by pointing out the means to avoid or produce any event. Feigned Events and the causes contrived for them, as they did not exist, can not inform us of what happened in former times, nor of consequence assist us in a plan of future conduct" (*LRBL* ii.19). In *LRBL*, Smith seems to hold the view that the instructive goal of historical writing would be undermined by fictitiousness. What, then, of the status of those "fictitious histories" he recommends some thirty years later?

Some guidance can come from Smith's classification of these genres in terms of their subject matter and descriptive modes. Smith notes that early "Romances," like early "Histories" had as their subject "the marvellous." These were tales of "withches [sic] and fairies," of "Heroes and centaurs and different monsters" (*LRBL* ii.61). But the "Novell," here marked out as a different form, turns away from these fantastic accounts and endeavors instead to "unfold | the tender emotions or more violent passions in the characters they bring before us" (*LRBL* ii.61). Smith goes on to associate the novel with "internall" description, or the description of internal states: "the thoughts sentiments or designs of men, which pass in their minds" (*LRBL* ii.64; i.150). Smith associates "internal" description with "indirect" description, or the description of the effects of a quality on those who behold it, claiming that "Internall objects as passions and affections can be well described only by their effects" (*LRBL* i.160; i.182). Smith associates both internal and indirect description with the historical form of writing:

> The ancients carry us as it were into the very circumstances of the actors, we feel for them as it were for ourselves. {They show us the feelings and agitation of Mind in the Actors previous to and during the Event. They Point to us also the Effects and Consequences of the Event not only in the intrinsick change it made on the Situation of the Actors but the manner of behaviour with which they supported them}.
>
> (LRBL ii.28)

While Smith is describing historians, like Thucydides, who wrote history by focusing on the motives and sentiments of the actors involved, this could stand very well as a description of what the early novelist took herself to be doing.

Richardson's *Clarissa* is subtitled "The History of a Young Lady," and in *Pamela* he advocates for the morally instructive capacity of the novel, at least when it narrates its history in a "probable" and "natural" way (2011, p. 3). Collyer writes in the preface of her translation of *Marianne*,

> The reading of that part of history that relates to human life and manners has been always considered by allowed judges as one of the best methods of instructing and improving the mind. When we see the heart laid open, and the secret springs and movements that actuate it exposed and set in one impartial light with their different good and evil tendencies, we are enabled to form a true estimate of human nature and are taught what ought or ought not to be our own conduct in every similar instance.
>
> (Marivaux, 1965, p. 3)

Collyer adds that in a nonfictional history, "the scene of action is generally laid in exalted and public life among *deep politicians* and *martial heroes*" rendering it such that "few readers ... will ever have occasion to reduce the example into practice" (1965, p. 3, emphasis original). Collyer suggests that the instructive function of a history depends on the probability and accessibility of the characters and events, along with the internal and indirect forms through which it is narrated. The internal narrative description lays the heart of a character open, and the indirect form focuses on how that character is affected by the events of their life and the qualities of the people to whom they are related. In *LRBL*, Smith agrees that the novelist employs the methods of indirect, internal description, even lauding Marivaux for being "Allways at great pains to account for every event by the temper and internall disposition of the several actors" (*LRBL* ii.64). Arguably, then, Smith would recognize that a probable but fictitious history does more than merely entertain, producing the instructive effects of a history by borrowing the formal modes of that genre.

Thus, we do not need to posit that Smith changed his mind about novels between the discussion in *LRBL* and the recommendation of three authors of epistolary novels in the sixth edition of *TMS*. Genre categories at this time were fluid and imprecise, but nonetheless, the fictitious history, relying on the techniques of indirect and internal narrative description that Smith praises for their instructive capacities, would have elevated it above the "Fabulous" romance or a fantastic novel of adventure. Moreover, as early as the first edition of *TMS*, in 1759, Smith used examples of our sympathy with characters of "tragedy and romance," implying that fictionality is not a bar to our being able to enter into their situations (e.g. *TMS* I.i.1.4, I.ii.1.11, I.ii.2.3–4, I.ii.3.2, III.6.12). Finally, it is important to remember that we have been focusing on a specific kind of instruction. Some novelists and some novel-readers may have sought to treat the novel as a handbook to the virtuous conduct of a young servant-girl, or as a descriptive guide to how to survive after you have been shipwrecked on an island, such that fictionality might undermine such instructive functions. But our focus has been on how the novel provides access to sentiments and relationships otherwise blocked to the spectator, and on how the novel trains the reader's moral capacities. In the specific authors Smith mentions, this work is accomplished through the epistolary form, which makes special claims to the intimacy and authenticity of what is being reported.

Taking all of these aspects of the epistolary form together – the first-personal, present-tense narration, which produces an immersive experience, and the pretenses of authenticity and veracity, which produce an expectation of insight into realistic characters – we can see how this form produces the processes of sympathy and spectatorship. The reader of the epistolary novel is positioned as the spectator of the protagonist, listening to their account of what has befallen them, being entreated to sympathize with their situation and sentiments, and to approve of their motives and actions. But we need to be careful here. Some scholars have described this effect of the epistolary novel as encouraging "identification" with the characters of the novel, but this can misleadingly suggest a *collapse* of the reader and their own character into that of the literary character with whom they are engaging (Watt, 1957, p. 201; Hunt, 2007, p. 38 ff.). While some of Smith's descriptions of the spectator's imaginative efforts suggest that this is what he has in mind (*TMS* VII.iii.1.4), there is an important limit to these imaginative efforts. The morally relevant sympathetic interaction is essentially dialogic and comparative, and it requires the retention of at least two perspectives in the exchange. In the sympathetic interaction, the spectator retains a "secret consciousness" that the imaginary change of situations is *imaginary*. Moreover, Smith stresses that although sympathy will never produce "unisons" of sentiment, it may produce "concords," and "this is all that is wanted or required" (*TMS* I.i.4.7).

Retaining the distinction between the spectator and the person principally concerned is also crucial for allowing perspective-switching:

> In order to produce this concord, as nature teaches the spectators to assume the circumstances of the person principally concerned, so she teaches this last in some measure to assume those of the spectators. As they are continually placing themselves in his situation, and thence conceiving emotions similar to what he feels; so he is as constantly placing himself in theirs, and thence conceiving some degree of that coolness about his own fortune, with which he is sensible that they will view it. As they are constantly considering what they themselves would feel, if they actually were the sufferers, so he is as constantly led to imagine in what manner he would be affected if he was only one of the spectators of his own situation.
>
> (*TMS* I.i.4.7)

Moving between perspectives, as Smith describes here, enables the spectator to feel a moral sentiment, which is produced upon the comparison of the agent's "original passion" with the "sympathetic emotion" felt by the spectator after imagining the situation of the agent (*TMS* I.iii.1.9, note). Moving between perspectives also enables the agent's efforts of self-command. Moral sympathy, or the kind of sympathy that can produce a well-formed moral sentiment, whether with a real person or with a fictional character, cannot be a collapsing kind of identification, or it would fail to produce *Smithian* sympathy, spectatorship, and self-command.

A further subtlety is brought out by attending to how the sympathetic interaction involves perspective-switching. Obviously, when I read *Clarissa*, I do not imagine that Clarissa is responding to my efforts to imagine her situation. The sympathetic interaction is not "live" as it is in Smith's description above, nor is it strictly dyadic, with one spectator and one person principally concerned. But sympathetic perspective-switching is still enabled by the novel, and especially by the epistolary novel. The format of the letter, written by one person, addressed to a second person, and being read by yet a third person, the reader of the novel, produces a *triadic* sympathetic interaction. Further complexities introduce even more perspectives and more perspective-switching, as when, in *Clarissa*, Clarissa reports a conversation with her brother to Anna, representing that conversation as dialogue, or when, in *Juliette Catesby*, Juliette forwards to Henrietta a letter written by Lady Sunderland to Sir William Manly, which was given to Juliette by Sir William as a representation of Lady Sunderland's character.

The epistolary novels we are examining proliferate with different perspectives and different characters, many of whom clamor to have their voice heard and their situation sympathized with. As scholars have noted, those perspectives do not always coincide or complement one another, and the reader is placed in the position of adjudicating between competing claims for sympathy and approval. As Spacks notes, an epistolary novel "demand[s] of its readers alertness to the implications and ambiguities of individual points of view" (2006, p. 93). In the case of *Clarissa*, where the central relationship is antagonistic, clouded by deception and threatened by violence, the reader is in an even more challenging interpretive position. Clarissa and Lovelace each relate the same encounters and conversations to their respective correspondents, revealing how different perspectives produce different narrations of the same event. The reader is thus faced with the challenges of assessing how perspective and character influence narration, and of assessing the propriety and merit of the different narrations and what they reveal about the perspectives that produced them.

The epistolary novel thus produces multi-positional sympathetic structures, with the reader of the novel in the more detached and removed position, addressed by the letter-writers through at least one mediating perspective, the addressee of the letter. As such, the sympathetic structure produced by the epistolary novel most closely resembles Smith's description of sympathizing through the device of the "supposed impartial spectator." On his first account of the sympathetic interaction in *TMS* Part I, Smith focuses on one spectator, one person principally concerned, and one target feeling, broadly taken as any affective response to any object that might affect one of those two people in some particular way (*TMS* I.i.4.5). But in *TMS* Part III, Smith complicates and specifies this account. He targets a specific class of passions, the "selfish and original passions of human nature," which are strong and recalcitrant passions that threaten our ability to sympathize with the misfortunes and fortunes of other people (*TMS* III.3.3). In order to balance and "correct the otherwise natural inequality of our sentiments," we must learn to suppose and occupy a third position. Smith writes, "before we can make any proper comparison of those opposite interests, we must change our position. We must view them, neither from our own place nor yet from his, neither with our own eyes nor yet with his, but from the place and with the eyes of a third person, who has no particular connexion with either, and who judges with impartiality between us" (*TMS* III.3.3). In this more complex sympathetic interaction, there are at least three perspectives involved – the perspective of the subject, the perspective of the person the subject is interacting with, and the perspective of a third person who is impartial to the first two. In the attempt to sympathize, the subject toggles between all three of these perspectives, but relies on the third, impartial one as that from which to sympathize, feel moral sentiments, and judge.

The ability to suppose and occupy the perspective of an impartial spectator, and so to correct for the natural imbalance in our sentiments, is learned and developed. But we need no gloomy browbeating or "metaphysical sophisms" to develop this skill, as Smith claims some philosophers have thought (*TMS* III.3.9, III.3.14). Instead, Smith holds that we develop it fairly easily: "habit and experience have taught us to do this so easily and so readily, that we are scarce sensible that we do it" (*TMS* III.3.3). And a few pages later, after arguing against the views that would make this into arduous and unnatural work, he recommends the epistolary novels of Richardson, Marivaux, and Riccoboni. Smith's recommendation is not an offhand remark, but placed in a discussion about how we learn the lessons of morality through habit and experience. This recommendation of literature, and of epistolary novels especially, is embedded in Smith's own account of how we learn to regulate our selfish, personal passions through the device of the supposed impartial spectator, a device which requires one to regularly imaginatively suppose the perspective of someone else, and to see and feel from that perspective. The three epistolary novelists are "much better instructors" than the Stoic philosophers because they help the novel-reader to "easily" and "readily" train their skills of sympathetic and imaginative spectatorship in the engaging and instructive worlds they create.

12.4 Conclusion

While Smith's recommendation of several modern literary authors is often noted, little work has yet been done on why he recommends epistolary novelists as "much better instructors" on the private and domestic affections that are so important in our lives.[13] This chapter has argued that Smith's recommendation is motivated by the need for access to situations, relationships, and sentiments that are otherwise difficult to observe, and by the general need to train one's spectatorial capacities in a variety of venues. The training of the Smithian spectator will involve the imaginative supposition of other characters and perspectives, of different types of situations, and of different sentiments and relationships. The epistolary novels of Marivaux, Richardson, and Riccoboni, with their thematic focus on the private and domestic relationships of family, friendship, and romantic love, and with their use of forms that engage the reader's imagination and sympathy, inform their understanding, and persuade and challenge their judgment, provide highly effective venues for such training.[14]

---

[13] Further research is needed on whether Smithian moral education could be similarly aided by other forms, like the sentimental novel, and by other narrative techniques, like free indirect discourse. See Kopajtic (2022) for discussion of free indirect discourse and focalized narrative.

[14] I am grateful to Fordham University for the fellowship that provided support during the research and writing of this chapter. I am also grateful to Paul Sagar for the invitation to write this piece, and to Deidre Lynch and Yoon Sun Lee for welcoming me into the virtual *Clarissa* reading group that helped to shape my thoughts for this chapter. This chapter has benefitted from the feedback of the Virtue Ethics and Moral Psychology working group in NYC, and from fellow volume contributors.

13

Sophie de Grouchy as an Activist Interpreter of Adam Smith

KATHLEEN MCCRUDDEN ILLERT

13.1 Introduction

Sophie de Grouchy (1763–1822) was, by some measures, the most important commentator in the Francophone world on Adam Smith's *TMS* for the whole of the nineteenth, and most of the twentieth, century. Her translation of *TMS*, published in 1798, was the third into French. It quickly became viewed as the "definitive" French text, and was not supplanted until Michaël Biziou, Claude Gautier and Jean-François Pradeau produced a new critical edition in 1999 (Bréban and Delamotte, 2016, p. 667). Yet more than that, everyone who picked up a copy of *Théorie des sentiments moraux* – at least until 1981 – would also be exposed to Grouchy's own criticism of, interpretation of, and adaptations to, Smith's theory. Alongside her translation, she published her own treatise, the *Lettres sur la sympathie* (*Letters on Sympathy*), which was reproduced in both the 1830 and 1860 reeditions of her translation of *TMS* (Faccarello and Steiner, 2002, p. 62; Bonnet, 2016, p. 14).

Newspapers in 1798 described these *Letters* as a "complement" to Smith (Mercure Français, 1798). Historians today have labelled them somewhat dismissively as a "commentary" on *TMS* (Whatmore, 2002, p. 87). Yet the *Letters* are in fact a combination of an analysis of Smith and other thinkers, and a presentation of Grouchy's own complex philosophy. Indeed, Grouchy made no bones about the fact that she intended to massage the message delivered in *TMS* for a French audience, informing her readers that the *Letters* were intended to "examine," "modify," and "even combat" some of Smith's ideas (Condorcet, 1798a, p. viii). In the face of this clear statement of purpose, various scholars have analysed the changes that Grouchy made to Smith's theory: both implicitly in her translation, and explicitly in her *Letters* (Dumouchel, 2010; Seth, 2010; Biziou, 2013; Tegos, 2013; Bréban and Delamotte, 2016; Schliesser, 2019). However, the emphasis has been on the intellectual reasons for the adaptations. There is little focus on more directly political motivations. This is despite the fact that we know that Grouchy was actively involved in Revolutionary politics beside her husband, the marquis de Condorcet (1743–1794). In 1791, for example, she co-founded, along with Condorcet, and possibly Thomas Paine (1737–1809), Achille du Chastellet

(1759–1794), Étienne Clavière (1735–1793), and Jacques Pierre Brissot (1754–1793), a short-lived radical republican journal, *Le Républicain* (Martin, 1927). Indeed, Sandrine Bergès, one of the few scholars who does link Grouchy's project in the *Letters* to a direct political context, points to 1791 as the crucial year for its drafting. She argues that the *Letters* were written in part to provide the ethical theory behind the type of republicanism forwarded in *Le Républicain*, a theory that she describes as founded on the ideal of "neorepublicanism," or nondomination (Bergès, 2015, pp. 103–104). The general reluctance to ascribe political motives to Grouchy's "modifications" is due, in large part, to a lack of clarity over when exactly Grouchy wrote her *Letters* and began her translation. Debates continue to flourish over which came first, and when in the period 1790–1793 work began (Forget, 2001, p. 230; Whatmore, 2002, p. 84; Sonenscher, 2007, p. 324; Scurr, 2009, p. 444; Badinter, 2010, p. 124; Bréban and Delamotte, 2016, p. 703; Bergès and Schliesser, 2019, p. 23). Although a seemingly insignificant date range, these three years covered a tumultuous period of French history: from the abolition of the hereditary nobility, the Civil Constitution of the Clergy, the uprising of black slaves in Saint-Domingue, the flight of Louis XVI to Varennes, the declaration of war in Europe, the September massacres, the trial and execution of the King, and the beginning of the Terror. Grouchy was in Paris to witness all these events, and she could have been reacting, potentially or in part, to any one of them. It is this difficulty in pinning down a convincing timeline for Grouchy's engagement with Smith that has led to vagueness about Grouchy's possible political motivations, or the temptation to dismiss them altogether. Eric Schliesser summed up this tendency when he argued that "[t]here is no evidence that in 1798," when her translation and *Letters* were published, "De Grouchy [sic] had any hope she could influence the development of Napoleonic France. Rather, by systematising and radicalising Smithian principles, De Grouchy is offering us a model to aspire to ... [she] in no sense has to take into account the interests of established powers" (Schliesser, 2019, p. 218).

This chapter will argue that treating Grouchy as a utopian thinker, motivated in her interpretation of Smith entirely by intellectual aims, is the wrong approach. Rather, the "modifications" she made to his theory, presented most explicitly in her *Letters*, were directly spurred by the period in which she was writing, and were often deeply political. This is not to draw a false dichotomy between the "political" and the "intellectual": the two are, of course, deeply interconnected. Rather, it is to argue that by missing her political motivations, we risk essentialising Grouchy as an ivory-tower translator and commentator, and portraying the French version of Smith that she produced as a timeless philosophical artefact. It is here useful to draw on the concept of "activist translation." Rebecca Ruth Gould and Kayvan Tahmasebian have recently defined activist translation as that which "stirs readers and audiences to actions," a goal which "may stand in tension with – and even contradict – a literal rendering of words on the page" (Gould and Tahmasebian, 2020, p. 4). Grouchy was, of course, more than a translator of Smith. She was also an "activist interpreter." She criticised and adapted Smith in order to stir her contemporaries to action. Crucially, as Gould and Tahmasebian point out, a crucial element of activist translations are their "timeliness": "Translations can only be activist at certain times and within certain social circumstances." Grouchy's translation and interpretation of Smith was a product of its time: she was trying to do specific things with it.

Grasping the fact of the "timeliness" of Grouchy's presentation of Smith in turn affects our understanding of the intellectual impact in France of *TMS*. If we are to correctly understand the diffusion of Smith in France, his influence on Francophone philosophy, and the relationship between modern French thought and Smithian moral philosophy, it is vital to grasp in what role Grouchy originally cast Smith in the texts that would be the main entry-point to his philosophy for the Francophone public between 1798 and 1999.

This argument draws on that made by Bergès, when she sought to connect Grouchy's *Letters* to *Le Républicain* (Bergès, 2015). However, I will suggest that Bergès misidentified the correct context for the composition of Grouchy's *Letters*. I will argue, based on hitherto undiscovered archival evidence, that Grouchy in fact wrote this treatise during the period 1786–1789. Her target was not the Bourbon monarchy, but the unjust *ancien régime* court system, and the lack of knowledge among the common people of morality and their natural rights. Where she disagreed with Smith, and where she made changes to his theory, were on these points: how to make morality more accessible, and how to make society more equal.

This chapter will focus on Grouchy's *Letters*, as her most explicit statement of how she hoped to "combat" Smith's ideas. The conclusions found here may, however, be used in future to analyse the choices she made in her translation. It is not the aim of this chapter to establish whether or not Grouchy was normatively or philosophically "right" in her criticisms of Smith's theory: but rather to explore what they were, why they arose, and what changes she proposed in their place. Section 13.2 will describe two key critiques that Grouchy made of Smith's *Theory of Moral Sentiments* in her *Letters*: the need for an impartial spectator, and the tendency for humans to sympathise more with those higher in the socio-economic hierarchy than themselves. Section 13.3 will demonstrate that Grouchy focused on these elements due to two parallel contexts: her desire to write an educational treatise for an Académie française competition, and her involvement, together with her new husband Condorcet, with an *ancien régime cause célèbre*, the affair of the *trois roués*. Section 13.4 will explore how Grouchy constructed an alternative theory which she saw as better suited to these demands. Section 13.5 concludes that seeing Grouchy as an "activist commentator" on Smith helps us to re-interpret the influence of his *TMS* in nineteenth- and twentieth-century France.

13.2

In the 1798 version of Grouchy's *Letters*, the earliest extant text, Grouchy notes that she is indebted to Smith for the concept of sympathy. In reading his *TMS*, and in particular "the chapters on sympathy," she informs her readers, "I had other ideas on the same subject" (Condorcet, 1798b, p. 356). Indeed, she initially provides a broadly similar definition to Smith. While the first chapter of *TMS* defines the emotion as "our fellow-feeling with any passion whatever," Grouchy describes "sympathy" as "the disposition that we have to feel in a way similar to that of others" (*TMS* I.i.1.5; Condorcet, 1798b, p. 357). Nevertheless, she is also explicit that while engaging with *TMS*, "instead of following the ideas of the philosopher of Edinburgh, I allowed myself to follow my own." This is clear when she turns to directly criticising elements of Smith's philosophy.

In this section, I will outline two key critiques that Grouchy makes of Smith's theory in her *Letters*. The first is the removal of Smith's impartial spectator. Smith's basic description of a moral man is someone who considers "what will be the sentiments of the cool and impartial spectator," and chooses his actions as those most fitting or suitable to these sentiments (*TMS* I.ii.3.8). This device is central to his moral system. Grouchy, however, is deeply critical of this move. She equates what she calls Smith's "inhabitant of the breast, the man within," with the "moral sense" of fellow Scottish philosopher Francis Hutcheson (Hutcheson, 1725):

> Smith, (she states) ... claims that our knowledge of justice and injustice, or virtue and vice, derives in part from their suitability [*convenance*] or their lack of suitability [*disconvenance*] with a type of intimate sense [*sens intime*].

This, she suggests, is a "monstrous fable" (Condorcet, 1798b, p. 464).

Grouchy's main objection to Smith's impartial spectator seems to be that it introduces an unhelpful degree of emotional distance into moral calculations. This was, of course, precisely Smith's intention: being too close to our own emotions inevitably clouds our assessment of them. "We can never survey our own sentiments and motives ... [or] form any judgment concerning them," he argues, "unless we remove ourselves ... from our own natural station" (*TMS* III.1.2). Grouchy, on the other hand, wants to reverse the trend she claims to have identified in Smith, of "seek[ing] outside of nature and always far from her, the motives for being good." There is no need to invent a "*sens intime*," she argues. These motives can be found much closer at hand: by consulting our "direct and close interest" (Condorcet, 1798b, p. 466).

Grouchy, in other words, wants to trace all moral impulses back to self-interest. In this inclination she was not, of course, alone. John Robertson has identified a project of "moral Epicureanism" which defined the work of Enlightenment philosophers including David Hume and Giambattista Vico, who also integrated sentiments such as sympathy into their arguments (Robertson, 2005). This trend was alive and well in the intellectual circles in which Grouchy moved from the time of her marriage to Condorcet in 1786. It is hard to believe, for example, that Grouchy would not have been familiar with the controversial work of Claude Adrien Helvétius (1715–1771). Although unlikely to have known him personally, she was intimate with the group surrounding his widow, Anne-Catherine de Ligniville (1722–1800), at Auteuil (Guillois, 1894, p. 66). Helvétius, in *De l'Esprit* (1758) and the posthumously published *De l'Homme* (1773), argued that physical sensitivity was the sole principle of mental activity, so that the basic law of human behaviour was the self-interested search for pleasurable sensations. Unlike previous thinkers, such as Thomas Hobbes, however, Helvétius did not think that such human egoism would necessarily lead to anarchy without powerful state control; instead, he suggested that self-interest could itself be a driver of human sociability. The need to find one's own judgment confirmed by others, and the pleasure that came about when it was, Helvétius suggested, served to give rise to relatively stable societies (Sonenscher, 2007, pp. 266–281). As will be seen in the next section, Grouchy bases her account of morality on a similar foundation.

Grouchy's second objection considered here was to take aim at Smith's argument that we have a tendency to sympathise more with those higher in the political or socioeconomic hierarchy than ourselves. "[E]very injury that is done to them," Smith argues in *TMS*, "excites in the breast of the spectator ten times more compassion and resentment than he would have felt had the same thing happened to other men. It is the misfortunes of Kings only which afford the proper subjects for tragedy" (*TMS* I.iii.2.2). Grouchy demurs, declaring "I do not think that Smith has indicated the real reason which makes us pity dethroned kings." It was not, as she interprets Smith as arguing, "because the idea of grandeur . . . disposes us by a sort of affection and deference for [kings'] happiness to sympathise more particularly with them," but rather because "kings seem to us to have been preserved from misfortune by their elevation, and thus we judge that they must be more sensitive to it" (Condorcet, 1798b, p. 408). Indeed, in reality, such sympathy with kings, and the upper classes in general, barely exists. Sympathy for superiors, Grouchy argues, is "absolutely opposed to the sentiment of natural equality, which leads us to regard with jealousy, or at least severity, all that is above us" (Condorcet, 1798b, p. 408).

Moreover, she is scathing about the idea, expressed by Smith, that inequality could be useful for the stability of society. Describing those who are "recommended to our benevolent attention and good offices," Smith lists "the rich and the powerful, the poor and the wretched." "[T]he peace and order of society," he goes on, "are, in a great measure, founded upon the respect which we naturally conceive for the former." He even warns against tampering with this socioeconomic hierarchy, suggesting that "Nature has wisely judged that the distinction of ranks, the peace and order of society, would rest more securely upon the plain and palpable difference of birth and fortune, rather than upon the invisible and often uncertain difference of wisdom and virtue" (*TMS* VI.ii.1.20). Grouchy, on the other hand, states explicitly that it is "equality" that is "necessary" for the maintenance of "security in all the relations of the social order" (Condorcet, 1798b, p. 416). To this end, she declares baldly, "[o]ne of the principal objects of the laws, must thus be to give birth to, and to maintain among citizens, the equality of fortunes" (Condorcet, 1798b, p. 372).

Grouchy's argument here is reminiscent of the case that her husband would make in his 1793–1794 *Esquisse d'un tableau historique des progrès de l'esprit humain*. While in hiding from the Jacobin Terror, Condorcet suggested that the "final end of the social art" would be "real equality" (Condorcet, 1795, pp. 328–329). To this end, Condorcet proposed a scheme, subsidised by public *caisses d'accumulation*, which would support widows, orphans, and labourers past the age of work (Condorcet, 1795, p. 306; Stedman Jones, 2005, p. 24). Gareth Stedman Jones and Michael Sonenscher have shown how Condorcet's argument about inequality and the need for redistribution owed much, in its outline, to Smith: in particular to Smith's conception of "the science of the legislator," and his ideas about the social usefulness of investment and insurance (Sonenscher, 2015, p. 693). Nevertheless, Stedman Jones admits that Condorcet – and by implication, Grouchy – took these insights in a radically different direction from Smith. Smith was deeply suspicious of any "man of system" who sought to impose a preconceived plan of improvement on society (*TMS* VI.ii.2.17). In particular, "[f]or Smith," Stedman Jones argues, "the progress of 'natural liberty' stood in place of a politics of redistribution" (Stedman Jones, 2005, pp. 25, 30–31). In place of the state, the "invisible hand," as Smith described in *TMS*, would ensure that the rich would "make nearly the same distribution of the necessaries of life, which would have been made, had the earth been divided into equal portions among all its inhabitants" (*TMS* IV.i.10). It is here, in fact, that Grouchy's divergence from Smith becomes clear. While "natural liberty" was at the heart of his political vision, Grouchy's emphasis lay instead on "natural equality" (Condorcet, 1798b, p. 408).

13.3

Grouchy, therefore, took issue with the elements of Smith's *TMS* that seemed to remove moral decisions too far from the individual's self-interest, and those which promoted a social and economic hierarchy over equality. But why were these her targets? And what did she propose in their place? To answer these questions, we must establish the context in which Grouchy was first drafting her *Letters*. And, as has been indicated, this is no easy feat. Three pieces of evidence are generally called upon by historians wishing to date this text. The first is a letter, written by Grouchy between March and May 1792 to her friend Étienne Dumont (1759–1829), the Swiss writer and editor of Jeremy Bentham. Grouchy sent Dumont a manuscript which she stated was part of her *Lettres sur la sympathie*. This has led Bergès and Schliesser to argue for 1791 as the original composition date (Grouchy, 1792; Bergès and Schliesser, 2019, p. 23). Pierre Louis Roederer (1754–1835), deputy to the Estates General, and later an influential politician under Napoleon's Empire, provides two further accounts of when he first saw the manuscript of the *Letters*, giving varying dates of 1789 or 1790 (Roederer, 1798, 1859, p. 194; Sonenscher, 2007, p. 324; Scurr, 2009, p. 444).

Yet none of these accounts take stock of the claim made consistently by Grouchy's daughter, Eliza Condorcet O'Connor (1790–1859), in various manuscript biographies of Grouchy, that her mother's "letters on sympathy" were "written before the revolution" (Condorcet O'Connor, no date a, fol. 26). Grouchy and Condorcet O'Connor remained close throughout Grouchy's lifetime, so it seems surprising that Condorcet O'Connor would be mistaken. And indeed, there is a fourth set of documents, hitherto ignored by scholars, that bolster the case for an earlier date for the original composition. In the *Bibliothèque de l'Institut*, amongst Condorcet's papers, lies a collection of – undated and untitled – notes written by Condorcet about an unknown work. The subject of this work is the moral education of children. "A father who grasps the principles established in this work," Condorcet wrote about the treatise on which he is commenting, "will direct the education [of his son] towards the development of his son's moral faculties." It is, moreover, a text that argues that the "sensibility of good and bad" is "born of the sympathy which we have for the unhappiness of others" (Condorcet, no date b).

A close comparison of this manuscript and the earliest extant copy of Grouchy's *Lettres sur la sympathie*, the 1798 version, reveals that it is extremely likely that Condorcet was here commenting on an early draft of Grouchy's *Letters*. The content of the text on which Condorcet was commenting – which he helpfully summarises – is so close to the argument of the published *Letters* as to be instantly recognisable. What is more, the following document in the archive provides a clue as to the original purpose of this draft. This second text is apparently a set of instructions written by Condorcet in 1783 for entrants to an essay competition offered by the Académie française between 1781–1786 for the best "Traité élémentaire de morale sur les devoirs de l'homme et du citoyen." (Condorcet, no date b).[1] I therefore suggest that Grouchy originally conceived her *Letters* in 1786, at Condorcet's prompting and under Condorcet's guidance, as a pedagogical treatise, written in response to this Académie française competition. In this interpretation, Condorcet, who had been named secretary of the Académie in 1782, recommended the prize to Grouchy after meeting her in August 1786, over the course of their courtship. Grouchy had dismissed previous suitors for not being sufficiently open, as her uncle put it, to her "taste for study" (Guillois, 1897, p. 48). It is therefore plausible that this was Condorcet's way of demonstrating his commitment to the intellectual side of her character.

This interpretation would explain Condorcet O'Connor's insistence that the *Letters* were an *ancien régime* text. There are both textual and historical reasons why it is convincing. It was not unheard of for women to participate in academic essay competitions during this period, particularly in those related to education. In 1783, the *Prix Montyon*, established the previous year as a prize for the *"ouvrage le plus utile"* was awarded to Louise d'Épinay's (1726–1783) *Les Conversations d'Emilie* (first published in 1774), narrowly beating Stéphanie-Félicité de Genlis's (1746–1830) *Adèle et Théodore, ou lettres sur l'éducation* (Smart, 2011, p. 90). On the textual front, it is worth noting that Grouchy's *Letters* often reproduces Condorcet's demands in his instructions for the competition word for word. While Condorcet asks that morality should be based on "the painful sentiment [*sentiment pénible*] that one feels in doing harm to another," Grouchy tells us that seeing the misfortune of another makes us feel a "very painful sentiment [*sentiment très pénible*]," that "this sentiment is more vivid when we are the voluntary or even the involuntary cause of this misfortune," and this feeling thus makes us want to avoid doing harm to others (Condorcet, 1798b, pp. 436–437, no date b, fol. 153). Condorcet further prompts that potential applicants to the prize should begin with an account of "particular sentiments [*sentiments particulières*]," and Grouchy describes in her first Letter "a particular sympathy [*sympathie particulière*] between those who are brought together by their tastes and habits" (Condorcet, 1798b, p. 378, no date b, fol. 153; McCrudden, 2021, pp. 43–48).

Nevertheless, while elements of Grouchy's *Letters* certainly do read like a pedagogical treatise, intended to help develop the moral faculties of children, other parts do not. Those sections, already cited, where she argues for government-sponsored redistribution of wealth, for example, seem out of place in this interpretation: as do those where she discusses the foundations of "reasonable laws" – whether "criminal" or "civil" – or launches into an

---

[1] For a more detailed analysis and dating of both of these manuscripts, as well as the text of Condorcet's "Fragment d'une letter sur l'opinion," see McCrudden, 2021 Appendix I and II.

invective against those who want to "substitute the wheel [*la roue*] and the scaffold for the true foundations of morality" (Condorcet, 1798b, pp. 490–492; 496). Elsewhere, she rails against economic and social "prerogatives" and "privileges" (Condorcet, 1798b, p. 452.).

To explain these elements, we must therefore modify our origin story of the *Letters*. While the text began life as an educational treatise in 1786, Grouchy added to it and adapted it in light of a pressing political crisis in which she was involved over the next two years: the affair of the *trois roués*. This *cause célèbre* (literally translated as "the three men who are to be broken on the wheel") unfolded thus (see also Maza, 1993, pp. 243–247). On the night of January 29–30 1783, three men forced their way into the house of a couple named Thomassin, farmers in the Champagne region. The couple were tied up, possibly tortured, and robbed. Three suspects were quickly arrested: Charles Bradier, Nicolas Lardoise, and Jean-Baptiste Simare. Their case ground through various jurisdictions, and it was not until June 1785, after the three men had been sitting in prison for over two years, that the regional authorities began to investigate. Nevertheless, only two months later four judges in Chaumont had condemned them to life in the galleys. The *procureur du roi* – the prosecution lawyer – protested the comparative lightness of the sentence, and lodged an appeal with the Parlement of Paris. On October 20, 1785, the majority of the Parlement condemned Lardoise, Bradier, and Simare to death on the wheel. This meant strangulation, after their limbs had been broken with a steel bar.

In a move that would change the course not only of the lives of the three *roués*, but also of both Grouchy and Condorcet, one of the three dissenting judges of the Parlement, and an uncle of Grouchy, Emmanuel-Marie-Michel-Philippe Fréteau de Saint-Just (1745–1794), unhappy with the verdict, decided to break the rules. He illegally showed the trial papers to his brother-in-law, Charles Dupaty (1746–1788), a magistrate from Bordeaux. Dupaty, horrified by the case, became convinced of the three men's innocence. He persuaded Fréteau to petition the keeper of the seals for a stay of execution and to appeal to the Royal Council, and in the meantime set about producing a public defence of the three men. His *Mémoire justicatif pour trois hommes condamnés à la roue*, published in February 1786, proved immensely popular – the queen herself and three royal princes were said to have purchased it – and Dupaty followed it up with another pamphlet in July (Dupaty, 1786a, 1786b). The Parlement of Paris was not, however, impressed. Interpreting his texts as a direct attack on their prerogative, they came down harshly on Dupaty, voting on August 18 to have his first *mémoire* publicly burnt. Into this maelstrom stepped the marquis de Condorcet, who in June 1796 published his own intervention. In his *Réflexions d'un citoyen non-gradué sur un procès très-connu*, he defended Dupaty, and echoed the calls Dupaty had made in his pamphlets for a reform of the legal system (Condorcet, 1786). The stage was set not only for Grouchy and Condorcet's encounter, but also Grouchy's first sustained exposure to the political injustices of *ancien régime* France.

It is clear what a large part the *trois roués* played in Condorcet and Grouchy's courtship and early marriage. It was, indeed, directly through his defence of the men that Condorcet met his future bride. A few days after their wedding, in December 1786, Condorcet wrote to his friend Josef Mikuláš, Count Windischgrätz (1744–1802), a member of a noble Bohemian family and himself a mathematician and *philosophe*. He explained how through the printing of his *Réflexions d'un citoyen*, Condorcet was able to strengthen his former friendship with Dupaty, which in turn gave him "the opportunity to meet one of [Dupaty's] nieces, beautiful, only twenty-three years old." Despite the difference in age – Condorcet was then forty-three – and his own professed "lack of agreeable attributes," Condorcet told his friend, "[m]y zeal for the affair that occupied her uncle, and for everything that can enlighten men or make them happier," led Grouchy to agree to "share my feelings, my work, and reward me for it" (Condorcet, 1787a). Contemporaries gossiped that it was only because of "the daughter of Madame the marquise de Grouchy" that Condorcet "defended the three Roués and the two magistrates, their protectors" with such "zeal" (Bachaumont and Mouffle d'Angerville, 1788, p. 304). If there was any doubt about the importance of this case to their relationship, it was dispelled on their wedding day. At the chapel of Villette, Grouchy's family home, Condorcet presented his young bride with the son of Charles Bradier, gift-wrapped in the costume of an English jockey (Maza, 1993, p. 257).

And as the fate of the three men was not finally resolved until December 1787 – when Bradier, Simarre, and Lardoise were declared innocent and allowed to sue their accusers – Grouchy and Condorcet's interest in the case continued into the first year of their marriage. Grouchy was passionately outspoken in her defence of the three men, and outraged at the legal personalities and systems that had caused them to suffer. On one occasion, in the presence of Guillaume-Chrétien de Lamoignon de Malesherbes (1721–1794), Grouchy became so carried away as to claim to want to kiss two of the imprisoned men. "You surely did not give too much faith, Monsieur," Condorcet wrote to Malesherbes, "to the accolade given by my wife to the three accused men ... I can guarantee that my wife has no more desire to embrace [*embrasser*] Simarre or Bradier than M. Séguier or the President d'Ormesson: and that says it all" (Condorcet, 1787b). The reference to Grouchy's disdain for Antoine-Louis Séguier (1726–1792) and Louis Lefèvre d'Ormesson de Noyseau (1718–1789), both conservative members of the Parlement of Paris, and her admiration for two of the three *roués*, demonstrates that Grouchy was in full support of the position taken by her embattled uncle and her new husband in the case, and that she continued to take a vivid interest in the affair.

It is this context, I suggest, that accounts for the more pointed critiques of the status quo, and particularly of unjust laws and "the wheel," that are to be found in Grouchy's Letters. Although it was first conceived in 1786 as an educational treatise, passages that supported the public position of Condorcet and Dupaty in the affair of the *trois roués* – in which Grouchy was involved from 1786–1787 – were soon added. Indeed, there are elements in the published Letters which echo those found in the pamphlets of this period of her new husband and uncle almost exactly. At one point, for example, Grouchy argues that people are less likely to turn in the perpetrator of a crime if they know the punishment for that crime will be unnecessarily brutal: thus, crime increases. This precise claim was also made in Condorcet's *Essai sur quelque changemens à faire dans les loix criminelles de France* (1786), another text written in response to the affair (Condorcet, 1904, p. 556). Equally, she launches a defence of those "philosophers *in the last few years*" who have "demanded just laws," and insists that it is time to "stop calumniating them and wanting to reduce them to silence": vividly recalling the burning of Dupaty's *mémoire* (Condorcet, 1798b, pp. 491, 496 emphasis added).

13.4

This new knowledge of the contexts in which Grouchy was first drafting her Letters, and her various motivations for putting pen to paper, throws fresh light on her reasons for critiquing Smith. Let us first consider her removal of the impartial spectator, and her promotion instead of our "direct and close interest" as at the foundation of morality (Condorcet, 1798b, p. 466). This desire was motivated, I suggest, by her initial aim of writing an educational manual explicitly aimed at the children of the common people. In his instructions for the Académie française prize, which I have argued was the initial spur for Grouchy to begin drafting her Letters, Condorcet is clear that the treatise should be intended for children of commoners as opposed to noblemen. The style should be made "simple and clear," perhaps by "importing ... forms of conversation" into the text (Condorcet, no date b, p. 154).

Grouchy embraces this demand in her Letters. She adopts a chatty style throughout, drawing her interlocutor, "my dear C," into conversation. She also criticises other moralists not necessarily for being wrong, but for being too esoteric. For example, she suggests that although she fundamentally agrees with the moral system of Luc de Clapiers, marquis de Vauvenargues (1715–1747), hers is superior, simply because his is "more difficult to understand, because [his moral rule] does not correspond to the idea that common men have of moral good and evil" (Condorcet, 1798b, p. 443).

Grouchy, in contrast, wanted to describe a slimmed-down route to making moral decisions that would be easily accessible to the children of uneducated commoners. She begins with the basic feeling of physical pain and pleasure

(Condorcet, 1798b, p. 357). This feeling is reproduced in us when we see others experiencing these feelings, through the mechanism of sympathy (Condorcet, 1798b, p. 359). The next step that Grouchy takes is to argue that the general pain or pleasure that is produced by the *sight* of others in pain can also be reproduced by the "abstract idea" of pain (Condorcet, 1798b, pp. 359–360). Simply the *idea* of someone else in pain can make us experience pain. It is here that, for Grouchy, reason enters the equation: we have to reflect in order to develop this abstract idea of pain, for "reflection draws out the ideas which our senses provide to us, it extends and conserves in us the effects of the sight of pain" (Condorcet, 1798b, p. 370).[2] This sympathising with the physical and moral pains and pleasures of others, whether immediate or abstract, is initially, for Grouchy, confined to those to whom we are physically and emotionally close. She labels this sympathetic relationship "particular sympathy" (Condorcet, 1798b, pp. 376–379).

It is from "particular sympathy" that the first stirrings of morality begin. The fact that it makes us happy when those to whom we are close are happy, and sad when they are sad, leads us to want to *cause* that happiness or help avoid that sadness. To get from particular sympathy to true morality, two further steps are required: to make this feeling of happiness of doing and having done good *abstract* and *general*. Just as you could be made to feel pain by the abstract idea of a tragic loss, Grouchy argues, you can be made to feel joy at the abstract idea of good being done. It no longer needs to be attached to a particular deed to produce the same feeling of pleasure. Equally, it is possible – and necessary – to escape simply from the desire to do good to those directly around you, and learn to desire to do good to *everyone*. Sentiments are, again, made abstract and general through "reflection." Once one has developed an *abstract* and *general* desire to do good – as well as an *abstract* and *general* desire to avoid evil – they have developed a sense of morality (Condorcet, 1798b, p. 441).

Grouchy is clear that reason must play a role in discerning moral right and wrong. Indeed, she defines "the idea of moral evil" as "*an action harmful to*

---

[2] Eric Schliesser has suggested that Karin Brown and James Edward McClellan are mistaken in identifying "reflection" with "reason" in Grouchy's *Letters*, arguing that in the Lockean philosophic tradition, "reflection" is a distinct faculty, where impressions and ideas are re-directed (Schliesser, 2019, p. 207). However, Grouchy herself does not seem to draw this distinction, and indeed conflates the two faculties. In describing her theory, she states that "it was necessary to show the origin of our moral sentiments in natural and unreflective sympathy for the physical pain of others; the origin of our moral ideas in reflection … One cannot say, however, that morality is founded on sentiment alone, because it is reason which shows us what is just or unjust; but one can even less support that it is founded uniquely on reason, because the judgment of reason is almost always preceded and followed by a sentiment which announces and confirms it" (Condorcet, 1798b, pp. 463–464).

another and which reason disavows" (Condorcet, 1798b, p. 442, emphasis in original). And yet, despite the importance of reason to her definition of morality, the crucial first step is always the emotional reaction. Indeed, ideally, the element of reasoning will at some point drop out, once the habit of acting morally has been acquired. The idea of good will automatically be associated with a "secret satisfaction" and bad with "remorse," without having to make any "calculations" (Condorcet, 1798b, p. 444).

It is thus, Grouchy believes, through this appeal to basic, individual, and personal passions, that morality can be taught to the populace at large. There exist, she argues "elevat[ed]" minds who have "acquired by reflection or by a sort of instinct the habit of increasing and generalising their ideas." But the mind of the "multitude" is "difficult to enlighten." It is therefore "necessary to ... seek in their passions, forces which extend and renew their intelligence" (Condorcet, 1798b, p. 449).

It is for this reason that Grouchy rejects Smith's impartial spectator. Of course, Smith also traced moral judgment, ultimately, to feelings. In his *TMS* he argued that while "reason is undoubtedly the source of the general rules of morality ... first perceptions, as well as all other experiments upon which any general rules are founded, cannot be the object of reason, but of immediate sense and feeling" (*TMS* VII.iii.2.7). Smith's impartial spectator is supposed to be free of partial feelings, but not free of sentiment altogether, nor derive judgments from reason alone. Here, they are fundamentally in agreement, with Grouchy making an almost identical point: "One cannot say ... that morality is founded on sentiment alone, because it is reason which shows us what is just or unjust; but one can even less maintain that it is founded uniquely on reason, because the judgment of reason is almost always *preceded* and followed by a sentiment which announces and confirms it" (Condorcet, 1798b, pp. 463–464, emphasis mine).

Yet, as D.D. Raphael and others have pointed out, Smith's concept of the impartial spectator as a mechanism for discerning moral right and wrong requires a complex feat of imagination (Festa, 2006, p. 27). In Smith's theory:

> An agent who consults his conscience in judging his own conduct has to imagine himself in the position of an uninvolved spectator who in turn imagines himself to be in the position of the involved agent; and, having performed this feat of imagination doubling back on its tracks, the agent has to ask himself whether the feelings that he imagines he would then experience do or do not correspond to the feelings that he actually experiences now.
>
> (Raphael, 2007, p. 52)

Grouchy rejected Vauvenargues's moral theory, despite the fact that "at heart" they had "the same definition" of morality, because his was too complex for educating "the least enlightened men" (Condorcet, 1798b, p. 443). This consideration, I suggest, was also uppermost in her mind when she stripped away Smith's impartial spectator. Why introduce a convoluted "man within," when a much simpler and easier route was available: appealing directly to each person's desire to feel pleasure and avoid pain? Grouchy was adapting Smith for what she saw as the lowest common denominator, and the impartial spectator had no place in that scheme. In doing so, whether intentionally or not, she refashioned Smith in the direction of earlier Epicurean accounts. Indeed, she could even be seen as bringing Smith closer to Bernard Mandeville, one of the most prominent interlocutors from whom Smith explicitly wanted to distinguish his own sentimentalist account (Sagar, 2018a). Although it began and ended with the self, the impartial spectator had allowed self-approval to be the reigning sentiment in Smith's moral system (Hont, 2015, pp. 41–42). Grouchy, in stripping away the "man within" to create an ecumenical moral code, replaced this with self-interest.

Grouchy's second major revision of Smith had less to do with her aim of providing an educational manual for the children of commoners. Her insistence on social and economic equality – and a state that ensured this fact – was prompted by her engagement with the inequities of the *ancien régime* legal system. A veritable cottage industry had developed in France in reform-minded circles by the 1780s: the production of tracts which linked specific calls for reforms to the judicial system to broader appeals to natural rights. This had arguably begun with Voltaire's defence, in 1763, of the Calvinist Jean Calas (1698–1762), who had been accused of murdering his son to prevent his conversion to Catholicism.[3] During the 1770s and 1780s, a pamphlet campaign for the abolition of torture and the moderation of punishment gained momentum, spurred on by the publication in Italian in 1764 and translation in French in 1766 of Cesare Beccaria's *On Crimes and Punishments*. Lynn Hunt has shown that although Beccaria himself did not stress the connection between his views on the need for a reformed criminal justice system and a discourse of natural rights, others were prepared to do so on his behalf. The abbé André Morellet (1727–1819), who translated *On Crimes and Punishment* into French, took Beccaria's only reference to supporting "the rights of man" out of the end of chapter 11 in the original 1764 Italian edition and moved it into the introduction. Thus, defending the rights of man was made to appear to be Beccaria's chief aim (Hunt, 2007, pp. 102–103). Both Dupaty and Condorcet explicitly positioned themselves as participating in this discourse. Condorcet, for example, claimed that in defending the *trois roués*, and demanding a reform of the legal code, he was not even asking for "a legislation worthy of an enlightened people, but [simply] the enjoyment of the first rights of humanity" (Condorcet, 1786, p. 17). Grouchy's critique of Smith's hierarchical thinking

---

[3] Smith himself makes reference to the Calas affair (*TMS* III.ii.11).

was also intended as a contribution to this call for a reformed society based on natural rights. I have shown elsewhere how Grouchy in her *Letters* further develops her conception of morality to explain how people can also gain an understanding of their natural rights through a reflection on their sentiments (McCrudden, 2021, pp. 74–87). In brief, she adds the criterion of universalizability to her definition of morality to come to a definition of justice (Condorcet, 1798b, p. 453). Importantly for our purposes, however, she also explains why any significant distinction in status or wealth has the potential to disrupt the mechanism by which individuals in society are able to act morally or with justice.

Due to the unequal distribution of fortunes, "the greatest part of the human race is doomed to a narrow dependence on all the beings which can help them to satisfy their needs"(Condorcet, 1798b, p. 376). This was to echo Jean-Jacques Rousseau, another key interlocutor of Grouchy, who in *Émile* (1762) stated that "[d]ependence of men ... engenders all the vices, and by it, master and slave are mutually corrupted" (Rousseau, 1991, p. 85). However, Grouchy goes further, and explains precisely *why* this dependence is so pernicious. "It follows," she tells her readers, "that each individual, soon contemplating those to whom he owes the greatest part of his existence, as the close and permanent cause of his pains and his enjoyments, their presence and the idea alone of them cannot be indifferent to him" (Condorcet, 1798b, p. 376). This emotional proximity is crucial. Recall that the vital first step in Grouchy's chain of reasoning was the experiencing of "particular sympathy" for those with whom one was physically and emotionally close. This was an important move, but in order to progress to true morality, and thus onto rights, one had to be able to *generalise* this feeling, so that it could apply not just to those with whom one was intimate, but to everyone. Dependence meant that men remained trapped in this particular sympathy with the person on whom they were dependent for survival. The consequences of thus being unable to generalise sympathy are momentous. If the "greatest part of the human race" are unable to generalise their emotions, they will be entirely incapable of knowing their own natural rights, or recognising those of others.

Sandrine Bergès describes this emotional stiltedness as the effect of domination (Bergès, 2015, p. 107, 2019, p. 352ff). However, Grouchy is explicit that it is caused by *dependency*, particularly of an economic kind. This is a fine distinction, but an important one, as it shifts the focus of Grouchy's argument. It is possible to be dominated (say, by a monarch), but not be directly economically dependent on them. Conversely, a tenant could be financially dependent on a landowner, but due to the master's laxity or absenteeism, not feel himself to be dominated by his lord. By taking aim at dependency, Grouchy was therefore not in her *Letters*, as Bergès has argued, making an explicitly anti-monarchic argument. She was focused above all on the creation of an equal society, the opposite of Smith's community held together by hierarchy. "[T]he extreme inequality of fortunes," Grouchy argues, "the great distance which is found between one class and another, makes men strangers to one another." They are no longer able to recognise each other's common humanity, and they can thus no longer sympathise with one another. This does harm to both sides: "the one can oppress the other almost without remorse, and the other can deceive him in his turn with impunity" (Condorcet, 1798b, p. 501). The rich, she tells her readers, are unable to feel compassion, because they are "separated from even the idea of misery and misfortune by the almost insurmountable barrier of riches" (Condorcet, 1798b, p. 361). While the poor who are dependent on the rich become too emotionally close to their benefactors to be able to properly use their sympathy, the rich, in turn, become too distant.

Ironically, Grouchy is here drawing – consciously or not – on an argument that Smith himself made. He had suggested in *TMS* that sympathy is most effective for things and beings close for us, and becomes increasingly "feeble" the further away we get. We thus, he dryly puts it, find losing a finger more distressing than the idea of the whole of China, with all its inhabitants, disappearing under the sea (*TMS* III.3.4). Yet while Smith was talking about physical distance, Grouchy applied the same logic to emotional distance: "the great distance which is to be found between one class and another makes men strangers to one another" (Condorcet, 1798b, p. 175). As Smith had pointed out, those at a great distance were unable to sympathise: and thus, Grouchy argued, they could neither act morally nor justly. It was therefore fundamental to the working of society that extremes of fortune were removed, and that status barriers were dismantled. If those who made up society were unable to recognise justice, and thus could not act in a just manner, justice could not exist.

And this was precisely the world Grouchy saw surrounding her. In criticising economic and social "prerogatives" and "privileges," she was taking aim at the last vestiges of the unreformed feudal system. Such was, for example, the deeply unpopular *taille* tax, intended as a payment for military services, from which the First and Second Estates were exempted and the burden of which fell predominantly on peasants and nonnoble rural landholders. This levy was not abolished until August 4, 1789. This hierarchical and unequal society – just like the one Grouchy interpreted Smith as advocating – could never deliver justice for the *trois roués*, or for any of its other members.

13.5

It is beyond the scope of this chapter to assert which nineteenth- and twentieth-century Francophone thinkers imbibed Grouchy's ideas alongside Smith's while perusing their copy of *Théorie des sentiments moraux*. It may be impossible to ever know for sure. Yet we do know that it was Grouchy's version of Smith – refracted through the lens of both her translation and her *Letters* – that was the most readily available to French audiences. As we have seen, the *Letters on Sympathy* contained not only a light commentary on Smith, but radical adaptations to his ideas, and her own original theorising.

Moreover, these adaptations were not simply founded on abstract differences of opinion with Smith, or as Michaël Biziou has even suggested, a "misunderstanding" of Smith's theory (Biziou, 2013, p. 24). Grouchy was engaging in a clear and directed political project when she first took on the project of criticising and adapting Smith in the 1780s. She wanted, firstly, to radically simplify his moral theory to make it accessible to the children of the uneducated. Secondly, she aimed at critiquing the social and economic inequalities of the *ancien régime* with a view to strengthening her case for a reform of French society on the basis of natural rights.

Grouchy's engagement with Smith continued into the 1790s. It seems likely that it was not until 1795 that she began her translation of *TMS*, which she then published together with her *Letters*, "written earlier" (Condorcet O'Connor, 1893, p. 370). A question remains as to why Grouchy continually associated her ideas with those of a philosopher with whom she, on some matters, vehemently disagreed. Although outside the purview of this chapter, the answer likely lies, at least in part, with Smith's concept of "sympathy." This was central to Grouchy's thinking, and had rarely been used in Francophone philosophy before this date, eclipsed by the alternative, and conceptually distinct, *pitié* (Larrère, 2002; Hurtado, 2005). Nevertheless, an understanding of how this crucial disseminator of Smith first engaged with and moulded his ideas is a vital initial step in discerning how and why later Francophone audiences reacted to the Scottish philosopher. Far from a timeless and impartial presentation, Grouchy offered a reading of Smith that was heavily Epicurean and egalitarian precisely because it was motivated by her pressing political concerns. This, however, was the interpretation that would be read side-by-side with *TMS* in France for the next two hundred years.

This chapter does not offer an exhaustive re-reading of two hundred years of reception history. Yet it does suggest that an awareness of Grouchy and her aims will have an important impact on how we interpret Smith's legacy in France. I offer here two brief examples. Richard Whatmore has noted that *TMS* was seen as less significant than *WN* in France in the early years of the nineteenth century, reflecting the perceived failure of republican constitutionalism and a move away from debates about forming national manners (Whatmore, 2002, pp. 87–88). It seems extremely plausible that the link that Grouchy drew between Smith and educating the populace, as well as her insistence on a more egalitarian reading of his theory, significantly influenced the association of Smith with republican education, and thus the subsequent rejection of his *TMS*. Equally, although the importance of Grouchy's influence on Pierre Jean George Cabanis' (1757–1808) interpretation of Smith is beginning to be recognised, much more could be done to dissect how her depiction of an alternative, Epicurean Smithian theory affected the broader Idéologue emphasis on self-interest as a moral instrument (Saad, 2015). These two examples are just the contemporary thinkers who may have been impacted by Grouchy's *Letters* and interpretation of Smith. The list stretches on.

Grouchy's interpretation of Smith was far from timeless; nor was it intended to be. We have simply, until now, put it in the wrong time. She was not a utopian thinker, intentionally disconnecting herself from the horrors of the recent past (Tegos, 2013). She merely could not allude to a Revolution that had not yet happened. She could, however – and did – make a pointed intervention in the context of the 1780s. She moulded Smith for her own purposes. This activist agenda must, in the future, be taken into consideration if we are to fully understand the Francophone Smith.

14

Adam Smith and the Limits of Philosophy[1]

CRAIG SMITH

One of the most lasting legacies of the 1976 celebrations of the 200th anniversary of the *Wealth of Nations* and the production of the Glasgow Edition of Adam Smith's Works was the impetus it gave to scholarship on Smith's writing beyond political economy.[2] The rediscovery of Adam Smith's moral philosophy and an increasing exploration of his conception of himself as, first and foremost, a moral philosopher, has produced a series of studies that have deepened our understanding of Smith and given us a better appreciation of the richness and systematic nature of his oeuvre.[3] In a series of papers over the last few years I have been trying to grasp what Smith understood the discipline of philosophy to entail, and what its relationship was to religion, social science, and politics.[4] Throughout I have been struck by the thought that Smith was distinctly wary about the discipline in which he operated. In this chapter I explore Smith's understanding of the role of philosophy in moral decision-making and, more particularly, what this means for teaching moral philosophy (as Smith did for many years at the University of Glasgow). I argue that Smith saw philosophy as a specific and limited activity that formed but a small part of the moral life of the individual. Moreover, I argue that Smith cautioned against over-ambition in philosophical thinking and warned of the intellectual, social, and political dangers of too much philosophy. In pedagogical terms this brings him closer to the typical view of the function of moral philosophy held by his fellow 'Professors of Virtue' in the Scottish Universities of the eighteenth century than is sometimes supposed (Sher, 1990). Smith, so I will argue, did not want to make philosophers of his students, instead he wanted to

---

[1] An alternative title for this chapter might be 'Why the Impartial Spectator Is Not a Philosopher, Nor Should We Wish Him to Be'. Indeed this is taken from a note scrawled in the margin of some notes. I have an uneasy feeling that it may not be my own thought, but rather a paraphrase of someone else. However I have been unable to trace the phrase and so offer apologies in advance to its inspiration for the failure to cite them by name.
[2] The author would like to thank the editor of this collection and the participants in an online workshop of contributors for their very helpful comments.
[3] See, for example Griswold, 1999; Fleischacker, 2004b; Darwall, 2006; Sen, 2009; Schliesser, 2017; McHugh, 2021
[4] See Smith 2015, 2018, 2022.

produce thoughtful individuals who would play a practical role in improving their society.

This leads to my contention that the impartial spectator of those raised in the real world was a more reliable judge of moral questions than the moral philosopher. When it comes to his vision of the virtuous character, Smith stresses that self-command is the virtue that should predominate in ordinary moral conduct, while diffidence, I suggest, ought to predominate in the conduct of moral philosophy. I proceed by considering Smith's conception of philosophy and of its benefits, before stressing the many places where he is openly derogatory about the discipline of moral philosophy. I then argue that the root of his doubts about philosophy as a discipline came from its arrogance and presumption in the face of the complexity of moral life. This explains why Smith believed that the impartial spectator of actual moral agents was to be preferred to the reasonings of philosophers when it comes to moral decision-making. I conclude by exploring the implications of this for the role of moral philosophy in education.

14.1 The Case for the Defence: The Strengths of Philosophy

We should begin by noting that Smith is not some sort of crude sub-Burkean critic of philosophy who sees it as disconnected from reality or futile in its aspirations. That Smith has a novel and sophisticated account of philosophy (and science) is another commonplace in the scholarship that has developed in modern Smith studies. Authors such as Andrew Skinner (1996) and Eric Schliesser (2017) have stressed the importance of grasping Smith's conception of the discipline within which he operated. Perhaps the strongest case for this reading of Smith as a systematic, empirical thinker inspired by his friend David Hume's 'science of man' is that provided in the late Nicholas Phillipson's biography (2010). The Smith we see here is very much an enlightenment figure keen to build a body of systematic knowledge that would prove useful in the improving projects that marked the Scottish Enlightenment. Philosophy is understood as 'the science of the connecting principles of nature' (*HA* II.2). The philosopher is engaged in a process of 'rendering familiar to the imagination' (*HA* IV.65) chains of events that appear, initially at least, to be chaotic and unsettling. Smith's persuasive account of the emotional and psychological forces that prompt us to philosophy and the subsequent illustration of the evolution of philosophy through systems of thinking in the field of astronomy, are a masterly account of the gradual emergence of the self-conscious pursuit of knowledge for its own sake that characterises modern philosophy. For Smith the increasing sophistication and reach of our explanations of the universe, led as they are through improving systems of ideas where gaplessness and parsimony prove criteria for adopting new ideas, was one of the great achievements of civilisation. His own works – the *Theory of Moral Sentiments* and the *Inquiry into the Nature and Causes of the Wealth of*

Nations – are self-consciously cast as philosophical explorations. There seems little doubt then that Smith was a keen adherent of a particular, empirically based, Newtonianly inspired, form of systematic inquiry that he understood as moral philosophy. And yet, for all that, Smith is pretty uncharitable in his description of his fellow philosophers.

14.2 The Case for the Prosecution: The Vices of Philosophers

For all of his enthusiasm about the benefits of philosophy there remain some significant passages that indicate that Smith had doubts about the place of philosophy in human life. Moreover, these comments do not appear simply to be directed at 'bad' philosophers. Smith is indeed scathing about 'quacks and imposters' (*TMS* VI.ii.27), and dismissive of those such as Rousseau who mistake passionate rhetoric for careful analysis (*EPS* 250), but he also seems to see that there is something about the nature of philosophy, something that it does to people who engage in it, that has the potential to be very troubling. As a matter of biography we know that Smith, like Hume before him and J. S. Mill after him, had suffered a form of mental crisis brought on by excessive study.[5] And it may be worth speculating here whether his worry about philosophy came from personal experience of its nature as a poor consolation in adversity.

Some of Smith's observations focus on the character of philosophers. He observes that they are poor company and preoccupied by their speculations (*TMS* I.ii.2.6). This is compounded by the distance between these speculations and the ordinary experience of moral judgment. Smith argues that philosophical differences are less animating to us than absence of fellow-feeling (*TMS* I.i.4.6) when it comes to the consideration of moral matters. A point which leads him to observe that philosophy itself is a poor path to contentment; it is the society of everyday life rather than philosophy that soothes the mind (*TMS* I.i.4.9). Philosophers are at risk of becoming detached from common life if they retreat into the company of those like them and shun everyday society.

As a result philosophy can prove a misleading guide to judgment in real life. In *TMS* Smith stresses that his examples are chosen from everyday life precisely to avoid our view of them being perverted by 'wrong systems' (*TMS* I.i.3.3). We can be misled by a 'refinement of philosophy' (*TMS* VII.ii.i.34), and it is typical of philosophers to overestimate the role of reason in human life (*TMS* II.ii.3.5). When these two things combine, the practice of moral philosophy poses a threat to moral conduct. These arguments culminate in Smith's attack on the 'man of system', where enthusiasm for a system of thought passes over into the madness of fanaticism with disastrous political consequences (*TMS* VI.ii.2.16–17).

---

[5] For a discussion of this, see Ross 2010, pp. 70–71.

Other of Smith's criticisms are directed at the incentives which govern the professional lives of philosophers. This view is particularly prominent in *WN*. Like everything else in modern society the discipline of philosophy has become a distinct profession. Philosophers 'whose trade it is, not to do anything, but to observe everything' (*WN* I.i.9: 21) become a trade like any other and subject to the same temptations towards rent-seeking and monopoly control. Book V of *WN* includes an analysis of the evolution of philosophy (*WN* V.i.f.24–34) within Smith's analysis of the perverse incentives of the European university system. Smith describes how the academic disciplines have separated out through the same process as the division of labour has operated in other areas of society (*WN* V.i.f.28). But in the case of moral philosophy this led to the development of a scholastic and antiquarian philosophy that was not 'likely either to improve the understanding, or to mend the heart' (*WN* V.i.32) and of almost no practical use to the students upon whom it was inflicted.

Before printing, philosophers could only make a living as teachers (*WN* I.x. c.38) and many of them found their homes in the universities. The existence of tenured fellowships meant that teaching there was poor or non-existent (*WN* V.i.f. 14) and the colleges designed for the benefit of the teachers rather than the students (*WN* V.i.f.15). Smith's proposals to reform the universities along the lines of the Scottish system are aimed at introducing direct incentives for teachers to teach well and to research the latest knowledge in their specialism. As Smith points out, this is simply a particular case of the more general point that people perform a task with diligence if their income depends on it. Private tutors can't teach useless and poor material. If they were to teach 'a mere useless and pedantick heap of sophistry and nonsense' (*WN* V.i.f.46), they would not long have any students.

It is here that Smith observes that the financial incentives of the professional philosophers align with their desire to protect their own systems of thought from criticism that he identified in *EPS* (*HA* IV.35). The learned societies act like trades guilds and protect 'exploded systems and obsolete prejudices' (*WN* V.i.f.34) encouraging the teaching of 'sham lectures' 'written in a foreign or dead language' (*WN* V.i.f.14) to protect the lazy philosophers in their sinecures. Such 'little clubs and cabals, who, in the superior arts and sciences, so often erect themselves into the supreme judges of merit; and who make it their business to celebrate the talents and virtues of one another, and to decry whatever can come into competition with them' (*TMS* VI.i.7) are a barrier to good scholarship. Scholarship for Smith should not be 'the vain parade of erudition and quotation' (*EPS* 249) that demonstrates familiarity with and conformity to the systems of others; but rather a display of active and critical thought.

The most serious charge against philosophers is their recurring confidence in the scope of their systems of ideas. This 'overweening conceit' (*WN* I.x.b.26) arises from the 'vanity of the philosopher' (*WN* I.ii.4), a mistaken confidence in their superiority and the strength of their ideas that has retarded rather than advanced philosophical understanding. This vice is not restricted to bad philosophers or to those who would like to insulate their ideas from criticism, but rather seems to be embedded in the very practice of philosophy itself. The clearest discussion of this lies in *EPS*. Here Smith explains how, in the early ages of philosophy, thinkers were tempted to extend their ideas from a single area of study to a systematic or universal level. For example, in the essay on *Ancient Physics* he writes:

> This natural anticipation, too, was still more confirmed by such a slight and inaccurate analysis of things, as could be expected in the infancy of science, when the curiosity of mankind, grasping at an account of all things before it had got full satisfaction with regard to any one, hurried on to build, in imagination, the immense fabric of the universe.
>
> (*EPS* 107–108)

The desire to develop a 'theory of everything' is a pervasive one among philosophers and inspires a kind of scholarly arrogance that elevates the system above the evidence concerning the phenomena that it is supposed to explain. This, coupled with the desire to preserve the universal claims of the system, leads to increasingly convoluted revisions to the system or a simple denial of the reality of contrary evidence. The preservation of the system of ideas becomes more important than its explanatory reach, and to riff on a comment that Smith makes with reference to Copernicus it becomes amazing '... how easily the learned give up the evidence of their senses to preserve the coherence of the ideas of their imagination ...' (*HA* IV.35). This, together with another universal feature of human psychology, the fact that 'Mankind have had, at all times, a strong propensity to realise their own abstractions ...' (*EPS* 125), produces a heady mix of institutional, reputational, and psychological vices common in intellectual circles. The result is that 'Gross sophistry has scarce ever had any influence upon the opinions of mankind, except in matters of philosophy and speculation; and in these it has frequently had the greatest' (*WN* V.i.f.26).

14.3 Moral Pluralism

Two recent moves in the interpretation of Smith's moral philosophy seem to share a similar sense that his approach is sceptical about previous schools of philosophy. The first is the scholarship on Smith's moral philosophy that has dwelt on the eclectic nature of this thinking. Scholars such as Colin Heydt and Aaron Garrett (2015) and Leonidas Montes (2004) have suggested that Smith draws on and combines elements drawn from across the ancient and modern schools of philosophy displaying a non-doctrinaire and pragmatic attitude to the existing schools of thought. The second approach, championed by Michael

Gill (2014), argues that Smith's moral philosophy, like that of David Hume, is characterised by an acceptance of the fact of moral pluralism. Moral pluralism leaves open the possibility that different modes of moral thinking can issue in incommensurable conclusions and, following Isaiah Berlin (1969, pp. lv–lvi), that these contradictions may prove insurmountable. In other words, moral philosophy will never generate a single systematic approach that will answer all moral questions in a clear and decisive fashion.

Both of these interpretations are persuasive and make sense in the light of what Smith says about other schools of philosophy in Part VII of *TMS*. His argument is that the schools of ancient and modern philosophy all contain some grain of truth, but that they are based on a 'partial and imperfect view of nature' (*TMS* VII.i.i). The reason for this, in Smith's view, is that they fall prey to a vice that is peculiar to philosophers, one that we saw in the last section: the over-extension of single principles of explanation that succeed in particular and limited areas to universal principles governing all of morality.

This, as Smith was aware, was a vice inherent in the act of philosophy – stemming from the desire for clarity and for explanatory reach in the fashion that Smith had praised Newton for in *EPS*. Writing of Epicurus he noted:

> Epicurus indulged a propensity, which is natural to all men, but which philosophers in particular are apt to cultivate with a peculiar fondness, as the great means of displaying their ingenuity, the propensity to account for all appearances from as few principles as possible.
>
> (*TMS* VII.ii.2.14)

Philosophers should be aware of this vice inherent in their discipline and ensure that their theories do not sacrifice accuracy in their description of how we make moral judgments for principled simplicity. It follows that for Adam Smith a pure consequentialism, a pure deontology, and a pure virtue theory are all false: false as descriptions of how individuals make judgments and false as normative principles that seek to be definitive of moral experience.[6]

So Smith's theory is eclectic and accepts the fact of moral pluralism, but he does not give up on the idea of presenting a systematic analysis of moral judgment. This is because for Smith morality itself is eclectic. Humans draw on a number of approaches to make moral judgments and these differ depending on the circumstances. This provides us with insight into two significant features of Smith's moral theory. The first of these is his mode of presentation. In both *TMS* and *WN* Smith arranges his argument around a single explanatory principle that provides a connecting point for his narrative.

---

[6] This, I suggest, but will not explore here, means that those who seek to understand Smith's contextualised account of morality as a virtue theory are mistaken. Smith is not a virtue theorist properly understood either because both utility and rules also play a part in our moral judgments.

In *WN* it is the division of labour, in *TMS* it is sympathy. But we need to be clear that this is not a case of the philosophical vice that we have just been discussing. Smith is well aware that whatever the scope of these principles as a means to provide a coherent explanatory account of the phenomenon in question, they are not master principles that provide the key to all matters economic or moral. Smith is using them to arrange his arguments and not suggesting that they are definitive of all that we need know of those matters. This is about the systematic presentation of an argument within a work, not about thinking that we have cracked the theory of everything.[7]

The second insight concerns Smith's development of the impartial spectator in his explanations of how humans make moral judgments. The impartial spectator lies at the heart of Smith's account of moral experience (*TMS* III.2.3). His description of it makes very clear that consultation of the spectator provides us with the self-approbation that is definitive of virtue and represents the authority of conscience (*TMS* III.2.8). As he does this he also makes clear that the process of developing and consulting the impartial spectator is not 'rational'. Echoing Hume he argues that:

> it is altogether absurd and unintelligible to suppose that the first perceptions of right and wrong can be derived from reason, even in those particular cases upon the experience of which the general rules are formed ... It is by finding in a vast variety of instances that the one tenor of conduct constantly pleases in a certain manner, and that another as constantly displeases the mind, that we form the general rules of morality.
>
> (*TMS* VII.iii.2.7)

Moral judgment, on this account, is not to be understood as a detached process of rational argumentation, rather it is an emotional and imaginative experience where we reflect on what to do in the light of past moral judgments. This, it is vital to note, means that moral judgment guided by the impartial spectator, as understood by Smith, is distinct from moral philosophy.

14.4 Real Life and Not Moral Philosophy Teaches Moral Judgment

Smith begins Part VII of *TMS* by outlining the two questions that lie at the heart of moral philosophy. These are 'wherein does virtue consist?' and 'How and by what means does it come to pass, that the mind prefers one tenour of conduct to another, denominates the one right and the other wrong; considers the one as the object of approbation, honour, and reward, and the other blame,

---

[7] For a discussion of a similar interpretation of Smith's view on systematic thought see Phillipson 2010. This is a line of argument that I make in a recent book on Smith and which Ryan Hanley (2021) rightly points out is less clearly developed than it ought to have been.

censure, and punishment' (*TMS* VII.i.I). Both of these questions are distinct from particular acts of moral judgment. They represent reflections upon what it is like to judge and how we ought to judge and are in this sense abstracted from the job of getting on with judging ourselves and our peers. This, so I would like to suggest, is no bad thing in Smith's view.[8] As he puts it:

> When a philosopher goes to examine why humanity is approved of, or cruelty condemned, he does not always form to himself, in a very clear and distinct manner, the conception of any one particular action either of cruelty or of humanity, but is commonly contented with the vague and indeterminate idea which the general names of those qualities suggest to him. But it is in particular instances only that the propriety or impropriety, the merit or demerit of actions is very obvious and discernable.
>
> (*TMS* IV.2.2)

The result of this is that:

> When we consider virtue and vice in an abstract and general manner, the qualities by which they excite these several sentiments seem in a great measure to disappear, and the sentiments themselves become less obvious and discernible.
>
> (*TMS* IV.2.2)

The reflection and generalisation that the philosopher pursues necessarily removes him from the judgment of the particulars of a given case. But this is precisely what lies at the heart of the moral experience of sympathy and spectatorship. The point here being that the philosophical mode of thought is ill-suited to the fine-grained, contextual appreciation that Smith believes is constitutive of moral life. Moreover it is also unsuccessful as a means of educating the individual in the exercise of moral judgment. Smith points out that:

---

[8] In *WN* Smith describes moral philosophy as the methodical ordering of the 'Maxims of common life' (*WN* V.i.f). While in *LRBL* he notes: 'This you'll say is no more than common sense, and indeed it is no more. But if you'll attend to it all the Rules of Criticism and morality when traced to their foundation, turn out to be some Principles of Common Sense which every one assents to; all the business of those arts is to apply these Rules to the different subjects and show what their conclusions are when so applied.' (*LRBL* 11.135). In pointing this out I am not suggesting that Smith is a Common Sense thinker in the mould of Thomas Reid or his successors. Smith has no list of universal basic principles of mind, and so he does not aspire to derive the content of normative moral philosophy from descriptive psychology in the fashion of the Aberdeen School. His aim is to explain judgment in context, because judgment in context is what we in fact do when we engage in moral judgments. The task of the philosopher is to distil some general observations on types of context that might then aid the individual in the exercise of their particular judgments.

> If we examine the different shades and gradations of weakness and self-command, as we meet with them in common life, control of our passive feelings must be acquired, not from the abstruse syllogisms of a quibbling dialectic, but from that great discipline which Nature has established for the acquisition of this and of every other virtue; a regard to the sentiments of the real or supposed spectator of our conduct.
>
> (*TMS* III.3.21)[9]

This, then, helps us make sense of Smith's criticism of philosophers who have taken their 'doctrines a good deal beyond' 'the just standard of nature and propriety' (*TMS* III.3.8). Their problem is that they see philosophy as their guide rather than ordinary moral judgment in consultation with the impartial spectator. Philosophers are people of retreat and introspection, they lack experience of the world and their judgments are cramped by this lack of active participation and awareness of the sentiments of others. As a result their judgments are often skewed, driven by the over-extension of a single principle that has proved helpful in other connections. The impartial spectator, contextually sensitive, yet disinterested, is a more reliable guide and this is because it has been habituated by living in society and experiencing the lives of others.

Smith goes further than this and suggests that the confusions that philosophy can introduce into moral judgment can ultimately be dispelled by the force or nature of ordinary experience: 'The reasonings of philosophy, it may be said, though they may confound and perplex the understanding, can never break down the necessary connection which Nature has established between causes and their effects' (*TMS* VII.ii.47). This, then, is what Smith means when he says that previous philosophers worked with a 'partial and imperfect view of nature' (*TMS* VII.i.1) that led them to develop a partial understanding of moral experience. An understanding that bordered on the truth, but which was unable to capture and reconcile the truths that emerge from the other principles in as effective a fashion as Smith's account. For example, the case against Mandeville's system is that it could not be maintained because it misdescribed a process that was familiar to all individuals. Mandeville's view must, in some respect, have bordered on the truth for us to even consider it, but it departed from our experience of self-regarding and other-regarding behaviours and so was ultimately unpersuasive to all but philosophers.

Such a check issued by ordinary experience was less applicable in the more abstract realms of philosophy. In his discussion of Descartes's system in natural philosophy, Smith points out that it could be believed because it described phenomena beyond everyday experience and observation even though it turned out to have 'no foundation in nature, nor any sort of

---

[9] See Smith's view that the rules of morality come first from Nature, are then attributed to God, and only after that 'informed by reasoning and philosophy' (*TMS* III.5.3).

resemblance to the truth' (*TMS* VII.ii.4.14). The reason Smith believes this to be the case is that all of us have a personal experience of the act of moral judgment and so are immediately aware of the insufficiency of Mandeville's account as an explanation of something that is familiar to us (*TMS* VII.ii.4.13–14), while few of us have a sufficient grasp of astronomy to so easily dismiss Descartes's inventions.

Smith's criticism of the 'whining and melancholy moralists' (*TMS* III.3.9) who would lose all sense of perspective in the face of the miseries of the universe and wish the world or human nature to be other than it is, is based on an appreciation that philosophy encourages such mania. Thinkers like this are considered ridiculous by their fellows and by Smith. The 'splenetic philosophers' are 'peevish individuals' whose cynical view of the love of praise-worthiness generated by consultation with the impartial spectator leads them to interpret it as vanity (*TMS* II.ii.27). But such splenetic philosophy can only be maintained in a philosophical mode of reflection and not in the application of ordinary moral judgment. The sheer weight of the experience of ordinary life tells against miserabilism and cynicism. So for Smith it is a good thing that 'we rarely view it in this abstract and philosophical light' (*TMS* IV.i.9), and that when we do so it is equally good that we meet with the ridicule of our peers.

Moral philosophy requires a degree of modesty in its ambitions. Smith demonstrates what he has in mind here in his rejection of casuistic rules. The need for discretion in judgment means that such rules are arid schoolroom exercises unable to capture: 'all the different shades and gradations of circumstance, character, and situation, to differences and distinctions which, though not imperceptible, are, by their nicety and delicacy, often altogether indefinable' (*TMS* VI.ii.I.2.1). Instead Smith's theory explains to us how each individual evolves their own guide to judgment based on their own experience and the observation of those around them. The impartial spectator creates idea of a good person in us and we use that to judge (*TMS* VI.iii.23–25) how we and others should act. As a result 'We shall stand in need of no casuistic rules to direct our conduct' (*TMS* VI.ii.2.1).

There is a further element to this critique of the usefulness of philosophy as a guide to practical moral judgment and that is to be found in Smith's distinction between the ideal and the practicable or ordinary exercise of virtue. Individuals are conscious of a difference between the actions of a perfectly virtuous individual and those of everyday people. His distinction between 'what principles a perfect being would approve of the punishment of bad actions' and 'what principles so weak a creature as man actually and in fact approves of' (*TMS* II.i.5.10) involves both an epistemic distinction between the ideal and the practicable and a recognition that the former is not something that can be supported as a useful guide to human life. The point of this is not to diminish the pursuit of the ideal on an intellectual level, but to recognise that the ideal is rarely attainable and that humans tend to judge themselves against a lower standard of perfection, one that recognises fallibility and justified partiality. The ideal, then, is of limited use in making moral judgments and educating those who will make them. Moreover this is not a case of a second-best scenario for Smith. He thinks that it is both good and appropriate that we do not aim to live our lives according to philosophical ideals. The problem, once again, lies with philosophy rather than ordinary life. Contemplation of the 'sublime' is no excuse for ignoring the 'humbler department' of everyday good behaviour (*TMS* VI.ii.3.6).

14.5 Individual Judgment and the Professor of Virtue

One way of understanding the distinction that Smith is making here is to see him as following the line of argument that one finds in David Hume's distinction between the 'anatomist' or 'painter' in moral philosophy (Hume, 1978, pp. 620–621).[10] Here the painter seeks to inspire virtue by painting an idealised picture of the beauty of right conduct, an approach that Hume criticised as it was not sufficiently grounded in the reality of human nature and resulted in a philosophy and pedagogy that was detached from experience. Smith seems to share this view, and to recognise that if he was to develop a successful moral pedagogy, then it would have to be directed towards the reality of moral judgment.

There is an extensive literature on the role of the Scottish moral philosophy professor as a moral educator. Gordon Graham (2007), for example, argues that education is central to the self-conception of Smith and his contemporaries.[11] It is in this context, I wish to suggest, that we ought to understand Smith's conception of himself as a moral philosopher in a manner that is perhaps deeper than we might previously have thought. The point I have been labouring to make so far is that philosophy is not, in Smith's view, an appropriate mode through which to engage in practical moral judgments. Moreover, given that this is the case, then the Professor of Moral Philosophy who wants to provide his students with help in making moral judgments needs to present their argument in a clear and concise fashion while recognising that the phenomenon under consideration is not amenable to precise definitions, and that those faced with making the judgments will not reach them through philosophical argument.[12]

---

[10] For a discussion of Hume's distinction, see Abramson 2007.
[11] See also Garrett and Heydt 2015 and Sher 1985.
[12] Elsewhere in this volume Lauren Kopajtic discusses the role of imaginative fiction in Smith's account of the development of our moral thinking. That reading is an excellent complement to the argument advanced here. Imaginative contemplation of scenarios where judgment is exercised is a more reliable form of moral education than immersing oneself in existing works of moral philosophy precisely because it is contextual rather than abstract.

Smith's moral pedagogy as we find it in *TMS* is not one which seeks to provide us with an abstracted or idealised version of what can be achieved by moral philosophy. Instead it is one which focuses on ordinary examples and everyday character sketches to illustrate virtuous behaviour in concrete situations. His sketches of parsimony versus prodigality (*WN* II.iii.16–22) or of the prudent man (*TMS* VI.i.4–14) give practical instances of the exercise of particular virtues without believing or implying that their efficacy extends beyond the circumstances in which he raises them. And again, the desire is to illustrate by everyday example to avoid the distractions of philosophy.[13]

What, then, is the correct disposition for individuals when it comes to their moral judgments, and how might the philosopher help them to realise this? The answer to this is to be found in the modesty of Smith's vision of the practical moral virtues that he discusses in *TMS*. It is having the self-command to consult the impartial spectator and identify the right thing to do that we should expect of individuals in their everyday lives. For the most part we can trust people to do that. Smith clearly thought that most people, most of the time, want to do the right thing. It was the role of education to help them to think about what that was and, crucially, to instil them with the self-command to follow through on the judgments of the impartial spectator.

Smith's view of moral philosophy, on the other hand, remains suspicious when it comes to moral judgment. He prefers 'men of the world' to 'men of retirement and speculation' (*TMS* I.i.4.10) when it comes to forming an accurate moral compass. And here, perhaps, he might agree with his great friend David Hume's advice to the sceptical philosopher to 'be diffident of his philosophical doubts, as well as of his philosophical convictions' (Hume, 1978, p. 271). Smith, like Hume, had a great horror of fanaticism and enthusiasm in religion and saw science as 'the great antidote' (*WN* V.i.g.14) to them, but those are vices that can mislead the philosopher should he come to think of himself as a suitable guide to the actual moral judgments we experience in everyday life.[14]

Circumstances require fine-grained judgments, and that is what Smith's impartial spectator gives us. The character of the impartial spectator is developed gradually from our own experience of moral judgment and is thus educated in the exercise of judgment by undertaking such judgment. The role of the philosopher is not to guide moral judgment, but rather to prepare his students for a life of participation and judgment. It is to help them reflect on what it is to judge rather than to prejudge the circumstances in which they will try to do the right thing. Understanding that it is the impartial spectator and

---

[13] For a clear account of this aspect of Smith's style, see Heydt 2012.
[14] As Paul Sagar pointed out on reading a draft of this chapter, Smith thinks that there is no obvious connection between being good at moral philosophy and being good at being good.

not the moral philosopher who is the most reliable arbiter of moral judgment will save us from potential errors of judgment.

We should, then, be thankful that the impartial spectator is not a moral philosopher. Moral philosophy cannot do our moral judgment for us, and philosophers who set out with the ambition to make it do just that are doing a disservice to both philosophy and morality. This, however, is not to say that philosophy has no role to play in Smith's view. Philosophical reasoning and the clarity of thought that can come with it have a place in a pedagogy designed to encourage the thoughtful development of each individual's impartial spectator. So long as we do not mistake an aid to moral judgment for an authority on moral judgment, then we might safely philosophise alongside our active moral life. Smith is not rejecting philosophy as a practice; indeed he is engaged in a philosophical reflection on the limits of philosophical enquiry as an aid to moral decision-making. Philosophy can help us to be better judges of behaviour, but its rigidity, desire for precision, and sense of its own importance as a mode of enquiry need to be reined in. Thinking imaginatively about the moral implications of various scenarios helps us to fine-tune our spectatorial and sympathetic abilities and it is this development of the impartial spectator that lies at the heart of Smith's vision of moral education.

BIBLIOGRAPHY

Abramson, K. (2007) "Hume's Distinction between Philosophical Anatomy and Painting," *Philosophy Compass*, 2(5), pp. 680–698. Available at: https://doi.org/10.1111/j.1747-9991.2007.00096.x.

Acemoglu, D. and Robinson, J. A. (2006) "Economic Backwardness in Political Perspective," *American Political Science Review*, 100(1), pp. 115–131. Available at: https://doi.org/10.1017/S0003055406062046.

——— (2012) *Why Nations Fail: The Origins of Power, Prosperity, and Poverty*. New York: Crown Business.

Adair, D. (1957) "'That Politics May Be Reduced to a Science': David Hume, James Madison, and the Tenth Federalist," *Huntington Library Quarterly*, 20(4), pp. 343–360. Available at: https://doi.org/10.2307/3816276.

Anderson, E. (2016) "Adam Smith on Inequality," in R. P. Hanley (ed.) *Adam Smith: His Life, Thought and Legacy*. Princeton: Princeton University Press, pp. 152–172.

——— (2017) *Private Government: How Employers Rule Our Lives (and Why We Don't Talk about It)*. Princeton: Princeton University Press.

Anderson, G. M. (1988) "Mr. Smith and the Preachers: The Economics of Religion in the Wealth of Nations," *Journal of Political Economy*, 96(5), pp. 1066–1088.

Aristotle (1984) "Politics," in J. Barnes (ed.) *The Complete Works of Aristotle*. Princeton: Princeton University Press, pp. 1986–2129.

Armstrong, N. (2005) *How Novels Think: The Limits of Individualism from 1719–1900*. New York: Columbia University Press.

Ashraf, N., Camerer, C. F. and Loewenstein, G. (2005) "Adam Smith, Behavioral Economist," *Journal of Economic Perspectives*, 19(3), pp. 131–145. Available at: https://doi.org/10.1257/089533005774357897.

Aspromourgos, T. (2009) *The Science of Wealth: Adam Smith and the Framing of Political Economy*. London: Routledge.

Bachaumont, L. P. de P. de M. M. F. and Mouffle d'Angerville, B.-F.-J. (1788) *Mémoires secrets pour servir à l'histoire de la République des Lettres en France, depuis MDCCLXII, ou Journal d'un observateur, contenant les analyses des pièces de théâtre qui ont paru durant cet intervalle, les relations des assemblée littéraires*. London: John Adamson.

Bacon, F. (1853) *The Physical and Metaphysical Works of Lord Bacon*. Edited by J. Devey. London: Bohn Library.

Badinter, E. (2010) "'Esquisse d'un portrait'," in M. A. Bernier and D. Dawson (eds.) *Les Lettres sur la sympathie (1798) de Sophie de Grouchy, philosophie morale et réforme sociale*. Oxford: Voltaire Foundation, pp. 107–126.

Barber, W. J. (1993) *Breaking the Academic Mould: Economists and Higher Learning in the Nineteenth Century*. New Brunswick: Transaction Publishers.

Barro, R. J. and McCleary, R. M. (2003) "Religion and Economic Growth across Countries," *American Sociological Review*, 68(5), pp. 760–781.

Bates, R. H. (2001) *Prosperity & Violence: The Political Economy of Development*. New York: W.W. Norton & Co.

Bator, P. G. (1996) "The Entrance of the Novel into the Scottish Universities," in R. Crawford (ed.) *The Scottish Invention of English Literature*. Cambridge: Cambridge University Press, pp. 89–102.

Baumol, W. J., Panzar, J. C. and Willig, R. D. (1982) *Contestable Markets and the Theory of Industry Structure*. New York: Harcourt Brace Jovanovich, Inc.

Baysinger, Barry, Robert B. Ekelund, Jr., and Robert D. Tollison. 2008. "Mercantilism as a Rent-Seeking Society," in Roger Hillman Congleton and Arye Konrad Kai (ed.), *40 Years of Research on Rent Seeking 2. Applications: Rent Seeking in Practice*. Heidelberg: Springer.

Beccaria, C. (1965) *Dei Delitti e delle Pene*. Edited by F. Venturi. Turin: Einaudi.

Becker, J. F. (1961) "Adam Smith's Theory of Social Science," *Southern Economic Journal*, 28(1), pp. 13–21.

Bell, D. (2014) "What Is Liberalism?," *Political Theory*, 42(6), pp. 682–715. Available at: https://doi.org/10.1177/0090591714535103.

Bentham, J. (1948) *Principles of Morals and Legislation*. Edited by W. Harrison. Oxford: Blackwell.

Bergès, S. (2015) "Sophie de Grouchy on the Cost of Domination in the Letters on Sympathy and Two Anonymous Articles in Le Republicain," *The Monist*, 98 (1), pp. 102–112. Available at: https://doi.org/10.1093/monist/onu011.

(2019) "Revolution and Republicanism: Women Political Philosophers of Late Eighteenth-Century France and Why They Matter," *Australasian Philosophical Review*, 3(4), pp. 351–370. Available at: https://doi.org/10.1080/24740500.2020.1840647.

Bergès, S. and Schliesser, E. (2019) "Introduction" in S. Berges and E. Schliesser (eds.) *Letters on Sympathy: A Critical Engagement with Adam Smith's the Theory of Moral Sentiments*. Oxford: Oxford University Press, pp. 3–22.

Berlin, I. (1969) *Four Essays on Liberty*. London: Fontana.

Berns, L. (1994) "Aristotle and Adam Smith on Justice: Cooperation between the Ancients and Moderns?" *The Review of Metaphysics*, 49(1), pp. 71–90.

Berry, C. J. (1997) *The Social Theory of the Scottish Enlightenment*. Edinburgh: Edinburgh University Press.

(2006) "Smith and Science," in Knud Haakonssen (ed.) *The Cambridge Companion to Adam Smith*. Cambridge: Cambridge University Press, pp. 112–135.

(2013) *The Idea of Commercial Society in the Scottish Enlightenment*. Edinburgh: Edinburgh University Press.

(2018a) "Adam Smith's 'Science of Human Nature,'" in *Essays on Hume, Smith and the Scottish Enlightenment*. Edinburgh: Edinburgh University Press, pp. 364–384.

(2018b) "Smith and Science," in *Essays on Hume, Smith and the Scottish Enlightenment*. Edinburgh: Edinburgh University Press, pp. 303–325.

(2020a) "O Problema da Coesão na Sociedada Comercial," *Discurso: Revista da Filosofia*, 50(1), pp. 9–23.

(2020b) "Out of the Coffee House, or How Political Economy Pretended to Be a Science from Montchrétien to Steuart," *Social Philosophy and Policy*, 37(1), pp. 10–29. Available at: https://doi.org/10.1017/S0265052520000023.

Besley, T. and Persson, T. (2011) *Pillars of Prosperity: The Political Economics of Development Clusters*. Princeton: Princeton University Press.

Bittermann, H. J. (1940) "Adam Smith's Empiricism and the Law of Nature," *Journal of Political Economy*, 48(5), pp. 487–520. Available at: https://doi.org/10.1086/255612.

Biziou, M. (2013) "Traductions et retraductions françaises de la Théorie des sentiments moraux d'Adam Smith. L'insoutenable légèreté de (re)traduire," *Noesis*, 21, pp. 229–263.

Blair, H. (2005) *Lectures on Rhetoric and Belles Lettres*. Edited by S. M. Halloran and L. Ferreira-Buckley. Carbondale: Southern Illinois University Press.

Bonnet, J.-C. (2016) "Preface," in J.-C. Bonnet (ed.) *Lettres sur la sympathie*. Paris: Payot & Rivages, pp. 7–14.

Boucoyannis, D. (2013) "The Equalizing Hand: Why Adam Smith Thought the Market Should Produce Wealth without Steep Inequality," *Perspectives on Politics*, 11(4), pp. 1051–1070. Available at: https://doi.org/10.1017/S153759271300282X.

Bourne, E. G. (1894) "Alexander Hamilton and Adam Smith," *Quarterly Journal of Economics*, 8(3), pp. 328–344. Available at: https://doi.org/10.2307/1883458.

Bray, J. (2003) *The Epistolary Novel: Representations of Consciousness*. London: Routledge.

Bréban, L. and Delamotte, J. (2016) *From One Form of Sympathy to Another: Sophie de Grouchy's Translation of and Commentary on Adam Smith's Theory of Moral Sentiments*. Available at: https://hal.archives-ouvertes.fr/hal-01435828 (accessed: July 28, 2022).

Broadie, A. (2006) "Sympathy and the impartial spectator," in K. Haakonnsen (ed.) *The Cambridge Companion to Adam Smith*. Cambridge: Cambridge University Press, pp. 158–188.

Brooke, C. (2020) "Nonintrinsic Egalitarianism, from Hobbes to Rousseau," *Journal of Politics*, 82(4), pp. 1406–1417. Available at: https://doi.org/10.1086/708502.

Brown, V. (2016) "The Impartial Spectator and Moral Judgment," *Econ Journal Watch*, 13(2), pp. 232–248.

Buchan, J. (2016) "The Biography of Adam Smith," in R. P. Hanley (ed.) *Adam Smith: His Life, Thought and Legacy*. Princeton: Princeton University Press, pp. 3–16.

Buchanan, J. M. (1978) "The Justice of Natural Liberty," in F. R. Glahe (ed.) *Adam Smith and the Wealth of Nations: Bicentrnnial Essays 1776-1976*. Boulder: Colorado Associated University Press, pp. 61–82.

(1990) "The Domain of Constitutional Economics," *Constitutional Political Economy*, 1(1), pp. 1–18. Available at: https://doi.org/10.1007/BF02393031.

Buck, P. (1977) "Seventeenth-Century Political Arithmetic: Civil Strife and Vital Statistics," *Isis*, 68(1), pp. 67–84.

Burgin, A. (2012) *The Great Persuasion: Reinventing Free Markets since the Great Depression*. Cambridge MA: Harvard University Press.

Business Roundtable (2019) *Statement on the Purpose of a Corporation*, www.businessroundtable.org/business-roundtable-redefines-the-purpose-of-a-corporation-to-promote-an-economy-that-serves-all-americans.

Butler, J. (2017) *Fifteen Sermons and Other Writings on Ethics*. Edited by D. McNaughton. Oxford: Oxford University Press.

Cantillon, R. (2001) *Essai sur la nature du Commerce en général*. Edited by S. Couvreur. Paris: Coppet.

Casal, P. (2007) "Why Sufficiency Is Not Enough," *Ethics*, 117(2), pp. 296–326. Available at: https://doi.org/10.1086/510692.

Chamberlain, S. (2017) *Character in the Age of Adam Smith*. Berkeley: University of California Press.

Chandra, R. (2021) "Adam Smith, Allyn Young, Amartya Sen and the Role of the State," *History of Economics Review*, 78(1), pp. 17–43. Available at: https://doi.org/10.1080/10370196.2020.1863005.

Cheney, P. (2022) "István Hont, the Cosmopolitan Theory of Commercial Globalization, and Twenty-First-Century Capitalism," *Modern Intellectual History*, 19(3), pp. 883–911. Available at: https://doi.org/10.1017/S147924432100007X.

Cicero (1961) *De Finibus Bonorum et Malorum*. Edited by H. Rackham. London: William Heinemann Ltd.

(1967) *De Natura Deorum*. Edited by H. Rackham. London: William Heinemann Ltd.

(1988) *De Re Publica and De Legibus*. Edited by C. W. Keyes. Cambridge, MA: Harvard University Press.

(1990) *De Officiis*. Edited by W. Miller. Cambridge MA: Harvard University Press.

Clarke, P. H. (2000) "Adam Smith, Stoicism and Religion in the 18th Century," *History of the Human Sciences*, 13(4), pp. 49–72. Available at: https://doi.org/10.1177/09526950022120863.

Collini, S. (1991) *Public Moralists: Political Thought and Intellectual Life in Britain, 1850–1930*. Oxford: Clarendon Press.

Condillac, E. B. de (1947) *Oeuvres Complètes, 3 vols*. Edited by G. le Roy. Paris: Presses Universitaires de France.

Condorcet (1798a) "Avertissement," in S. Condorcet (ed.) *Théorie des sentiments moraux [. . .] [septième édition]*. Paris: Buisson.

(1798b) "Lettres sur la sympathie," in S. Condorcet (ed.) *Théorie des sentiments moraux [. . .] [septième édition]*. Paris: Buisson.

Condorcet, M. J. A. N. C. de (1786) *Réflexions d'un citoyen non gradué sur un procès très connu*. London [Brussels].

(1787a) "'Announcing marriage to Grouchy,'" *[Letter] Held at: Státní oblastní archiv v Plzni. RAW, no. 1562, f. 17*.

(1787b) "'Letter to Malesherbes,'" *[Letter] Held at: Bibliothèque de l'Institut. Ms 854, F. 419*.

(1795) *Esquisse d'un tableau historique des progrès de l'esprit humain*. Paris: chez Agasse.

(1904) "'Essai sur quelques changemens à faire dans les loix criminelles de France,'" in L. Cahen (ed.) *Condorcet et la Révolution française*. Paris: Germer Baillière, pp. 549–559.

(no date a) "'Rapport sur un concours (sur le meilleur livre de morale à l'usage des enfants),'" *[Manuscript] Held at: Bibliothèque de l'Institut. Ms 884, F. 153–154*.

(no date b) "'Fragment d'une lettre sur l'opinion,'" *[Manuscript] Held at: Bibliothèque de l'Institut. Ms 884, F. 150–153*.

Condorcet O'Connor, E. (1893) "'Note biographique sur Mme de Condorcet,'" in *Condorcet: Sa Vie, Son Oeuvre (1743-1794)*. Paris: Librairies-Imprimeries réunies, pp. 369–371.

(no date) "'Note biographique,'" *[Manuscript] Held at: Bibliothèque de l'Institut. Ms 848, F. 26*.

Congressional Record (1893). 53rd Congress, 2nd Session, Senate. December 13, p. 203.

Conkin, P. K. (1980) *Prophets of Prosperity: America's First Political Economist*. Bloomington: Indiana University Press.

Conn, S. (2018) "Business Schools Have No Business in the University," *Chronicle of Higher Education*, 20 February.

D'Alembert, J. le R. (2011) *Discours Préliminaire à l'Encyclopédie [1752]*. Paris: Les Échoes de Maquis.

Darwall, S. (1999) "Sympathetic Liberalism: Recent Work on Adam Smith," *Philosophy and Public Affairs*, 28(2), pp. 139–164. Available at: https://doi.org/10.1111/j.1088-4963.1999.00139.x.

(2004) "Equal Dignity in Adam Smith," *The Adam Smith Review*, 1, pp. 129–134.

(2006) *The Second Person Standpoint: Morality, Respect, and Accountability*. Cambridge, MA: Harvard University Press.

Dawson, D. (1991) "Is Sympathy so Surprising? Adam Smith and the French Fictions of Sympathy," *Eighteenth Century Life*, 15, pp. 47–62.

Debes, R. (2016) "Adam Smith and the Sympathetic Imagination," in R. P. Hanley (ed.) *Adam Smith: His Life, Thought and Legacy*. Princeton: Princeton University Press, pp. 192–207.

Debes, R. and Stueber, K (eds.) (2017) *Ethical Sentimentalism*. Cambridge: Cambridge University Press.

Degooyer, S. (2018) "'The Eyes of Other People': Adam Smith's Triangular Sympathy and the Sentimental Novel," *ELH - English Literary History*, 85 (3), pp. 669–690. Available at: https://doi.org/10.1353/elh.2018.0024.

DeMartino, G. F. (2011) *The Economist's Oath: On the Need for and Content of Professional Economic Ethics*. New York: Oxford University Press.

Deneen, P. J. (2018) *Why Liberalism Failed*. New Haven: Yale University Press.

Diderot, D. (1751) *Encyclopédie ou dictionnaire raisonné des sciences, des arts et des métiers, etc*. Paris.

Diogenes Laertius. (1925) *Lives of Eminent Philosophers*. Edited by R. D. Hicks. Cambridge, MA: Harvard University Press.

Douglass, R. (2017) "Morality and Sociability in Commercial Society: Smith, Rousseau-And Mandeville," *Review of Politics*, 79(4), pp. 597–620. Available at: https://doi.org/10.1017/S0034670517000584.

⸻ (2018) "Theorising Commercial Society: Rousseau, Smith and Hont," *European Journal of Political Theory*, 4(17)pp. 501–511. Available at: https://doi.org/10.1177/1474885118782390.

Dumouchel, D. (2010) "Une éducation sentimentale: sympathie et construction de la morale dans les Lettres sur la sympathie de Sophie de Grouchy," in M. A. Bernier and D. Dawson (eds) *Les Lettres sur la sympathie (1798) de Sophie de Grouchy, philosophie morale et réforme sociale*. Oxford: Voltaire Foundation, pp. 139–150.

Duncan, I. (1998) "Adam Smith, Samuel Johnson and the Institutions of English," in R. Crawford (ed.) *The Scottish Invention of English Literature*. Cambridge: Cambridge University Press, pp. 37–54.

Dupaty, C.-M.-J.-B.M. (1786a) *Mémoire justificatif pour trois hommes condamnés à la roue*. Paris: Philippe-Denys Pierres.

⸻ (1786b) *Moyens de droit pour Bradier, Simare, Lardoise, condamnés à la roue*. Paris: Philippe-Denys Pierres.

Easterly, W. (2021) "Progress by Consent: Adam Smith as Development Economist," *Review of Austrian Economics*, 34(2), pp. 179–201. Available at: https://doi.org/10.1007/s11138-019-00478-5.

Ekelund, R. B., Jr., et al. (1996) *Sacred Trust: The Medieval Church as an Economic Firm*. Oxford: Oxford University Press.

Ekelund, R. B., Jr. and Hébert, R. F. (2007) *A History of Economic Theory and Method*, 5th edition. Long Grove: Waveland Press, Inc.

Ekelund, R. B., Jr., Hébert, R. F. and Tollison, R. D. (2006) *The Marketplace of Christianity*. Cambridge: MIT Press.

Elster, J. (2004) "Two for One? Reciprocity in Seneca and Adam Smith," *Adam Smith Review*, 6, pp. 152–171.

Endres, A. M. (1991) "Adam Smith's Rhetoric of Economics," *Journal of Scottish Political Economy*, 38(1), pp. 76–95.

Epictetus (1989) *The Discourses as Reported by Arrian, the Manual and Fragments*. Edited by W. A. Oldfather. Cambridge MA: Harvard University Press.

Erskine, A. (1990) *The Hellenistic Stoa*. London: Duckworth.

Evensky, J. (2005a) *Adam Smith's Moral Philosophy: A Historical and Contemporary Perspective on Markets, Law, Ethics, and Culture*. Cambridge: Cambridge University Press.

(2005b) "'Chicago Smith' versus 'Kirkaldy Smith,'" *History of Political Economy*, 37(2), pp. 197–203. Available at: https://doi.org/10.1215/00182702-37-2-197.

Faccarello, G. and Steiner, P. (2002) "The Diffusion of the Work of Adam Smith in the French Language: An Outline History," in K. Tribe (ed.) *A Critical Bibliography of Adam Smith*. London: Pickering and Chatto, pp. 61–119.

Farrant, A. and Paganelli, M. P. (2016) "Romance or No Romance? Adam Smith and David Hume in James Buchanan's 'Politics without Romance,'" *Research in the History of Economic Thought and Methodology*, 34A, pp. 357–372. Available at: https://doi.org/10.1108/S0743-41542016000034A013.

Fawcett, E. (2014) *Liberalism: The Life of an Idea*. Princeton: Princeton University Press.

Festa, L. M. (2006) *Sentimental Figures of Empire in Eighteenth-Century Britain and France*. Baltimore: Johns Hopkins University Press.

Fiori, S. (2012) "Adam Smith on Method: Newtonianism, History, Institutions, and the 'Invisible Hand,'" *Journal of the History of Economic Thought*, 34(3), pp. 411–435. Available at: https://doi.org/10.1017/S1053837212000405.

Fleischacker, S. (1999) *A Third Concept of Liberty*. Princeton: Princeton University Press.

(2002) "Adam Smith's Reception among the American Founders, 1776–1790," *William and Mary Quarterly*, 59(4), pp. 897–924. Available at: https://doi.org/10.2307/3491575.

(2004a) *A Short History of Distributive Justice*. Cambridge MA: Harvard University Press.

(2004b) *On Adam Smith's Wealth of Nations: A Philosophical Companion*. Princeton: Princeton University Press.

(2013) "Adam Smith on Equality," in C. J. Berry, P. P. Maria, and C. Smith (eds) *The Oxford Handbook of Adam Smith*. Oxford: Oxford University Press, pp. 485–501.

(2016) "Adam Smith and the Left," in R. P. Hanley (ed.) *Adam Smith: His Life, Thought and Legacy*. Princeton: Princeton University Press, pp. 478–493.

(2019a) *Being Me Being You*. Chicago: University of Chicago Press.

(2019b) "The Impact on America," in A. Broadie and C. Smith (eds.) *The Cambridge Companion to the Scottish Enlightenment*. Cambridge: Cambridge University Press, pp. 313–333.

(2021) *Adam Smith*. New York: Routledge.

Forbes, D. (1975) "Sceptical Whiggism, Commerce and Liberty," in A. S. Skinner and T. Wilson (eds) *Essays on Adam Smith*. Oxford: Clarendon Press, pp. 179–201.

Force, P. (2003) *Self-Interest before Adam Smith: A Genealogy of Economic Science*. Cambridge: Cambridge University Press.

Fordyce, J. (1766) *Sermons to Young Women*. London: A. Millar and T. Cadell.

Forget, E. L. (2001) "Cultivating Sympathy: Sophie Condorcet's Letters on Sympathy," *Journal of the History of Economic Thought*, 23(3), pp. 319–337. Available at: https://doi.org/10.1080/10427710120073609.

Forman-Barzilai, F. (2010) *Adam Smith and the Circles of Sympathy*. Cambridge: Cambridge University Press.
Forrester, K. (2019) *In the Shadow of Justice: Postwar Liberalism and the Remaking of Political Philosophy*. Princeton: Princeton University Press.
Frank, R. H. (1988) *Passions within Reason: The Strategic Role of the Emotions*. New York: W.W. Norton & Co.
Frankfurt, H. (1987) "Equality as a Moral Ideal," *Ethics*, 98(1), pp. 21–43. Available at: https://doi.org/10.1086/292913.
Frecer, R. (2015) *Stoicism in Practice: The Cosmopolitanism of Cicero and the Development of Roman Citizenship*. Prague: Charles University in Prague.
Fricke, C. (2013) "Adam Smith: The Sympathetic Process and the Origin and Function of Conscience," in C. J. Berry, C. Smith, and M. P. Paganelli (eds) *The Oxford Handbook of Adam Smith*. Oxford: Oxford University Press, pp. 177–200.
Friedman, Milton (1977). "The Invisible Hand", in *The Collected Works of Milton Friedman*, Hoover Institution Archives. Available at http://miltonfriedman.hoover.org/objects/57602 (accessed: March 8, 2022).
Frye, N. (1957) *Anatomy of Criticism*. Princeton: Princeton University Press.
Galiani, F. (1975a) "Della Moneta," in F. Diaz and L. Guerci (eds) *Opere di Ferdinando Galiani*. Milan: Ricciardi.
   (1975b) "Dialogues sur le commerce des bleds," in F. Diaz and L. Guerci (eds) *Opere di Ferdinando Galiani*. Milan: Ricciardi.
Garrett, A. and Hanley, R. P. (2015) "Adam Smith: History and Impartiality," in J. Harris and A. Garrett (eds) *Scottish Philosophy in the Eighteenth Century*. Oxford: Oxford University Press, pp. 239–282.
Garrett, A. and Heydt, C. (2015) "Moral Philosophy: Practical and Speculative," in A. Garrett and J. Harris (eds) *Scottish Philosophy in the Eighteenth Century*. Oxford: Oxford University Press, pp. 77–130.
Gill, M. B. (2014) "Moral Pluralism in Smith and His Contemporaries," *Revue Internationale de Philosophie*, 269(3), pp. 275–306.
Goddard, C. (2018) *Ten Lectures on the Natural Semantic Metalanguage*. Leiden: Brill.
Goddard, C. and Wierzbicka, A. (2014) *Words and Meanings. Lexical Semantics across Domains, Languages and Cultures*. Oxford: Oxford University Press.
   (2016) "'It's mine!' Re-thinking the Conceptual Semantics of 'Possession' through NSM," *Language Sciences*, 56, pp. 93–104.
   (2019) "Cognitive Semantics, Linguistic Typology and Grammatical Polysemy: 'Possession' and the English Genitive," *Cognitive Semantics*, 5(2), pp. 224–247. Available at: https://doi.org/10.1163/23526416-00502003.
Gorski, P. (2003) *The Disciplinary Revolution: Calvinism and the Rise of the State in Early Modern Europe*. Chicago: University of Chicago Press.
Gould, R. R. and Tahmasebian, K. (2020) "Introduction: Translation and Activism in the Time of the Now," in R. R. Gould and K. Tahmasebian (eds) *The Routledge Handbook of Translation and Activism*. Abingdon: Routledge, pp. 1–9.

Graham, Gordon. (2007) "The Ambition of Scottish Philosophy," *The Monist*, 90, pp. 157–169.
Greiner, R. (2010) "The Art of Knowing Your Own Nothingness," *ELH - English Literary History*, 77(4), pp. 893–914.
— (2012) *Sympathetic Realism in Nineteenth-Century British Fiction*. Baltimore: Johns Hopkins University Press.
Griswold, C. L. (1991) "Rhetoric and Ethics: Adam Smith on Theorizing about the Moral Sentiments," *Philosophy and Rhetoric*, 24(3), pp. 213–237.
— (1999) *Adam Smith and the Virtues of Enlightenment*. Cambridge: Cambridge University Press.
— (2010) "Smith and Rousseau in Dialogue: Sympathy, pitié, Spectatorship and Narrative," *The Adam Smith Review*, 5, pp. 59–84.
— (2018) *Jean-Jacques Rousseau and Adam Smith: A Philosophical Encounter*. London: Routledge.
Grotius, H. (2005) *The Rights of War and Peace*. Edited by R. Tuck. Indianapolis: Liberty Fund.
Grouchy, S. de (1792) "Sending Manuscript of Lettres," *[Letter] Held at: Bibliothèque de Genève. Ms Dumont 74, f. 174.*
Guillois, A. (1894) *Le salon de Madame Helvétius: Cabanis et les idéologues*. Paris: Calmann Lévy.
— (1897) *La marquise de Condorcet: sa famille, son salon, ses amis, 1764–1822*. Paris: P. Ollendorff.
Haakonssen, K. (1981) *The Science of a Legislator: The Natural Jurisprudence of David Hume and Adam Smith*. Cambridge: Cambridge University Press.
— (1996) *Natural Law and Moral Philosophy: From Grotius to the Scottish Enlightenment*. Cambridge: Cambridge University Press.
Hacker, L. M. (1957) *Alexander Hamilton and the American Tradition*. New York: McGraw-Hill.
Haeffele, S. and Storr, V. H. (2019) "Adam Smith and the Study of Ethics in a Commercial Society," in M. D. White (ed.) *The Oxford Handbook of Ethics and Economics*. Oxford: Oxford University Press, pp. 13–33.
Halikias, D. I. (2020) "Adam Smith on the Scottish Highlands and the Origins of Commercial Society," *History of Political Thought*, 41(4), pp. 622–647.
Hamilton, Alexander (1963). "Second Report on the Further Provision Necessary for Establishing Public Credit" in *The Papers of Alexander Hamilton*, vol. 7, September 1790–January 1791. Edited by H. C. Syrett. New York: Columbia University Press, pp. 236–256.
Hanley, R. P. (2006) "From Geneva to Glasgow: Rousseau and Adam Smith on the Theater and Commercial Society," *Studies in Eighteenth Century Culture*, 35, pp. 177–202. Available at: https://doi.org/10.1353/sec.2010.0051.
— (2008) "Commerce and Corruption: Rousseau's Diagnosis and Adam Smith's Cure," *European Journal of Political Theory*, 7(2), pp. 137–158. Available at: https://doi.org/10.1177/1474885107086445.

(2009) *Adam Smith and the Character of Virtue.* Cambridge: Cambridge University Press.

(2014) "The Wisdom of the State: Adam Smith on China and Tartary," *American Political Science Review*, 108(2), pp. 371–382. Available at: https://doi.org/10.1017/S0003055414000057.

(2018) "On the Place of Politics in Commercial Society," in M. P. Paganelli, D. C. Rasmussen, and C. Smith (eds) *Adam Smith and Rousseau: Ethics, Politics, Economics.* Edinburgh: Edinburgh University Press, pp. 16–31.

(2021) "Review of Craig Smith, 'Adam Smith,'" *History of Political Economy*, 53(4), pp. 793–795. Available at: https://doi.org/10.1215/00182702-9309009

Heath, E. (2013) "Adam Smith and Self-Interest," in C. J. Berry, M. P. Paganelli, and C. Smith (eds) *The Oxford Handbook of Adam Smith.* Oxford: Oxford University Press, pp. 242–264.

Heath, J. (2020) *The Machinery of Government: Public Administration and the Liberal State.* Oxford: Oxford University Press.

Heckscher, Eli Filip. (1994). "Mercantilism as a conception of society," in *Mercantilism, vol. II: 5.* London: Routledge.

Herzog, L. (2011) "Higher and Lower Virtues in Commercial Society: Adam Smith and Motivation Crowding Out," *Politics, Philosophy and Economics*, 10(4), pp. 370–395. Available at: https://doi.org/10.1177/1470594X10386564.

(2013) *Inventing the Market: Smith, Hegel and Political Theory.* Oxford: Oxford University Press.

(2014) "Adam Smith on Markets and Justice," *Philosophy Compass*, 9(12), pp. 864–875. Available at: https://doi.org/10.1111/phc3.12183.

Hetherington, N. S. (1983) "Isaac Newton's Influence on Adam Smith's Natural Laws in Economics," *Journal of the History of Ideas*, 44(3), pp. 497–505.

Heydt, C. (2012) "'A Delicate and an Accurate Pencil': Adam Smith, Description, and Philosophy as Moral Pedagogy," in W. L. Robison and D. B. Suits (eds) *New Essays on Adam Smith's Moral Philosophy.* Rochester: RIT Press, pp. 212–227.

Hill, L. (2001) "The Hidden Theology of Adam Smith," *European Journal of the History of Economic Thought*, 8(1), pp. 1–29. Available at: https://doi.org/10.1080/713765225.

(2011) "Social Distance and the New Strangership in Adam Smith," *Adam Smith Review*, 6, pp. 166–183.

(2017) "'The Poor Man's Son' and the Corruption of Our Moral Sentiments: Commerce, Virtue and Happiness in Adam Smith," *Journal of Scottish Philosophy*, 15(1), pp. 9–25. Available at: https://doi.org/10.3366/jsp.2017.0149.

(2020) *Adam Smith's Pragmatic Liberalism, Adam Smith's Pragmatic Liberalism.* Cham: Palgrave Macmillan.

Hill, L. and Blazejak, E. (2021) *Stoicism and the Western Political Tradition.* New York: Palgrave Macmillan.

Hill, L. and McCarthy, P. (1999) "Hume, Smith and Ferguson: Friendship in Commercial Society," *Critical Review of International Social and Political*

Philosophy, 2(4), pp. 33–49. Available at: https://doi.org/10.1080/13698239908403290.
Hill, M. and Montag, W. (2014) *The Other Adam Smith*. Stanford: Stanford University Press.
Hobbes, T. (1991) *Leviathan*. Edited by R. Tuck. Cambridge: Cambridge University Press.
Hollander, S. (1973) *The Economics of Adam Smith*. Toronto: University of Toronto Press.
   (1977) "Adam Smith and the Self-Interest Axiom," *The Journal of Law and Economics*, 20(1), pp. 133–152. Available at: https://doi.org/10.1086/466895.
Honneth, A. (2021) *Recognition: A Chapter in the History of European Ideas*. Cambridge: Cambridge University Press.
Hont, I. (2005) *Jealousy of Trade: International Competition and the Nation State in Historical Perspective*. Cambridge MA: Harvard University Press.
   (2015) *Politics in Commercial Society*. Edited by M. Sonenscher and B. Kaposy. Cambridge MA: Harvard University Press.
Hont, I. and Ignatieff, M. (1983a) "Needs and Justice in the Wealth of Nation," in I. Hont and M. Ignatieff (eds) *Wealth and Virtue: The Shaping of Political Economy in the Scottish Enlightenment*. Cambridge: Cambridge University Press.
Hont, I. and Ignatieff, M. (eds) (1983b) *Wealth and Virtue: The Shaping of Political Economy in the Scottish Enlightenment*. Cambridge: Cambridge University Press.
Hume, D. (1978) *A Treatise of Human Nature*. Edited by P. Nidditch and L. Selby-Bigge. Oxford: Clarendon Press.
   (1987) *Essays Moral, Political and Literary*. Edited by E. F. Miller. Indianapolis: Liberty Fund.
   (2001) *An Enquiry Concerning Human Understanding*. Edited by T. L. Beauchamp. Oxford: Oxford University Press.
Hunt, L. (2007) *Inventing Human Rights: A History*. New York: W.W. Norton & Co.
Hurtado, J. (2005) "Pity, Sympathy and Self-Interest: Review of Pierre Force's Self-Interest before Adam Smith," *European Journal of the History of Economic Thought*, 12(4), pp. 713–721. Available at: https://doi.org/10.1080/09672560500370409.
Hutcheson, F. (1725) *An Inquiry into the Original of Our Ideas of Beauty and Virtue*. London: J. Darby.
   (1755) *A System of Moral Philosophy*. Glasgow and London.
Iannaccone, L. R. (1990) "Religious Participation: A Human Capital Approach," *Journal for the Scientific Study of Religion*, 29(3), pp. 297–314.
   (1991) "The Consequences of Religious Market Structure: Adam Smith and the Economics of Religion," *Rationality and Society*, 3(2), pp. 156–77.
Iannacone, L. R. (1997) "Rational Choice: Framework for the Scientific Study of Religion," in L. A. Young (ed.) *Rational Choice Theory and Religion: Summary and Assessment*. New York: Routledge, pp. 25–44.

Iannaccone, L. R. and Bainbridge, W. S. (2009) "Economics of Religion," in J. Hinnells (ed.) *Routledge Companion to the Study of Religion*, 2nd Edition. Florence: Routledge, pp. 475–489.

Ince, O. U. (2021) "Adam Smith, Settler Colonialism, and Limits of Liberal Anti-imperialism," *Journal of Politics*, 83(3), pp. 1080–1096. Available at: https://doi.org/10.1086/711321.

Innes, J. (2009) *Inferior Politics: Social Problems and Social Policies in Eighteenth-Century Britain*. Oxford: Oxford University Press.

Jefferson, T. (1961) "Letter from Thomas Jefferson to Thomas Mann Randolph, Jr., 30 May 1790," in J. P. Boyd (ed.) *The Papers of Thomas Jefferson, vol. 16, 30 November 1789–4 July 1790*. Princeton: Princeton University Press, pp. 448–450.

Jeffrey, F. (1844) *Contributions to the Edinburgh Review*, 3 vols. London: Longman, Brown, Green, and Longmans.

Johnson, S. (2000) "The Rambler no. 4 ['The New Realistic Novel']," in D. Greene (ed.) *The Major Works*. Oxford: Oxford University Press, pp. 175–9.

Jones, D. S. (2014) *Masters of the Universe: Hayek, Friedman, and the Birth of Neoliberal Politics*. Princeton: Princeton University Press.

Jones, E. (2017) *Edmund Burke and the Invention of Modern Conservatism, 1830–1914: An Intellectual History*. Oxford: Oxford University Press.

Jubb, R. (2015) "The Real Value of Equality," *Journal of Politics*, 77(3), pp. 679–691. Available at: https://doi.org/10.1086/681262.

Kames, H. H. L. (2005) *Essays on the Principles of Morality and Natural Religion*. Edited by K. Haakonssen. Indianapolis: Liberty Fund.

Kaplan, S. L. (1976) *Bread, Politics and Political Economy in the Reign of Louis XV*. The Hague: M. Nijhoff.

Kelly, C. (2006) "Rousseau's 'peut-etre': Reflections on the Status of the State of Nature," *Modern Intellectual History*, 3(1), pp. 75–83. Available at: https://doi.org/10.1017/S1479244305000697.

Kelly, D. (2013) "Adam Smith and The Limits of Sympathy," in C. J. Berry, M. P Paganelli and C. Smith (eds.) *The Oxford Handbook of Adam Smith*. Oxford: Oxford University Press, pp. 201–218.

Kennedy, G. (2005) *Adam Smith's Lost Legacy*. London: Palgrave Macmillan.

 (2008) *Adam Smith: A Moral Philosopher and His Political Economy*. London: Palgrave Macmillan.

Klein, D. (1985) "Deductive Economic Methodology in the French Enlightenment: Condillac and Destutt de Tracy," *History of Political Economy*, 17(1), pp. 51–71. Available at: https://doi.org/10.1215/00182702-17-1-51.

Klein, D. and Humphries, A. G. (2019) "Foreword and Supplement to 'Adam Smith's Library: General Checklist and Index," *Econ Journal Watch*, 16(2), pp. 374–474.

Klein, D. B. (2018) "Dissing *The Theory of Moral Sentiments*: Twenty-Six Critics, from 1765 to 1949," *Econ Journal Watch*, 15(2), pp. 201–254.

Kopajtic, L. (2020) "Smith's Sentimentalist Conception of Self-Command," *Adam Smith Review*, 12, pp. 7–27.

(2022) "Learning to Read: A Problem for Adam Smith and a Solution from Jane Austen," in G. Hagberg (ed.) *Philosophical Reflection in Fictional Worlds*. London: Palgrave Macmillan, pp. 49–78.
Krueger, A. O. (1974) "The Political Economy of the Rent-Seeking Society," *The American Economic Review*, 64(3), pp. 291–303.
Lai, C.-C. (2000) *Adam Smith across Nations: Translations and Receptions of the Wealth of Nations*. Oxford; New York: Clarendon Press.
Larrère, C. (1992) "L'Arithémetiques des physiocrates," *Histoire et Mesure*, 7(1–2), pp. 5–24.
(2002) "Adam Smith et Jean-Jacques Rousseau: sympathie et pitié," *Kairos: revue de la Faculté de philosophie de l'Université de Toulouse-Le Mirail*, 20, pp. 73–94.
Leddy, N. (2009) "Adam Smith's Moral Philosophy in the Context of Eighteenth Century French Fiction," *Adam Smith Review*, 4, pp. 158–180.
Levy, J. T. (2015) *Rationalism, Pluralism, and Freedom*. Oxford: Oxford University Press.
Lindgren, R. J. (1973) *The Social Philosophy of Adam Smith*. The Hague: Martinus Nijhoff.
Lippert-Rasmussen, K. (2021) "Relational Sufficientarianism and Frankfurt's Objections to Equality," *Journal of Ethics*, 25(1), pp. 81–106. Available at: https://doi.org/10.1007/s10892-020-09344-0.
List, G. F. (1827) *Outlines of American Political Economy*. Philadelphia: Samuel Parker.
Liu, G. M. (2018) "'The Apostle of Free Trade:' Adam Smith and the Nineteenth-Century American Trade Debates," *History of European Ideas*, 44(2), pp. 210–223. Available at: https://doi.org/10.1080/01916599.2018.1429709.
(2020) "Rethinking the Chicago Smith Problem: Adam Smith and the Chicago School, 1929–1980," *Modern Intellectual History*, 4(17), pp. 1041–1068. Available at: https://doi.org/10.1017/S147924431900009X.
(2022) *Adam Smith's America: How A Scottish Philosopher Became an Icon of American Capitalism*. Princeton: Princeton University Press.
Long, A. A. (2008) "The Concept of the Cosmopolitan in Greek & Roman Thought," *Daedalus*, 137(3), pp. 50–58. Available at: https://doi.org/10.1162/daed.2008.137.3.50.
Luban, D. (2012) "Adam Smith on Vanity, Domination, and History," *Modern Intellectual History*, 2(9)pp. 275–302. Available at: https://doi.org/10.1017/S1479244312000042.
Lynch, D. S. (1998) *The Economy of Character: Novels, Market Culture, and the Business of Inner Meaning*. Chicago: University of Chicago Press.
Macdonald, K. (2019) "Did British Sociology Begin with the Scottish Enlightenment?" in P. Panayatova (ed.) *The History of Sociology in Britain*. London: Palgrave Macmillan, pp. 37–69.
Machovec, F. (2012) "Adam Smith: Early Public-Choice Theorist," *Journal of Political Economy*, 120(4), p. 4. Available at: https://doi.org/10.1086/668966.
Mackenzie, H. (1987) *The Man of Feeling*. Edited by B. Vickers. Oxford: Oxford University Press.

Madison, James (1979). "Import Tonnage and Duties, 9 April 1789," in M. E. Rachal, R. A. Rutland and J. K. Sisson (eds) *The Papers of James Madison*, vol. 12. Charlottesville: University of Virginia Press, pp. 69–74.
Magnusson, Lars. (1994). *Mercantilism: The Shaping of an Economic Language*. Taylor & Francis.
Mandeville, B. (1988) *The Fable of the Bees: or, Private Vices, Publick Benefits, in two volumes*. Edited by F. B. Kaye. Indianapolis: Liberty Fund.
Manent, P. and Seigel, J. E. (1996) *An Intellectual History of Liberalism*. Translated by R. Balinski. Princeton: Princeton University Press.
Marcus Aurelius (1987) *The Meditations*. Edited by C. R. Haines. Cambridge MA: Harvard University Press.
Marivaux, P. (1965) *The Virtuous Orphan, or, The Life of Marianne, Countess of *****: An Eighteenth-Century English Translation by Mrs. Mary Mitchell Collyer of Marivaux's La vie de Marianne*. Edited by W. H. McBurney and M. F. Shugrue. Carbondale: Southern Illinois University Press.
Marshall, D. (1986) *The Figure of Theater: Shaftesbury, Defoe, Adam Smith, and George Eliot*. New York: Columbia University Press.
Martin, J. (1927) "Achille du Chastellet et le premier mouvement républicain en France d'après les lettres inédites (1791–1792)," *La Révolution française*, 80, pp. 104–132.
Maurer, C. (2016) "Stoicism and the Scottish Enlightenment," in J. Sellars (ed.) *The Routledge Handbook of the Stoic Tradition*. New York: Routledge, pp. 254–269.
  (2019) *Self-Love, Egoism and the Selfish Hypothesis*. Edinburgh: Edinburgh University Press.
Mayer, C. (2018) *Prosperity: Better Business Makes the Greater Good*. Oxford: Oxford University Press.
Maza, S. (1993) *Private Lives and Public Affairs: the causes célèbres of prerevolutionary France*. Berkeley: University of California Press.
McBurney, W. H. and Shugrue, M. F. (1965) "Introduction," in W. H. McBurney and M. F. Shugrue (eds) *The Virtuous Orphan, or, The Life of Marianne, Countess of *****: An Eighteenth-Century English Translation by Mrs. Mary Mitchell Collyer of Marivaux's La vie de Marianne*. Carbondale: Southern Illinois University Press, pp. xi–xliv.
McCloskey, D. N. (1998) "The Good Old Coase Theorem and the Good Old Chicago School: A Comment on Zerbe and Medema," in S. G. Medeman (ed.) *Coasean Economics Law and Economics and the New Institutional Economics*. Boston: Kluwer Academic Publishers, pp. 239–248.
  (2016) "Adam Smith Did Humanomics: So Should We," *Eastern Economic Journal*, 42(4), pp. 503–513. Available at: https://doi.org/10.1057/s41302-016-0007-8.
McCloskey, D. N. and DeMartino, G. F. (eds) (2016) *The Oxford Handbook of Professional Economic Ethics*. Oxford: Oxford University Press.
McCrudden, K. (2021) Fraternité, Liberté, Égalité: Sophie de Grouchy, Moral Republicanism, and the History of Liberalism, 1785–1815. PhD Dissertation. Yale University.

McCulloch, J. R. (1889) *Preface to Adam Smith Wealth of Nations [1828]*. Edinburgh: A & C. Black.
McHugh, J. (2021) *Adam Smith's 'The Theory of Moral Sentiments' A Critical Commentary*. London: Bloomsbury.
McLean, I. (2006) *Adam Smith, Radical and Egalitarian: An Interpretation for the 21st Century*. Edinburgh: Edinburgh University Press.
Medema, S. G. (2010) "Adam Smith and the Chicago School," in R. B. Emmet (ed.) *The Elgar Companion to the Chicago School of Economics*. Cheltenham and Northampton: Edward Elgar, pp. 40–51.
Mercier de la Rivière (1910) *L'ordre natural et essentiel des sociétés politiques*. Edited by E. Depitre. Paris: Librairie Paul Guethner.
Mercure Français (1798) "Announcement of publication of Lettres sur la sympathie," *Mercure Français*, p. 38.
Minowitz, P. (1993) *Profits, Priests and Princes: Adam Smith's Emancipation of Economics from Politics and Religion*. Stanford: Stanford University Press.
Mirabeau (1759) *L'Ami des Hommes*. Amsterdam.
——— (1769) "Suite de la Seizième Lettre de M. B.A M***," in *Éphémérides du Citoyen*. Paris.
Mizuta, H. (1976) "Towards a Definition of the Scottish Enlightenment," *Studies in Voltaire*, 154, pp. 1459–1464.
——— (2000) *Adam Smith's Library: A Catalogue*. Oxford: Clarendon Press.
Mizuta, H. and Sugiyama, C. (1993) *Adam Smith: International Perspectives*. London: Palgrave Macmillan UK.
Montes, L. (2003) "Das Adam Smith Problem: Its Origins, the Stages of the Current Debate, and One Implication for Our Understanding of Sympathy," *Journal of the History of Economic Thought*, 25(1), pp. 63–90. Available at: https://doi.org/10.1080/1042771032000058325.
——— (2004) *Adam Smith in Context: A Critical Reassessment of Some Central Components of His Thought*. New York: Palgrave Macmillan.
——— (2013) "Newtonianism and Adam Smith," in C. J. Berry, M. P. Paganelli, and C. Smith (eds) *The Oxford Handbook of Adam Smith*. Oxford: Oxford University Press, pp. 36–53.
Montesquieu (1961) *De l'Esprit des Lois, 2 vols*. Paris: Garnier.
Mullan, J. (1988) *Sentiment and Sensibility: The Language of Feeling in the Eighteenth Century*. Oxford: Oxford University Press.
——— (1996a) "Feelings and Novels," in R. Porter (ed.) *Rewriting the Self: Histories from the Middle Ages to the Present*. London: Routledge, pp. 119–131.
——— (1996b) "Sentimental Novels," in J. Richetti (ed.) *The Cambridge Companion to the Eighteenth-Century Novel*. Cambridge: Cambridge University Press, pp. 236–254.
Muller, J. Z. (1993) *Adam Smith in His Time and Ours*. Princeton: Princeton University Press.
Musonius, Rufus C. (2011) *Musonius Rufus, Lectures and Sayings*. Edited by C. King and W. B. Irvine. CreateSpace Independent Publishing.

Muthu, S. (2008) "Adam Smith's Critique of International Trading Companies: Theorizing 'Globalization' in the Age of Enlightenment," *Political Theory*, 36(2), pp. 185–212. Available at: https://doi.org/10.1177/0090591707312430.

Neem, J. N. (2019) "Abolish the Business Major! Anti-Intellectual Degree Programs Have No Business in Colleges," *Chronicle of Higher Education*, 13 August.

Norman, J. (2018) *Adam Smith: Father of Economics*. New York: Basic Books.

North American Review (1823). "Review: *Considerations sur l'Industrie et la Législation sous le Rapport de leur Influence sur la Richesse des Etats, et Examen Critique des Principaux Ouvrages, Qui ont para sur l'Economie Politique by Louis Say*", 17(41), pp. 424–436.

North, D. C. (1992) Transaction Costs, Institutions, and Economic Performance. *Economic Inquiry*, 25(3), pp. 419–428. Available at: https://onlinelibrary.wiley.com/doi/abs/10.1111/j.1465-7295.1987.tb00750.x (accessed: February 8, 2022).

North, D. C., Wallis, J. J. and Weingast, B. R. (2009) *Violence and Social Orders: A Conceptual Framework for Interpreting Recorded Human History*. Cambridge: Cambridge University Press.

Nussbaum, M. C. (2019) *The Cosmopolitan Tradition: A Noble but Flawed Ideal*. Cambridge MA: Harvard University Press.

O'Connor, M. J. L. (1944) *Origins of Academic Economics in the United States*. New York: Columbia University Press.

Olson, M. (1971) *The Logic of Collective Action: Public Goods and the Theory of Groups, Second Printing with a New Preface and Appendix*. Cambridge MA: Harvard University Press.

Oncken, A. (1897) "The Consistency of Adam Smith," *The Economic Journal*, 7 (27), pp. 443–450. Available at: https://doi.org/10.2307/2957137.

O'Neill, M. (2008) "What Should Egalitarians Believe?," *Philosophy and Public Affairs*, 36(2), pp. 119–156. Available at: https://doi.org/10.1111/j.1088-4963.2008.00130.x.

Oprea, A. (2022) "Adam Smith on Political Judgment: Revisiting the Political Theory of the Wealth of Nations," *Journal of Politics*, 84(1), pp. 18–32. Available at: https://doi.org/10.1086/715249.

Otteson, J. R. (2016) "Adam Smith and the Right," in R. P. Hanley (ed.) *Adam Smith: His Life, Thought and Legacy*. Princeton: Princeton University Press, pp. 494–511.

Pack, S. J. (1991) *Capitalism as a Moral System: Adam Smith's Critique of the Free Market Economy*. Aldershott: Edward Elgar.

Paganelli, M. P. (2008) "The Adam Smith Problem in Reverse: Self-Interest in the *Wealth of Nations* and the *Theory of Moral Sentiments*," *History of Political Economy*, 40(2), pp. 365–382. Available at: https://doi.org/10.1215/00182702-2008-006.

(2010) "The Moralizing Role of Distance in Adam Smith: The Theory of Moral Sentiments as Possible Praise of Commerce," *History of Political Economy*, 42 (3), pp. 425–441. Available at: https://doi.org/10.1215/00182702-2010-019.

(2017) "240 Years of Adam Smith's Wealth of Nations," *Nova Economia*, 27(2), pp. 7–19.

(2020) *The Routledge Guidebook to Smith's Wealth of Nations*. London: Routledge.

(2021) "Adam Smith and Dying Peacefully," in E. A. Dolgoy, K. Hurd Hale, and B. Peabody (eds) *Political Theory on Death and Dying*. London: Routledge, pp. 292–298.

Paganelli, M. P. and Schumacher, R. (2019) "Do Not Take Peace for Granted: Adam Smith's Warning on the Relation between Commerce and War," *Cambridge Journal of Economics*, 43(3), pp. 785–797. Available at: https://doi.org/10.1093/cje/bey040.

Paganelli, M. P., Smith, C. and Rasmussen, D. C. (2018) "Introduction," in M. P. Paganelli, C. Smith, and D. C. Rasmussen (eds) *Adam Smith and Rousseau: Ethics, Politics, Economics*. Edinburgh: Edinburgh University Press, pp. 1–15.

Palen, M. W. (2016) *The "Conspiracy" of Free Trade: The Anglo-American Struggle over Empire and Economic Globalisation, 1846–1896*. Cambridge: Cambridge University Press.

Peart, S. and Levy, D. (2005) *The Vanity of the Philosopher: From Equality to Hierarchy in Postclassical Economics*. Ann Arbour: Michigan University Press.

Perrot, J.-C. (1992) *Une Histoire Intellectuelle de l'Économie Politique*. Paris: Éditions de l'École des Hautes Études en Sciences Social.

Petty, W. (1899) *Economic Writings of Sir William Petty, 2 Vols*. Edited by C. Hull. Cambridge: Cambridge University Press.

Phillips, A. (2021) *Unconditional Equals*. Princeton: Princeton University Press.

Phillipson, N. (1983) "Adam Smith as Civic Moralist," in I. Hont and M. Ignatieff (eds) *Wealth and Virtue: The Shaping of Political Economy in the Scottish Enlightenment*. Cambridge: Cambridge University Press, pp. 179–202.

(2010) *Adam Smith: An Enlightened Life*. London: Penguin.

Pignol, C. and Walraevens, B. (2017) "Smith and Rousseau on Envy in Commercial Societies," *European Journal of the History of Economic Thought*, 24(6), pp. 1214–1246. Available at: https://doi.org/10.1080/09672567.2017.1378693.

Pitts, Jennifer. (2005). *A Turn to Empire: The Rise of Imperial Liberalism in Britain and France*. Princeton University Press.

Plato (1992) *The Republic*. Edited by C. D. C. Reeve and G. M. A. Grube. Indianapolis: Hackett.

Pocock, J. G. A. (1983) "Cambridge Paradigms and Scotch Philosophers," in I. Hont and M. Ignatieff (eds) *Wealth and Virtue: The Shaping of Political Economy in the Scottish Enlightenment*. Cambridge: Cambridge University Press, pp. 235–252.

(1985) *Virtue, Commerce, and History*. Cambridge: Cambridge University Press.

du Pont de Nemours (1768) *De l'Origine et des Progrès d'une Science Nouvelle*. Paris.

Powell, B. and Zwolinski, M. (2012) "The Ethical and Economic Case against Sweatshop Labor: A Critical Assessment," *Journal of Business Ethics*, 107(4) pp. 449–472. Available at: https://doi.org/10.1007/s10551-011-1058-8.

Quesnay, F. (1764) *Philosophie rurale ou économie générale et politique de l'agriculture*, 3 vols. Amsterdam.
  (1767a) "Despotisme de la Chine," in *Éphémérides du Citoyen*. Paris.
  (1767b) "Lettre de M. Alpha," in *Éphémérides du Citoyen*, 1st edition. Paris.
Raphael, D. D. (1973) "Hume and Adam Smith on Justice and Utility," *Proceedings of the Aristotelian Society*, 73(1), pp. 87–103. Available at: https://doi.org/10.1093/aristotelian/73.1.87.
  (2007) *The Impartial Spectator: Adam Smith's Moral Philosophy*. Oxford: Oxford University Press.
Raphael, D. D. and Macfie, A. L. (1976) "Introduction," in D. D. Raphael and A. L. Macfie (eds) *The Theory of Moral Sentiments*. Oxford: Oxford University Press, pp. 1–52.
Rashid, S. (1982) "Adam Smith's Rise to Fame: A Reexamination of the Evidence," *The Eighteenth Century*, 23(1), pp. 64–85.
Rasmussen, D. C. (2006) "Does 'Bettering Our Condition' Really Make Us Better Off? Adam Smith on Progress and Happiness," *American Political Science Review*, 100(3), pp. 309–318. Available at: https://doi.org/10.1017/S0003055406062204.
  (2008) *The Problems and Promise of Commercial Society*. University Park: Penn State University Press.
  (2016) "Adam Smith on What Is Wrong with Economic Inequality," *American Political Science Review*, 110(2), pp. 342–352. Available at: https://doi.org/10.1017/S0003055416000113.
Recktenwald, H. C. (1978) "An Adam Smith Renaissance anno 1976? The Bicentenary Output: A Reappraisal of His Scholarship," *Journal of Economic Literature*, 16(1), pp. 56–83.
Redman, D. A. (1993a) "Adam Smith and Isaac Newton," *Scottish Journal of Political Economy*, 40(2), pp. 210–230. Available at: https://doi.org/10.1111/j.1467-9485.1993.tb00651.x.
  (1993b) *The Rise of Political Economy as Science*. Cambridge, MA: Harvard University Press.
Richardson, S. (1985) *Clarissa, or The History of a Young Lady*. Edited by A. Ross. London: Penguin.
  (2011) *Pamela: Or, Virtue Rewarded*. Edited by A. J. Rivero. Cambridge: Cambridge University Press.
Ridley, M. (2010) *The Rational Optimist: How Prosperity Evolves*. New York: Harper.
Robertson, J. (2005) *The Case for The Enlightenment*. Cambridge: Cambridge University Press.
Roederer, P.-L. (1798) "Des Lettres de la Citoyenne Condorcet sur la Sympathie," *Journal de Paris*.
  (1859) "Cours d'organisation sociale," in A.-M. Roederer (ed.) *Oeuvres du Comte Pierre Louis Roederer*. Paris: Firmin Didot Frères, pp. 129–304.
Rose, D. C. (2011) *The Moral Foundation of Economic Behavior*. New York: Oxford University Press.

Rosenblatt, H. (2019) *The Lost History of Liberalism: From Ancient Rome to the Twenty-First Century*. Princeton: Princeton University Press.

Ross, I. S. (2010) *The Life of Adam Smith*, Second edition. Oxford: Oxford University Press.

Rothschild, E. (1992) "Adam Smith and Conservative Economics," *The Economic History Review*, 45(1), pp. 74–96. Available at: https://doi.org/10.1111/j.1468-0289.1992.tb01292.x.

(2002) *Economic Sentiments: Adam Smith, Condorcet and the Enlightenment*. Cambridge, MA: Harvard University Press.

Rousseau, J.-J. (1991) *Emile, or On Education*. Edited by A. Bloom. London: Penguin.

Rousseau, J. J. (1992) *Discourse on the Origins of Inequality (Second Discourse), Polemics, and Political Economy*. Edited by R. D. Masters and C. Kelly. Hanover: University Press of New England.

(1997) *The Discourses and Other Early Political Writings*. Edited by V. Gourevitch. Cambridge: Cambridge University Press.

Ryan, A. (2012) *The Making of Modern Liberalism*. Princeton: Princeton University Press.

Saad, M. (2015) "Sentiment, Sensation and Sensibility: Adam Smith, Pierre Jean Georges Cabanis and Wilhelm von Humboldt," *History of European Ideas*, 41 (2), pp. 205–220. Available at: https://doi.org/10.1080/01916599.2014.921474.

Sagar, P. (2018a) "Smith and Rousseau, after Hume and Mandeville," *Political Theory*, 46(1), pp. 29–58. Available at: https://doi.org/10.1177/0090591716656459.

(2018b) *The Opinion of Mankind: Sociability and the Theory of the State from Hobbes to Smith*. Princeton: Princeton University Press.

(2021a) "Adam Smith and the Conspiracy of the Merchants," *Global Intellectual History*, 6(4), pp. 463–483.

(2021b) "On the Liberty of the English: Adam Smith's Reply to Montesquieu and Hume," *Political Theory*, 50(3), pp. 381–404. Available at: https://doi.org/10.1177/00905917211039763.

(2022) *Adam Smith Reconsidered: History, Liberty and the Foundations of Modern Politics*. Princeton: Princeton University Press.

Say, J.-B. (1972) *Traité d'Économie Politique*. Paris: Calman-Levy.

Schabas, M. and Wennerlind, C. (2020) *A Philosopher's Economist: David Hume and the Rise of Capitalism*. Chicago: University of Chicago Press.

Schliesser, E. (2006) "Adam Smith's Benevolent and Self-Interested Conception of Philosophy," in L. Montes and E. Schliesser (eds) *New Voices on Adam Smith*. London: Routledge, pp. 328–357.

(2017) *Adam Smith: Systematic Philosopher and Public Thinker*. Oxford: Oxford University Press.

(2019) "Sophie de Grouchy, Adam Smith, and the Politics of Sympathy," in E. O'Neill and M. P. Lascano (eds) *Feminist History of Philosophy: The Recovery and Evaluation of Women's Philosophical Thought*. Cham: Springer International Publishing, pp. 193–219.

(2021) "Adam Smith on Political Leadership," in R. J. W. Mills and C. Smith (eds) *The Scottish Enlightenment: Human Nature, Social Theory and Moral Philosophy: Essays in Honour of Christopher J. Berry*. Edinburgh: Edinburgh University Press, pp. 132–163.

Schliesser, E. and Bergé, S. (2019) *Sophie de Grouchy's Letters on Sympathy: A Critical Engagement with Adam Smith's The Theory of Moral Sentiments*. New York: Oxford University Press.

Schwab, K. (2021) *Stakeholder Capitalism: A Global Economy That Works for Progress, People and Planet*. Hoboken: John Wiley & Sons.

Schwarze, M. (2020) *Recognizing Resentment: Sympathy, Injustice and Liberal Political Thought*. Cambridge: Cambridge University Press.

Schwarze, M. A. and Scott, J. T. (2015) "Spontaneous Disorder in Adam Smith's Theory of Moral Sentiments: Resentment, Injustice, and the Appeal to Providence," *Journal of Politics*, 77(2), pp. 463–476. Available at: https://doi.org/10.1086/679750.

(2019) "Mutual Sympathy and the Moral Economy: Adam Smith Reviews Rousseau," *Journal of Politics*, 81(1), pp. 66–80. Available at: https://doi.org/10.1086/700003.

Scott, W. (1995) *Rob Roy*. Hammondsworth: Penguin.

Scurr, R. (2009) "Inequality and Political Stability from Ancien Régime to Revolution: The Reception of Adam Smith's Theory of Moral Sentiments in France," *History of European Ideas*, 35(2), pp. 441–449.

Sebastiani, S. (2013) *The Scottish Enlightenment; Race, Gender, and the Limits of Progress*. New York: Palgrave Macmillan.

Sen, A. (1986) "Adam Smith's Prudence," in S. Lall and F. Stewart (eds) *Theory and Reality in Development*. London: Macmillan, pp. 28–37.

(1987) *On Ethics and Economics*. Malden: Blackwell.

(2009) *The Idea of Justice*. Cambridge, MA: Harvard University Press.

(2013) "The Contemporary Relevance of Adam Smith," in C. J. Berry, M. P. Paganelli, and C. Smith (eds) *The Oxford Handbook of Adam Smith*. Oxford: Oxford University Press, pp. 581–592.

(2016) "Adam Smith and Economic Development," in R. P. Hanley (ed.) *Adam Smith: His Life, Thought and Legacy*. Princeton: Princeton University Press, pp. 281–301.

Seneca (1917) *Epistles*, in Three Volumes. Edited by R. Gummere. Cambridge, MA: Harvard University Press.

(2003) *Moral Essays*, in Three Volumes. Edited by J. W. Basore. Cambridge, MA: Harvard University Press.

Seth, C. (2010) "Un double service rendu à la postérité: la Théorie des sentiments moraux par Adam Smith, suivie des Lettres sur la sympathie," in M. A. Bernier and D. Dawson (eds) *Les 'Lettres sur la sympathie' (1798) de Sophie de Grouchy, marquise de Condorcet*. Oxford: Voltaire Foundation, pp. 127–137.

Sher, R. B. (1985) *Church and University in the Scottish Enlightenment: The Moderate Literati of Edinburgh*. Edinburgh: Edinburgh University Press.

(1990) "'Professors of Virtue: The Social History of the Edinburgh Moral Philosophy Chair in the Eighteenth Century,'" in M. A. Stewart (ed.) *Studies in the Philosophy of the Scottish Enlightenment*. Oxford: Oxford University Press, pp. 87–126.

(2010) *The Enlightenment and the Book: Scottish Authors and Their Publishers in Eighteenth-Century Britain, Ireland, and America*. Chicago: Chicago University Press.

Shields, L. (2020) "Sufficientarianism," *Philosophy Compass*, 15(11), pp. 1–10. Available at: https://doi.org/10.1111/phc3.12704.

Shklar, J. (1990) *The Faces of Injustice*. New Haven: Yale University Press.

Silver, A. (1997) "'Two Different Sorts of Commerce': Friendship and Strangership in Civil Society," in K. Kumar and J. Weintraub (eds) *Public and Private in Thought and Practice*. Chicago: University of Chicago Press, pp. 43–74.

Skinner, A. F. (1975) "Adam Smith: An Economic Interpretation of History," in A. S. Skinner and T. Wilson (eds) *Essays on Adam Smith*. Oxford: Oxford University Press, pp. 154–178.

(1996) *A System of Social Science: Papers Relating to Adam Smith*, Second edition. Oxford: Clarendon Press.

Slack, P. (2015) *The Invention of Improvement: Information and Material Progress in Seventeenth-Century England*. Oxford: Oxford University Press.

Smart, A. K. (2011) *Citoyennes: Women and the Ideal of Citizenship in Eighteenth-Century France*. Newark, DE: University of Delaware Press.

Smith, A. (1983) *The Glasgow Edition of the Works and Correspondence of Adam Smith: Volume IV – Lectures on Rhetoric and Belles Lettres* [LRBL]. Edited by J. C. Bryce. Oxford: Clarendon Press.

Smith, C. (2013a) "Adam Smith and the New Right," in C. J. Berry, M. P. Paganelli, and C. Smith (eds) *The Oxford Handbook of Adam Smith*. Oxford: Oxford University Press, pp. 539–558.

(2013b) "Adam Smith: Left or Right?," *Political Studies*, 61(4), pp. 784–798. Available at: https://doi.org/10.1111/j.1467-9248.2012.00985.x.

(2015) "Adam Smith: Moral Judgment versus Moral Theory," in A. G. Sison, G. R. Beabout, and I. Ferrero (eds) *The Handbook of Virtue Ethics in Business and Management*. Dordrecht: Springer, pp. 143–150.

(2018) "Adam Smith on Philosophy and Religion," *Ruch Filozoficzny*, 73(3), pp. 23–39.

(2020) *Adam Smith*. London: Polity.

(2022) "Adam Smith, Adam Ferguson and the Reconceptualization of Philosophy in Eighteenth-Century Scotland," *History of Political Economy*, 54(5), pp. 921–934.

Smith, V. L. and Wilson, B. J. (2019) *Humanomics: Moral Sentiments and the Wealth of Nations for the Twenty-First Century*. Cambridge. Cambridge University Press.

Somos, M. (2011) "'A Price Would Be Set Not Only upon Our Friendship, but upon Our Neutrality': Alexander Hamilton's Political Economy and Early

American State-Building," *Studies across Disciplines in the Humanities and Social Sciences, Helsinki Collegium for Advanced Studies*, 10, pp. 184–211.

Sonenscher, M. (2007) *Before the Deluge: Public Debt, Inequality, and the Intellectual Origins of the French Revolution*. Princeton: Princeton University Press.

——— (2015) "Sociability, Perfectibility and the Intellectual Legacy of Jean-Jacques Rousseau," *History of European Ideas*, 41(5), pp. 683–698. Available at: https://doi.org/10.1080/01916599.2014.987563.

Spacks, P. M. (2006) *Novel Beginnings: Experiments in Eighteenth-Century English Fiction*. New Haven: Yale University Press.

Stark, A. and Davis, M. (eds) (2001) *Conflict of Interest in the Professions*. New York: Oxford University Press.

Stark, R. and Bainbridge, W. S. (1989) *A Theory of Religion*. New Brunswick: Rutgers University Press.

Stedman Jones, G. (2005) *An End to Poverty?: A Historical Debate*. New York: Columbia University Press.

Stein, J. A. (2020) *When Novels Were Books*. Cambridge MA: Harvard University Press.

Steiner, P. (1998) *La 'Science Nouvelle' de l'Économie Politique*. Paris: Presses Universitaires de France.

Sterne, L. (2009) *The Life and Opinions of Tristram Shandy, Gentleman*. Edited by I. C. Ross. Oxford: Oxford University Press.

Stigler, G. J. (1975) "Smith's Travels on the Ship of State," in A. S. Skinner and T. Wilson (eds) *Essays on Adam Smith*. Oxford: Clarendon Press, pp. 232–248.

——— (1976) "The Successes and Failures of Professor Smith," *Journal of Political Economy*, 84(6), pp. 1199–1213. Available at: https://doi.org/10.1086/260508.

Stimson, S. C. (2015) "The General Will after Rousseau: Smith and Rousseau on Sociability and Inequality," in J. Farr and D. Lay Williams (eds) *The General Will: The Evolution of a Concept*. Cambridge: Cambridge University Press, pp. 350–381.

Tegos, S. (2013) "Sympathie morale et tragédie sociale: Sophie de Grouchy lectrice d'Adam Smith," *Noesis*, 21, pp. 265–292.

——— (2014) "Friendship in Commercial Society Revisited," in Hardwick David F. and L. Marsh (eds) *Propriety and Prosperity: New Studies on the Philosophy of Adam Smith*. London: Palgrave Macmillan, pp. 37–53.

Teichgraeber, R. F. (1987) "'Less Abused Than I Had Reason to Expect': The Reception of the Wealth of Nations in Britain, 1776–90," *The Historical Journal*, 30(2), pp. 337–366. Available at: https://doi.org/10.1017/S0018246X00021476.

Thayer, H. (ed.) (1953) *Newton's Philosophy of Nature: Selections from His Writing*. New York: Hafner.

Thomson, H. F. (1965) "Adam Smith's Philosophy of Science," *Quarterly Journal of Economics*, 79(2), pp. 212–233. Available at: https://doi.org/10.2307/1880627.

Tribe, K. (1995) *Strategies of Economic Order: German Economic Discourse, 1750-1950*. Cambridge: Cambridge University Press.

(2008) "'Das Adam Smith Problem' and the Origins of Modern Smith Scholarship," *History of European Ideas*, 34(4), pp. 514-525. Available at: https://doi.org/10.1016/j.histeuroideas.2008.02.001.

(2021) "The 'System of Natural Liberty': Natural Order in the Wealth of Nations," *History of European Ideas*, 47(4), pp. 573-583. Available at: https://doi.org/10.1080/01916599.2020.1793516.

Tullock, G. (1967) "The Welfare Costs of Tariffs, Monopolies, and Theft," *Economic Inquiry*, 5(3), pp. 224-232. Available at: https://doi.org/10.1111/j.1465-7295.1967.tb01923.x.

(1975) "The Transitional Gains Trap," *The Bell Journal of Economics*, 6(2), pp. 671-678. Available at: https://doi.org/10.2307/3003249.

Valihora, K. (2016) "Adam Smith's Narrative Line," in R. P. Hanley (ed.) *Adam Smith: His Life, Thought, and Legacy*. Princeton: Princeton University Press, pp. 405-421.

Waldron, J. (1993) "Liberal Rights: Two Sides of the Coin," in *Liberal Rights: Collected Papers 1981-1991*. Cambridge: Cambridge University Press, pp. 1-34.

(2008) "Basic Equality," *SSRN Electronic Journal* [Preprint]. Available at: https://doi.org/10.2139/ssrn.1311816.

Waszek, N. (1984) "Two Concepts of Morality: A Distinction of Adam Smith's Ethics and Its Stoic Origin," *Journal of the History of Ideas*, 45(4), pp. 591-606. Available at: https://doi.org/10.2307/2709375.

Waterman, A. M. C. (2002) "Economics as Theology: Adam Smith's Wealth of Nations," *Southern Economic Journal*, 68(4), pp. 907-921. Available at: https://doi.org/10.2307/1061499.

Watt, I. (1957) *The Rise of the Novel: Studies in Defoe, Richardson and Fielding*. Berkeley: University of California Press.

Weingast, B. R. (2017) "Adam Smith's Theory of Violence and the Political Economics of Development," in J. J. Wallis and N. Lamoreaux (eds) *Organizations, Civil Society, and the Roots of Development*. Chicago: University of Chicago Press, pp. 51-82.

(2022) "Adam Smith's Theory of the Persistence of Slavery and Its Abolition in Western Europe. Stanford. Available at: www.researchgate.net/publication/315450839_Adam_Smith%27s_Theory_of_the_Persistence_of_Slavery_and_its_Abolition_in_Western_Europe (accessed: August 2, 2022).

Weinstein, J. R. (2013) *Adam Smith's Pluralism: Rationality, Education, and the Moral Sentiments*. New Haven: Yale University Press.

Werhane, P. H. (1991) *Adam Smith and His Legacy for Modern Capitalism*. New York: Oxford University Press.

West, E. G. (1990) *Adam Smith and Modern Economics: From Market Behavior to Public Choice*. Aldershot: Edward Elgar.

Whatmore, R. (2002) "Adam Smith's Role in the French Revolution," *Past & Present*, 175(1), pp. 65–89. Available at: https://doi.org/10.1093/past/175.1.65.

Wierzbicka, A. (1972) *Semantic Primitives*. Frankfurt: Athenäum-Verl.

——— (1980) *Lingua Mentalis*. Sydney: Academic Press.

——— (1992) *Semantics, Culture and Cognition: Universal Human Concepts in Culture-Specific Configurations*. New York: Oxford University Press.

——— (1996) *Semantic Primes and Universals*. New York: Oxford University Press.

Wight, J. B. (2002) "The Rise of Adam Smith: Articles and Citations, 1970–1997," *History of Political Economy*, 34(1), pp. 55–82. Available at: https://doi.org/10.1215/00182702-34-1-55.

Williams, O. F. (2014) *Corporate Social Responsibility: The Role of Business in Sustainable Development*. New York: Routledge.

Willis, K. (1979) "The Role in Parliament of the Economic Ideas of Adam Smith, 1776–1800," *History of Political Economy*, 11(4), pp. 505–544. Available at: https://doi.org/10.1215/00182702-11-4-505.

Wills, G. (1978) "Benevolent Adam Smith," *New York Review of Books*, 9 February.

Wilson, B. J. (2015) "Humankind in Civilization's Extended Order: A Tragedy, The First Part," *Supreme Court Economic Review*, 23(1), pp. 35–58. Available at: https://doi.org/10.1086/686471.

——— (2020) *The Property Species: Mine, Yours, and the Human Mind*. New York: Oxford University Press.

Winch, D. (1978) *Adam Smith's Politics: An Essay in Historiographic Revision*. Cambridge: Cambridge University Press.

——— (1992) "Adam Smith: Scottish Moral Philosopher as Political Economist," *The Historical Journal*, 35(1), pp. 91–113. Available at: https://doi.org/10.1017/S0018246X00025620.

——— (1996) *Riches and Poverty: An Intellectual History of Political Economy in Britain, 1750–1834*. Cambridge: Cambridge University Press.

Wooton, D. (2018) *Power, Pleasure, and Profit: Insatiable Appetites from Machiavelli to Madison*. Cambridge, MA: Harvard University Press.

Young, A. (1999) "Combination and Monopoly," in P. M. Mehrling and R. Sandilands (eds) *Money and Growth: Selected Papers of Allyn Abbott Young*. London: Routledge, pp. 244–251.

Young, J. T. and Gordon, B. (1996) "Distributive Justice as a Normative Criterion in Adam Smith's Political Economy," *History of Political Economy*, 28(1), pp. 1–25. Available at: https://doi.org/10.1215/00182 702-28-1-1.

INDEX

accidental variations, 30
Account of the Life and Writings of Adam Smith, LL.D. (Stewart), 7
activist commentator
   Grouchy on Smith, 217
activist interpreter
   Grouchy as, 216
activist translation
   concept of, 215
   Smith's *TMS*, 2
Adam Smith and the Circles of Sympathy (Barzilai), 16
Adam Smith, Sa vie, ses travaus, ses doctrines (Delatour), 10
Adam Smith's Moral Philosophy (Evensky), 13
Adam Smith's Pluralism (Weinstein), 13
advantage
   concept, 92
affairs
   concern for self and others, 195
   interest in others, 201
affections, 201
agreement
   gaming an, 106
altruism, 70, 187
American Founding Era, 19
amiable principle
   pity, 134
amour propre, 144, 151, 152, 156
An Inquiry into the Human Mind (Reid), 5
ancien régime, 216, 221, 223, 227, 230
ancien régime cause célèbre, 216
Ancient Physics (Smith), 236

Anderson, Elizabeth, 18, 125
apprenticeships, 98
Aristotle, 26, 33, 62, 72, 162, 177
   commutative justice, 162
   distributive justice, 163
   elitism, 74
Armstrong, Nancy, 194
astronomy, 233, 241
ataraxia
   individual pleasure, 182
Aurelius, Marcus, 177
   theodicy and, 179
Author of Nature, 183
authority
   Smith, 8–10
authority of fortune, 138
authority of riches, 137

Baconianism, 23, 25
barbarians
   term, 128
   virtues of, 133
bargain
   concept, 92
Barzilai, Fonna Forman, 16
Beccaria, Cesare, 227
Bell, Duncan, 15
beneficence, 98
   justice and, 168
   Smith dismissing Stoic, 182
   violations of, 174
benevolence
   impartial, 180–181
   universal, 187
Bentham, Jeremy, 15, 220
Bergès, Sandrine, 215, 228
Berlin, Isaiah, 237

270   INDEX

betterment principle, 28, 29, 32
Bibliothèque de l'Institut, 220
Biziou, Michaël, 214, 230
Blair, Hugh, 6, 197
blood and treasure
   citizens, 112, 118, 122
Bonar, James, 10
Bradier, Charles, 222, 223
Brissot, Jacques Pierre, 215
Britain
   Corn Laws of, 120
British Empire, 119
Brooke, Frances, 196
Brown, Karin, 225
Buchanan, James, 117, 122
Buckle, Henry, 10
Burke, Edmund, 15
business. *See* virtuous business
   malfeasance and corruption, 96
businesspeople
   code of ethics for, 105–108
   commercial society and, 96
   moral guidance for, 109
   promises and responsibilities, 107–108
   refraining from coercion, threats, ad exploitation, 105–107
butcher
   case of, 33
   conduct of, 34
   exchange and speech, 68–71
   kosher, 70
   self-interest and exchange, 62–68
Butler, Joseph, 165

Cabanis, Pierre Jean George, 230
Calas, Jean, 227
canonization
   Smith, 10–12
Cantillon, Richard, 36
capitalism, 71, 124, 140
   commercial society, 126
   commercial society and, 17, 129
   Roman Church impeding, 51
captatio benevolentiae, 92
Carey, Henry C., 8
Catalogue of Adam Smith's Library (Bonar), 10
Cathars, 46

Catholic Church, 60, *See* Church
   centralized hierarchy of, 57
   existential threats from, 58
   religious sects competing with, 55
Catholicism, 227
causes, 22, 29–31
   explicit references to, 29
   identification of, 30
   natural, 30
caveat emptor
   principle of, 106
Chicago Price Theory, 9
Chicago School
   economics, 9
   Stigler and, 112
Chicago Smith, 11, 19
Chicago Smith Problem, 12
chimerical
   Hume's term, 37
China, 119, 127
Church
   competition among religions, 55–56
   financial support of, 48
   landowner, 51
   leases and, 51
   leverage over the masses, 41
   Lord and, 52–53
   luxury and, 54, 56, 57, 58, 60
   monopoly of, 42, 44–46, 53, 54, 55, 58, 59
   political exchange and equilibrium with lords, 47–50
   predatory behavior of, 54
   understanding behavior of, 44
Church's authority
   challenging, 49, 50, 55, 58, 60, 61
   environmental changes eroding, 54–55
   violence to capture, 59
   weakening, 60
   weakening of, 42
Cicero, 178, 184, 188
Cicero's *De Finibus*, 177
citizens
   blood and treasure of, 112, 122
   true world, 181
Civil Constitution of the Clergy, 215
civil magistrate, 45

civilization
    state of, 128
civilized
    term, 129
Clapiers, Luc de, 224
Clarissa (Richardson), 195, 204, 205, 206, 207, 209, 211
Clavière, Étienne, 215
coercion
    firms refraining from, 105–107
Collini, Stefan
    four stages model, 3–4
colonial trade, 121
    monopoly of, 115, 122
Comanche
    language, 82
commerce
    bond of union and friendship, 118
    form of speech, 75
    peace and, 192
    regulation of, 123
Commerce et le Gouvernement (Condillac), 35
commercial
    term, 129, 189
commercial countries, 127
commercial friendship, 190
commercial modernity
    term, 126
commercial nation
    principal virtues of, 139
commercial nations, 127
commercial society
    capitalism and, 129
    concept of, 126, 140
    conjectural history of, 132
    economic success of, 192
    modern, 126, 127, 131, 133, 137, 140
    morality of, 136–138
    phrase, 124, 127
    prudence and, 138–140
    savage vs. civilized states, 135
    Smith's concept of, 17
    term, 125, 126, 127, 129
    TMS and, 126–131
commitments
    fulfilling, 107–108

communication
    speech and, 73
community
    important and excellent thing, 180
commutative justice, 186
    Aristotle, 162
competition, 39
    industrial organization of religion and rise of, 56–58
    monopoly and, 40
    rise of, among religions, 55–56
    wealth and, 64
competitive psychological self-harm, 152
Condorcet O'Connor, Eliza, 220, 221
consequentialism, 237
conspiracies of merchants, 104
Constant, Benjamin, 15
consumption
    deception of, 148
    imbalances in economic production and, 151
    motor of, 145–149
    psychology of endless, 148
    quirk of rationality, 144, 146
    quirk of rationality driving, 152
    Rousseau's view, 144
contentment
    happiness and, 149
    splenetic philosophy, 147
contracts
    reneging on, 106
    society protecting, 98
conveniences
    necessaries and, 84
conversations
    speech and exchange, 70
cooperation
    exchange and speech, 68–71
cooperative exchange, 109
Copernicus, 236
Corn Laws, 120
corporate social responsibility
    business ethics, 109
corporations
    interests of, 112–117
corrective justice
    Aristotle's, 162
corruption
    commercial, 138

corruption of our moral sentiments, 140
　Smith on, 136, 137, 138
cosmopolitanism, 187
　economic, 189, 192
　Epicurean, 187–188
　Stoic, 187–188
Count Windischgrätz, 223
country
　indifference to faraway, 119
　inhabitants of, 113
Creator
　errors and evils intended by, 180
　perfection, 179
crime syndicate
　cooperation and purpose, 104
Critical Review (journal), 5
cronyism, 111, 112
　deaths by mercantilist, 118
cynicism, 241

d'Épinay, Louise, 221
Das Adam Smith Problem, 10, 12, 13, 19, 140
Dawson, Deirdre, 194
De Finibus (Cicero), 177
De Rerum Natura (Lucretius), 177
definitionism, 36
Degooyer, Stephanie, 194
Delatour, Albert, 10
Die Nationalökonomie der Gegenwart und Zukunft ("The National Economy of the Present and Future") (Hildebrand), 8
Diogenes Laertius' *Lives and Opinions of Eminent Philosophers*, 177
discipleship
　Smith, 7–8
Discours préliminaire à l'Encyclopédie (D'Alembert), 23
Discourse on the Origins of Inequality among Men (Rousseau), 131
distributions
　egalitarianism in terms of, 142
distributive injustice, 170
distributive justice, 158
　Aristotle, 163
　egalitarians and, 143
　right to, 186

divine intelligence
　universe design, 181
Divine Masterplan, 187
division of labor, 238
　all people living well, 89–90
　differences in, 87–89
　protecting 3 Ps, 99
　term, 87
domestic affections, 195
domination, 154
　material distribution and, 155
　material inequality and, 154
　rule of law against, 153
　slavery and love of, 173
Draco
　laws of, 118
du Chastellet, Achille, 214
Dumont, Étienne, 220
Duncan, Ian, 194
Dupaty, Charles, 222, 224

earthquake
　being swallowed by, 119
　ease of body and peace of mind
　poor achieving, 150
East India Company
　monopoly of, 119
ecclesiastic lords
　political accommodation between secular and, 52–53
economic consumption
　psychology of, 147
　Rousseau on, 152
economic equality
　social and, 227
economic exchange
　self-interest and, 62–68
economic growth, 25
　violence and predation, 44
economic growth and development
　society's long-term, 50–51
economic inequality
　Smith's concern, 137
　stages of society and, 137
economic nationalism, 8
economic principles
　necessaries and conveniences of life, 81–82
economics, 78

based on feeling good, 85
discipline of, 1
organization, 40
people exchanging things, 91–93
people, places and things, 81
Plan of the Work, 83–87
re-humanizing study of, 95
study of, 90–95
Economizer Argument, 102
   Smith's, 101
   Smith's political economy, 100
economy
   comparison to sick body, 122
Edinburgh Belles Lettres Society, 197
Edinburgh Review (journal), 131, 133, 206
education, 194, *See* moral education
   literature for, 198
efficiency
   Smith's concerns about, 117
egalitarian
   forms of theory, 156
   Smith as basic, 142
egalitarianism
   distributions, 142
   merely arithmetic, 156
   non-intrinsic, 157
   political value, 144
   Smith's, 74
   sufficientarianism and, 144
Egypt, ancient, 127
Elements of Criticism (Kames), 5
Elements of the Philosophy of the Human Mind (Stewart), 5
elitism
   Aristotle's, 74
Émile (Rousseau), 228
England, 128
English
   eighteenth-century King's, 82
Enlightenment, 23, 29, 38
environment, social, and governance (ESG), 109
Epicureanism, 177, 178
   Smith returning to, 181
   Stoicism and, 178, 193
Epicureans
   conception of justice, 185
   duties to others, 186–187
   pleasure, 181–182
   prudence, 182
   self-regard, 182–184
   Stoics and, 178
Epicurus, 177, 178, 182, 186, 192, 237
   pleasure, 181–182
Epicurus' "Principal Doctrines", 177
epistolary novel, 200, 210, 211, 212
epistolary novels, 213
equality
   Grouchy on necessity of, 219
   social and economic, 227
ESG (environment, social, and governance), 109
Esquisse d'un tableau historique des progrès de l'esprit humain (Condorcet), 219
Essays on Philosophical Subjects (*EPS*) (Smith), 21
Essays on the Principles of Morality and Natural Religion (Kames), 163
Evensky, Jerry, 13, 112
evil
   prevalence of, 179
exchange
   fair, 69
   networks of cooperative, 99
   people doing different things for, 93–94
   placeholder, 79
   self-interest and, 62–68
   semantic basis of, 81
   speech and freedom, 71–72
   things and people, 91–93
exploitation
   firms refraining from, 105–107
extractive exchange, 109

fair
   exchange as, 69
familiarity criterion, 33
fanaticism, 234, 243
father of capitalism, 96
father of economics
   Smith as, 1, 4
felicity
   distant idea of, 148

feudal political system
    Church in, 47
feudalism, 50, 59
    commerce and, 54
    European transition from, 129
Fifteen Sermons Preached at the Rolls Chapel (Butler), 165
filial piety, 195
Financial Crisis (2008), 14
firms
    mission of, 103–105
    origin and purpose of, 104
First Rule, Newton's, 27
Fleischacker, Samuel, 13, 17, 18, 194
Forbes, Duncan, 11
Fordyce, James, 198
four-stages model, 19
Frankfurt, Harry, 144, 150
free competition
    monopolies versus, 104
free market
    natural liberty, 190
free trade
    champions of, 7
free will
    exercise of, 179
freedom
    importance of civic, 74
    speech and, 71–72
French audience
    Grouchy on *TMS* for, 214
Fréteau de Saint-Just, Emmanuel-Marie-Michel-Philippe, 222
Friedman, Milton, 9, 10
friendship
    happiness and, 192

Galiani, 26
Garrett, Aaron, 236
Garrick, David, 199
Gassendi, Pierre, 177
Gautier, Claude, 214
general welfare of the society, 82
Genlis, Stéphanie-Félicité de, 221
Germany
    reformation birth in, 56
Gill, Michael, 237
God
    divine masterplan and, 179
    original purpose, 184
    perfect confidence in, 184
God is good, 179
good being done
    abstract idea of, 225
good will
    idea of, 226
Gould, Rebecca Ruth, 215
governments
    inequalities, 158
Graham, Gordon, 242
gratitude
    resentment of denied, 172
Great Britain, 123
great revolution
    consequences of, 134
    inequality growth from, 132
Greiner, Rae, 194
greyhounds, 63, 72
Griswold, Charles, 194
Grotius, Hugo, 162
    justice and beneficence, 162
    understanding of justice, 168
    utility and justice, 175
Grouchy, Sophie de, 2, 5, 214
    courtship and marriage of Condorcet and, 223
    marriage to Condorcet, 218
    objection to impartial spectator, 217
    sympathizing with kings, 218
Grouchy's *Letters*, 5, 216, 217, 220, 221, 224, 225, 231
Grumbling Hive
    allusion to England, 131
guardians of justice, 168

Haakonssen, Knud, 11
Hamilton. Alexander, 6
Hanley, Ryan, 14, 125, 238
happiness
    benevolence and, 184
    contentment and, 149
    ease of body and peace of mind, 149
    friendship and, 192
    human life and, 135
    prosperity and, 191
    Smith on, 155

Stoics living for others, 181
wealth and greatness and, 148
Helvétius, Claude Adrien, 218
Henry VIII, 57
Heydt, Colin, 194
Hildebrand, Bruno, 8
Hippocratic Oath, 102
historical writing, 208
History of Civilization in England (Buckle), 10
History of Philosophy (Stanley), 177
Hobbes, Thomas, 218
homo economicus, 14
Hont, István, 11, 17, 112, 125
human beings
  self-interest as motivation, 63
  self-regard, 182–184
  speech and freedom, 71–72
human equality
  Smith describing, 173
human life
  guide to moral judgement, 238–242
  real happiness of, 149
human nature
  naturalization of, 31
  passions of, 212
  science of, 31–34
  self-interest motivation, 97
humanity, 32
Humanomics (Smith), 14
humbling
  language of, 167
Hume, David, 6, 30, 31, 65, 145, 153, 165, 175, 218, 234, 238
  advice to sceptical philosopher, 243
  moral philosophy, 197, 237, 242
  science of man, 233
Hunt, Lynn, 208, 227
Hutcheson, Francis, 5, 23, 65, 217

Ignatieff, Michael, 11, 17, 112
imagination
  experiences and sensations, 201
  observational tool, 202
impartial spectator, 169, 176
  character of, 243
  Grouchy on removal of, 224
  Grouchy rejecting Smith's, 226
  Grouchy's objection to Smith's, 217

indignation and, 171
judgment of, 175
reliability of, 240
Smith's development of, 238
sympathy of, 170
imperialism
  critique of, 15
  European, 129, 190
import restrictions, 119
improvement
  Baconian goal of, 29
imprudence, 182
indignation
  anger and resentment, 166
  impartial spectator, 171
  ingratitude and, 171
  language of, 171
  proper object of, 186
  resentment and, 171
individual ethic, 144
  material wealth, 143
industrial organization
  religion, 42–51
  term on Church, 41
industrial organization of religion
  rise of competition and, 56–58
industrialization, 8
inequality
  economic, 135
  fortune, 138
  great revolution and, 132
  growth of, 137
  material distributions, 142
  material holdings vs. relations, 153, 154
  personal vs. political implications, 155
  problem of relational, 154
  Smith's discussion of, 135
  wealth, 138
ingratitude
  indignation and, 171
  resentment and, 170
  resentment of, 174
  response to, 170
injury
  object of resentment, 169
injustice
  conception of, 160

injustice (cont.)
  injury and, 170
  resentment and, 164–169
  resentment of, 174
innovations
  Smith on, 104
insolence, 75
institutionalized religion
  Smith's theory of, 42
instrumental friendship, 191
interest
  colonies, 121
  unjust, 117–122
interest of the dealers, 113
invisible hand, 219
Invisible Hand Argument
  Smith's political economy, 101–102

Jacobin Terror, 219
Jeffrey, Francis, 206
Johnson, Samuel, 198
Juliette Catesby (Riccoboni), 196, 205, 206, 211
jurisprudence
  systematic theory of natural, 162
justice
  3 Ps of, 105, 109, 110
  beneficence and, 168
  conception of, 98, 160
  definition and scope of, 161
  efficiency and, 112
  Epicurean conception of, 185
  guardians of, 168
  law and, 184–186
  promises and, 107
  protection of 3 Ps, 98
  punishment and improper resentment, 172–176
  resentment and, 167–169
  resentment motivating concern, 160
  rules of, 174
  Smith's conception of, 186
  Smith's discussion in TMS, 161–164
  Smith's principles of, 107
  Stoic conception of, 184
  wealth and, 122
justitia attributrix
  Grotius, 162

justitia expletrix
  Grotius, 162

kallipolis
  good city-state, 97
Kames, Lord, 5
  definition of justice, 163
  justice, 163
King of England, 58
Kirkaldy Smith, 112

La Vie du Marianne (Marivaux), 195
labor
  division of, 25, 27, 44
  productivity of, 25
labor markets
  monopolizing, 121
labour
  word, 87
laissez-faire, 7, 9, 96, 143
  policy of, 9
language
  theory of, 73
Lardoise, Nicolas, 222, 223
Larrère, Catherine, 36
law
  avoiding reputational harm, 186
  forbidding harm to others, 185
  justice and, 184–186
  obeying the, 185
law of unintended consequences
  Nature's, 183
laws of commerce, 26
Le Républicain (journal), 215
Lectures on Jurisprudence (Smith), x, 10, 11, 43
Lectures on Rhetoric and Belles Lettres (Blair), 197
Leddy, Neven, 194
Lee, Yoon Sun, 213
Lefèvre d'Ormesson de Noyseau, Louis, 223
Left Smith, 17
legislators
  love of system blinding, 115
Letters on Sympathy (Grouchy), 5
Lettres de Milady Juliette Catesby (Riccoboni), 196

Lettres sur la sympathie (*Letters on Sympathy*) (Grouchy), 214, 220
liberal egalitarianism, 16
liberal pluralism, 16
liberal rationalism, 16
liberal-capitalist societies, 124
liberalism, 15
  array of, 16
liberty
  Church and, 51
life
  guide to moral judgement, 238–242
Life of Adam Smith (Rae), 10
Ligniville, Anne-Catherine de, 218
List, Friedrich, 7
  critique of Smith, 8
literature
  role in Smith's pedagogy, 198
living creatures, 79
living well
  ideal of people, 89–90
Local Knowledge Argument, 102
  Smith's, 107
  Smith's political economy, 100–101
Lord
  Church and, 52–53
Louis XVI
  flight to Varennes, 215
Lucretius' *De Rerum Natura*, 177
Lynch, Deidre, 213

Mackenzie, Henry, 199
Madison, James, 6
mafia
  cooperation and purpose, 104
Malesherbes, Guillaume-Chrétien de Lamoignon de, 223
Mandeville, Bernard, 131, 240
  TMS as response to, 131–136
manufacturers
  interests of, 112–117, 121
  lobbying power, 116
  monopolies of, 115
  unjust interest, 117–122
Marianne (Marivaux), 205, 206, 207
Marivaux, Pierre, 195
market, 81
  exchange and speech, 68–71
  form of speech, 69
market price
  natural price and, 25
material distributions
  egalitarianism, 143
material inequality, 149
  domination and, 154
  psychological response to, 154
  Smith on living in world of, 155
material resources
  distribution of, 142
material wealth
  individual ethic, 143
mathematization of evidence, 36
McClellan, James Edward, 225
McCloskey, Deirdre, 14, 112
McCulloch, J.R., 24
mean rapacity, 123
measure
  advantage over opinion, 35
Medema, Steven, 112
medicine
  Hippocratic Oath of, 102
medieval Church
  industrial organization of, 42
  Smith's views on, 40
Meditations (Aurelius), 177
Mémoire justicatif pour trois hommes condamnés à la roue (Dupaty), 222
mercantile empires
  creation of, 116
mercantile system
  condemnations of, 122
  Smith's condemnation of, 116
  violent attacks against, 123
mercantilism
  conceptual error of, 190
  condemnation of, 117
  state capture of, 112
  WN as attack against, 112
merchants
  interests of, 112–117, 121
  lobbying power, 116
  monopolies of, 115
  unjust interest, 117–122
metaphysical sophisms, 195, 212
Mikuláš, Josef, 223
Mill, John Stuart, 15, 234
Millar, James, 198

miserabilism, 241
misreadings, 11
modern economy, 33
modernity, 140
Momus
  Greek god, 201
  magical window, 207
monopolies
  East India Company, 119
  interest of producer or consumer, 115
  merchants and manufacturers, 115
  Smith on, 104
  wars in protecting, 118
monopolists
  unjust interest of, 117–122
monopolization
  Church's, 45
monopoly
  Roman Catholic Church, 44–46
  spirit of, 113
Montes, Leonidas, 236
Monthly Review, 6
moral agents
  equal status of individuals as, 172
moral economy
  Smith's version of, 17
moral education
  literature in project of, 195
  literature of Momus's glass, 200–205
  novels contributing to, 196
  painting sentiments, 197–200
  Smithian, 213
  Smith's framework, 199
  spectatorial training, 196, 205–213
  value of literature, 196
moral Epicureanism, 218
moral judgment
  real life teaching, 238–242
moral philosophers
  Smith's conception of self as, 242–244
moral philosophy, 22, *See* philosophy
  discipline of, 233
  function of, 232
  individual judgment, 242–244
  interpretation of Smith's, 236
  modesty in ambitions, 241
  moral pluralism, 236–238
  practice of, 234

real life teaching moral judgment, 238–242
rediscovery of Smith's, 232
Smith's, 14, 15, 16
Smith's view of, 243
moral pluralism
  moral philosophy, 236–238
moral psychology
  Smith's, 194
moral right and wrong
  role of reason in, 225
moral science, 21–23
moral sentimentalism, 13
moral sentiments, 137
  admiring rich and powerful, 136
  corruption of, 137
moral spectator
  work of lifetime, 200
moral spectatorship
  resentment and, 164–167
  Smith's account of, 202
  Smith's theory of, 165
moral virtue
  Plato's theory of, 162
moral virtues
  Smith's vision of, 243
moralists
  whining and melancholy, 195, 241
morality, 39
  definition of, 226
  lessons of, 195
morals
  experimental approach to, 165
  Smith's theory of, 125
Morellet, André, 227
Mullan, John, 194
multinational monopoly, 45

Napoleon's Empire, 220
nations
  civilized versus barbarous, 128
  commercial, 127
natural authority
  deferring to superiors, 153
natural equality
  Grouchy's emphasis, 219
  sentiment of, 218
natural jurisprudence
  systematic theory of, 162

natural liberty, 24
  free market, 190
  label as system, 28
  obvious and simple system of, 105
  Smith vision, 219
  term, 29
natural order of things, 130
natural price
  market price and, 25
Natural Semantic Metalanguage, 2, 78, 79, 83
  economic principles, 79–81
  English exponents of semantic primes, 79–80
  mini-language of, 80
  syntax of, 79
naturalization
  human nature, 31
necessaries
  conveniences and, 84
necessaries and conveniences of life, 83
  economic principle, 81–82
necessary consequence, 94
neoliberalism, 15
Neoplatonism, 177
neorepublicanism
  ideal of, 215
new economic science
  term, 35
new economics of organization, 40
New Organon (Bacon), 25
new Smith scholarship, 12, 14, 15, 16
Newton, Isaac, 26, 34, 237
Newton's *Principia*, 34
Norman, Jesse, 19
North American colonies, 121
NSM. *See* Natural Semantic Metalanguage
Nussbaum, Martha, 15

O'Neill, Martin, 156, 157
objects
  utility of, 145
Oceana, 123
oikeiosis, 180
On Benefits (Seneca), 174
On Crimes and Punishments (Beccaria), 227

opium
  Bengal, 119
opportunism, 106
Orthodox Jewish population, 70
Osbaldistone, Frank, 75

pain
  Grouchy on seeing, 225
Paine, Thomas, 214
parental love, 201, 204
parental tenderness, 195
Parlement of Paris, 222, 223
parsimony, 27
particular sympathy, 221, 225, 228
pastoral countries, 127
patrimony of poor, 56, 121
peasants
  Church and, 55
people
  advantages and benefits of work, 89–90
  differences allowing exchange, 93–94
  different and different things, 94–95
  different kinds of labor, 87–89
  exchanging things, 91–93
  protection from coercion, threats, and exploitation, 105–107
people's work
  produce of, 83
perfect rights, 186
person
  society protecting, 98
perspectives
  sympathizing with, 212
perspective-switching
  spectator and, 211
  sympathetic, 211
persuasion, 71
  speech and, 72
  word, 74
Petty, William, 34
Phèdre (Racine), 203
philanthropia, 181
  Stoic, 192
Phillipson, Nicholas, 12, 67, 125, 126, 233
philosophers
  character of, 234
  financial incentives of, 235

philosophers (cont.)
　incentives governing, 235
　Smith's criticism of, 240
　splenetic, 241
　vanity of, 235
　vice of, 234–236
philosophy, 12, See moral philosophy
　Descartes's system in natural, 240
　discipline of, 232
　evolution of, 233, 235
　moral pluralism, 236–238
　Smith on development of, 22
　Smith's conception of, 233
　strengths of, 233–234
　usefulness as guide, 241
　vices of philosophers, 234–236
Pitjantjatjara
　language, 82
Pitts, Jennifer, 15
pity
　amiable principle of, 134
Plato, 97
　theory of moral virtue, 162
pleasure
　Epicureans, 181–182
pluralism, 97
　Smith's, 16
Pocock, J.G.A., 11
poets and romance writers, 194, 196, 204
political arithmetic
　term, 35
political economy
　Adam Smith's, 97–102
　economizer argument, 100
　invisible hand argument, 101–102
　local knowledge argument, 100–101
　Smith's, 178
　system of, 30
political exchange
　Church and the Lords, 47–50
political motivations
　Grouchy on TMS, 214
　Grouchy's possible, 215
political value, 144
poor
　Church's revenue and, 47
poor man's son
　avoiding pitfalls of, 157

　example of wasting one's life, 147
　famous parable of, 145
　happiness thinking, 147
　life of toil of, 150
　perils of, 145–149
　pursuit of wealth, 135
　Smith's example, 152
　Smith's parable of, 134
　trap of seeking utility, 145
porter
　ambition of street, 150
possession
　semantics of, 83
poverty
　problem of, 120
power
　synonyms for, 74
Pownall, William, 6
Pradeau, Jean-François, 214
pragmatic liberalism, 16
pride, 75
Principia (Newton), 34
principles, 22, 26–29, See also betterment principle
　desire for betterment, 32
　identification of, 27
　illustration of, 21
　system connections, 26
　truck, barter, and exchange, 27
Principles of Common Sense, 239
private property
　respecting, 98
professional ethics
　law code of, 102
promises
　justice and, 107
　principle of, 107–108
　reneging on, 106
　society protecting, 98
promittee, 107
property
　concept of, 85
　society protecting, 98
property rights
　rich on idea of, 151
prosperity
　business firms, 105
　hapiness and, 191
　positive production of, 109

prosperity of the commonwealth, 175
protectionism, 8
Protestant Reformation, 55
prudence
 virtue of, 27, 65, 126, 138, 139, 163, 178, 181, 182, 187, 202
psychology
 consumption, 144
 economic consumption, 147
 endless consumption, 148
 response to material inequality, 155
 vanity, 153
Public Choice, 112, 122
 warning, 123
Public Choice perspective, 2
Public Choice problems
 Stigler on Smith of not seeing, 111
public finance
 principles of, 25
public institutions
 protecting virtuous business, 108
public social institutions
 human beings administering, 98
publick interest, 101
punishment
 justice and improper resentment, 172–176
 natural consequence of resentment, 169
 resentment and, 170

quirk of rationality
 consumption, 146, 152
 consumption as, 144
 frivolous objects, 145

Rae, John, 10
Rambler (Johnson), 198
Rand, Ayn, 64
Raphael, D. D., 226
Rasmussen, Dennis, 14, 126
Rawls, John, 156
redistribution of wealth
 Grouchy arguing for governmental, 221
refinement of philosophy, 234
reflection
 idea of pain, 225
 sentiments through, 225

Réflexions d'un citoyen non-gradué sur un procès très-connu (Condorcet), 222
reform liberalism, 16
Reformation, 53, 56, 59, 60, 61
Reid, Thomas, 5, 239
relational inequality
 problem of, 154
relationships
 individuals, 142
religion
 Catholic monopoly, 55
 industrial organization of, 42–51
 political exchange and equilibrium between Church and lords, 47–50
 rise of competition among, 55–56
 secular lords and the Church, 47–52
religious services
 demand side of market for, 47
rent seeking
 concentrated interests, 113
 moral condemnation of, 112
republicanism, 215
resentment
 Butler on sorts of, 165
 concern with justice, 164
 gratitude denied and, 172
 indignation and, 171
 ingratitude and, 170
 injustice, 174
 justice and, 160, 167–169
 justice, punishment and problem of improper, 172–176
 moral spectatorship and, 164–167
 motivating concern for justice, 160
 narrowing the scope of, 169–172
 proper objects of gratitude and, 167
 punishment as consequence of, 169, 172
 Smith's account of, 161
 Smith's theory, 164–169
 "unsocial" passion, 173
rhetoric, 194
 literature, 197
 pedagogical value of, 198
Riccoboni, Marie Jeanne, 195
rich
 selfishness of, 148
Richardson, Samuel, 195

Right Smith, 17
rights
   person, reputation and estate, 186
rights of man
   Beccaria on defending, 227
Robertson, John, 218
Roederer, Pierre Louis, 220
Roman Catholic Church. *See* Church
   organization of, 40
   Smith on, 39
   wealth and power, 40
romantic love, 196, 202, 203, 204, 213
romantic passion, 201
Rousseau, Jean-Jacques, 131, 144, 228, 234
   challenge, 151–155
   radical egalitarian critique, 151
   TMS as response to, 131–136
rule of law
   against domination, 153
rule of natural justice, 130
Rules of Criticism, 239

Sagar, Paul, 112, 127
salvation
   Church providing, 48, 50
savages
   depictions of life of, 133
   term, 128
   virtues of, 133
Say, Jean-Baptiste, 24
Scanlon, Thomas, 156
Schliesser, Eric, 13, 215, 225, 233
Scholastics, 162
science
   moral, 21–23
   question of, 33
   society, 34–37
science of economics, 37
science of human nature, 31–34
science of man, 31
science of the legislator
   Smith's conception of, 219
Scott, Sir Walter, 75
Scottish Enlightenment, 38, 233
Scottish Highlands, 120, 127
Second Discourse (Rousseau), 131, 151
secret satisfaction, 226

secular lords
   Church and, 47–52, 60
   exchange between Church and, 48
   political accommodation between ecclesiastic and, 52–53
   power grabs by, 56
   redefining Church, 58
Séguier, Antoine-Louis, 223
self-command
   development of, 66
   market for training in, 66
self-interest
   charitable actions and, 62
   exchange and, 33, 62–68
   general principle of, 32
   Grouchy on, 218
   principle of, 27, 33
   Stigler on, 111
   with betterment and trucking, 32
selfish gratification
   means of utility, 148
self-love, 64, 184
   concept, 92
   cooperation and, 68
   moderating, 66
self-preservation, 182
self-protection, 185
semantic molecules
   Natural Semantic Metalanguage, 79
semantic primes, 78
Sen, Amartya, 15, 124
Sermons to Young Women (Fordyce), 198
Silver, Allan, 66
Simare, Jean-Baptiste, 222, 223
Skinner, Andrew, 233
slavery, 59
   condemnation of, 142
   Smith on, 173
Smith scholarship
   future, 19
   idea of, 4
   past, 5–12
   present, 12–19
Smith, Adam
   anniversary (300th), 1
   authority, 8–10
   canonization, 10–12
   comprehensibility of text, 82–83
   discipleship, 7–8

INDEX 283

early engagements with, 5–7
future studies, 19
misinterpretation of, 62
modern economics and, 95
political economy, 97–102
present, 12–19
well-being of humankind, 122
Smith, Craig, 18
Smith, Elihu Hubbard, 5
Smith, Vernon, 14
Smith's Lectures on Justice, Police, and Arms, 10
Smithian concepts, 12
Smithian theodicy, 179–180
social science
    science of society, 34–37
society
    civilized and commercial, 128
    general welfare of, 82
    interest of, 112–117
    long-term economic growth and development, 50–51
    system of, 178
    virtuous business, 97
Sonenscher, Michael, 219
Spacks, Patricia, 207
Spanish Armada, 123
special interest groups, 112
    government capture, 120
    inefficiency problem of, 117
    lobbying from, 111
    lobbying of, 112
    monopolistic privileges and, 118
    state capture, 122
    unjust interest, 117–122
spectator
    imagination and, 210
    perspective-switching, 211
    training of Smithian, 213
spectatorship
    moral experience of, 239
    sympathy and, 210
speech
    communication and, 73
    exchange and, 68–71
    freedom and, 71–72
    persuading with, 72
    persuasion and, 74

splenetic philosophy
    adoption of, 147
Stanley, Thomas, 177
Stedman Jones, Gareth, 219
Sterne, Laurence, 201
Stewart, Dugald, 5, 7, 198
Stigler, George, 9, 10, 62, 111
Stoic cosmopolitanism, 187–188
Stoic theodicy, 179–180
Stoic theology, 178
Stoicism, 177, 178
    duties to others, 186–187
    Epicureanism and, 178, 193
Stoics
    benevolent and moral diety, 180
    conception of justice, 184
    self-regard, 182–184
sufficiency
    equality vs., 156
sufficientarian
    achieving contentedness, 149
    individual ethic, 144
    individual-level motivations, 158
    perspective in *TMS*, 155
    Smith as, 154
    Smith on Rousseau's analysis, 151
sufficientarianism
    argument for, 144
    egalitarianism over, 150
    Smith's, 149–151
sufficientarians, 143
summum bonum
    highest good, 181
sympatheia
    Stoic, 192
sympathetic liberalism, 16
sympathia, 181
sympathy, 238
    characters of tragedy and romance, 210
    concept of, 217
    effectiveness of, 229
    experiencing feelings, 225
    function of imagination, 201
    Grouchy on, 217
    imagination and, 213
    moral, 211

sympathy (cont.)
  moral experience of, 239
  Smith defining, 164
  Smithian, 203
  Smith's concept of, 5
  with superiors, 218
system, 22
  concept of, 26
  term, 24
System of Moral Philosophy (Hutcheson), 5, 23
systematic spirit
  D'Alembert's, 25

Tahmasebian, Kayvan, 215
theodicy
  description of, 179
  Smith, 183
  Stoic, Epicurean desires and Smithian, 179–180
theology, 39
Théorie des sentiments moraux (Grouchy), 214, 229
Theory of Moral Sentiments (Smith), 5, 6, 10, 13, 15, 77, 216
  commercial society and, 126–131
  response to Mandeville and Rousseau, 131–136
threats
  firms refraining from, 105–107
Thucydides, 209
trade
  interactions between nations, 83
trade laws, 119
trade restrictions
  inefficiency of, 121
trade unions movements, 158
Traité des Systèmes (Condillac), 26
tranquility
  restoration of, 34
Tribe, Keith, 4
Tristram Shandy (Sterne), 201
trois roués, 216, 222, 223, 224, 227, 229
truck, barter, and exchange
  propensity to, 25, 68, 69, 71, 121, 122, 183, 189
Turn to Empire (Pitts), 15
Twain, Mark, 3

universal opulence, 85, 99
University of Glasgow, 232
unjust exploitation
  firms refraining from, 105–107
utility
  futility of pursuing means of, 147
  poor man's son in search of, 146
  selfish gratification, 148
  wealth and greatness, 146
Utopia, 123

Valihora, Karen, 194
vanity, 144
  psychology of, 153
  wealth and greatness, 146
Vauvenargues, marquis de, 224, 226
Vico, Giambattista, 218
violence
  competition and, 43
  decentralized sources of, 43
  feudalism and, 50
  Intra-Church, 44
  threat from poor and rich, 49
violent attacks
  mercantile system, 123
  Smith's, 122
virtuous behavior
  institutions protecting, 108
virtuous business, 96
  code of ethics for businessperson, 105–108
  concept of, 102, 110
  firm's mission, 103–105
  promises and responsibilities, 107–108
  refraining from coercion, threats and exploitation, 105–107
  Smithian version of, 108–110
virtuous life, 181
Voltaire, 227

Waldron, Jeremy, 142
Watt, Ian, 204
wealth
  justice and, 122
  means to utility, 146
  pleasures of, 147
  Smith's definition of, 99

wealth creation
  principles of, 78
Wealth of Nations (Smith), 1, 5, 6, 7, 9, 11, 17, 18, 41, 43, 54, 62, 71, 77, 78, 112, 122, 173, 232, 234
Weber, Max, 55
Weinstein, Jack Russell, 13
well-being
  humankind, 122
well-governed society
  government's main duties, 108
  mutual benefit of people in, 99
  projecting justice, 98
  standards of living increasing, 101

Whatmore, Richard, 230
whining and melancholy moralists, 195, 241
Willis, Kirk, 6
Wills, Garry, 11
Winch, Donald, 11, 13, 67
world peace, 192

xenophobia, 192

Young, Allyn, 111

Zeno, 187, 190, 194
Zeus, 185, 186, 187, 188

For EU product safety concerns, contact us at Calle de José Abascal, 56–1°,
28003 Madrid, Spain or eugpsr@cambridge.org.

www.ingramcontent.com/pod-product-compliance
Ingram Content Group UK Ltd.
Pitfield, Milton Keynes, MK11 3LW, UK
UKHW021542200725
460969UK00015B/145